The Way We Lived

Volume I
1492–1877

The Way We Lived

Essays and Documents
in American Social History
Fourth Edition

Frederick M. Binder
City University of New York, College of Staten Island

David M. Reimers
New York University

Houghton Mifflin Company   Boston   New York

Editor-in-Chief: Jean Woy
Sponsoring Editor: Colleen Kyle
Associate Project Editor: Amy Johnson
Associate Production/Design Coordinator: Jodi O'Rourke
Senior Manufacturing Coordinator: Sally Culler
Senior Marketing Manager: Sandra McGuire

Cover Design: Wing Ngan/Stoltze Design
Cover Painting Detail: John Lewis Krimmel, *Country Wedding, Bishop White Officiating.* Courtesy of the Pennsylvania Academy of Fine Arts, Philadelphia. Gift of Paul Beck, Jr.

Photos: p. 3, Carolina Indian man and woman sharing food by John White (Copyright The British Museum); p. 19 (left), Nova Britannia ad, 1609 (Rare Book Division, New York Public Library; Aster, Lenox and Tilden Foundations); p. 19 (right), Page from a New England Primer (American Antiquarian Society); p. 38, *Isaac Royall & Family* by Robert Feke (Fogg Art Museum, Harvard University, Harvard); p. 56, Description of a Slave Ship, 1789 (Peabody Essex Museum); p. 77, *George Whitfield Preaching* (National Portrait Gallery, London); p. 95, Abraham Godwin engraving from a 1787 fireman's certificate (Museum of the City of New York); p. 112, Drawing of the British troops firing on the Americans at Lexington (North Wind Picture Archives); p. 135, Merrimack Manufacturing Company, Lowell, MA (American Textile History Museum) Label #P1235.1; p. 150, *Trail of Tears* by Robert Lindneux (Woolarac Museum, Bartlesville, Oklahoma); p. 169, *The Promised Land—The Grayson Family*, 1850 by William Smith Jewett (Daniel J. Terra Collection courtesy Terra Museum of American Art, Chicago); p. 184, Camp meeting during the Great Awakening (The Granger Collection, NY); p. 204, *Bay & Harbor of New York*, 1855 by Samuel B. Waugh (Museum of the City of New York. Gift of Mrs. Robert M. Littlejohn) #33.169.1; p. 227, Illustration from *Six Nights with the Washingtonians*, 1871 by Arthur; p. 247, African-American group, 1861–62 (Library of Congress); p. 268, Civil War hospital (Library of Congress); p. 287, Former slaves picking cotton (The Valentine Museum, Richmond, Virginia).

Printed in the U.S.A.

Library of Congress Catalog Number: 99-72018

ISBN: 0-395-95960-8

123456789-CS-03 02 01 00 99

Contents

Contents

Contents

Preface

History courses have traditionally emphasized the momentous events of our past. Wars and laws, technological advances and economic crises, ideas and ideologies, and the roles of famous heroes and infamous villains have been central to these studies. Yet what made events momentous is the impact they had on society at large, on people from all walks of life. Modern scholars' growing attention to social history is in part a recognition that knowledge of the experiences, values, and attitudes of these people is crucial to gaining an understanding of our past.

America's history as reflected in the everyday lives of its people provides the focus of these volumes. In preparing a work of selected readings, we have had to make choices as to which episodes from our past to highlight. Each of those included, we believe, was significant in the shaping of our society. Each of the essays is followed by original documents that serve several purposes. They provide examples of the kinds of source materials used by social historians in their research; they help to illuminate and expand upon the subject dealt with in the essays; and they bring the reader into direct contact with the people of the past—people who helped shape, and people who were affected by, the "momentous events."

Our introduction to each essay and its accompanying documents is designed to set the historical scene and to call attention to particular points in the selections, raising questions for students to ponder as they read. A list of suggested readings follows after each of the major divisions of the text. We trust that these volumes will prove to be what written history at its best can be—interesting and enlightening.

We are pleased to note that favorable comments by faculty and students as well as the large number of course adoptions attest to the success of our first three editions. Quite naturally, we thus have no desire in our fourth edition to alter the basic focus, style, and organization of *The Way We Lived*. Those essays that we and our readers consider to have been the earlier editions' very best remain intact. We believe that the new selections will identify and clarify significant issues in America's social history even more effectively than those they replaced.

F. M. B.

D. M. R.

Part I

*Colonial Society
1492–1783*

Chapter 1

The First Americans

Up until a few short decades ago, students of history were taught that the story of America began with Columbus's voyage of discovery, followed by settlement of the land by Europeans. Native Americans were depicted primarily as part of the unfamiliar, exotic, and somewhat threatening natural landscape that had to be tamed. Fortunately, scholars in recent years have come to appreciate and to illustrate that American history predated European colonization by thousands of years. America's first settlers had begun their migration—one that would continue for centuries—across the land bridge that emerged periodically in the Bering Sea. Drawing from a variety of Asiatic peoples, the hundreds of native tribes that settled across America prior to the arrival of Europeans differed profoundly in language, religion, economy, and social and political organization. Before the first white men set foot on American soil, Indian nations used the land effectively and flourished.

The essay that follows, from Peter Nabokov and Dean Snow's "Farmers of the Woodlands," illustrates the complexity and vitality of the societies and cultures of two groups of Indians, the Algonquians and Iroquoians, as they existed in 1492. Situated between the Atlantic coastline and the foothills of the Appalachians, both groups figured prominently in the drama of initial contact between Europeans and Native Americans. As you read, make note of the ways in which the Indians, in the authors' words, "made extremely efficient use of the natural resources in their river and forest world." What factors appeared to be most significant in leading some Eastern Indians toward a primarily seminomadic hunting-and-gathering pattern of existence and others toward an agrarian, semisedentary, village-based way of life? In what ways do the descriptions of Indian culture found in the essay complement or contrast with popular film depictions of Native Americans?

The image of the Indian portrayed by the early English colonists differs in many respects from that of modern scholars. Using their own culture as the guideline by which to evaluate others, colonists found some aspects of Indian life exotic, some even admirable, but on the whole they deemed Indians inferior savages. Thus, the prevailing attitude of the Europeans was that the Indians had to adopt white man's civilization or be vanquished. One of the earliest and most influential proponents of this view was Captain John Smith, swashbuckling adventurer and a leader of the Jamestown, Virginia, settlement of 1607. In his A Generall Historie of Virginia, published in 1624, Smith describes the land and native people of England's first North American colony. The first document includes some of Smith's descriptions of Virginia's "Naturall Inhabitants." What evidence is there that Smith evaluated these people's culture by European standards?

The Indians' resistance to attempts to subjugate them both culturally and physically during the colonial period contributed to the general consensus among the European settlers that they faced a truly barbarous and savage people. However, while few Indians embraced white society, evidence exists of a considerable number of English colonists who ran off to join the Indians and of white captives who, when given the opportunity to return home, chose to remain among the Indians. Look for clues to explain these phenomena in the experiences of Mary Jemison, related in the second document. The daughter of colonists, Jemison was captured and adopted by Seneca Indians in 1755, when she was twelve years old. Mary, in turn, assimilated the Seneca's way of life. When she related the story of her adventure to Dr. James Seaver in 1823, she still lived among the Seneca. In the excerpt that follows, she recalls her thoughts and experiences after four years in captivity.

The Seneca Indians were members of the New York–based League of the Iroquois, a confederation that was able—through their unity, courage, and military and diplomatic skills—to withstand European incursions for more than a hundred years. Their ill-fated alliance with the British during the Revolutionary War led to their downfall. By 1805, the time of the final document, the once mighty Iroquois shared the fate of other Indians before them: encroachment on their lands and pressure to abandon their religion and way of life. The final document presents a speech by Red Jacket, a Seneca warrior and subchief. Born in 1751, Red Jacket was old enough to have served during the years when Iroquois power and prestige were at their height. Now he headed what detractors called the "pagan faction"—Iroquois

4

who sought to maintain their traditional culture and to keep European influences outside the borders of their reservation. In his speech, Red Jacket responds to Missionary Cram's suggestion that Native Americans convert to Christianity and accept European ways. What is Red Jacket's view of the European assault on Indian life?

ESSAY

Algonquians and Iroquoians: Farmers of the Woodlands

Peter Nabokov with Dean Snow

When the hunting party of three Penobscot River Indian families arrived at the frozen creek in the spring of 1492, the men tested the ice with their five-foot staves. It would support them today, but not much longer. The wintry season which they called "still-hunting and stalking" was ending quickly. A warm spell a few days earlier caused sticky snow to cling to their moose-hide snowshoes, slowing them down.

It was time to head downstream, following creeks to the broad river and continuing to where it widened to the sea. Other hunters and their families, whom they had not seen since autumn, would also be returning to the summer villages. The warmer evenings would offer time for recounting the past winter—all the deaths, births, hunts, and tragic, funny, and supernatural happenings of which human memory and history are made.

The hunting parties were traversing a well-watered and heavily forested landscape which white men would one day call Maine. In their own language they knew themselves as "people of the white rocks country," a phrase which Europeans would later shorten to Penobscot. They were one of six loosely organized eastern Algonquian-speaking tribes who would become known colloquially as Wabanakis, or "daybreak land people." Their territory marked the northern limits of Indian farming, for late thaws and early frosts permitted them to produce only a little corn, squash, and beans.

The annual shifts between seasonal camps up and down the Penobscot River valley were determined by the time-honored habits of fishing and hunting on which their survival depended. Branching out from this great stream were innumerable tributaries that were familiar to the hunters who revisited them, usually more than once, throughout the year. Each of these

SOURCE: Peter Nabokov with Dean Snow, "Farmers of the Woodlands," *America in 1492: The World of the Indian People Before the Arrival of Columbus*, Alvin M. Josephy Jr. ed. Copyright © 1992 by Alfred A. Knopf, Inc. Reprinted by permission of the publisher.

natural domains was dubbed a "river," which, to the Penobscot hunting families, evoked a stretch of stream and adjoining lands on which they held relatively exclusive hunting and fishing privileges. Deep in the heart of their homeland loomed their sacred Mount Katahdin, home to the fearsome spirit known as Pamola. Few hunters ventured above the tree line to trespass on his territory.

Waterways, and the well-trodden trails that connected them, served as the hunters' routes into the dense interior forests, where their arrows, snares, and deadfalls yielded moose, deer, beavers, muskrats, and otters in their "rivers." The central river was their highway down to the coast, where they collected clams and lobsters, speared seals, and caught porpoises.

Mobility was a necessity for the hunting life of the Penobscot. Hence, their social groups were small, and rules of residence were rather loose. Generally, it was up to the husband whether his family lived with his own or with his wife's parents. The opportunities and dictates of the hunt dominated all other concerns; social organization had to be flexible enough to let men make the most of the availability of game or shifts in the weather.

The hunters were not unhappy to leave winter behind. The "master of the animals" had blessed this group with a late-season moose cow, her unborn still in its slick, wet pouch. Their hunting had yielded enough beaver and other pelts, thick with luxuriant winter hair, to weigh down the toboggans the men dragged behind them. Their dogs also sniffed spring, and seemed happier. Ahead, everyone anticipated spearing and netting the shad, salmon, alewives, and sturgeon during their spring spawning runs.

This was also a time to harvest bark. It is hard to imagine northeastern Algonquian culture without the paper birch tree. Thin, speckled flats were peeled from the trunks at different times of year. Spring bark was thickest and was preferred for canoes, so the entire trunk would be cut down and the bark separated in the largest pieces possible. Then it would be sewn onto a canoe frame of steam-bent cedar wood and waterproofed at the seams with white-pine pitch colored with charcoal.

Summer bark was thinner, and was earmarked for roofing mats and receptacles. It could be stripped from the trunk in smaller flats without killing the tree. Then it could be folded and sewn into maple-sap buckets, baby craddleboards, and pitch-caulked cooking vessels in which heated stones were dropped to bring water to a boil. For more decorative items, floral designs were produced by careful scraping away to the darker, inner layer of the bark. Porcupine-quill or moose-hair embroidery might also ornament the bark surfaces.

In late spring, families planted gardens before heading for the coast and the pleasures of seabird eggs, escape from blackflies, summer berry picking, flirting among the young, easier fishing along the saltwater bays, and extended twilights. At summer's end, the "going about to find something" time, the forest lured them once more.

Hunting opened in earnest with moose mating season. To entice the fat summer bulls within arrow range, hunters trumpeted through birch-bark megaphones, imitating the sounds of cow moose. Then came winter, story-telling season, when a few families collected within wigwams and lulled children to sleep with the exploits of Glooskap, the trickster figure of Wabanaki folklore.

For Penobscot Indians in 1492, this cycle of tasks and pleasures seemed as predictable and everlasting as the seasons themselves. Their way of life also made extremely efficient use of the natural resources in their river and forest world. Woodlands, waterways, and—south of Penobscot country—open fields remain the ecological hallmarks of all of the North American East. However, in 1492, there was probably far more local variation in plant and animal life than we have today.

Indeed, if we are to believe the earliest European eyewitnesses, New England, for instance, resembled a checkerboard of natural preserves with dramatically contrasting ecological features. "It did all resemble a stately Parke, wherein appeare some old trees with high withered tops, and other flourishing with living green boughs," wrote James Rosier in 1605, after walking through the forests and fields not far from Indian Island in Maine. Yet in this stroll of less than four miles, the modern-day environmental historian William Cronon pointed out, Rosier's party actually passed beneath the leafy canopies of a number of quite different micro-environments.

The sylvan paradise of northern New England, lying at the northern-most extreme of the corn-growing region, was but one section of nearly one million square miles of the eastern half of North America that is commonly called the Woodland culture area. Farther west might be added 400,000 square miles of intermixed river foliage and tallgrass prairie, where—except on strips of narrow floodplain—Indians usually were not able to sustain substantial gardening.

By 1492, the native people of this huge eastern mass of the continent occupied a world already rich and complex in human history—many different histories, in fact. At least sixty-eight mutually unintelligible tongues, representing five of the twenty known language families of North America, were spoken in the region. The net effect of over 10,000 years of adaptation by contrasting native peoples who had grown deeply tied to a great diversity of environmental regions of the eastern woodlands had produced a complex cultural mosaic. . . .

It had taken time, new ideas, and experimentation for the woodland Indian peoples of 1492 to develop this annual round of land-use customs and mixed strategies of subsistence. Indian occupancy of the East is now believed to go back as far as 16,000 B.C., when Paleo-Indian foragers and hunters began settling the region in highly mobile bands. As these groups established local residency, they developed almost imperceptibly into the Indian world that archaeologists label the Archaic period, which lasted until about 700 B.C.

The domesticated dogs that accompanied the Penobscot hunters were introduced during Archaic times and were found throughout the East by 1492. Inherited from their Paleo-Indian forerunners, a principal Archaic weapon was the spear thrower. Archaic hunters improved this device to gain increased velocity during a throw by adding flexible shafts and by weighting the throwing stick with a ground stone to add leverage. . . .

By 1492, Indians in the East had been growing vegetables in two different ways for a long time. Both the Iroquoians and Algonquians practiced what is known as swidden, or slash-and-burn, horticulture. A plot of preferably well-drained land was cleared of its canopy of leaves and branches. The area was then burned and nutrient-rich ashes and organic materials were hoed into the forest floor. Seeds were dispersed within hand-formed mounds. The resulting fields did not have a very kempt appearance; generally, the corn stalks and squash vines flourished greenly amid a scatter of scorched or dead brush.

Among the semi-nomadic hunting-and-gathering Algonquian bands, who traveled relatively light and who fished, foraged, hunted, and gathered maple syrup, growing vegetables was but one subsistence activity. If a season's garden was beset by insects, or a hunt came up empty, the people generally could rely on stored foods or other options. The Iroquoians, however, who elevated swidden agriculture to their dominant means of support, might be considered true "farmers," rather than part-time "gardeners." Their sizable hillside lots were the mainstay for their matrilineal social system and for a semi-sedentary, village-based way of life. . . .

Prior to the advent of gardening, food foraging among woodland Indians had probably been the responsibility of women. The heightened importance of plant cultivation, processing, and storage steadily enhanced their role. By the time of Columbus, women were clearly the primary food producers in a number of woodland cultures whose political and religious systems reflected their status.

South of the northeastern territories of the Wabanaki peoples, the weather softened. Among the Indian groups of central and southern New England, the length of the summer allowed greater attention to gardening and so promoted a more settled village way of life. While for Penobscot hunters corn was a sometime delicacy, for the south it became a basic food staple. In present-day New Hampshire and Vermont, the western Abenakis were marginal farmers and fishermen. Among the Mahicans of eastern New York, like the Pocumtucks of the interior Connecticut River valley, work in the fields was still augmented by hunting in the woods and trapping migratory fish in local rivers.

Not surprisingly, this more temperate world had a larger native population than did the northern forests. It is estimated that the Massachusett, Wampanoag, and other Indian nations of southern New England possessed a population density of five people per square mile—ten times that of the hunters of Maine. Population densities at this high level also obtained for other eastern Algonquian-speakers farther south, the Lenapes (Delawares) and Nanticokes, and their linguistic kinfolk in coastal Delaware, Maryland, Virginia, and North Carolina. There, also, among the Powhatans and others, were permanent villages and more stable intertribal alliances.

All central and southern New England Indians spoke languages belonging to the same language family—Algonquian. Commonly, a tribesman was conversant with the words and pronunciation of his immediate neighbors, but communicated with decreasing fluency as trade, hunting, or warfare drew him farther from his home territory.

By 1492, techniques for growing and storing vegetables had been developing in the Northeast for four or five centuries. Wampanoag men cleared fields from the forests of oak, elm, ash, and chestnut. They felled the smaller trees and burned the thicker trunks at the base together with their branches, which left a coating of ash to enrich the soil. In Wampanoag society, rights to these cleared plots were inherited through the female line of descent.

Women broke up the ground with hoes edged with deer scapulae or clamshells. Around April, they began planting the seed corn in little mounds, often counting four kernels per hillock and perhaps adding heads of alewife fish for fertilizer. The corn came in many colors and kinds—flint, flour, dent, and pop.

By midsummer, an early crop yielded squash and beans and green corn, but the major harvest occurred in September. Apparently these crops helped each other out. The beans growing amid the corn added nitrogen, which corn consumes, while the heavy stalks offered support for the climbing bean vines. Finally, the corn provided the shade that the low-lying squash needed to reach maximum maturity.

When eaten together, beans, corn, and squash produced a greater protein intake, and Indians developed the mixed-vegetable dish which is still known by its Algonquian name, "succotash."

While garden caretakers weeded roots and protected the emerging crops from birds and pests, the majority of villagers headed for the coast to gather clams and oysters and to catch lobsters and fish. Wild greens, nuts, and fruits, which were also important to their diet, varied with season and habitat. They included blackberries, blueberries, raspberries, strawberries, and wild grapes, and walnuts, chestnuts, and acorns, which could also be dried and stored for leaner times.

In autumn, the Indians divided their time between preparing their agricultural surplus for winter storage and dispersing in hunting parties before winter set in. Deer were stalked by individuals, or were flushed into special game pens by communal drivers. For warm skins as well as meat, Indians stalked moose, elk, bears, bobcats, and mountain lions in late fall, winter, and early spring. In midwinter, they dangled lines into local ponds through the ice, but dipped nets or repaired fish weirs in milder seasons.

Villages came alive in summertime, their long, mat-covered multifamily structures busy with social activity. Those villages near cultural frontiers were surrounded by a protective stockade of fire-hardened, sharpened posts. A typical settlement included storage pits, menstrual huts, and sometimes special religious structures. Plaza-like areas were used for public feasts, and for dancing performed to the accompaniment of song, drum, and rattle.

Religious specialists among the Wampanoag of present-day Massachu-setts were known as "powwows." Admired and feared for their association with extraordinarily strong "manitou," or spirits, they exhibited their spirit-bestowed powers at special events to benefit hunters, control weather, prophesy the future, cure the sick, or bewitch their enemies. They also me-diated between the community and the spirit world at green-corn harvest feasts and at special midwinter rituals and memorials for the dead, and they concocted war magic against tribal enemies. Among some southern New England tribes, religious specialists who behaved more like formal priests maintained temples in which bones of the chiefly class were treasured.

Exchange was lively among these different peoples and probably bound them together in personal and group alliances. The eastern woods and riversides were laced with well-used trail systems along which goods and messages were conveyed. Individuals fortunate enough to be related to the resident "sachem," or chief, as well as powwows who were on intimate terms with them, benefited from the exchange of values and goods that moved back and forth.

In 1492, these Algonquian-speaking hunter-farmers were neighbors to more militarily powerful tribes who were representatives of another major eastern Indian language family, Iroquoian. Dwelling along the Carolina and Virginia portions of the Appalachian foothills were such Iroquoian-speaking peoples as the Nottoways, Meherrins, and Tuscaroras. The last of these would later migrate north to become the sixth member of the famous Iroquois confederacy in the eighteenth century.

Among the mountains, valleys, and flatlands that lay across what is now central New York State, the principal beacon of Iroquoian-speaking culture was positioned in the midst of a more extensive territory of Al-gonquian-speaking groups. What these upper Iroquoian peoples may have lost in terms of sheer acreage, however, they more than made up for in the fertility of their agricultural lands, which they utilized most efficiently.

Inhabiting the mountains of eastern Tennessee and western North Car-olina were southern Iroquoians, the ancestors of the populous Cherokees. Tutelos, who lived in Virginia, were speakers of the Siouan language, while the Catawbas, farther south, possessed a language with a more distant rela-tionship to mainstream Siouan. West of Cherokee country were the Yuchis, whose language was vaguely related to Siouan.

If the birch was the emblematic tree of Algonquian culture, it was the white pine for the Iroquoians. In their cosmology, a cosmic evergreen was believed to stand at the center of the earth. Elm served more pragmatic purposes. Slabs of its heavy bark, sewn onto stout sapling frames, shrouded their barrel-roofed longhouses, which extended up to 300 feet or more in length.

These dormitorylike buildings were also an embodiment of the Iroquois social order, for women and children under one roof were linked by membership in the same clan, which was traced through the female line. Each of the ten or so Iroquois clans took its name from a particular animal or bird that was considered to be the original ancestor of the clan's members—thus there were, for example, the Eagle, Snipe, and Heron clans. Over the door at one end of a longhouse would be a depiction of the reigning clan animal of the house's inhabitants.

The year 1492 probably found this group of woodland Indians undergoing a profound social and political transformation. Sometime between 1450 and 1550, it is believed, the five major Iroquoian-speaking tribes south of the St. Lawrence River were developing an altogether innovative form of political union—a multitribal federation with members allied for mutual defense—and were deliberating with elaborately democratic rules of order. The story of the formation of the Iroquois League provides a strong argument against the notion that pre-contact Indian societies existed in a timeless vacuum and did not experience "history" until Columbus imported it.

At the dawn of this transformation, around A.D. 1450, northern Iroquoian groups were found across southern Ontario, New York, and central Pennsylvania in villages of slightly over 200 people each. As with the New England horticulturists, they practiced swidden agriculture, only to a far more intensive degree. Lacking direct access to coastal resources, they were more dependent upon gardening for survival. These tribes also appear to have been highly competitive and politically assertive.

Early Iroquoian life was divided into two domains, the clearings with their longhouses and gardens and the wider wilderness with its game and dangers. The clearings were the responsibility of women, and over each longhouse presided the oldest "clan mother." By contrast, the forests were a male domain, where the men gave offerings to the masked spirits, who responded by "giving" wild animals to respectful hunters.

Iroquois fields were cleared by hacking and burning around the base of tree trunks so that the heavier foliage died and, if necessary, the entire tree could be felled easily the following year. This also allowed sunlight to shine on the forest floor and provided ashes to energize the soil. Maize, beans, and squash were planted in hills among the fallen trees. Firewood was gathered as dead limbs dropped during the course of the year. Within a few years, however, the garden soil began to decline in productivity, and new acreage had to be opened up. Every twenty years or so, infestation from worms and other pests, plus depletion of easily available wood for fires and stockade or longhouse construction, forced relocation of the village. The entire community would rebuild not far away, often an easy walk from the old site.

For the Iroquoians, growing crops was not simply one of a number of food-gathering options; their fields were their lifeline. They were considerably more sedentary than their Algonquian neighbors. This heightened reliance upon cultigens and reliable food storage decisively elevated the prominence of women in political life. By 1492, not only was each longhouse under the authority of the eldest clan mother resident, but it was Iroquois women who handpicked candidates for the office of sachem.

However, the pattern of communities containing only a dozen or so longhouses changed by 1492, when Iroquois towns each began sheltering from 500 to 2,000 inhabitants. Perhaps a rise in intertribal warfare inspired consolidation for mutual defense, or improved farming strategies allowed for a dramatic aggregation of population. But the new social and political institutions that arose to cope with these mega-villages grew directly out of the old social fabric and residence patterns.

Traditionally, the center aisles of the Iroquoian longhouse split the buildings lengthwise. Paired family quarters faced each other like compartments in a sleeping car, with a shared cooking hearth in the central aisle. Men married "into" these longhouses—which were expanded if all existing quarters were spoken for. Although men appointed from senior households ran the affairs of the village as a council of equals, sometime around 1492 this changed. The matrilineal clans, which seem to have served originally as units that facilitated trade and exchange within the tribe, became the building blocks of a brand-new political institution. Within the century between 1450 and 1550, the Iroquois proper became known as the Five Nations, which held sway across present-day New York State. They consisted of the Seneca, Cayuga, Onondaga, Oneida, and Mohawk peoples.

According to Iroquois tradition, two legendary figures, Deganawidah and Hiawatha, conceived of a "great peace" among the incessantly feuding Iroquois peoples. They persuaded the Iroquois tribes, one by one, to accept their "good news of peace and power." Among the reforms they instituted was the abolition of cannibalism. The old social importance of the communal longhouse made it a perfect symbol for their political creation. All the member tribes talked of themselves as "fires" of an imagined "longhouse" that spanned the extent of Iroquois territory.

To its participants, this Iroquoian fraternity meant strength in numbers and security through allies. To outsiders such as the Hurons, neighboring Algonquians, and eventually the European powers, it meant a formidable foe. The full drama of Iroquois political destiny would actually unfold in the three centuries after 1492, but if Columbus had ventured northward, he would have witnessed a truly Native American representative government in the making. . . .

DOCUMENTS

"Of the Naturall Inhabitants of Virginia," 1624

The land is not populous, for the men be fewe; their far greater number is of women and children. Within 60 miles of *James* Towne there are about some 5000 people, but of able men fit for their warres scarse 1500. To nourish so many together they have yet no means, because they make so small a benefit of their land, be it never so fertill.

6 or 700 have beene the most [that] hath beene seene together, when they gathered themselves to have surprised *Captaine Smyth at Pamaunke,* having but 15 to withstand the worst of their furie. As small as the proportion of ground that hath yet beene discovered, is in comparison of that yet unknowne. The people differ very much in stature, especially in language, as before is expressed.

Since being very great as the *Sesquesahamocks,* others very little as the *Wighcocomocoes:* but generally tall and straight, of a comely proportion, and of a colour browne, when they are of any age, but they are borne white. Their haire is generally black; but few have any beards. The men weare halfe their heads shaven, the other halfe long. For Barbers they use their women, who with 2 shels will grate away the haire, of any fashion they please. The women are cut in many fashions agreeable to their yeares, but ever some part remaineth long.

They are very strong, of an able body and full of agilitie, able to endure to lie in the woods under a tree by the fire, in the worst of winter, or in the weedes and grasse, in *Ambuscado* in the Sommer.

They are inconstant in everie thing, but what feare constraineth them to keepe. Craftie, timerous, quicke of apprehension and very ingenious. Some are of disposition fearefull, some bold, most cautelous, all *Savage.* Generally covetous of copper, beads, and such like trash. They are soone moved to anger, and so malitious, that they seldome forget an injury: they seldome steale one from another, least their conjurors should reveale it, and so they be pursued and punished. That they are thus feared is certaine, but that any can reveale their offences by conjuration I am doubtful. Their women are carefull not to bee suspected of dishonesty without the leave of their husbands.

Each household knoweth their owne lands and gardens, and most live of their owne labours.

For their apparell, they are some time covered with the skinnes of wilde beasts, which in winter are dressed with the haire, but in sommer without.

SOURCE: Edward Arber, ed., *Captain John Smith Works* (Birmingham, Eng.: The English Scholars Library, No. 16, 1884), 65–67.

The better sort use large mantels of deare skins not much differing in fashion from the Irish mantels. Some imbrodered with white beads, some with copper, other painted after their manner. But the common sort have scarce to cover their nakedness but with grasse, the leaves of trees, or such like. We have seen some use mantels made of Turkey feathers, so prettily wrought and woven with threeds that nothing could bee discerned but the feathers, that was exceeding warme and very handsome. But the women are alwaies covered about their midles with a skin and very shamefast to be seene bare.

They adorne themselves most with copper beads and paintings. Their women some have their legs, hands, breasts and face cunningly imbrodered with diverse workes, as beasts, serpentes, artificially wrought into their flesh with blacke spots. In each eare commonly they have 3 great holes, whereat they hange chaines, bracelets, or copper. Some of their men weare in those holes, a smal greene and yellow coloured snake, neare halfe a yard in length, which crawling and lapping her selfe about his necke often times familiarly would kiss his lips. Others wear a dead Rat tied by the tail. Some on their heads weare the wing of a bird or some large feather, with a Rattell. Those Rattels are somewhat like the chape of a Rapier but lesse, which they take from the taile of a snake. Many have the whole skinne of a hawke or some strange fowle, stuffed with the wings abroad. Others a broad peece of copper, and some the hand of their enemy dryed. Their heads and shoulders are painted red with the roote *Pocone* braied to powder mixed with oyle; this they hold in somer to preserve them from the heate, and in winter from the cold. Many other formes of paintings they use, but he is the most gallant that is the most monstrous to behould.

Their buildings and habitations are for the most part by the rivers or not farre distant from some fresh spring. Their houses are built like our Arbors of small young springs bowed and tyed, and so close covered with mats or the barkes of trees very handsomely, that notwithstanding either winde raine or weather, they are as warme as stooves, but very smoaky, yet at the toppe of the house there is a hole made for the smoake to goe into right over the fire.

Against the fire they lie on little hurdles of Reedes covered with a mat, borne from the ground a foote and more by a hurdle of wood. On these round about the house, they lie heads and points one by thother against the fire: some covered with mats, some with skins, and some starke naked lie on the ground, from 6 to 20 in a house.

Their houses are in the midst of their fields or gardens; which are smal plots of ground, some 20, some 40, some 100, some 200, some more, some lesse. Some times from 2 to 100 of these houses [are] togither, or but a little separated by groves of trees. Neare their habitations is little small wood, or old trees on the ground, by reason of their burning of them for fire. So that a man may gallop a horse amongst these woods any waie, but where the creekes or Rivers shall hinder.

14

Men women and children have their severall names according to the severall humor of their Parents. Their women (they say) are easilie delivered of childe, yet doe they love children verie dearly. To make them hardy, in the coldest mornings they wash them in the rivers, and by painting and ointments so tanne their skins, that after year or two, no weather will hurt them.

The men bestowe their times in fishing, hunting, wars, and such manlike exercises, scorning to be seene in any woman like exercise, which is the cause that the women be verie painefull and the men often idle. The women and children do the rest of the worke. They make mats, baskets, pots, morters, pound their corne, make their bread, prepare their victuals, plant their corne, gather their corne, beare all kind of burdens, and such like. . . .

Recollections of a "White Indian" (1759), 1823

I had then been with the Indians four summers and four winters, and had become so far accustomed to their mode of living, habits and dispositions, that my anxiety to get away, to be set at liberty, and leave them, had almost subsided. With them was my home; my family was there, and there I had many friends to whom I was warmly attached in consideration of the favors, affection and friendship with which they had uniformly treated me, from the time of my adoption. Our labor was not severe; and that of one year was exactly similar, in almost every respect, to that of the others, without that endless variety that is to be observed in the common labor of the white people. Notwithstanding the Indian women have all the fuel and bread to procure, and the cooking to perform, their task is probably not harder than that of white women, who have those articles provided for them; and their cares certainly are not half as numerous, nor as great. In the summer season, we planted, tended and harvested our corn, and generally had all our children with us; but had no master to oversee or drive us, so that we could work as leisurely as we pleased. We had no ploughs on the Ohio; but performed the whole process of planting and hoeing with a small tool that resembled, in some respects, a hoe with a very short handle.

Our cooking consisted in pounding our corn into samp or hommany,* boiling the hommany, making now and then a cake and baking it in the ashes, and in boiling or roasting our venison. As our cooking and eating utensils consisted of a hommany block and pestle, a small kettle, a knife or two, and a few vessels of bark or wood, it required but little time to keep them in order for use.

SOURCE: James E. Seaver, *A Narrative of the Life of Mrs. Mary Jemison* (Canandaigua, N.Y.: J. D. Bemis and Co., 1824), 46–49.
Hominy (hommany) is shucked corn with the germ removed; *samp* is a boiled cereal made from hominy. (Eds.)

Spinning, weaving, sewing, stocking knitting, and the like, are arts which have never been practised in the Indian tribes generally. After the revolutionary war, I learned to sew, so that I could make my own clothing after a poor fashion; but the other domestic arts I have been wholly ignorant of the application of, since my captivity. In the season of hunting, it was our business, in addition to our cooking, to bring home the game that was taken by the Indians, dress it, and carefully preserve the eatable meat, and prepare or dress the skins. Our clothing was fastened together with strings of deer skin, and tied on with the same.

In that manner we lived, without any of those jealousies, quarrels, and revengeful battles between families and individuals, which have been common in the Indian tribes since the introduction of ardent spirits amongst them.

The use of ardent spirits amongst the Indians, and the attempts which have been made to civilize and christianize them by the white people, has constantly made them worse and worse; increased their vices, and robbed them of many of their virtues; and will ultimately produce their extermination. I have seen, in a number of instances, the effects of education upon some of our Indians, who were taken when young, from their families, and placed at school before they had had an opportunity to contract many Indian habits, and there kept till they arrived to manhood; but I have never seen one of those but what was an Indian in every respect after he returned. Indians must and will be Indians, in spite of all the means that can be used for their cultivation in the sciences and arts.

One thing only marred my happiness, while I lived with them on the Ohio; and that was the recollection that I had once had tender parents, and a home that I loved. Aside from that consideration, or, if I had been taken in infancy, I should have been contented in my situation. Notwithstanding all that has been said against the Indians, in consequence of their cruelties to their enemies—cruelties that I have witnessed, and had abundant proof of—it is a fact that they are naturally kind, tender and peaceable towards their friends, and strictly honest; and that those cruelties have been practised, only upon their enemies, according to their idea of justice.

An Indian's View, 1805

Friend and brother, it was the will of the Great Spirit that we should meet together this day. He orders all things, and He has given us a fine day for our council. He has taken His garment from before the sun, and caused it to shine with brightness upon us; our eyes are opened, that we see clearly; our

SOURCE: Red Jacket's reply to Missionary Cram at Buffalo, New York, in Samuel G. Goodrich, *Lives of Celebrated American Indians* (Boston: Bradbury, Soden and Co., 1843), 283–287.

ears are unstopped, that we have been able to hear distinctly the words that you have spoken; for all these favours we thank the Great Spirit, and Him only. . . .

Brother, you say you want an answer to *your talk,* before you leave this place. It is right you should have one, as you are a great distance from home, and we do not wish to detain you; but we will first look back a little, and tell you what our fathers have told us, and what we have heard from the White people.

Brother, listen to what we say. There was a time when our forefathers owned this great land. Their seats extended from the rising to the setting sun. The Great Spirit had made it for the use of Indians. He had created the buffalo, the deer, and other animals for food. He made the bear and the beaver, and their skins served us for clothing. He had scattered them over the country, and taught us how to take them. He had caused the earth to produce corn for bread.

All this He had done for His Red children because he loved them. If we had any disputes about hunting grounds, they were generally settled without the shedding of much blood.

But an evil day came upon us; your forefathers [the Europeans] crossed the great waters, and landed on this island. Their numbers were small; they found friends, and not enemies; they told us they had fled from their own country for fear of wicked men, and come here to enjoy their religion. They asked for a small seat; we took pity on them, granted their request, and they sat down amongst us; we gave them corn and meat; they gave us poison in return. The White people had now found our country, tidings were carried back, and more came amongst us; yet we did not fear them, we took them to be friends; they called us brothers; we believed them, and gave them a larger seat. At length their numbers had greatly increased; they wanted more land; they wanted our country. Our eyes were opened; and our minds became uneasy. Wars took place; Indians were hired to fight against Indians, and many of our people were destroyed. They also brought strong liquors among us; it was strong and powerful, and has slain thousands.

Brother, our seats were once large, and yours were very small; you have now become a great people, and we have scarcely a place left to spread our blankets; you have got our country, but are not satisfied; you want to force your religion upon us.

Brother, continue to listen. You say that you are sent to instruct us how to worship the Great Spirit agreeably to His mind, and if we do not take hold of the religion which you White people teach, we shall be unhappy hereafter; you say that you are right, and we are lost; how do we know this to be true? We understand that your religion is written in a book; if it was intended for us as well as you, why has not the Great Spirit given it to us, and not only to us, but why did He not give to our forefathers the knowledge of that book, with the means of understanding it rightly? We only

17

know what you tell us about it; how shall we know when to believe, being so often deceived by the White people?

Brother, you say there is but one way to worship and serve the Great Spirit; if there is but one religion, why do you White people differ so much about it? Why not all agree, as you can all read the book?

Brother, we do not understand these things; we are told that your religion was given to your forefathers, and has been handed down from father to son. We also have a religion which was given to our forefathers, and has been handed down to us, their children. We worship that way. It teaches us to be thankful for all the favours we receive; to love each other, and to be united; we never quarrel about religion.

Brother, the Great Spirit has made us all; but He has made a great difference between His White and Red children; He has given us a different complexion and different customs; to you He has given the arts; to these He has not opened our eyes; we know these things to be true. Since He has made so great a difference between us in other things, why may we not conclude that He has given us a different religion according to our understanding? The Great spirit does right; He knows what is best for his children; we are satisfied.

Brother, we do not wish to destroy your religion, or take it from you. We want only to enjoy our own.

Brother, you say you have not come to get our land or our money, but to enlighten our minds. I will now tell you that I have been at your meetings, and saw you collecting money from the meeting. I cannot tell what this money was intended for, but suppose it was for your minister, and if we should conform to your way of thinking, perhaps you may want some from us.

Brother, we are told that you have been preaching to White people in this place; these people are our neighbors, we are acquainted with them; we will wait a little while and see what effect your preaching has upon them. If we find it does them good, makes them honest, and less disposed to cheat Indians, we will then consider again what you have said.

Brother, you have now heard our answer to your talk, and this is all we have to say at present. As we are going to part, we will come and take you by the hand, and hope the Great Spirit will protect you on your journey, and return you safe to your friends.

Chapter 2

Conflicting Cultural Values in Early America

NOVA BRITANNIA.

OFFERING MOST

Excellent fruites by Planting in
VIRGINIA.

Exciting all such as be well affected
to further the same.

LONDON
Printed for SAMVEL MACHAM, and are to befold at
his Shop in Pauls Church-yard, at the
Signe of the Bul-head.
1 6 0 9.

(15)

T.
Young TIMOTHY
Learnt Sin to fly,

V.
VASHTI for Pride,
Was set aside.

W.
WHALES in the Sea,
GOD's Voice obey.

X.
XERXES did die,
And so must I.

Y.
While YOUTH do cheer
Death may be near.

Z.
ZACCHEUS he
Did climb the Tree,
Our Lord to see.

The colonial history of what today is the United States began in the early seventeenth century with the planting of settlements along the eastern seaboard. Almost all the early colonists were English; together, they suffered the hardships of the ocean voyage and the dangers and vicissitudes of frontier life. However, as T. H. Breen points out in his essay "Looking Out for Number One," significant differences existed among these newcomers, especially in terms of their motivation for coming to the New World and the societies that they established. Breen discusses early Virginia, a colony marked by greed and the exploitation of people and natural resources. The first document provides a vivid account of the early years of Virginia. Nathaniel Butler, governor of Bermuda, visited the colony in 1622, and wrote a report of the conditions he saw there. What evidence did he provide that human failings were as much or perhaps even more to blame than natural causes for the sufferings of the colonists? The second document, dated a year after Butler's report,

19

is a letter written by indentured servant Richard Frethorne to his parents in England, in which he reveals that the exploitation of human labor in Virginia was well under way by 1623.

As you read the third document, written by Governor John Winthrop of the Massachusetts Bay Colony, note the differences in what Breen termed "operative values" between the stated goals for that colony and conditions in Virginia. Composed during his journey to America in 1630, Winthrop's statement clearly expressed the religious motives of the Puritan adventurers and set forth the ideological objective that communal effort take precedence over individual ambition. What did Winthrop mean by his declaration that "wee shall be as a City upon a Hill"?

Within a generation of the founding of Virginia and Massachusetts, time and circumstances had done much to modify the original, and quite different, characters of the two colonies. The Virginia colonists ultimately realized that their dreams of getting rich quickly would not find fulfillment; eventually, the expansion of agriculture furthered the development of a more stable—but nonetheless prosperous—society. Massachusetts also represented a success story, though not the kind John Winthrop envisioned. By the end of the seventeenth century, profits from agriculture, fishing, and commerce had moved the eastern half of the colony beyond the "wilderness" status and diverted its citizens' attention from the mission of creating a new Zion. Although the Puritan spirit would long continue to influence the Massachusetts population, its dominance was broken.

ESSAY

Looking Out for Number One: Conflicting Cultural Values in Early Seventeenth-Century Virginia

T. H. Breen

Despite their common English background, the thousands of European men and women who migrated to Barbados, Virginia, and New England during the seventeenth century created strikingly different societies in the New World. . . .

This essay examines the creation of a distinct culture in Virginia roughly between 1617 and 1630. Although early Virginians shared certain general ideas, attitudes, and norms with other English migrants, their operative values were quite different from those that shaped social and institu-

SOURCE: T. H. Breen, "Looking Out for Number One: Conflicting Cultural Values in Early Seventeenth-Century Virginia," *South Atlantic Quarterly* 78:3, 342–360. Copyright Duke University Press, 1979. All rights reserved. Reprinted with permission.

tional behavior in places such as Massachusetts Bay. Virginia's physical environment, its extensive network of navigable rivers, its rich soil, its ability to produce large quantities of marketable tobacco, powerfully reinforced values which the first settlers carried to America. The interplay between a particular variant of Jacobean* culture and a specific New World setting determined the character of Virginia's institutions, habits of personal interaction, and patterns of group behavior that persisted long after the early adventurers had died or returned to the mother country. . . .

The early settlers in Virginia were an unusual group of Jacobeans. In no way did they represent a random sample of seventeenth-century English society or a cross section of English values. While little is known about the specific origins or backgrounds of most settlers, we do have a fairly clear idea of what sort of inducements persuaded men and women to move to Virginia. The colony's promotional literature emphasized economic opportunity, usually quick and easy riches. In his "True Relation of the State of Virginia" written in 1616, for example, John Rolfe pitied England's hard-working farmers who barely managed to make ends meet. "What happiness might they enjoy in Virginia," Rolfe mused, "where they may have ground for nothing, more than they can manure, reap more fruits and profits with half the labour." And in 1622 Peter Arundle, overlooking the colony's recent military setbacks at the hands of the Indians, assured English friends that "any laborious honest man may in a short time become rich in this Country." It was a compelling dream, one which certain Englishmen were all too willing to accept as truth. Indeed, so many persons apparently risked life and possessions in the elusive search for the main chance that John Harvey, a future Royal Governor of Virginia, begged men of integrity on both sides of the Atlantic to control "the rumors of plenty to be found at all tyme[s] in Virginia."

The lure of great wealth easily obtained held an especially strong appeal for a specific type of seventeenth-century Englishman, individuals who belonged to a distinct subculture within Jacobean society. By all accounts, early Virginia drew a disproportionately large number of street toughs, roughnecks fresh from the wars in Ireland, old soldiers looking for new glory, naive adventurers, mean-spirited sea captains, marginal persons attempting to recoup their losses. If contemporaries are to be believed, Virginia found itself burdened with "many unruly gallants packed thether by their friends to escape ill destinies." Even Sir Thomas Dale, himself a recent veteran of English military expeditions in Holland, was shocked by the colony's settlers, "so prophane, so riotous, so full of Mutenie and treasonable Intendments" that they provided little "testimonie beside their names that they are Christians."

Jacobean refers to the people and culture of England during the reign of James I, 1603–1625. (Eds.)

Even if Dale exaggerated, there is no reason to question that the colonists were highly individualistic, motivated by the hope of material gain, and in many cases, not only familiar with violence but also quite prepared to employ it to obtain their own ends in the New World. By and large, they appear to have been extremely competitive and suspicious of other men's motives. Mutiny and anarchy sometimes seemed more attractive than obeying someone else's orders. Few of the colonists showed substantial interest in creating a permanent settlement. For the adventurer, Virginia was not a new home, not a place to carry out a divine mission, but simply an area to be exploited for private gain. It was this "variant" strain of values—a sense of living only for the present or near future, a belief that the environment could and should be forced to yield quick financial returns, an assumption that everyone was looking out for number one and hence that cooperative ventures of all sorts were bound to fail—that help to account for the distinctive patterns of social and institutional behavior found in early Virginia.

The transfer of these variant values, of course, only partially explains Virginia's cultural development. The attitudes, beliefs, and ideas that the founders brought with them to the New World interacted with specific environmental conditions. The settlers' value system would certainly have withered in a physical setting that offered no natural resources capable of giving plausibility to the adventurers' original expectations. If by some chance the Virginians had landed in a cold, rocky, inhospitable country devoid of valuable marketable goods, then they would probably have given up the entire venture and like a defeated army, straggled home. That is exactly what happened in 1607 to the unfortunate men who settled in Sagadahoc, Maine, a tiny outpost that failed to produce instant wealth. Virginia almost went the way of Sagadahoc. The first decade of its history was filled with apathy and disappointment, and at several points, the entire enterprise seemed doomed. The privatistic values that the colonists had carried to Jamestown, a tough, exploitive competitive individualism, were dysfunctional—even counter-productive—in an environment which offered up neither spices nor gold, neither passages to China nor a subject population easily subdued and exploited. In fact, before 1617 this value system generated only political faction and petty personal violence, things that a people struggling for survival could ill afford.

The successful cultivation of tobacco altered the course of Virginia's cultural development. Clearly, in an economic sense, the crop saved the colony. What is less obvious but no less true, is that the discovery of a lucrative export preserved the founders' individualistic values. Suddenly, after ten years of error and failure, the adventurers' transported values were no longer at odds with their physical environment. The settlers belatedly stumbled across the payoff; the forests once so foreboding, so unpromising, could now be exploited with a reasonable expectation of quick return. By

1617 the process was well-advanced, and as one planter reported, "the streets, and all other spare places planted with Tobacco. . . . The Colonie dispersed all about, planting *Tobacco."*

The interplay between the settlers' value system and their environment involved more than economic considerations. Once a market for tobacco had been assured, people spread out along the James and York Rivers. Whenever possible, they formed what the directors of the Virginia Company* called private hundreds, small plantations frequently five or more miles apart which groups of adventurers developed for their own profit. By 1619 forty-four separate patents for private plantations had been issued, and by the early 1620s a dispersed settlement pattern, long to be a characteristic of Virginia society, was well established. The dispersion of the colony's population was a cultural phenomenon. It came about not simply because the Virginia soil was unusually well suited for growing tobacco or because its deep rivers provided easy access to the interior, but because men holding privatistic values regarded the land as an exploitable resource, and within their structure of priorities, the pursuit of private gain outranked the creation of corporate communities.

The scattering of men and women along the colony's waterways, their self-imposed isolation, obviously reduced the kind of ongoing face-to-face contacts that one associates with the villages of seventeenth-century New England. A migrant to Virginia tended to be highly competitive and to assume that other men would do unto him as he would do unto them—certainly an unpleasant prospect. Dispersion heightened this sense of suspicion. Because communication between private plantations was difficult, Virginians possessed no adequate means to distinguish the truth about their neighbors from malicious rumor, and lacking towns and well-developed voluntary organizations, without shared rituals, ceremonies, even market days, they drew increasingly distrustful of whatever lay beyond the perimeter of their own few acres.

The kind of human relationships that developed in colonial Virginia graphically reveal the effect of highly individualistic values upon social behavior. In this settlement only two meaningful social categories existed, a person was either free or dependent, either an exploiter or a resource. There was no middle ground. Those men who held positions of political and economic power treated indentured servants and slaves not as human beings, but as instruments to produce short-run profits. As a consequence of this outlook, life on the private plantations was a degrading experience for thousands of men and women who arrived in Virginia as bonded laborers. Whatever their expectations about the colony may have been before they migrated, the servants' reality consisted of poor food, meager clothing, hard

*The *Virginia Company* was the private corporate body, headquartered in London, that organized and financed the early settlement of Virginia. (Eds.)

work, and more often than not, early death. The leading planters showed little interest in reforming these conditions. The servants were objects, things to be gambled away in games of chance, beaten or abused, and then, replaced when they wore out.

But dependence has another side. In Virginia dominance went hand in hand with fear, for no matter how tractable, how beaten down, the servants may have appeared, both masters and laborers recognized the potential for violence inherent in such relationships. In the early 1620s several worried planters complained that Captain John Martin, a longstanding troublemaker for the Virginia Company, "hath made his owne Territory there a receptacle of Vagabonds and bankerupts & other disorderly persons." Whether the rumors of Martin's activities were accurate is not the point. In such a society a gathering of "Vagabonds" represented a grave threat, a base from which the exploited could harass their former masters. The anxiety resurfaced in 1624 when the Virginia Company lost its charter and no one in the colony knew for certain who held legitimate authority. In shrill rhetoric that over the course of a century would become a regular feature of Virginia statue books, the colony's Assembly immediately ordered that "no person within this Colonie upon the rumor of supposed change and alterations [may] presume to be disobedient to the presente Government, nor servants to theire privatt officers masters or overseers, at their utmost perills."

The distrust that permeated Virginia society poisoned political institutions. Few colonists seem to have believed that local rulers would on their own initiative work for the public good. Instead, they assumed that persons in authority would use their office for personal gain. One settler called Governor George Yeardley, a man who grew rich directing public affairs, "the right worthy statesman for his own profit." William Capps, described simply as an old planter, referred to the governor as an "old smoker" and claimed that this official had "stood for a cypher whilst the Indians stood ripping open our guts." Cynicism about the motives of the colony's leaders meant that few citizens willingly sacrificed for the good of the state. In fact, Virginia planters seem to have regarded government orders as a threat to their independence, almost as a personal affront. William Strachey, secretary of the colony, condemned what he labeled the general "want of government." He reported, "every man overvaluing his owne worth, would be a Commander: every man underprising anothers value, denied to be commanded." Other colonists expressed agreement with Strachey's views. During the famous first meeting of the House of Burgesses in 1619, the representatives of the various plantations twice commented upon the weakness of Virginia's governing institutions. Toward the end of the session, they declared that whatever laws they passed in the future should go into immediate effect without special authorization from London, "for otherwise this people . . . would in a shorte time growe so insolent, as they would shake off all government, and there would be no living among them."

The colonists' achievements in education and religion were meager. From time to time, Virginians commented upon the importance of churches and schools in their society, but little was done to transform rhetoric into reality. Church buildings were in a perpetual state of decay; ministers were poorly supported by their parishioners. An ambitious plan for a college came to nothing, and schools for younger children seem to have been nonexistent. The large distances between plantations and the pressure to keep every able-bodied person working in the fields, no doubt discouraged the development of local schools and parish churches, but the colony's dispersed settlement plan does not in itself explain the absence of these institutions. A colonywide boarding school could have been constructed in Jamestown, a Harvard of Virginia, but the colony's planters were incapable of the sustained, cooperative effort that such a project would have required. They responded to general societal needs as individuals, not as groups. Later in the seventeenth century some successful planters sent their sons at great expense to universities in England and Scotland, but not until the end of the century did the colonist found a local college.

An examination of Virginia's military policies between 1617 and 1630 provides the clearest link between social values and institutional behavior. During this important transitional period, military affairs were far better recorded than were other social activities, and the historian can trace with a fair degree of confidence how particular military decisions reflected the colonists' value system. And second, in any society military efforts reveal a people's social priorities, their willingness to sacrifice for the common good, and their attitudes toward the allocation of community resources. Certainly, in early Virginia, maintaining a strong defense should have been a major consideration. Common sense alone seemed to dictate that a group of settlers confronted with a powerful Indian confederation and foreign marauders would, in military matters at least, cooperate for their own safety. But in point of fact, our common sense was not the rule of the seventeenth-century Virginian. The obsession with private profits was a more compelling force than was the desire to create a dependable system of self-defense. This destructive individualism disgusted John Pory, at one time the colony's secretary of state. In 1620 he reported that Governor Yeardley asked the men of Jamestown "to contribute some labor to a bridge, and to certaine platformes to mounte greate ordinance upon, being both for the use and defense of the same Citty, and so of themselves; yet they repyned as much as if all their goods had been taken from them."

Virginians paid dearly for their failure to work together. On March 22, 1622, the Indians of the region launched a coordinated attack on the scattered, poorly defended white settlements, and before the colonists could react, 347 of them had been killed. . . . The Massacre and the events of the months that followed provide rare insight into the workings of the Virginia culture. The shock of this defeat called into question previous institutional policies—not just military ones—and some colonists even saw the setback as an opportunity to reform society, to develop a new set of values.

Virginia's vulnerability revealed to some men the need to transform the privatistic culture into a more tightly knit, cooperative venture. Local rulers bravely announced that "this Massacre will prove much to the speedie advancement of the Colony and much to the benefitt of all those that shall nowe come thither." No longer would the planters live so far apart. Short-sighted dreams of tobacco fortunes would be laid aside, and the people would join together in the construction of genuine towns. And most important, the settlers would no longer evade their military responsibilities. As the members of the Virginia Council wrote only a month after the Massacre, "our first and princypall care should have beene for our safetie . . . yet its very necessarie for us yett at last, to laye a better and surer foundation for the tyme to come." But despite the death and destruction and despite the bold declarations about a new start, the colonists proceeded to repeat the very activities that contemporary commentators agreed had originally caused the people's immense suffering.

Even though the Indians remained a grave threat to security throughout the 1620s, the settlers continued to grumble about the burden of military service. Each person seemed to assess the tragedy only in personal terms—how, in other words, had the Indian Massacre affected his ability to turn a profit. By the end of the summer of 1622, there were unmistakable signs that many people no longer regarded the defeat of the Indians as a community responsibility. Few men talked of the common good; fewer still seemed prepared to sacrifice their lives or immediate earning power in order to preserve the colony from a second disaster.

Even as the governor and his council were weighing the various military alternatives, colonists were moving back to their isolated frontier plantations. The dispersion of fighting men, of course, seemed to invite new military defeats. But the danger from the Indians, although clearly perceived, was not sufficient to deter Virginians from taking up possessions which one person declared were "larger than 100 tymes their Number were able to Cultivate." In a poignant letter to his parents in England, a young servant, Richard Frethorne, captured the sense of doom that hung over the private plantations. "We are but 32 to fight against 3000 [Indians] if they should Come" he explained, "and the nighest helpe that Wee have is ten miles of us, and when the rogues overcame this place last [Martin's Hundred], they slew 80 Persons how then shall wee doe for wee lye even in their teeth, they may easily take us but that God is mercefull." Frethorne wrote this letter in March 1623, just twelve months after the Massacre had revealed to all the survivors that consequences of lying in the Indians' teeth.

The Virginia Council protested to colonial administrators in England, "It is noe smale difficultie and griefe unto us to maintaine a warr by unwill-

inge people, who . . . Crye out of the loss of Tyme against their Commanders, *in a warr where nothinge is to be gained."* By contrast, the village militia
in Massachusetts Bay provided an effective fighting force precisely because
the soldiers trusted those persons who remained at home. In theory, at least,
most New Englanders defined their lives in terms of the total community,
not in terms of private advancement, and the troops had no reason to believe that their friends and neighbors would try to profit from their sacrifice.
But in Virginia long before the massive enslavement of black Africans,
human relationships were regarded as a matter of pounds and pence, and
each day one man chased the Indians through the wilderness or helped
build a fortification, another man grew richer growing tobacco. When
William Capps in 1623 attempted to organize a raiding party of forty men to
go against the Indians, he was greeted with excuses and procrastination. Almost in disbelief, he informed an English correspondent of the planters'
train of though, "take away one of my men, there's 2000 Plantes gone, thates
500 waight of Tobacco, yea and what shall this man doe, runne after the Indians. . . . I have perhaps 10, perhaps 15, perhaps 20, men and am able to secure my owne Plantacion; how will they doe that are fewer? let them first be
Crusht alittle and then perhaps they will themselves make up the Nomber
for theire own safeties." Perhaps Frethorne's anxiety grew out of the knowledge that no one beyond Martin's Hundred really cared what the Indians
might do to him and his comrades.

Such foot-dragging obviously did nothing to promote colonial security.
Regardless of the planters' behavior, however, Virginia leaders felt compelled to deal with the Indians. After all, these appointed officials did not
want to appear incompetent before the king and his councillors. But the Virginians soon discovered that in the absence of public-spirited citizen soldiers, their range of military responses was effectively reduced to three. The
governor and his council could make the business of war so lucrative that
Virginians would willingly leave the tobacco fields to fight, entrust private
contractors with the responsibility of defending the entire population, or
persuade the king to send English troops at his own expense to protect the
colonists from their Indian enemies. Unfortunately, each of these alternatives presented specific drawbacks that rendered them essentially useless as
military policies.

The first option was to make the conditions of service so profitable that
the planters or in their place, the planters' servants, would join in subduing
the common enemy. In times of military crisis, such as the one following the
Great Massacre, both Company and Crown officials tried their best to persuade the settlers that warfare was not all hardship and sacrifice—indeed,
that for some men, presumably not themselves, Indian fighting could be an
economic opportunity. For the majority, however, such arguments apparently rang hollow. The colonists had learned that local Indians made poor

slaves, and in a spacious colony like Virginia, the offer of free land was an inadequate incentive for risking one's life. The promise of plunder drew few men away from the tobacco fields, and with typical candor, Captain John Smith announced in 1624, "I would not give twenty pound for all the pillage . . . to be got amongst the Salvages in twenty yeeres."

A second possible solution for Virginia's military needs was to hire someone to defend the colonists. The merits of this approach seemed obvious. The state could simply transfer public funds to groups of enterprising individuals who in turn might construct forts along the rivers, build palisades to ward off Indian attacks, and even in some cases, fight pitched battles along the frontier. Unlike the New Englanders, who generally regarded matters of defense as a community responsibility, much like providing churches and schools, Virginians accepted the notion that private contractors could serve as an adequate substitute for direct popular participation in military affairs.

In this belief the Virginians were mistaken. A stream of opportunists came forward with schemes that would compensate for the colony's unreliable militia. Without exception, however, these plans drained the public treasury but failed to produce lasting results. Indeed, Virginia's social values spawned a class of military adventurers—perhaps military profiteers would be a more accurate description—who did their best to transform warfare into a profitable private business.

Some of the private military schemes of the 1620s were bizarre, others humorous, almost all misallocations of public revenues. In the summer of 1622 a sea captain named Samuel Each, whose military qualifications remain obscure, offered to construct a fort of oyster shells to guard the mouth of the James River. Each's project seemed a convenient way to secure the colony's shipping from possible foreign harassment. For his work, the captain was promised a handsome reward, but as was so often to be the case in the history of seventeenth-century Virginia, the contractor disappointed the settlers' expectations. The proposed site for the fortification turned out to be under water at high tide and "at low water with everie wynd washed over by the surges." One colonist sardonically described Each's pile of sea shells as "a Castle in the aire" and suggested that the captain had wisely died on the job "to save his Credit."

During the 1620s other adventurers followed, but their performance was no more impressive than Each's had been. These men sometimes couched their proposals in rhetoric about the common good. There was no question, however, about what considerations motivated the contractors. In 1628, for example, two of the colony's most successful planters, Samuel Mathews and William Claiborne, presented the king of England with what they called "A Proposition Concerning the Winning of the Forest." They humbly informed Charles I that their plan grew "not out of any private respects, or intent to gaine to our selves, but because in our owne mindes wee perceive [?] our selves bound to expend both our lives and fortunes in so good a service for this Plantation." One may be justly skeptical about the extent of their anticipated personal sacrifice, for in the next paragraph, the two Virginians demanded 1200 pounds "in readie monye" and 100 pounds sterling every year thereafter. Governor Francis Wyatt gave the project begrudging support. He explained that because of the planters' "too much affection to their private dividents" and their unwillingness to alter their pattern of settlement in the interest of defense, Mathews and Claiborne should be encouraged to construct a fortified wall running six miles between the Charles and James Rivers. The two men promised to build a palisade and staff it with their own armed servants. There is no record of what happened to this particular plan, but if it had been accepted, the servants most likely would have spent their days planting tobacco for two men already quite wealthy.

The reliance on military adventurers held dangers of which the Virginians of the 1620s were only dimly aware. As long as the price of tobacco remained relatively high, the colonists ignored much of the waste and favoritism associated with lucrative military contracts. But high taxes caused grumbling, even serious social unrest. In the early 1620s the members of the Virginia Council reported that when it came time to reimburse Captain Each, there was "a general unwillingness (not to say an opposition) in all almost but ourselves." As tobacco profits dropped over the course of the seventeenth century, small planters and landless freemen showed an increasing hostility to private military contractors. . . .

A second difficulty with the adventurers was no bigger than a man's hand during the 1620s. The colony needed every able-bodied defender that could be found, and no one seems to have worried much about arming indentured servants and poor freeman. But in later years, Virginians would have cause to reconsider the wisdom of creating mercenary bodies composed largely of impoverished recruits. The leading planters discovered, in fact, that one could not systematically exploit other human beings for private profit and then expect those same people to risk their lives fighting to preserve the society that tolerated such oppressive conditions. As privatism became the way of life, the colony's leading planters were less and less certain whether internal or external enemies posed a greater threat to Virginia's security.

A third possible solution to the settlement's early military needs lay in obtaining direct English assistance. During the 1620s Virginia leaders frequently petitioned the mother country for arms, men and supplies. In 1626—four years after the Massacre—the royal governor informed the Privy Council that the security of Virginia required "no less nombers then five hundred soldiers to be yearly sent over." On other occasions officials in Virginia admitted that as few as 50 or 100 troops would do, but however many men England provided, the colonists expected the king to pay the bill. Free protection would remove the necessity for high taxes. Understandably, the English administrators never found the settlers' argument persuasive, and royal policy makers may well have wondered what several thousand colonists were doing to defend themselves.

Before the 1670s not a single English soldier was dispatched to Virginia. Nevertheless, despite repeated failures in gaining English assistance, the dream of acquiring a cheap, dependable military force remained strong. Had the colony's own citizens been more involved in Virginia's defense, more willing to live closer together, there would have been no reason to plead for outside support. But the spirit of excessive individualism ironically bred a habit of dependence upon the mother country, and as soon as internal problems threatened the peace, someone was sure to call for English regulars.

Virginia's military preparedness was no more impressive in 1630 than it had been a decade earlier. The colony's rulers still complained that the planters "utterly neglected eyther to stand upon their guard or to keepe their Armes fitt." The Council admitted helplessly that "neyther proclamations nor other strict orders have remedied the same." The settlers were incorrigible. Forts remained unbuilt; the great palisade neither kept the colonists in nor the Indians out. And in 1644 the local tribes launched a second, even more deadly attack, revealing once again the fundamental weakness of Virginia's military system.

Virginia's extreme individualism was not an ephemeral phenomenon, something associated only with the colony's founding or a peculiar boomtown atmosphere. Long after the 1620s, values originally brought to the New World by adventurers and opportunists influenced patterns of social and institutional behavior, and instead of providing Virginia with new direction or a new sense of mission, newcomers were assimilated into an established cultural system. Customs became statute law, habitual acts tradition. . . . seventeenth-century Virginians never succeeded in forming a coherent society. Despite their apparent homogeneity, they lacked cohesive group identity; they generated no positive symbols, no historical myths strong enough to overcome individual differences. As one might expect, such a social system proved extremely fragile, and throughout the seventeenth century Virginians experienced social unrest, even open rebellion.

Nor should the grand life style of the great eighteenth-century planters, the Byrds, the Carters, the Wormeleys, mislead one into thinking that their value system differed significantly from that of Virginia's early settlers. These first families of the early eighteenth century bore the same relationship to Captain John Smith and his generation as Cotton Mather and his contemporaries did to the founders of Massachusetts Bay. The apparent political tranquility of late colonial Virginia grew not out of a sense of community or new value-orientations, but out of more effective forms of human exploitation. The mass of tobacco field laborers were now black slaves, men and women who by legal definition could never become fully part of the privatistic culture. In Byrd's Virginia, voluntaristic associations remained weak; education lagged, churches stagnated, and towns never developed. The isolation of plantation life continued, and the extended visits and the elaborate balls of the period may well have served to obscure the competition that underlay planter relationships. As one anthropologist reminds us, "in a society in which everyone outside the nuclear family is immediately suspect, in which one is at every moment believed to be vulnerable to the underhanded attacks of others, reliability and trust can never be taken for granted." In the course of a century of cultural development, Virginians transformed an extreme form of individualism, a value system suited for soldiers an adventurers, into a set of regional virtues, a love of independence, an insistence upon personal liberty, a cult of manhood, and an uncompromising loyalty to family.

DOCUMENTS

Virginia, A Troubled Colony, 1622

I found the plantations generally seated upon meer salt marshes, full of infectious boggy and muddy creeks and lakes, and hereby subjected to all those inconveniences and diseases which are so commonly found in the most unsound and most unhealthy parts of England, whereof every country and climate hath some.

I found the shores and sides of those parts of the main river, where our plantations are settled, every where so shallow that no boats can approach the shores; so that besides the difficulty, danger and spoil of goods in the landing of them, the poor people are forced to the continual wading and wetting themselves, and that in the prime of winter, when the ships commonly arrive, and thereby get such violent surfeits of cold upon cold as seldom leave them until they leave to live.

The new people that are yearly sent over, which arrives here for the most part very unseasonably in winter, find neither guest-house, inn, nor any the like place to shroud themselves in at their arrival; no, not so much as a stroke given towards any such charitable work, so that many of them, by want hereof, are not only seen dying under hedges, and in the woods, but being dead lye some of them for many days unregarded and unburied.

The colony was this winter in much distress of victual, so that English meal was sold at the rate of thirty shillings a bushel, their own native corn,

SOURCE: Report of Nathaniel Butler, Governor of Bermuda, 1622. Document from Bibliobase®, edited by Michael Bellesiles. Copyright © by Houghton Mifflin Company. Reprinted by permission.

called maize, at ten and fifteen shillings per bushel, the which, howsoever it lay heavy upon the shoulders of the generality, it may be suspected not to be unaffected by some of the chief, for they only having the means in those extremities to trade with the natives for corn, do hereby engross all into their own hands, and to sell it abroad at their own prices, and I myself have heard from the mouth of a prime one among them that he would never wish that their own corn should be cheaper amongst them than eight shillings the bushel.

Their houses are generally the worst that ever I saw, the meanest cottages in England being every way equal (if not superior) with the most of the best, and besides, so improvidently and scatteringly are they seated one from another, as partly by their distance, but especially by the interposition of creeks and swamps, as they call them, they offer all advantages to their savage enemies, and are utterly deprived of all sudden recollection of themselves upon any terms whatsoever.

I found not the least piece of fortification; three pieces of ordnance only mounted at James City, and one at Flowerde Hundreds, but never a one of them serviceable, so that it is most certain that a small bark of a hundred tun may take its time to pass up the river in spite of them, and coming to an anchor before the town may beat all their houses down about their ears, and so forcing them to retreat into the woods may land under the favour of their ordnance and rifle the town at pleasure.

Expecting, according to their printed books, a great forwardness of divers and sundry commodities at mine arrival, I found not any one of them so much as in any towardness of being, for the iron works were utterly wasted, and the men dead, the furnaces for glass and pots at a stay, and small hopes; as for the rest they were had in a general derision even amongst themselves, and the pamphlets that had published their, being sent thither by hundreds, were laughed to scorn, and every base fellow boldly gave them the lye in divers particulars; so that tobacco only was the business, and for ought that I could hear every man madded upon that little thought or looked for anything else.

I found the ancient plantations of Henrico and Charles City wholly quitted and left to the spoil of the Indians, who not only burnt the houses, said to be once the best of all others, but fell upon the poultry, hogs, cows, goats and horses, whereof they killed great numbers, to the great grief as well as ruin of the old inhabitants, who stick not to affirm that these were not only the best and healthiest parts of all others, but might also, by their natural strength of situation, have been the most easily preserved of all others.

Whereas, according to his Majesty's most gracious letters-patents, his people are as near as possibly may be to be governed after the excellent laws and customs of England, I found in the Government here not only ignorant and enforced strayings in divers particulars, but wilful and intended ones; in so much as some who urged due conformity have in contempt been termed men of law, and were excluded from those rights which by orderly proceedings they were elected and sworn unto here.

There having been, as it is thought, not fewer than ten thousand souls transported thither, there are not, thro' the aforementioned abuses and neglects, above two thousand of them to be found alive at this present . . . many of them also in a sickly and desperate state. So that it may undoubtedly be expected that unless the confusions and private ends of some of the Company here, and the bad execution in seconding them by their agents there, be redressed with speed by some divine and supream hand, that instead of a plantation it will get the name of a slaughter-house, and so justly become both odious to ourselves and contemptible to all the world.

The Experiences of an Indentured Servant, 1623

LOVING AND KIND FATHER AND MOTHER:

My most humble duty remembered to you, hoping in God of your good health, as I myself am at the making hereof. This is to let you understand that I your child am in a most heavy case by reason of the nature of the country, [which] is such that it causeth much sickness, [such] as the scurvy and the bloody flux and diverse other diseases, which maketh the body very poor and weak. And when we are sick there is nothing to comfort us; for since I came out of the ship I never ate anything but peas, and loblollie (that is, water gruel). As for deer or venison I never saw any since I came into this land. There is indeed some fowl, but we are not allowed to go and get it, but must work hard both early and late for a mess of water gruel and a mouthful of bread and beef. A mouthful of bread for a penny loaf must serve for four men which is most pitiful. [You would be grieved] if you did know as much as I [do], when people cry out day and night—Oh! that they were in England without their limbs—and would not care to lose any limb to be in England again, yea, though they beg from door to door. For we live in fear of the enemy every hour, yet we have had a combat with them . . . and we took two alive and made slaves of them. But it was by policy, for we are in great danger; for our plantation is very weak by reason of the death and sickness of our company. For we came but twenty for the merchants, and they are half dead just; and we look every hour when two more should go. Yet there came some four other men yet to live with us, of which there is but one alive; and our Lieutenant is dead, and [also] his father and his brother. And there was some five or six of the last year's twenty, of which

SOURCE: Richard Frethorne, Letter to his father and mother, March 20, April 2 & 3, 1623, in Susan M. Kingsbury, ed., *The Records of the Virginia Company of London* 4 (Washington, D.C.: Government Printing Office, 1935): 58–62.

there is but three left, so that we are fain to get other men to plant with us; and yet we are but 32 to fight against 3000 if they should come. And the nighest help that we have is ten miles of us, and when the rogues overcame this place [the] last [time] they slew 80 persons. How then shall we do, for we lie even in their teeth? They may easily take us, but [for the fact] that God is merciful and can save with few as well as with many, as he showed to Gilead.* And like Gilead's soldiers, if they lapped water, we drink water which is but weak.

And I have nothing to comfort me, nor is there nothing to be gotten here but sickness and death, except [in the event] that one had money to lay out in some things for profit. But I have nothing at all—no, not a shirt to my back but two rags (2), nor no clothes but one poor suit, nor but one pair of shoes, but one pair of stockings, but one cap, [and] but two bands [collars]. My cloak is stolen by one of my own fellows, and to his dying hour [he] would not tell me what he did with it; but some of my fellows saw him have butter and beef out of a ship, which my cloak, I doubt [not], paid for. So that I have not a penny, nor a penny worth, to help me to either spice or sugar or strong waters, without the which one cannot live here. For as strong beer in England doth fatten and strengthen them, so water here doth wash and weaken these here [and] only keeps [their] life and soul together. But I am not half [of] a quarter so strong as I was in England, and all is for want of victuals; for I do protest unto you that I have eaten more in [one] day at home than I have allowed me here for a week. You have given more than my day's allowance to a beggar at the door; and if Mr. Jackson had not relieved me, I should be in a poor case. But he like a father and she like a loving mother doth still help me.

For when we got to Jamestown (that is 10 miles of us) there lie all the ships that come to land, and there they must deliver their goods. And when we went up to town [we would go], as it may be, on Monday at noon, and come there by night, [and] then load the next day by noon, and go home in the afternoon, and unfold, and then away again in the night, and [we would] be up about midnight. Then if it rained or blowed never so hard, we must lie in the boat on the water and have nothing but a little bread. For when we go into the boat we [would] have a loaf allowed to two men, and it is all [we would get] if we stayed there two days, which is hard; and [we] must lie all that while in the boat. But that Goodman Jackson pitied me and made me a cabin to lie in always when I [would] come up, and he would give me some poor jacks [fish] [to take] home with me, which comforted me more than peas or water gruel. Oh, they be very godly folks, and love me very well, and will do anything for me. And he much marvelled that you would send me a servant to the Company; he saith I had been better

---

*Frethorne's "Gilead" is apparently a reference to the Biblical Gideon of the Book of Judges, chapters 6 and 7. (Eds.)

knocked on the head. And indeed so I find it now, to my great grief and misery; and [I] saith that if you love me you will redeem me suddenly, for which I do entreat and beg. And if you cannot get the merchants to redeem me for some little money, then for God's sake get a gathering or entreat some good folks to lay out some little sum of money in meal and cheese and butter and beef. Any eating meat will yield great profit. Oil and vinegar is very good; but, father, there is great loss in leaking. But for God's sake send beef and cheese and butter, or the more of one sort and none of another. But if you send cheese, it must be very old cheese; and at the cheesemonger's you may buy very good cheese for twopence farthing or halfpenny, that will be liked very well. But if you send cheese, you must have a care how you pack it in barrels; and you must put cooper's chips between every cheese, or else the heat of the hold will rot them. And look whatsoever you send me—be it never so much—look, what[ever] I make of it, I will deal truly with you. I will send it over and beg the profit to redeem me; and if I die before it come, I have entreated Goodman Jackson to send you the worth of it, who hath promised he will. If you send, you must direct your letters to Goodman Jackson, at Jamestown, a gunsmith. (You must set down his freight, because there be more of his name there.) Good father, do not forget me, but have mercy and pity my miserable case. I know if you did but see me, you would weep to see me; for I have but one suit. (But [though] it is a strange one, it is very well guarded.) Wherefore, for God's sake, pity me. I pray you to remember my love to all my friends and kindred. I hope all my brothers and sisters are in good health, and as for my part I have set down my resolution that certainly will be; that is, that the answer of this letter will be life or death to me. Therefore, good father, send as soon as you can; and if you send me any thing let this be the mark.

ROT

RICHARD FRETHORNE,
MARTIN'S HUNDRED

"Wee shall be as a Citty upon a Hill," 1630

It rests now to make some application of this discourse by the present designe which gave the occasion of writeing of it. Herein are 4 things to be propounded: first the persons, 2ly, the worke, 3ly, the end, 4ly, the meanes.

1. For the persons, wee are a Company professing our selves fellow members of Christ, In which respect onely though wee were absent from eache other many miles, and had our imploymentes as farre distant, yet wee

SOURCE: John Winthrop, "A Modell of Christian Charity," in *Winthrop Papers* 2 (Boston: Massachusetts Historical Society, 1929): 282–284.

ought to account our selves knitt together by this bond of love, and live in the exercise of it, if wee would have comforte of our being in Christ. . . .

2ly. For the worke wee have in hand, it is by a mutuall consent through a speciall overruleing providence, and a more then an ordinary approbation of the Churches of Christ to seeke out a place of Cohabitation and Consorteshipp under a due forme of Government both civill and ecclesiasticall. In such cases as this the care of the publique must oversway all private respects, by which not onely conscience, but meare Civill policy doth binde us; for it is a true rule that perticuler estates cannot subsist in the ruine of the publique.

3ly. The end is to improve our lives to doe more service to the Lord the comforte and encrease of the body of christe whereof wee are members that our selves and posterity may be the better preserved from the Common corrupcions of this evill world to serve the Lord and worke out our Salvacion under the power and purity of his holy Ordinances.

4ly. for the meanes whereby this must bee effected, they are 2fold, a Conformity with the worke and end wee aime at, these wee see are extraordinary, therefore wee must not content our selves with usuall ordinary meanes whatsoever wee did or ought to have done when wee lived in England, the same must wee doe and more allsoe where wee goe: That which the most in theire Churches maineteine as a truthe in profession onely, wee must bring into familiar and constant practise, as in this duty of love wee must love brotherly without dissimulation, wee must love one another with a pure hearte fevently wee must beare one anothers burthens, wee must not looke onely on our owne things, but allsoe on the things of our brethren, neither must wee think that the lord will beare with such faileings at our hands as hee dothe from those among whome wee have lived. . . . Thus stands the cause betweene God and us, wee are entered into Covenant with him for this worke, wee have taken out a Commission, the Lord have given us leave to drawe our owne Articles wee have professed to enterprise these Accions upon these and these ends, wee have hereupon besought him of favour and blessing: Now if the Lord shall please to heare us, and bring us in peace to the place wee desire, then hath hee ratified this Covenant and sealed our Commission, [and] will expect a strickt performance of the Articles contained in it, but if wee shall neglect the observacion of these Articles which are the ends wee have propounded, and dissembling with our God, shall fall to embrace this present world and prosecute our carnall intencions, seekeing great things for our selves and our posterity, the Lord will surely breake out in wrathe against us be revenged of such a periured people and make us knowe the price of the breache of such a Covenant.

Now the onely way to avoyde this shipwracke and to provide for our posterity is to followe the Counsell of Micah, to doe Justly, to love mercy, to walke humbly with our God, for this end, wee must be knitt together in this worke as one man, wee must entertaine each other in brotherly Afeccion,

wee must be willing to abridge our selves of our superfluities, for the supply of others necessities, wee must uphold a familiar Commerce together in
all meekenes, gentlenes, patience and liberallity, wee must delight in each
other, make others Condicions our owne reioyce together, mourne together,
labour, and suffer together, allwayes haveing before our eyes our Commission and Community in the worke, our Community as members of the same
body, soe shall wee keepe the unitie of the spirit in the bond of peace, the
Lord will be our God and delight to dwell among us, as his owne people
and will commaund a blessing upon us in all our wayes, soe that wee shall
see much more of his wisdome power goodnes and truthe then formerly
wee have beene acquainted with, wee shall finde that the God of Israell is
among us, when tenn of us shall be able to resist a thousand of our enemies, when hee shall make us a prayse and glory, that men shall say of suc-
ceeding plantacions: the lord make it like that of New England: for wee
must Consider that wee shall be as a Citty upon a Hill, the eies of all people
are uppon us; soe that if wee shall deale falsely with our god in this worke
wee have undertaken and soe cause him to withdrawe his present help
from us, wee shall be made a story and a byword through the world, wee
shall open the mouthes of enemies to speake evill of the wayes of god and
all professours for Gods sake; wee shall shame the faces of many of gods
worthy servants, and cause theire prayers to be turned in Cursses upon us
till wee be consumed out of the good land whether wee are goeing: And to
shutt upp this discourse with that exhortacion of Moses that faithful servant
of the Lord in his last farewell to Israell Deut. 30. Beloved there is now sett
before us life, and good, deathe and evill in that wee are Commaunded this
day to love the Lord our God, and to love one another to walke in his wayes
and keepe his Commaundements and his Ordinance, and his lawes, and the
Articles of our Covenant with him that wee may live and be multiplyed,
and that the Lord our God may blesse us in the land whether wee goe to
possesse it: But if our heartes shall turne away soe that wee will not obey,
but shall be seduced and worshipp [serve cancelled] other Gods our pleasures, and proffitts, and serve them; it is propounded unto us this day; wee
shall surely perishe out of the good Land whether wee passe over this vast
Sea to possesse it;

> Therefore lett us choose life,
> that wee, and our Seede,
> may live, by obeyeing his
> voyce, and cleaveing to him,
> for hee is our life, and
> our prosperity.

Chapter 3

Husbands and Wives, Parents and Children in Puritan Society

In sharp contrast to the privatism and individualism that marked seventeenth-century Virginia, a deep sense of cooperative commitment to building a new Zion characterized the society established in the Massachusetts Bay Colony. Nowhere was the notion of communal responsibility more fully developed or more clearly illustrated than in the Puritan family. As you read the essay "The Godly Family of Colonial Massachusetts" by Steven Mintz and Susan Kellogg, note the innumerable ways in which Puritan family life affected and was affected by the larger social, political, and economic community. How would you compare the role of the family in Massachusetts with that in Virginia during the same period?

Although few today would find Puritan notions regarding marriage and relations between the sexes appealing, Mintz and Kellogg remind us that these people were not as devoid of warmth and feeling as the term "Puritan" often implies. As evidence, the authors refer to sentiments expressed in the poems of Anne Bradstreet, the first important woman writer in the colonies. The document that follows the *essay presents two of Bradstreet's poems, "To My Dear and Loving Husband" and "Before the Birth of One of Her Children"—works that evoke a sense of deep and abiding love in a Puritan marriage. The poet's husband, Simon Bradstreet, served two terms as colonial governor of Massachusetts (1679–1686, 1689–1692).*

As the essay reveals, the Puritans considered the proper upbringing of children and the maintenance of a sound moral climate cardinal family responsibilities. They also believed that the state had a vital role to play in ensuring that families fulfill these obligations. The second document, an act passed by the colonial Massachusetts legislature, orders parents to educate their children. Such a legal step was highly unusual in the English-speaking world of the seventeenth century. Take note of all the items included under the term "good education" and the penalties imposed on parents who neglected their duties. The legislation in the third document describes the kinds of behavior deemed improper and the kinds of action deemed necessary to safeguard public morality. After reading these two documents, you should notice that the idea of a separation between church and state was totally absent from Puritan Massachusetts.

The final document is an excerpt from Eleazer Moody's The School of Good Manners, a well-known book of eighteenth-century children's literature. Which of the forty-two dicta that Moody lists might today's parents consider valid? Which, if any, would they likely reject? What conclusions can you draw regarding differences in attitudes toward children's behavior today and in colonial New England?

ESSAY

The Godly Family of Colonial Massachusetts

Steven Mintz and Susan Kellogg

The roughly twenty thousand Puritan men, women, and children who sailed to Massachusetts between 1629 and 1640 carried with them ideas about the family utterly foreign to Americans today. The Puritans never thought of the family as purely a private unit, rigorously separated from the surrounding community. To them it was an integral part of the larger political and social world; it was "the Mother Hive, out of which both those swarms of State and Church, issued forth." Its boundaries were elastic and inclusive, and it assumed responsibilities that have since been assigned to public institutions. ·

Although most Puritan families were nuclear in structure, a significant proportion of the population spent part of their lives in other families'

SOURCE: Reprinted with permission of The Free Press, a Division of Simon & Schuster, Inc. from *Domestic Revolutions: A Social History of American Family Life,* pp. 4–17, by Steven Mintz and Susan Kellogg. Copyright © 1988 by The Free Press.

homes, serving as apprentices, hired laborers, or servants. At any one time, as many as a third of all Puritan households took in servants. Convicts, the children of the poor, single men and women, and recent immigrants were compelled by selectmen to live within existing "well Governed families" so that "disorders may bee prevented and ill weeds nipt."

For the Puritans, family ties and community ties tended to blur. In many communities, individual family members were related by birth or marriage to a large number of their neighbors. In one community, Chatham, Massachusetts, the town's 155 families bore just thirty-four surnames; and in Andover, Massachusetts, the descendants of one settler, George Abbott I, had by 1750 intermarried into a dozen local families. The small size of the seventeenth-century communities, combined with high rates of marriage and remarriage, created kinship networks of astonishing complexity. In-laws and other distant kin were generally referred to as brothers, sisters, aunts, uncles, mothers, fathers, and cousins.

Today spousal ties are emphasized, and obligations to kin are voluntary and selective. Three centuries ago the kin group was of great importance to the social, economic, and political life of the community. Kinship ties played a critical role in the development of commercial trading networks and the capitalizing of large-scale investments. In the absence of secure methods of communication and reliable safeguards against dishonesty, prominent New England families, such as the Hutchinsons and Winthrops, relied on relatives in England and the West Indies to achieve success in commerce. Partnerships among family members also played an important role in the ownership of oceangoing vessels. Among merchant and artisan families, apprenticeships were often given exclusively to their own sons or nephews, keeping craft skills within the kinship group.

Intermarriage was also used to cement local political alliances and economic partnerships. Marriages between first cousins or between sets of brothers and sisters helped to bond elite, politically active and powerful families together. Among the families of artisans, marriages between a son and an uncle's daughter reinforced kinship ties.

In political affairs the importance of the kin group persisted until the American Revolution. By the early eighteenth century, small groups of interrelated families dominated the clerical, economic, military, and political leadership of New England. In Connecticut and Massachusetts, the most powerful of these kinship groups was made up of seven interrelated families. The "River Gods," as they were known, led regional associations of ministers, controlled the county courts, commanded the local militia, and represented their region in the Massachusetts General Court and Governor's Council. Following the Revolution, most states adopted specific reforms designed to reduce the power of kin groups in politics by barring nepotism, establishing the principle of rotation in office, prohibiting multiple officeholding, providing for the election of justices of the peace, and requiring officeholders to reside in the jurisdiction they served.

Unlike the contemporary American family, which is distinguished by its isolation from the world of work and the surrounding society, the Puritan family was deeply embedded in public life. The household—not the individual—was the fundamental unit of society. The political order was not an agglomeration of detached individuals; it was an organic unity composed of families. This was the reason that Puritan households received only a single vote in town meetings. Customarily it was the father, as head of the household, who represented his family at the polls. But if he was absent, his wife assumed his prerogative to vote. The Puritans also took it for granted that the church was composed of families and not of isolated individuals. Family membership—not an individual's abilities or attainments—determined a person's position in society. Where one sat in church or in the local meetinghouse or even one's rank at Harvard College was determined not by one's accomplishments but by one's family identity.

The Puritan family was the main unit of production in the economic system. Each family member was expected to be economically useful. Older children were unquestionably economic assets; they worked at family industries, tended gardens, herded animals, spun wool, and cared for younger brothers and sisters. Wives not only raised children and cared for the home but also cut clothes, supervised servants and apprentices, kept financial accounts, cultivated crops, and marketed surplus goods.

In addition to performing a host of productive functions, the Puritan family was a primary educational and religious unit. A 1642 Massachusetts statute required heads of households to lead their households in prayers and scriptural readings; to teach their children, servants, and apprentices to read; and to catechize household members in the principles of religion and law. The family was also an agency for vocational training, assigned the duty of instructing servants and apprentices in methods of farming, housekeeping, and craft skills. And finally the Puritan family was a welfare institution that carried primary responsibility for the care of orphans, the infirm, or the elderly.

Given the family's importance, the Puritans believed that the larger community had a compelling duty to ensure that families performed their functions properly. The Puritans did not believe that individual households should be assured freedom from outside criticism or interference. The Puritan community felt that it had a responsibility not only to punish misconduct but also to intervene within households to guide and direct behavior. To this end, in the 1670s, the Massachusetts General Court directed towns to appoint "tithingmen" to oversee every ten or twelve households in order to ensure that marital relationships were harmonious and that parents properly disciplined unruly children. Puritan churches censured, admonished, and excommunicated men and women who failed to maintain properly peaceful households, since, as minister Samuel Willard put it, "When husband and wife neglect their duties they not only wrong each other, but they provoke God by breaking his law." In cases in which parents failed properly to govern "rude, stubborn, and unruly" children, Puritan law permitted local authorities to remove juveniles from their families "and place them with some master for years . . . and force them to submit unto government." Men who neglected or failed to support their wives or children were subject to judicial penalties. In instances in which spouses seriously violated fundamental duties—such as cases of adultery, desertion, prolonged absence, or nonsupport—divorces were granted. In cases of fornication outside marriage, courts sentenced offenders to a fine or whipping; for adultery, offenders were punished by fines, whippings, brandings, wearing of the letter *A*, and in at least three cases, the death penalty.

The disciplined Puritan family of the New World was quite different from the English family of the sixteenth and seventeenth centuries that had been left behind. In fact, it represented an effort to re-create an older ideal of the family that no longer existed in England itself.

English family life in the era of New World colonization was quite unstable. Because of high mortality rates, three-generational households containing grandparents, parents, and children tended to be rare. The duration of marriages tended to be quite brief—half of all marriages were cut short by the death of a spouse after just seventeen to nineteen years. And the number of children per marriage was surprisingly small. Late marriage, a relatively long interval between births, and high rates of infant and child mortality meant that just two, three, or four children survived past adolescence. Despite today's mythical vision of stability and rootedness in the preindustrial world, mobility was rampant. Most Englishmen could expect to move from one village to another during their adult lives, and it was rare for an English family to remain in a single community for as long as fifty years. Indeed, a significant proportion of the English population was denied the opportunity to *have* a family life. Servants, apprentices, and university lecturers were forbidden from marrying, and most other young men had to wait to marry until they received an inheritance on their father's death.

The English migrants who ventured to New England sought to avoid the disorder of English family life through a structured and disciplined family. They possessed a firm idea of a godly family, and they sought to establish it despite the novelty of American circumstances. Puritan religion had a particularly strong appeal to these men and women who were most sensitive to the disruptive forces transforming England during the sixteenth and seventeenth centuries—such forces as an alarming increase in population, a rapid rise in prices, the enclosure of traditional common lands, and the sudden appearances of a large class of propertyless men and women who flocked to the growing cities or took to the woods. To the Puritans, whose spiritual community was threatened by these developments, establishment of a holy commonwealth in New England represented a desperate effort to restore order and discipline to social behavior. And it was the family through which order could most effectively be created.

Migration to the New World wilderness intensified the Puritan fear of moral and political chaos and encouraged their focus on order and discipline. In the realm of economics, Puritan authorities strove to regulate prices, limit the rate of interest, and fix the maximum wages—at precisely the moment that such notions were breaking down in England. And in the realm of family life, the Puritans, drawing on the Old Testament and classical political theory, sought to reestablish an older ideal of the family in which the father was endowed with patriarchal authority as head of his household. Their religion taught that family roles were part of a continuous chain of hierarchical and delegated authority descending from God, and it was within the family matrix that all larger, external conceptions of authority, duty, and discipline were defined.

Puritans organized their family around the unquestioned principle of patriarchy. Fathers represented their households in the public realms of politics and social leadership; they owned the bulk of personal property; and law and church doctrine made it the duty of wives, children, and servants to submit to the father's authority. The colonies of Connecticut, Massachusetts, and New Hampshire went so far as to enact statutes calling for the death of children who cursed or struck their fathers.

Patriarchal authority in the Puritan family ultimately rested on the father's control of landed property or craft skills. Puritan children were dependent upon their father's support in order to marry and set up independent households. Since Puritan fathers were permitted wide discretion in how they would distribute their property, it was important that children show a degree of deference to their father's wishes. The timing and manner in which fathers conveyed property to the next generation exerted a profound influence upon where children decided to live and when and whom they decided to marry. In many cases fathers settled sons on plots surrounding the parental homestead, with title not to be surrendered until after their deaths. In other instances fathers conveyed land or other property when their sons became adults or were married. Not uncommonly such wills or deeds contained carefully worded provisions ensuring that the son would guarantee the parent lifetime support. One deed, for example, provided that a son would lose his inheritance if his parents could not walk freely through the house to go outdoors.

Such practices kept children economically dependent for years, delayed marriage, and encouraged sons to remain near their fathers during their lifetimes. In Andover, Massachusetts, only a quarter of the second-generation sons actually owned the land they farmed before their fathers died. Not until the fourth generation in mid-eighteenth-century Andover had this pattern noticeably disappeared. In Plymouth, Massachusetts, and Windsor, Connecticut, fathers gave land to children on marriage. Among Quaker families in Pennsylvania, fathers who were unable to locate land for sons in the same town bought land in nearby communities. In order to replicate their parents' style of life, sons had to wait to inherit property from their fathers. In most cases ownership and control of land reinforced the authority of fathers over their children.

A corollary to the Puritan assumption of patriarchy was a commitment to female submission within the home. Even by the conservative standards of the time, the roles assigned to women by Puritan theology were narrowly circumscribed. The premise guiding Puritan theory was given pointed expression by the poet Milton: "God's universal law gave to man despotic power/Over his female in due awe." Women were not permitted to vote or prophesy or question church doctrine. The ideal woman was a figure of "modesty" and "delicacy," kept ignorant of the financial affairs of her family. Her social roles were limited to wife, mother, mistress of the household, seamstress, wet nurse, and midwife. Although there was no doubt that she was legally subordinate to her husband, she had limited legal rights and protections.

Puritan doctrine did provide wives with certain safeguards. Husbands who refused to support or cohabit with their wives were subject to legal penalties. Wives, in theory, could sue for separation or divorce on grounds of a husband's impotence, cruelty, abandonment, bigamy, adultery, or failure to provide, but divorce was generally unavailable, and desertion was such a risky venture that only the most desperate women took it as an option. Colonial statutes also prohibited a husband from striking his wife, "unless it be in his own defense." Before marriage single women had the right to conduct business, own property, and represent themselves in court. Upon marriage, however, the basic legal assumption was that of "coverture"—that a woman's legal identity was absorbed in her husband's. Spouses were nevertheless allowed to establish antenuptial or postnuptial agreements, permitting a wife to retain control over her property.

For both Puritan women and men, marriage stood out as one of the central events in life. Despite their reputation as sexually repressed, pleasure-hating bigots, the Puritans did not believe that celibacy was a condition morally superior to marriage. The only thing that Saint Paul might have said in favor of marriage was that it is "better to marry than to burn," but the Puritans extolled marriage as a sacrament and a social duty. John Cotton put the point bluntly: "They are a sort of Blasphemers then who dispise and decry" [women as a necessary evil,] "for they are a necessary Good; such as it was not good that man should be without."

For the Puritans love was not a prerequisite for marriage. They believed that the choice of a marriage partner should be guided by rational considerations of property, religious piety, and family interest, not by physical attraction, personal feelings, or romantic love. Affection, in their view, would develop after marriage. This attitude reflected a recognition of the essential economic functions of the colonial family. Marriage was a partnership to which both bride and groom were expected to bring skills and resources. A prospective bride was expected to contribute a dowry (usually in the form of money or household goods) worth half of what the bridegroom brought to the marriage. Artisans tended to choose wives from families that practiced the same trade precisely because these women would be best able to assist them in their work. In New England the overwhelming majority of men and women married—and many remarried rapidly after the death of a spouse—because it was physically and economically difficult to live alone.

According to Puritan doctrine, a wife was to be her husband's helpmate, not his equal. Her role was "to guid the house &c. not guid the Husband." The Puritans believed that a wife should be submissive to her husband's commands and should exhibit toward him an attitude of "reverence," by which they meant a proper mixture of fear and awe; not "a slavish Fear, which is nourished with hatred or aversion; but a noble and generous Fear, which proceeds from Love."

The actual relations between Puritan spouses were more complicated than religious dogma would suggest. It was not unusual to find mutual love and tenderness in Puritan marriages. In their letters Puritan husbands and wives frequently referred to each other in terms suggesting profound love for each other, such as "my good wife . . . my sweet wife" or "my most sweet Husband." Similarly, the poems of Anne Bradstreet refer to a love toward her husband that seems deeply romantic: "To My Dear and Loving Husband/I prize thy love more than whole Mines of gold." It is also not difficult, however, to find evidence of marriages that failed to live up to the Puritan ideal of domestic harmony and wifely submissiveness. In 1686, a Boston spinster, Comfort Wilkins, publicly spoke out about the "Tears, and Jars, and Discontents, and Jealousies" that marred many Puritan marriages.

Puritan court records further reveal that wife abuse is not a recent development. Between 1630 and 1699, at least 128 men were tried for abusing their wives. In one case a resident of Maine kicked and beat his wife with a club when she refused to feed a pig; in another case an Ipswich man poured poison into his wife's broth in an attempt to kill her. The punishments for wife abuse were mild, usually amounting only to a fine, a lashing, a public admonition, or supervision by a town-appointed guardian. Two colonists, however, did lose their lives for murdering their wives.

Even in cases of abuse, Puritan authorities commanded wives to be submissive and obedient. They were told not to resist or strike their husbands but to try to reform their spouses' behavior. Some women refused to conform to this rigid standard. At least thirty-two seventeenth-century Puritan women deserted their husbands and set up separate residences, despite such risks as loss of their dower rights and possible criminal charges of adultery or theft. Another eight women were brought to court for refusing to have sexual relations with their husbands over extended periods. Seventy-six New England women petitioned for divorce or separation, usually on grounds of desertion, adultery, or bigamy.

Women who refused to obey Puritan injunctions about wifely obedience were subject to harsh punishment. Two hundred seventy-eight New England women were brought to court for heaping abuse on their husbands, which was punishable by fines or whippings. Joan Miller of Taunton, Massachusetts, was punished "for beating and reviling her husband and egging her children to healp her, biding them knock him in the head." One wife was punished for striking her husband with a pot of cider, another for scratching and kicking her spouse, and a third for insulting her husband by claiming he was "no man." How widespread these deviations from Puritan ideals were, we do not know.

Within marriage, a woman assumed a wide range of responsibilities and duties. As a housewife she was expected to cook, wash, sew, milk, spin, clean, and garden. These domestic activities included brewing beer, churning butter, harvesting fruit, keeping chickens, spinning wool, building fires, baking bread, making cheese, boiling laundry, and stitching shirts, petticoats, and other garments. She participated in trade—exchanging surplus fruit, meat, cheese, or butter for tea, candles, coats, or sheets—and manufacturing—salting, pickling, and preserving vegetables, fruit, and meat and making clothing and soap—in addition to other domestic tasks. As a "deputy husband," she was responsible for assuming her husband's responsibilities whenever he was absent from home—when, for example, he was on militia duty. Under such circumstances she took on his tasks of planting corn or operating the loom or keeping accounts. As a mistress she was responsible for training, supervising, feeding, and clothing girls who were placed in her house as servants.

Marriage also brought another equally tangible change to women's lives: frequent childbirth. Childlessness within marriage was an extreme rarity in colonial New England, with just one women in twelve bearing no children. Most women could expect to bear at least six children and delivered children at fairly regular intervals averaging every twenty to thirty months, often having the last child after the age of forty. The process of delivery was largely in the hands of women and took place within the home. Labor was typically attended by a large number of observers. When one of Samuel Sewall's daughters gave birth in January 1701, at least sixteen women were in attendance in the lying-in room to offer encouragement and give advice. Often a midwife would intervene actively in the birth process by breaking the amniotic sac surrounding the infant in the uterus, steering the infant through the birth canal, and later removing the placenta.

Death in childbirth was frequent enough to provoke fear in many women. It appears that almost one delivery in thirty resulted in the death of the mother. Among the complications of pregnancy that could lead to maternal death were protracted labor, unusual presentation of the infant (such as a breech presentation), hemorrhages and convulsions, and infection after delivery. The sense of foreboding that was felt is apparent in the words of a Massachusetts woman, Sarah Stearns, who wrote in her diary, "Perhaps this is the last time I shall be permitted to join with my earthly friends."

After childbirth, infants were commonly breast-fed for about a year and were kept largely under their mother's care. Not until a child reached the age of two or three is there evidence that fathers took a more active role in child rearing.

Unlike marriages in contemporary England—where a late age of marriage and short life expectancy combined to make the average duration of marriage quite short—colonial unions tended to be long-lived, even by modern standards. A detailed study of one New England town found that an average marriage lasted almost twenty-four years. The extended duration of New England marriages gave such unions a sense of permanence that contrasted sharply with the transience characteristic of English marriages. In contrast to the pattern found today, however, the death of a spouse did not usually lead to the creation of households composed of a widow or widower living alone. Single adults of any age living alone were very unusual, and lifelong bachelors and spinsters were a rarity. Remarriage after the death of a spouse was common, particularly among wealthier men, and even individuals of very advanced ages (into their seventies or eighties) often remarried. Among those least likely to remarry were wealthy widows. If these women did remarry, they generally made an antenuptial agreement allowing them to manage their own property. The remarriage of a spouse often led to the rearrangement of families; the fostering out of children from an earlier marriage was not uncommon.

The experience of widowhood did give a small number of colonial women a taste of economic independence. Legally, a widow in seventeenth-century New England was entitled to at least a third of her husband's household goods along with income from his real estate until she remarried or died. Actual control of the house and fields—and even pots and beds— usually fell to a grown son or executor. But, in a number of cases, widows inherited land or businesses and continued to operate them on their own, assuming such jobs as blacksmith, silversmith, tinsmith, beer maker, tavernkeeper, shoemaker, shipwright, printer, barber, grocer, butcher, and shopkeeper—occupations and crafts usually monopolized by men.

Of all the differences that distinguish the seventeenth-century family from its present-day counterpart, perhaps the most striking involves the social experience of children. Three centuries ago, childhood was a much less secure and shorter stage of life than it is today. In recent years it has become fashionable to complain about the "disappearance of childhood," but historical perspective reminds us that—despite high divorce rates—childhood is more stable than it was during the colonial era. For a child to die during infancy was a common occurrence in colonial New England; more deaths occurred among young children than in any other age group. In Plymouth, Andover, or Ipswich, Massachusetts, a family could anticipate an infant death rate of one out of ten; in less-healthy towns such as Salem or Boston, three of every ten children died in infancy. It cannot be emphasized too strongly that high infant death rates did not necessarily make parents indifferent toward their young children. Cotton Mather, who lost eight of his fifteen children before they reached their second birthdays, suggests the depth of feeling of parents: "We have our children taken from us; the Desire of our Eyes taken away with a stroke."

Not only were children more likely to die in infancy or to be orphaned than today, they were raised quite differently. In certain respects young children were treated, by our standards, in a casual way. Child rearing was not the family's main function; the care and nurture of children were subordinate to other family interests. In colonial New England newborn infants of well-to-do families were sometimes "put out" to wet nurses who were responsible for breast-feeding, freeing mothers to devote their time to their household duties. As in Europe, new babies were sometimes named for recently deceased infants. In contrast to Europeans, however, New Englanders did not wrap infants in tightly confining swaddling clothes, and carelessly supervised children sometimes crawled into fires or fell into wells.

The moral upbringing of Puritan children was never treated casually. The Puritan religion taught that even newborn infants were embodiments of guilt and sin (traceable to Adam's transgression in Eden), who, unless saved by God, were doomed to writhe in Satan's clutches for eternity. This belief in infant depravity and original sin exerted a powerful influence on methods of child rearing. In their view the primary task of child rearing was to break down a child's sinful will and internalize respect for divinely instituted authority through weekly catechisms, repeated admonitions, physical beatings, and intense psychological pressure. "Better whipt, than damned," was Cotton Mather's advice to parents.

Although Calvinists could be indulgent with very small children, among many parents their religious faith led to an insistence that, after the age of two, any assertion of a child's will be broken. A Pilgrim pastor eloquently defined a parent's responsibility to combat the inherent evil of a child's nature: "Surely," he affirmed, "there is in all children (though not alike) a stubbernes and stoutnes of minde arising from naturall pride which must in the first place be broken and beaten down so the foundation of their education being layd in humilitie and tractablenes other virtues may in turne be built thereon." A child's willfulness could be suppressed through fierce physical beatings, exhibition of corpses, and tales of castration and abandonment—techniques designed to drive out "the old Adam" and produce traits of tractableness and peaceableness highly valued by Calvinists. The Puritans would strongly have rejected the twentieth-century "progressive" child rearing advice that the goal of parents should be to draw out their children's innate potentialities.

Without a doubt the most striking difference between seventeenth-century child rearing and practices today was the widespread custom of sending children to live with another family at the age of fourteen or earlier, so that a child would receive the proper discipline its natural parents could not be expected to administer. Children of all social classes and both sexes were frequently fostered out for long periods in order to learn a trade, to work as servants, or to attend a school. Since the family was a place of work and its labor needs and its financial resources often failed to match its size and composition, servants or apprentices might temporarily be taken in or children bound out.

If childhood is defined as a protected state, a carefree period of freedom from adulthood responsibilities, then a Puritan childhood was quite brief. Childhood came to an end abruptly around the age of seven when boys adopted adult clothing (prior to this both boys and girls wore frocks or petticoats) and were prevented from sleeping any longer with their sisters or female servants. By their teens most children were largely under the care and tutelage of adults other than their own parents. They were fostered out as indentured servants or apprentices or, in rare cases, sent to boarding schools.

While childhood ended early and abruptly, adulthood did not begin right away. Around the age of seven, young Puritans entered into a prolonged intermediate stage of "semi-dependency" during which they were expected to begin to assume a variety of productive roles. Young boys wove garters and suspenders on small looms, weeded flax fields and vegetable gardens, combed wool and wound spools of thread, and were taught to be blacksmiths, coopers, cordwainers (shoemakers), tanners, weavers, or shipwrights. Teenage girls received quite different training from their brothers. They were taught "housewifery" or spinning, carding, sewing, and knitting. Girls customarily helped their mothers or another mistress by hoeing gardens, spinning flax and cotton, tending orchards, caring for domestic animals, and by making clothing, lye, soap, and candles. Like their mothers, teenage girls might also assist their fathers in the fields or in a workshop.

For both young men and women, marriage, economic independence, and establishment of an independent household would come much later. For young men, the transition to full adulthood only occurred after they had received a bequest of property from their father. Marriage took place relatively late. The average age of marriage for men was over twenty-five years, and few women married before the age of twenty.

For New Englanders, migration across the Atlantic gave the family a significance and strength it had lacked in the mother country. In the healthful environment of New England, family ties grew tighter than they had ever been in the Old World. The first settlers lived much longer than their contemporaries in England and were much more likely to live to see their grandchildren. Marriages lasted far longer than they did in contemporary England, and infant mortality rates quickly declined to levels far below those in the old country. Migration to the New World did not weaken paternal authority; it strengthened it by increasing paternal control over land and property.

Even when individuals did move around in New England, they almost always migrated as part of a family group. Few sons moved farther than sixteen miles from their paternal home during their father's lifetime. Contrary to an older view that the New World environment dissolved extended family ties, it now seems clear that the family in early-seventeenth-century New England was a more stable, disciplined, and cohesive unit than its English counterpart in the Old World.

DOCUMENTS

Two Poems, 1678

To My Dear and Loving Husband

If ever two were one, then surely we;
If ever man were loved by wife, then thee;
If ever wife was happy in a man,
Compare with me, ye women, if you can.
I prize thy love more than whole mines of gold,
Or all the riches that the East doth hold.

My love is such that rivers cannot quench,
Nor aught but love from thee give recompense.
Thy love is such I can no way repay;
The heavens reward thee manifold, I pray.
Then while we live in love let's so persevere
That when we live no more we may live ever.

Before the Birth of One of Her Children

All things within this fading world have end.
Adversity doth still our joys attend;

SOURCE: Anne Bradstreet, *Poems of Mrs. Anne Bradstreet* (Boston, 1758).

No ties so strong, no friends so dear and sweet,
But with death's parting blow are sure to meet.
The sentence passed is most irrevocable,
A common thing, yet, oh, inevitable.
How soon, my dear, death may my steps attend,
How soon it may be thy lot to lose thy friend,
We both are ignorant; yet love bids me
These farewell lines to recommend to thee,
That when the knot's untied that made us one
I may seem thine who in effect am none.
And if I see not half my days that are due,
What nature would God grant to yours and you.
The many faults that well you know I have
Let be interred in my oblivion's grave;
If any worth or virtue were in me,
Let that live freshly in thy memory,
And when thou feelest no grief, as I no harms,
Yet love thy dead, who long lay in thine arms;
And when thy loss shall be repaid with gains
Look to my little babes, my dear remains,
And if thou love thyself, or lovedst me,
These oh protect from stepdam's injury.
And if chance to thine eyes shall bring this verse,
With some sad sighs honor my absent hearse;
And kiss this paper for thy love's dear sake,
Who with salt tears this last farewell did take.

A Law for "the good education of children," 1642

Forasmuch as the good education of children is of singular behoof and benefit to any commonwealth, and whereas many parents and masters are too indulgent and negligent of their duty in that kind:

It is ordered, that the selectmen of every town, in the several precincts and quarters where they dwell, shall have a vigilant eye over their brethren and neighbours, to see, first that none of them shall suffer so much barbarism in any of their families, as not to endeavour to teach, by themselves or others, their children and apprentices, so much learning, as may enable them perfectly to read the English tongue, and knowledge of the capital laws: upon penalty of twenty shillings for each neglect therein.

SOURCE: The Charter and General Laws of the Colony and Province of Massachusetts Bay *(Boston: T. B. Waite and Co., 1814), 73–74.*

Also that all masters of families do once a week (at the least) catechise their children and servants in the grounds and principles of religion; and if any be unable to do so much, that then at the least they procure such children and apprentices to learn some short orthodox catechism without book, that they may be able to answer unto the questions that shall be propounded to them out of such catechism, by their parents or masters, or any of the selectmen when they shall call them to a trial, of what they have learned in that kind.

And farther that all parents and masters do breed and bring up their children and apprentices in some honest lawful calling, labour or employment, either in husbandry or some other trade, profitable for themselves and the commonwealth, if they will not or cannot train them up in learning, to fit them for higher employments.

And if any of the selectmen, after admonition by them given to such masters of families, shall find them still negligent of their duty in the particulars aforementioned, whereby children and servants become rude, stubborn, and unruly: the said selectmen with the help of two magistrates, or the next county court for that shire, shall take such children or apprentices from them, and place them with some masters for years, (boys till they come to twenty-one, and girls eighteen years of age complete) which will more strictly look unto, and force them to submit unto government, according to the rules of this order, if by fair means and former instructions they will not be drawn unto it. [May, 1642.]

Monitoring Style and Behavior in Puritan Massachusetts, 1675

Whereas there is manifest pride openly appearing amongst us in that long hair, like women's hair, is worn by some men, either their own or others hair made into periwigs, and by some women wearing borders of hair, and their cutting, curling, and immodest laying out their hair, which practise doth prevail and increase, especially among the younger sort:

This Court* doth declare against this ill custom as offensive to them, and divers sober Christians among us, and therefore do hereby exhort and advise all persons to use moderation in this respect; and further, do empower all grand juries to present to the County Court such persons, whether male or female, whom they shall judge to exceed in the premises; and the County Courts are hereby authorized to proceed against such delinquents either by admonition, fine, or correction, according to their good discretion. . . .

SOURCE: Nathaniel B. Shurtleff, ed., *Records of the Governor and Company of Massachusetts Bay, 1628–1686* 5 (Boston, 1853–1854): 60–61.
*"Court" refers to the General Court, the legislature of colonial Massachusetts. (Eds.)

Whereas there is much disorder and rudeness in youth in many congregations in time of the worship of God, whereby sin and profaneness is greatly increased, for reformation whereof:

It is ordered by this Court, that the selectmen do appoint such place or places in the meeting house for children or youth to sit in where they may be most together and in public view, and that the officers of the churches, or selectmen, do appoint some grave and sober person or persons to take a particular care of and inspection over them, who are hereby required to present a list of the names of such who, by their own observance or the information of others, shall be found delinquent, to the next magistrate or Court, who are empowered for the first offense to admonish them, for the second offense to impose a fine of five shillings on their parents or governors, or order the children to be whipped, and if incorrigible, to be whipped with ten stripes or sent to the house of correction for three days.

Good Manners for Colonial Children, 1772

When at Home

1. Make a bow always when you come home, and be immediately uncovered.
2. Be never covered at home, especially before thy parents or strangers.
3. Never sit in the presence of thy parents without bidding, tho' no stranger be present.
4. If thou passest by thy parents, and any place where thou seest them, when either by themselves or with company, bow towards them.
5. If thou art going to speak to thy parents, and see them engaged in discourse with company, draw back and leave thy business until afterwards; but if thou must speak, be sure to whisper.
6. Never speak to thy parents without some title of respect, viz., Sir, Madam, &c.
7. Approach near thy parents at no time without a bow.
8. Dispute not, nor delay to obey thy parents commands.
9. Go not out of doors without thy parents leave, and return within the time by them limited.
10. Come not into the room where thy parents are with strangers, unless thou art called, and then decently; and at bidding go out; or if strangers come in while thou art with them, it is manners, with a bow to withdraw.

SOURCE: Eleazer Moody, *The School of Good Manners. Composed for the Help of Parents in Teaching Their Children How to Carry It in Their Places During Their Minority* (Boston: Fleets, 1772), 17–19.

11. Use respectful and courteous but not insulting or domineering carriage or language toward the servants.
12. Quarrel not nor contend with thy brethren or sisters, but live in love, peace, and unity.
13. Grumble not nor be discontented at anything thy parents appoint, speak, or do.
14. Bear with meekness and patience, and without murmuring or sullenness, thy parents reproofs or corrections: Nay, tho' it should so happen that they be causeless or undeserved.

In Their Discourse

1. Among superiors speak not till thou art spoken to, and bid to speak.
2. Hold not thine hand, nor any thing else, before thy mouth when thou speakest.
3. Come not over-near to the person thou speakest to.
4. If thy superior speak to thee while thou sittest, stand up before thou givest any answer.
5. Sit not down till thy superior bid thee.
6. Speak neither very loud, nor too low.
7. Speak clear, not stammering, stumbling nor drawling.
8. Answer not one that is speaking to thee until he hath done.
9. Loll not when thou art speaking to a superior or spoken to by him.
10. Speak not without, Sir, or some other title of respect.
11. Strive not with superiors in argument or discourse; but easily submit thine opinion to their assertions.
12. If thy superior speak any thing wherein thou knowest he is mistaken, correct not nor contradict him, nor grin at the hearing of it; but pass over the error without notice or interruption.
13. Mention not frivolous or little things among grave persons or superiors.
14. If thy superior drawl or hesitate in his words, pretend not to help him out, or to prompt him.
15. Come not too near two that are whispering or speaking in secret, much less may'st thou ask about what they confer.
16. When thy parent or master speak to any person, speak not thou, nor hearken to them.
17. If thy superior be relating a story, say not, "I have heard it before," but attend to it as though it were altogether new. Seem not to question the truth of it. If he tell it not right, snigger not, nor endeavor to help him out, or add to his relation.
18. If any immodest or obscene thing be spoken in thy hearing, smile not, but settle thy countenance as though thou did'st not hear it.
19. Boast not in discourse of thine own wit or doings.
20. Beware thou utter not any thing hard to be believed.

21. Interrupt not any one that speaks, though thou be his familiar.
22. Coming into company, whilst any topic is discoursed on, ask not what was the preceding talk but hearken to the remainder.
23. Speaking of any distant person, it is rude and unmannerly to point at him.
24. Laugh not in, or at thy own story, wit or jest.
25. Use not any contemptuous or reproachful language to any person, though very mean or inferior.
26. Be not over earnest in talking to justify and avouch thy own sayings.
27. Let thy words be modest about those things which only concern thee.
28. Repeat not over again the words of a superior that asketh thee a question or talketh to thee.

Chapter 4

Crossing the Atlantic:
The Experiences of Slaves
and Servants

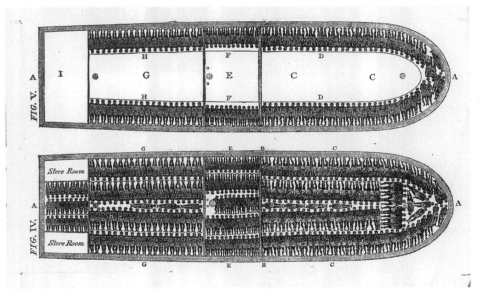

Africans contributed significantly to the population of the developing American colonies. Although the first blacks brought to Virginia in 1619 were forcibly removed from West Africa, the English colonists probably did not view them as slaves; slavery at this date did not exist in the laws of the colonies. Thus the fate of blacks brought to the colonies before the 1660s varied. Some, like white servants, eventually gained their freedom and obtained land and even servants of their own. Others spent their lives in servitude. But as the need for labor grew acute, and as the advantages of the services of lifetime bondsmen over indentured servants (who served for a limited time) became apparent, the institution of slavery began to evolve in law and practice.

Gradually the colonists tightened the grip of slavery on blacks, making it ever more difficult for them to gain their freedom. Slavery existed in the northern colonies, though it was not as crucial to their economies as it was in the South. Southern colonists depended on slave labor to cultivate tobacco, rice, and indigo. By the eighteenth century, slaves were legally property—to be bought, maintained, and sold according to the whim and financial position of their masters.

Hundreds of thousands of Africans were ultimately uprooted and brought to the American colonies. Daniel Mannix's and Malcolm Cowley's essay "The Middle Passage" vividly describes the brutality of the slave trade. Many blacks perished resisting capture and traveling on shipboard during the voyage to the New World. What do the practices of "loose-packing" and "tight-packing," discussed in the essay, reveal about the ship captains' attitudes?

Only a few slaves left reports of their experiences on the Middle Passage, as the voyage from Africa to the Americas was called. One who did was Gustavus Vasa; the first document presents an excerpt from his autobiography.

The voyage to the colonies could also bring hardship for Europeans destined for servitude. Such was certainly the case for the German emigré Gottlieb Mittelberger, who recounts his experiences in the second document. Why would Europeans in similar circumstances continue to come to America, despite Mittelberger's advice?

ESSAY
The Middle Passage
Daniel P. Mannix and Malcolm Cowley

As soon as an assortment of naked slaves was taken aboard a Guineaman [slave ship], the men were shackled two by two, the right wrist and ankle of one to the left wrist and ankle of another. Then they were sent to the hold or, at the end of the eighteenth century, to the "house" that the sailors had built on deck. The women—usually regarded as fair prey for the sailors—and the children were allowed to wander by day almost anywhere on the vessel, though they spent the night between decks in other rooms than the men. All the slaves were forced to sleep without covering on bare wooden floors, which were often constructed of unplaned boards. In a stormy passage the skin over their elbows might be worn away to the bare bones.

William Bosman says, writing in 1701, "You would really wonder to see how these slaves live on board; for though their number sometimes amounts to six or seven hundred, yet by careful management of our masters of ships"—the Dutch masters, that is—"they are so regulated that it seems incredible: And in this particular our nation exceeds all other Europeans; for as the French, Portuguese and English slave-ships are always foul and stinking; on the contrary ours are for the most part clean and neat." Slavers of every nation insisted that their own vessels were the best in the trade. . . .

There were two schools of thought among the Guinea captains, called the "loose-packers" and the "tight-packers." The former argued that by giving the slaves a little more room, with better food and a certain amount of liberty, they reduced the mortality among them and received a better price for each slave in the West Indies. The tight-packers answered that, although the loss of life might be greater on each of their voyages, so too were the net receipts from a larger cargo. If many of the survivors were weak and emaciated, as was often the case, they could be fattened up in a West Indian slave yard before being offered for sale. The argument between the two schools continued as long as the trade itself, but for many years after 1750 the tight-packers were in the ascendant. So great was the profit on each slave landed alive in the West Indies that hardly a captain refrained from loading his vessel to her utmost capacity. The hold of a slaving vessel was usually about five feet high. That seemed like waste space to the Guinea merchants, so they built a shelf or platform in the middle of it, extending six feet from each side of the vessel. When the bottom of the hold was completely covered with flesh, another row of slaves was packed on the platform. If there was as much as six feet of vertical space in the hold, a second platform might be installed above the first, sometimes leaving only twenty inches of headroom for the slaves; they could not sit upright during the whole voyage. The Reverend John Newton writes from personal observation:

> The cargo of a vessel of a hundred tons or a little more is calculated to purchase from 220 to 250 slaves. Their lodging rooms below the deck which are three (for the men, the boys and the women) besides a place for the sick, are sometimes more than five feet high and sometimes less; and this height is divided toward the middle for the slaves lie in two rows, one above the other, on each side of the ship, close to each other like books upon a shelf. I have known them so close that the shelf would not easily contain one more.
>
> The poor creatures, thus cramped, are likewise in irons for the most part which makes it difficult for them to turn or move or attempt to rise or to lie down without hurting themselves or each other. Every morning, perhaps, more instances than one are found of the living and the dead fastened together.

Dr. Falconbridge stated . . . that "he made the most of the room," in stowing the slaves, "and wedged them in. They had not so much room as a man in his coffin either in length or breadth. When he had to enter the slave deck, he took off his shoes to avoid crushing the slaves as he was forced to crawl over them." Taking off shoes on entering the hold seems to have been a widespread custom among surgeons. Falconbridge "had the marks on his feet where [the slaves] bit and pinched him."

In 1788 Captain Parrey of the Royal Navy was sent to measure such of the slave vessels as were then lying at Liverpool and to make a report to the

House of Commons. He discovered that the captains of many slavers possessed a chart showing the dimensions of the ship's half deck, lower deck, hold, platforms, gunroom, orlop, and great cabin, in fact of every crevice into which slaves might be wedged. Miniature black figures were drawn on some of the charts to illustrate the most effective method of packing in the cargo.

On the *Brookes*, which Captain Parrey considered to be typical, every man was allowed a space six feet long by sixteen inches wide (and usually about two feet, seven inches high); every woman, a space five feet, ten inches long by sixteen inches wide; every boy, five feet by fourteen inches; every girl, four feet, six inches by twelve inches. The *Brookes* was a vessel of 320 tons. By the law of 1788 it was permitted to carry 454 slaves, and the chart, which later became famous, showed how and where 451 of them could be stowed away. Captain Parrey failed to see how the captain could find room for three more. Nevertheless, Parliament was told by reliable witnesses, including Dr. Thomas Trotter, formerly surgeon of the *Brookes*, that before the new law was passed she had carried 600 slaves on one voyage and 609 on another.

Taking on slaves was a process that might be completed in a month or two at Bonny or Luanda. On the Gold Coast [present-day Ghana], where slaves were less plentiful, it might last from six months to a year or more. Meanwhile the captain was buying Negroes, sometimes one or two a day, sometimes a hundred or more in a single lot, while haggling over each purchase.

Those months when a slaver lay at anchor off the Guinea Coast, taking on her cargo, were the most dangerous stage of her triangular voyage. Not only was her crew exposed to African fevers and the revenge of angry natives; not only was there the chance of her being taken by pirates or by a hostile man-of-war; but also there was the constant threat of a slave mutiny. Captain Thomas Phillips says, in his account of a voyage made in 1693–1694:

When our slaves are aboard we shackle the men two and two, while we lie in port, and in sight of their own country, for 'tis then they attempt to make their escape, and mutiny; to prevent which we always keep centinels upon the hatchways, and have a chest full of small arms, ready loaden and prim'd, constantly lying at hand upon the quarter-deck, together with some granada shells; and two of our quarter-deck guns, pointing on the deck thence, and two more out of the steerage, the door of which is always kept shut, and well barr'd; they are fed twice a day, at 10 in the morning, and 4 in the evening, which is the time they are aptest to mutiny, being all upon deck; therefore all that time, what of our men are not employ'd in distributing their victuals to them, and settling them, stand to their arms; and some with lighted matches at the great guns that yaun upon them, loaden with partridge, till they have done and gone down to their kennels between decks.

. . . In spite of such precautions, mutinies were frequent on the coast, and some of them were successful. Even a failed mutiny might lead to heavy losses among the slaves and the sailors. James Barbot, Sr., of the *Albion-Frigate,* made the mistake of providing his slaves with knives so they could cut their meat. The slaves tore pieces of iron from the forecastle door, broke off their shackles, and killed the guard at the entrance to the hatchway. Before the mutiny was quelled, twenty-eight slaves either had been shot dead or had thrown themselves overboard. . . .

Mutinies were frequent during the years from 1750 to 1788, when Liverpool merchants were trying to save money by reducing the size of their crews. A small crew weakened by fever was no match for the slaves, especially if it had to withstand a simultaneous attack from the shore. On January 11, 1769, the *Nancy* out of Liverpool, Captain Williams, was lying at anchor off New Calabar. She had 132 slaves on board, who managed to break their shackles and assail the crew. The slaves were unarmed, but "it was with great difficulty, though [the crew] attacked them sword in hand, to make them submit." Meanwhile the natives on shore heard the fighting and swarmed aboard the *Nancy* from their canoes. They seized the slaves (whom they later resold to other ships . . .) and looted the cargo. There was a wild scene of plunder, with black men running through the vessel, breaching rum casks, throwing ships' biscuit and salt beef into the canoes, and robbing the sailors of everything they possessed. Afterward they cut the cables and set the *Nancy* adrift. Another slaver lying in the river sent a boat to rescue Captain Williams and the surviving seamen. The vessel, however, was wrecked. . . .

There are fairly detailed accounts of fifty-five mutinies on slavers from 1699 to 1845, not to mention passing references to more than a hundred others. The list of ships "cut off" by the natives—often in revenge for the kidnaping of freemen—is almost as long. On the record it does not seem that Africans submitted tamely to being carried across the Atlantic like chained beasts. Edward Long, the Jamaica planter and historian, justified the cruel punishments inflicted on salves by saying, "The many acts of violence they have committed by murdering whole crews and destroying ships when they had it in their power to do so have made these rigors wholly chargeable on their own bloody and malicious disposition which calls for the same confinement as if they were wolves or wild boars." For "wolves or wild boars" a modern reader might substitute "men who would rather die than be enslaved."

As long as a vessel lay at anchor, the slaves could dream of seizing it. If they managed to kill the crew, as they did in perhaps one mutiny out of ten, they could cut the anchor cable and let the vessel drift ashore. That opportunity was lost as soon as the vessel put to sea. Ignorant of navigation, which they regarded as white man's magic, the slaves were at the mercy of the captain. They could still die, but not with any hope of regaining their freedom.

The captain, for his part, had finished the most dangerous leg of his triangular voyage. Now he had to face only the ordinary perils of the sea, most of which were covered by his owners' insurance against fire, shipwreck, pirates and rovers, letters of mart and counter-mart, barratry,* jettison, and foreign men-of-war. Among the risks not covered by insurance, the greatest was that the cargo might be swept away by disease. The underwriters refused to issue such policies, arguing that they would expose the captain to an unholy temptation. If insured against disease among his slaves, he might take no precautions against it and might try to make his profit out of the insurance. . . .

On a canvas of heroic size, Thomas Stothard, Esq., of the Royal Academy, depicted "The Voyage of the Sable Venus from Angola to the West Indies." His painting is handsomely reproduced in the second volume of Bryan Edwards' *History of the West Indies,* where it appears beside a poem on the same allegorical subject by an unnamed Jamaican author, perhaps Edwards himself. In the painting the ship that carries the Sable Venus is an immense scallop shell, in which she sits upright on a velvet throne. Except for bracelets, anklets, and a collar of pearls, she wears nothing but a narrow embroidered girdle. Her look is soft and sensuous, and in grace she yields nothing—so the poem insists—to Botticelli's white Venus,

> In FLORENCE, where she's seen;
> Both just alike, except the white,
> No difference, no—none at night
> The beauteous dames between.

The joint message of the poem and the painting is simple to the point of coarseness: that slave women are preferable to English girls at night, being passionate and accessible; but the message is embellished with a wealth of classical details, to show the painter's learning. Two legendary dolphins draw the bark of Venus toward the West. Triton leads one of them, while blowing his wreathèd horn. Two mischievous lovers gambol about the other dolphin. There are cherubs above the wooly head of Venus, fanning her with ostrich plumes. In the calm distance a grampus discharges his column of spray. Cupid, from above, is shooting an arrow at Neptune, who strides ahead bearing the Union Jack. As the poet (who calls the dolphins "winged fish") describes the idyllic scene:

---

*Barratry is a fraudulent act by a ship's captain or crew that causes damage to the vessel or cargo. (Eds.)

> The winged fish, in purple trace
> The chariot drew; with easy grace
> Their azure rein she guides:
> And now they fly, and now they swim;
> Now o'er the wave they lightly skim,
> Or dart beneath the tides.

Meanwhile the Sable Venus, if she was a living woman borne from Angola to the West Indies, was roaming the deck of a ship that stank of excrement, so that, as with any slaver, "You could smell it five miles down wind." She had been torn from her husband and her children, she had been branded on the left buttock, and she had been carried to the ship bound hand and foot, lying in the bilge at the bottom of a dugout canoe. Now she was the prey of the ship's officers, in danger of being flogged to death if she resisted them. Her reward if she yielded was a handful of beads or a sailor's kerchief to tie around her waist.

Here is how she and her shipmates spent the day.

If the weather was clear, they were brought on deck at eight o'clock in the morning. The men were attached by their leg irons to the great chain that ran along the bulwarks on both sides of the ship; the women and half-grown boys were allowed to wander at will. About nine o'clock the slaves were served their first meal of the day. If they were from the Windward Coast, the fare consisted of boiled rice, millet, or cornmeal, which might be cooked with a few lumps of salt beef abstracted from the sailors' rations. If they were from the Bight of Biafra, they were fed stewed yams, but the Congos and the Angolans preferred manioc or plantains. With the food they were all given half a pint of water, served out in a pannikin [a small pan or cup].

After the morning meal came a joyless ceremony called "dancing the slaves." "Those who were in irons," says Dr. Thomas Trotter, surgeon of the *Brookes* in 1783, "were ordered to stand up and make what motions they could, leaving a passage for such as were out of irons to dance around the deck." Dancing was prescribed as a therapeutic measure, a specific against suicidal melancholy, and also against scurvy—although in the latter case it was a useless torture for men with swollen limbs. While sailors paraded the deck, each with a cat-o'-nine-tails in his right hand, the men slaves "jumped in their irons" until their ankles were bleeding flesh. One sailor told Parliament, "I was employed to dance the men, while another person danced the women." Music was provided by a slave thumping on a broken drum or an upturned kettle, or by an African banjo, if there was one aboard, or perhaps by a sailor with a bagpipe or a fiddle. Slaving captains sometimes advertised for "A person that can play on the Bagpipes, for a Guinea ship." The slaves were also told to sing. Said Dr. Claxton after his voyage in the *Young Hero*, "They sing, but not for their amusement. The captain ordered them to sing, and they sang songs of sorrow. Their sickness, fear of being beaten, their hunger, and the memory of their country, &c, are the usual subjects."

While some of the sailors were dancing the slaves, others were sent below to scrape and swab out the sleeping rooms. It was a sickening task, and it was not well performed unless the captain imposed an iron discipline. James Barbot, Sr., was proud of the discipline maintained on the *Albion-Frigate*. "We were very nice," he says, "in keeping the places where the slaves lay clean and neat, appointing some of the ship's crew to do that office constantly and thrice a week we perfumed betwixt decks with a quantity of good vinegar in pails, and red-hot iron bullets in them, to expel the bad air, after the place had been well washed and scrubbed with brooms." Captain Hugh Crow, the last legal English slaver, was famous for his housekeeping. "I always took great pains," he says, "to promote the health and comfort of all on board, by proper diet, regularity, exercise, and cleanliness, for I considered that on keeping the ship clean and orderly, which was always my hobby, the success of our voyage mainly depended." Consistently he lost fewer slaves in the Middle Passage than the other captains, some of whom had the filth in the hold cleaned out only once a week. A few left their slaves to wallow in excrement during the whole Atlantic passage.

At three or four in the afternoon the slaves were fed their second meal, often a repetition of the first. Sometimes, instead of African food, they were given horse beans, the cheapest provender from Europe. The beans were boiled to a pulp, then covered with a mixture of palm oil, flour, water, and red pepper, which the sailors called "slabber sauce." Most of the slaves detested horse beans, especially if they were used to eating yams or manioc. Instead of eating the pulp, they would, unless carefully watched, pick it up by handfuls and throw it in each other's faces. That second meal was the end of their day. As soon as it was finished they were sent below, under the guard of sailors charged with stowing them away on their bare floors and platforms. The tallest men were placed amidships, where the vessel was the widest; the shorter ones were tumbled into the stern. Usually there was only room for them to sleep on their sides, "spoon fashion." Captain William Littleton told Parliament that slaves in the ships on which he sailed might lie on their backs if they wished—"though perhaps," he conceded, "it might be difficult all at the same time."

After stowing their cargo, the sailors climbed out of the hatchway, each clutching his cat-o'-nine-tails: then the hatchway gratings were closed and barred. Sometimes in the night, as the sailors lay on deck and tried to sleep, they heard from below "an howling melancholy noise, expressive of extreme anguish." When Dr. Trotter told his interpreter, a slave woman, to inquire about the cause of the noise, "she discovered it to be owing to their having dreamt they were in their own country, and finding themselves when awake, in the hold of a slave ship." . . .

In squalls or rainy weather, the slaves were never brought on deck. They were served their two meals in the hold, where the air became too thick and poisonous to breathe. Says Dr. Falconbridge, "For the purpose of admitting fresh air, most of the ships in the slave-trade are provided, between the decks, with five or six airports on each side of the ship, of about six inches in length and four in breadth; in addition to which, some few ships, but not one in twenty, have what they denominate wind-sails." These were funnels made of canvas and so placed as to direct a current of air into the hold. "But whenever the sea is rough and the rain heavy," Falconbridge continues, "it becomes necessary to shut these and every other conveyance by which the air is admitted. . . . The negroes' rooms very soon become intolerably hot. The confined air, rendered noxious by the effluvia exhaled from their bodies and by being repeatedly breathed, soon produces fevers and fluxes which generally carry off great numbers of them."

Dr. Trotter says that when tarpaulins were thrown over the gratings, the slaves would cry, "Kickeraboo, kickeraboo, we are dying, we are dying." "I have known," says Henry Ellison, a sailor before the mast, "in the Middle Passage, in rains, slaves confined below for some time. I have frequently seen them faint through heat, the steam coming through the gratings, like a furnace." . . .

Not surprisingly, the slaves often went mad. Falconbridge mentions a woman on the *Emilia* who had to be chained to the deck. She had lucid intervals, however, and during one of these she was sold to a planter in Jamaica. Men who went insane might be flogged to death, to make sure that they were not malingering. Some were simply clubbed on the head and thrown overboard.

While the slaves were on deck they had to be watched at all times to keep them from committing suicide. Says Captain Phillips of the *Hannibal,* "We had about 12 negroes did wilfully drown themselves, and others starv'd themselves to death; for," he explained, "'tis their belief that when they die they return home to their own country and friends again." This belief was reported from various regions, at various periods of the trade, but it seems to have been especially prevalent among the Ibo of eastern Nigeria. In 1788, nearly a hundred years after the *Hannibal's* voyage, Ecroide Claxton was the surgeon who attended a shipload of Ibo. "Some of the slaves," he testified, "wished to die on an idea that they should then get back to their own country. The captain in order to obviate this idea, thought of an expedient, viz. to cut off the heads of those who died intimating to them that if determined to go, they must return without heads. The slaves were accordingly brought up to witness the operation. One of them by a violent exertion got loose and flying to the place where the nettings had been unloosed in order to empty the tubs, he darted overboard. The ship brought to, a man was placed in the main chains to catch him which he perceiving, made signs which words cannot express expressive of his happiness in escaping. He then went down and was seen no more."

Dr. Isaac Wilson, a surgeon in the Royal Navy, made a Guinea voyage on the *Elizabeth* [under] Captain John Smith, who was said to be very humane. Nevertheless, Wilson was assigned the duty of whipping the slaves. "Even in the act of chastisement," Wilson says, "I have seen them look up at me with a smile, and, in their own language, say, 'presently we shall be no more.'" One woman on the *Elizabeth* found some rope yarn, which she tied to the armorer's vise; she fastened the other end round her neck and was found dead in the morning. On the *Brookes* when Thomas Trotter was her surgeon, there was a man who, after being accused of witchcraft, had been sold into slavery with his whole family. During his first night on shipboard he tried to cut his throat. Dr. Trotter sewed up the wound, but on the following night the man not only tore out the sutures but tried to cut his throat on the other side. From the ragged edges of the wound and the blood on his fingers, he seemed to have used his nails as the only available instrument. His hands were tied together after the second wound, but he then refused all food, and he died of hunger in eight or ten days.

"Upon the negroes refusing to take food," says Falconbridge, "I have seen coals of fire, glowing hot, put on a shovel and placed so near their lips as to scorch and burn them. And this has been accompanied with threats of forcing them to swallow the coals if they persisted in refusing to eat. This generally had the required effect"; but if the Negroes still refused, they were flogged day after day. Lest flogging prove ineffective, every Guineaman was provided with a special instrument called the "speculum oris," or mouth opener. It looked like a pair of dividers with notched legs and with a thumbscrew at the blunt end. The legs were closed and the notches were hammered between the slave's teeth. When the thumbscrew was tightened, the legs of the instrument separated, forcing open the slave's mouth; then food was poured into it through a funnel. . . .

One deadly scourge of the Guinea cargoes was a phenomenon called "fixed melancholy." Even slaves who were well fed, treated with kindness, and kept under relatively sanitary conditions would often die one after another for no apparent reason; they simply had no wish to live. Fixed melancholy seems to have been especially rife among the Ibo and among the food-gathering tribes of the Gaboon, but no Negro nation was immune to it. Although the disease was noted from the earliest days of the trade, perhaps the best description of it was written by George Howe, an American medical student who shipped on an illegal slaver in 1859:

Notwithstanding their apparent good health [Howe says] each morning three or four dead would be found, brought upon deck, taken by the arms and heels, and tossed overboard as unceremoniously as an empty bottle. Of what did they die? And [why] always at night? In the barracoons it was known that if a Negro was not amused and kept in motion, he would mope, squat down with his chin on his knees and arms clasped about his legs and in a very short time die. Among civilized races it is thought almost impossible to hold one's breath until death follows. It is thought the African can do so. They had no means of concealing anything and certainly did not kill each other. One of the duties of the slave-captains was when they found a slave sitting with knees up and head drooping, to start them up, run them about the deck, give them a small ration of rum, and divert them until in a normal condition.

It is impossible for a human being to hold his breath until he dies. Once he loses consciousness, his lungs fill with air and he recovers. The simplest explanation for the slaves' ability to "will themselves dead" is that they were in a state of shock as a result of their being carried through the terrifying surf into the totally unfamiliar surroundings of the ship. In certain conditions shock can be as fatal as physical injury. There may, however, be another explanation. The communal life of many tribes was so highly organized by a system of customs, relationships, taboos, and religious ceremonies that there was practically nothing a man or a woman could do that was not prescribed by tribal law. To separate an individual from this complex system of interrelationships and suddenly place him, naked and friendless, in a completely hostile environment was in some respects a greater shock than any amount of physical brutality.

Dr. Wilson believed that fixed melancholy was responsible for the loss of two-thirds of the slaves who died on the *Elizabeth*. "No one who had it was ever cured," he says; "whereas those who had it not and yet were ill, recovered. The symptoms are a lowness of spirits and despondency. Hence they refuse food. This only increases the symptoms. The stomach afterwards got weak. Hence the belly ached, fluxes ensued, and they were carried off." But flux, or dysentery, is an infectious disease spread chiefly by food prepared in unsanitary conditions. The slaves, after being forced to wallow in filth, were also forced to eat with their fingers. In spite of the real losses from fixed melancholy, the high death rate on Guinea ships was due to somatic more than to psychic afflictions.

Along with their human cargoes, crowded, filthy, undernourished, and terrified out of the wish to live, the ships also carried an invisible cargo of microbes, bacilli, spirochetes, viruses, and intestinal worms from one continent to another; the Middle Passage was a crossroads and marketplace of diseases. From Europe came smallpox, measles (less deadly to Africans than to American Indians), gonorrhea, and syphilis (which last Columbus's sailors had carried from America to Europe). The African diseases were yellow fever (to which the natives were more resistant than white men), dengue, blackwater fever, and malaria (which was not specifically African, but which most of the slaves carried in their bloodstreams). If anopheles mosquitoes were present, malaria spread from the slaves through any new territories to which they were carried. Other African diseases were amoebic and various forms of bacillary dysentery (all known as "the bloody flux"), Guinea worms, hookworm (possibly African in origin, but soon endemic in the warmer parts of the New World), yaws, elephantiasis, and leprosy.

The particular affliction of the white sailors after escaping from the fevers of the Guinea Coast was scurvy, a deficiency disease to which they were exposed by their monotonous rations of salt beef and sea biscuits. The daily tot of lime juice (originally lemon juice) that prevented scurvy was almost never served on merchantmen during the days of the legal slave trade, and in fact was not prescribed in the Royal Navy until 1795. Although the slaves were also subject to scurvy, they fared better in this respect than the sailors, partly because they made only one leg of the triangular voyage and partly because their rough diet was sometimes richer in vitamins. But sailors and slaves alike were swept away by smallpox and "the bloody flux," and sometimes they went blind from various forms of ophthalmia, the worst of which seems to have been a gonorrheal infection of the eyes.

Smallpox was feared more than other diseases, since the surgeons had no means of combating it until the end of the eighteenth century. One man with smallpox infected a whole vessel, unless—as sometimes happened—he was tossed overboard when the first scabs appeared. Captain Wilson of the *Briton* lost more than half his cargo of 375 slaves by not listening to his surgeon. It was the last slave brought on board who had the disease, says Henry Ellison, who made the voyage. "The doctor told Mr. Wilson it was the small-pox," Ellison continues. "He would not believe it, but said he would keep him, as he was a fine man. It soon broke out amongst the slaves. I have seen the platform one continued scab. We hauled up eight or ten slaves dead of a morning. The flesh and skin peeled off their wrists when taken hold of, being entirely mortified." But dysentery, though not so much feared, could cause as many deaths. Ellison testifies that he made two voyages on the *Nightingale*, Captain Carter. On the first voyage the slaves were so crowded that thirty boys "messed and slept in the long boat all through the Middle Passage, there being no room below"; and still the vessel lost only five or six slaves in all, out of a cargo of 270. On the second voyage, however, the *Nightingale* buried "about 150, chiefly of fevers and flux. We had 250 when we left the coast." . . .

The average mortality in the Middle Passage is impossible to state accurately from the surviving records. Some famous voyages were made without the loss of a single slave, as notably by Captains John Newton, William Macintosh, and Hugh Crow. On one group of nine voyages between 1766 and 1780, selected at random, the vessels carried 2362 slaves and there were no epidemics of disease. The total loss of slaves was 154, or about 6½ per cent. On another list of twenty voyages compiled by Thomas Clarkson the abolitionist, the vessels carried 7904 slaves and lost 2053, or 26 per cent. Balancing high and low figures together, the English Privy Council in 1789 arrived at an estimate of 12½ per cent for the average mortality in the Middle Passage. That comes close to the percentage reckoned long afterward from the manifests of French vessels sailing from Nantes. Between 1748 and 1782 the Nantes slavers bought 146,799 slaves and sold 127,133 on the other side of the Atlantic. The difference of 19,666 would indicate a loss of 13 per cent in the voyage.

Of course there were further losses. To the mortality in the Middle Passage, the Privy Council added 4½ per cent for the deaths of slaves in harbors before they were sold, and 33 per cent for deaths during the seasoning process, making a total of 50 per cent. If those figures are correct (U. B. Phillips, the author of *American Negro Slavery,* thinks they are somewhat high), then only one slave was added to the New World labor force for every two purchased on the Guinea Coast.

To keep the figures in perspective, it might be added that the mortality among slaves in the Middle Passage was possibly no greater than that of white indentured servants or even of free Irish, Scottish, and German immigrants in the North Atlantic crossing. On the better commanded Guineamen it was probably much less, and for a simple economic reason. There was no profit in a slaving voyage until the Negroes were landed alive and sold; therefore the better captains took care of their cargoes. If the Negroes died in spite of good care, the captains regarded their deaths as a personal affront. . . .

After leaving the Portuguese island of São Thomé—if he had watered there—a slaving captain bore westward along the equator for a thousand miles, and then northwestward toward the Cape Verde Islands. This was the tedious part of the Middle Passage. Along the equator the vessel might be delayed for weeks by calms or storms; sometimes it had to return to the African coast for fresh provisions. Then, "on leaving the Gulf of Guinea," says the author of a *Universal Geography* published in the early nineteenth century, " . . . that part of the ocean must be traversed, so fatal to navigators, where long calms detain the ships under a sky charged with electric clouds, pouring down by turns torrents of rain and of fire. This *sea of thunder,* being a focus of mortal diseases, is avoided as much as possible, both in approaching the coasts of Africa and those of America." It was not until reaching the latitude of the Cape Verde Islands that the vessel fell in with the Northeast Trades and was able to make a swift passage to the West Indies.

Ecroide Claxton's ship, the *Young Hero,* was one of those delayed for weeks before reaching the trade winds. "We were so streightened for provisions," he testified, "that if we had been ten more days at sea, we must either have eaten the slaves that died, or have made the living slaves *walk the plank,"* a term, he explained, that was widely used by Guinea captains. There are no authenticated records of cannibalism in the Middle Passage, but there are many accounts of slaves killed for various reasons. English captains believed that French vessels carried poison in their medicine chests, "with which they can destroy their negroes in a calm, contagious sickness, or short provisions." They told the story of a Frenchman from Brest who had a long passage and had to poison his slaves; only twenty of them reached Haiti out of five hundred. Even the cruelest English captains regarded this practice as Latin, depraved, and uncovered by their insurance policies. In an emergency they simply jettisoned part of their cargo.

The most famous case involving jettisoned slaves was that of the *Zong* out of Liverpool, Luke Collingwood master. The *Zong* had left São Thomé on September 6, 1781, with a cargo of four hundred and forty slaves and a white crew of seventeen. There was sickness aboard during a slow passage; more than sixty Negroes died, with seven of the seamen, and many of the remaining slaves were so weakened by dysentery that it was a question whether they could be sold in Jamaica. On November 29, after they had already sighted land in the West Indies, Captain Collingwood called his officers together. He announced that there were only two hundred gallons of fresh water left in the casks, not enough for the remainder of the voyage. If the slaves died of thirst or illness, he explained, the loss would fall on the owners of the vessel; but if they were thrown into the sea it would be a legal jettison, covered by insurance. "It would not be so cruel to throw the poor sick wretches into the sea," he argued, "as to suffer them to linger out a few days under the disorders to which they were afflicted."

The mate, James Kelsal, demurred at first, saying there was "no present want of water to justify such a measure," but the captain outtalked him. To quote from a legal document, "The said Luke Collingwood picked, or caused to be picked out, from the cargo of the same ship, one hundred and thirty-three slaves, all or most of whom were sick or weak, and not likely to live; and ordered the crew by turns to throw them into the sea; which most inhuman order was cruelly complied with." A first "parcel," as the sailors called them, of fifty-four slaves went overboard that same day, November 29. A second parcel, this time of forty-two, followed them on December 1, still leaving thirty-six slaves out of those condemned to be jettisoned. (One man seems to have died from natural causes.) Also on December 1 there was a heavy rain and the sailors collected six casks of water, enough to carry the vessel into port. But Collingwood stuck to his plan, and the last parcel of condemned slaves was brought on deck a few days later. Twenty-six of them were handcuffed, then swung into the sea. The last ten refused to let the sailors come near them; instead they vaulted over the bulwarks and were drowned like the others.

On December 22 the *Zong* dropped anchor in Kingston harbor after a passage of three months and sixteen days. Collingwood sold the remainder of his slaves, then sailed his vessel to England, where his owners claimed thirty pounds of insurance money for each of the one hundred and thirty-two jettisoned slaves. The underwriters refused to pay, and the case was taken to court. At a first trial the jury found for the owners, since "they had no doubt . . . that the case of slaves was the same as if horses had been thrown overboard." The underwriters appealed to the Court of Exchequer, and Lord Mansfield presided. After admitting that the law supported the owners of the *Zong,* he went on to say that "a higher law [applies to] this very shocking case." He found for the underwriters. It was the first case in which an English court ruled that a cargo of slaves could not be treated simply as merchandise. . . .

. . . Usually the last two or three days of the Middle Passage were a comparatively happy period. All the slaves, or all but a few, might be released from their irons. Where there was a remaining stock of provisions, the slaves were given bigger meals—to fatten them for market—and as much water as they could drink. Sometimes on the last day—if the ship was commanded by an easy-going captain—there was a sort of costume party on deck, with the women slaves dancing in the sailors' cast-off clothing. Then the captain was rowed ashore to arrange for the disposition of his cargo.

There were several fashions of selling the slaves. In a few instances the whole cargo was consigned to a single rich planter, or to a group of planters. More often a West Indian factor* took charge of retail sales, for a commission of 15 per cent on the gross amount and 5 per cent more on the net proceeds. When the captain himself had to sell his slaves, he ferried them ashore, had them drawn up in a ragged line of march, and paraded them through town with bagpipes playing, before exposing them to buyers in the public square. J. G. Stedman, a young officer in the Scots Brigade employed as a mercenary by the Dutch in their obstinate efforts to suppress the slave revolts in Surinam, witnessed such a parade. "The whole party was," he says, ". . . a resurrection of skin and bones . . . risen from the grave or escaped from Surgeon's Hall." The slaves exposed for sale were "walking skeletons covered over with a piece of tanned leather."

But the commonest method of selling a cargo was a combination of the "scramble"—to be described presently—and the vendue or public auction "by inch of candle." First the captain, probably with the West Indian factor at his side, went over the cargo and picked out the slaves who were maimed or diseased. These were carried to a tavern and auctioned off, with a lighted candle beside the auctioneer; bids were received until an inch of candle had burned. The price of these "refuse" slaves sold at auction was usually less

*A *factor* was a middleman between the suppliers and purchasers of slaves. (Eds.)

than half of that paid for a healthy Negro; sometimes it was as little as five or six dollars a head. "I was informed by a mulatto woman," Falconbridge says, "that she purchased a sick slave at Grenada, upon speculation, for the small sum of one dollar, as the poor wretch was apparently dying of the flux." There were some slaves who could not be sold for even a dollar, and they were often left to die on the wharfs without food or water.

There were horse traders' methods of hiding the presence of disease. Yaws, for example, could be concealed by a mixture of iron rust and gunpowder, a practice which Edward Long, the Jamaica historian, denounces as a "wicked fraud." Falconbridge tells of a Liverpool captain who "boasted of his having cheated some Jews by the following stratagem: A lot of slaves, afflicted with the flux, being about to be landed for sale, he directed the surgeon to stop the anus of each of them with oakum. . . . The Jews, when they examine them, oblige them to stand up, in order to see if there be any discharge; and when they do not perceive this appearance, they consider it as a symptom of recovery. In the present instance, such an appearance being prevented, the bargain was struck, and they were accordingly sold. But it was not long before a discovery ensued. The excruciating pain which the prevention of a discharge of such an acrimonious nature occasioned, not being to be borne by the poor wretches, the temporary obstruction was removed, and the deluded purchasers were speedily convinced of the imposition."

The healthy slaves remaining after an auction were sold by "scramble," that is, at standard prices for each man, each woman, each boy, and each girl in the cargo. The prices were agreed upon with the purchasers, who then scrambled for their pick of the slaves. During his four voyages Falconbridge was present at a number of scrambles. "In the *Emilia*," he says, "at Jamaica, the ship was darkened with sails, and covered round. The men slaves were placed on the main deck, and the women on the quarter deck. The purchasers on shore were informed a gun would be fired when they were ready to open the sale. A great number of people came on board with tallies or cards in their hands, with their own names upon them, and rushed through the barricado door with the ferocity of brutes. Some had three or four handkerchiefs tied together, to encircle as many as they thought fit for their purpose." For the slaves, many of whom thought they were about to be eaten, it was the terrifying climax of a terrifying voyage. Another of Falconbridge's ships, the *Alexander*, sold its cargo by scramble in a slave yard at Grenada. The women, he says, were frightened out of their wits. Several of them climbed over the fence and ran about Saint George's town as if they were mad. In his second voyage, while lying in Kingston harbor, he saw a sale by scramble on board the *Tyral*, Captain Macdonald. Forty or fifty of the slaves jumped overboard—"all of which, however," Falconbridge told the House of Commons, "he believes were taken up again."

DOCUMENTS

Voyage from Africa, 1756

The first object which saluted my eyes when I arrived on the coast was the sea, and a slaveship, which was then riding at anchor, and waiting for its cargo. These filled me with astonishment, which was soon converted into terror, which I am yet at a loss to describe, nor the then feelings of my mind. When I was carried on board I was immediately handled, and tossed up, to see if I were sound, by some of the crew; and I was now persuaded that I had got into a world of bad spirits, and that they were going to kill me. . . .

I was not long suffered to indulge my grief; I was soon put down under the decks, and there I received such a salutation in my nostrils as I had never experienced in my life; so that, with the loathsomeness of the stench, and crying together, I became so sick and low that I was not able to eat, nor had I the least desire to taste anything . . . but soon, to my grief, two of the white men offered me eatables; and, on my refusing to eat, one of them held me fast by the hands, and laid me across, I think, the windlass, and tied my feet, while the other flogged me severely. . . .

In a little time after, amongst the poor chained men, I found some of my own nation, which in a small degree gave ease to my mind. I inquired of them what was to be done with us? They gave me to understand we were to be carried to these white people's country to work for them. I then was a little revived, and thought, if it were no worse than working, my situation was not so desperate: but still I feared I should be put to death, the white people looked and acted, as I thought, in so savage a manner; for I had never seen among any people such instances of brutal cruelty; and this not only shewn towards us blacks, but also to some of the whites themselves. One white man in particular I saw, when we were permitted to be on deck, flogged so unmercifully with a large rope near the foremast, that he died in consequence of it; and they tossed him over the side as they would have done a brute. This made me fear these people the more; and I expected nothing less than to be treated in the same manner. . . .

The stench of the hold while we were on the coast, was so intolerably loathsome, that it was dangerous to remain there for any time, and some of us had been permitted to stay on the deck for the fresh air; but now that the whole ship's cargo were confined together, it became absolutely pestilential. The closeness of the place, and the heat of the climate, added to the number in the ship, which was so crowded that each had scarcely room to turn himself, almost suffocated us. . . .

SOURCE: Gustavus Vasa, *The Interesting Narrative of the Life of Olandah Equiano or Gustavus Vasa, Written by Himself* (London: Printed and sold by the author, 1793), 46–53.

The shrieks of the women, and the groans of the dying, rendered the whole a scene of horror almost inconceivable. Happily perhaps for myself I was soon reduced so low here that it was thought necessary to keep me almost always on deck; and from my extreme youth I was not put in fetters. In this situation I expected every hour to share the fate of my companions, some of whom were almost daily brought upon deck at the point of death which I began to hope would soon put an end to my miseries. . . .

One day, when we had a smooth sea, and moderate wind, two of my wearied countrymen, who were chained together (I was near them at the time), preferring death to such a life of misery, somehow made through the nettings, and jumped into the sea; immediately another quite dejected fellow, who, on account of his illness, was suffered to be out of irons, also followed their example; and I believe many more would very soon have done the same, if they had not been prevented by the ship's crew, who were instantly alarmed. Those of us that were the most active were in a moment put down under the deck; and there was such a noise and confusion amongst the people of the ship as I never heard before, to stop her, and get the boat out to go after the slaves. However, two of the wretches were drowned, but they got the other, and afterwards flogged him unmercifully, for thus attempting to prefer death to slavery. In this manner we continued to undergo more hardships than I can now relate. . . .

An Immigrant's Journey, 1750

Both in Rotterdam and in Amsterdam the people are packed densely, like herrings so to say, in the large sea vessels. One person receives a place of scarcely 2 feet width and 6 feet length in the bedstead, while many a ship carries four to six hundred souls; not to mention the innumerable implements, tools, provisions, water-barrels and other things which likewise occupy much space.

On account of contrary winds it takes the ships sometimes 2, 3 and 4 weeks to make the trip from Holland to Kaupp [Cowes] in England. But when the wind is good, they get there in 8 days or even sooner. Everything is examined there and the custom-duties paid, whence it comes that the ships ride there 8, 10 to 14 days and even longer at anchor, till they have taken in their full cargoes. During that time every one is compelled to spend his last remaining money and to consume his little stock of provisions which had been reserved for the sea; so that most passengers, finding themselves on the ocean where they would be in greater need of them, must

SOURCE: Gottlieb Mittelberger, *Journey to Pennsylvania in the Year 1750 and Return to Germany in the Year 1754*, trans. Carl Theo. Eben (Philadelphia: John Jos McVey, 1898), 19–20, 22, 24–31.

greatly suffer from hunger and want. Many suffer want already on the water between Holland and Old England.

When the ships have for the last time weighed their anchors near the city of Kaupp [Cowes] in Old England, the real misery begins with the long voyage. For from there the ships, unless they have good wind, must often sail 8, 9, 10 to 12 weeks before they reach Philadelphia. But even with the best wind the voyage lasts 7 weeks.

But during the voyage there is on board these ships terrible misery, stench, fumes, horror, vomiting, many kinds of seasickness, fever, dysentery, headache, heat, constipation, boils, scurvy, cancer, mouth-rot, and the like, all of which come from old and sharply salted food and meat, also from very bad and foul water, so that many die miserably.

Add to this want of provisions, hunger, thirst, frost, heat, dampness, anxiety, want, afflictions and lamentations, together with other trouble, as *c.v.* the lice abound so frightfully, especially on sick people, that they can be scraped off the body. The misery reaches the climax when a gale rages for 2 or 3 nights and days, so that every one believes that the ship will go to the bottom with all human beings on board. In such a visitation the people cry and pray most piteously. . . .

Many sigh and cry: "Oh, that I were at home again, and if I had to lie in my pig-sty!" Or they say: "O God, if I only had a piece of good bread, or a good fresh drop of water." Many people whimper, sigh and cry piteously for their homes; most of them get home-sick. Many hundred people necessarily die and perish in such misery and must be cast into the sea, which drives their relatives or those who persuaded them to undertake the journey, to such despair that it is almost impossible to pacify and console them. In a word, the sighing and crying and lamenting on board the ship continues night and day so as to cause the hearts even of the most hardened to bleed when they hear it. . . .

At length, when, after a long and tedious voyage, the ships come in sight of land, so that the promontories can be seen, which the people were so eager and anxious to see, all creep from below on deck to see the land from afar, and they weep for joy, and pray and sing, thanking and praising God. The sight of the land makes the people on board the ship, especially the sick and the half-dead, alive again, so that their hearts leap within them; they shout and rejoice, and are content to bear their misery in patience, in the hope that they may soon reach the land in safety. But alas!

When the ships have landed at Philadelphia after their long voyage, no one is permitted to leave them except those who pay for their passage or can give good security; the others, who cannot pay, must remain on board the ships till they are purchased, and are released from the ships by their purchasers. The sick always fare the worst, for the healthy are naturally preferred and purchased first; and so the sick and wretched must often remain on board in front of the city for 2 or 3 weeks, and frequently die, whereas many a one, if he could pay his debt and were permitted to leave the ship immediately, might recover and remain alive. . . .

The sale of human beings in the market on board the ship is carried on thus: Every day Englishmen, Dutchmen and High-German people come from the city of Philadelphia and other places, in part from a great distance, say 20, 30, or 40 hours away, and go on board the newly arrived ship that has brought and offers for sale passengers from Europe, and select among the healthy persons such as they deem suitable for their business, and bargain with them how long they will serve for their passage money, which most of them are still in debt for. When they have come to an agreement, it happens that adult persons bind themselves in writing to serve 3, 4, 5 or 6 years for the amount due by them, according to their age and strength. But very young people, from 10 to 15 years, must serve till they are 21 years old.

Many parents must sell and trade away their children like so many head of cattle; for if their children take the debt upon themselves, the parents can leave the ship free and unrestrained; but as the parents often do not know where and to what people their children are going, it often happens that such parents and children, after leaving the ship, do not see each other again for many years, perhaps no more in all their lives. . . .

It often happens that whole families, husband, wife, and children, are separated by being sold to different purchasers, especially when they have not paid any part of their passage money.

When a husband or wife has died at sea, when the ship has made more than half of her trip, the survivor must pay or serve not only for himself or herself, but also for the deceased.

When both parents have died over half-way at sea, their children, especially when they are young and have nothing to pawn or to pay, must stand for their own and their parents' passage, and serve till they are 21 years old. When one has served his or her term, he or she is entitled to a new suit or clothes at parting; and if it has been so stipulated, a man gets in addition a horse, a woman, a cow. . . .

If some one in this country runs away from his master, who has treated him harshly, he cannot get far. Good provision has been made for such cases, so that a runaway is soon recovered. He who detains or returns a deserter receives a good reward.

If such a runaway has been away from his master one day, he must serve for it as a punishment a week, for a week a month, and for a month half a year. But if the master will not keep the runaway after he has got him back, he may sell him for so many years as he would have to serve him yet. . . .

However hard he may be compelled to work in his fatherland, he will surely find it quite as hard, if not harder, in the new country. Besides, there is not only the long and arduous journey lasting half a year, during which he has to suffer, more than with the hardest work; he has also spent about

200 florins which no one will refund to him. If he has so much money, it will slip out of his hands; if he has it not, he must work his debt off as a slave and poor serf. Therefore let every one stay in his own country and support himself and his family honestly. Besides I say that those who suffer themselves to be persuaded and enticed away by the man-thieves, are very foolish if they believe that roasted pigeons will fly into their mouths in America or Pennsylvania without their working for them.

Chapter 5

Eighteenth-Century Religion: Progress and Piety

Religion pervaded the lives of American colonists. Indeed, the New England colonies, Pennsylvania, and Maryland were established by founders with religious purposes in mind. In the other colonies, as well, religion played a central role.

Eighteenth-century immigration, much of it non-English in origin, intensified and diversified the religious climate. German Mennonites, Dunkers, and Moravians established settlements in Pennsylvania. Lutherans from Scandinavia and Germany, by the time of the Revolution, had built some 130 churches throughout the middle and southern colonies. Scots-Irish settlers brought their Presbyterian faith with them as they settled the western regions of Pennsylvania and moved south along the Appalachian mountain chain. English Baptists established a strong foothold in Philadelphia and eventually spread throughout the colonies, gaining particular strength in the South during the latter half of the century. Because no one group dominated, religious toleration took root in colonial America.

Patricia Bonomi's essay describes the prevalence of churchgoing during the eighteenth century. As you read, notice the variety of ways in which the churches served the colonists, both in settled areas and on the frontier, particularly among women and the elderly. The essay also discusses initial attempts to convert blacks and Indians to Christianity. The first document provides an example of such endeavors. Why did both masters and slaves respond lukewarmly to missionaries' efforts to convert the slaves?

The Great Awakening, the evangelical revivalist movement described in the Bonomi essay, reveals a great deal about the condition and direction of American colonial society during the 1730s and 1740s. Revivalist preachers, often noted more for their piety and oratorical skill than for their learning, touched the emotions of the lonely, unchurched, and often unschooled settlers of the western frontier regions and southern backwoods. They also found a responsive audience in the more settled areas of the middle and northern colonies, particularly among Presbyterians and Congregationalists who had grown weary of the highly intellectual sermons emanating from the pulpits of their college-educated ministers. In colorful, emotional sermons, the Great Awakening leaders preached a religion of the heart, emphasizing a personal relationship with God and the individual's responsibility for his or her own salvation. Saving grace, they insisted, was available through repentance and rejection of sin, prayer, moral behavior, and, most essential, a spiritual conversion, or being "born again." Starting in the middle colonies in the mid-1730s, the Great Awakening spread up and down the coast during the following decade and thus became a truly intercolonial movement, reflecting the growing ties among Britain's American colonies.

The excitement engendered by the traveling ministers of the Great Awakening is described in the second document. In it Nathan Cole tells of events surrounding the appearance of the evangelist George Whitefield in Middletown, Connecticut, on October 23, 1740.

To win the attention of potential converts, revivalist preachers usually painted vivid verbal pictures of the Hell that awaited sinners, as well as the Heaven promised to those "born again." The most famous "hellfire" sermon of the Great Awakening was delivered by Jonathan Edwards to his Enfield, Connecticut, congregation in 1741. The final document is taken from this sermon, which Edwards entitled "Sinners in the Hands of an Angry God."

As Bonomi reveals, not everyone, particularly not the more traditional "old light" ministers, approved of the techniques of the revivalist or "new light" preachers. After reading the essay and documents, what do you think led many people, including previously resistant blacks, to embrace the Great Awakening, and others to condemn it strongly? Can you identify trends in modern religious life reminiscent of the eighteenth-century division between "new lights" and "old lights"?

ESSAY

————— •◆• —————

The Churchgoers

Patricia U. Bonomi

Recent estimates suggest that a majority of adults in the eighteenth-century colonies were regular church attenders. Though the worship of God was no doubt the primary motive for churchgoing, eighteenth-century worshipers, like those of today, found that church attendance served a number of non-spiritual needs. The quest for community, long recognized as an incentive for churchgoing, must have operated with particular force among inhabitants of the dispersed farming society of early America. Churches in both country and town were vital centers of community life, as government proclamations were broadcast from the pulpit and news of prices and politics were exchanged in the churchyard. In a society formed from the uprooted communities of the Old World, moreover, the church congregation served as a primary agency by which immigrants recovered something of what they had left behind. Family tradition was another strong stimulus to churchgoing. Pious colonial parents promoted the religious education of their children and instilled in them habits of regular church attendance. In some congregations the founding elders and their offspring gained such firm control over the church that newcomers or persons not descended from "Godly parents" were made to feel unwelcome. Such "tribalism" apparently characterized the early Puritan churches, and a similar turning inward has been detected among the Quakers of Pennsylvania.

Inhabitants living on the geographic periphery of colonial parishes found their churchgoing practices being shaped by circumstances over which they had little control. As towns expanded, owing to natural increase and in-migration, a rising proportion of the outlivers lost touch with the central church. Distance and bad weather made travel to Sabbath services so hazardous that outlying hamlets frequently were granted "winter privileges," or the right to conduct their own services under lay direction. As peripheral districts gained population additional parishes were formed, and soon the former outlivers emerged as pillars of newly gathered churches.

The factors just noted also were significant determinants of the degree of church adherence, that is, of whether individuals became communicants, half-way members, regular attenders, pew holders, irregular attenders, or in a very few cases "scoffers." In all eighteenth-century churches a minority of the adherents were communicants.* Self-imposed scrupulosity accounts for

SOURCE: From *Under the Cope of Heaven: Religion, Society and Politics in Colonial America* by Patricia U. Bonomi. Copyright © 1986 by Patricia U. Bonomi. Used by permission of Oxford University Press, Inc.

Communicants were entitled to receive communion, as full church members. (Eds.)

some of this, especially in the Congregational churches, where admission standards remained high, and the Anglican church, where the absence of an American bishop meant that only those confirmed in England were canonically qualified to take communion. . . .

The conventional ratio of one communicant for every three or four non-communicating church attenders is probably too low for most colonial churches, at least until the late eighteenth century. However that may be, many non-communicants participated vigorously in church life, serving as deacons or vestrymen and supporting their churches financially through the purchase of pews and contributions to the minister's salary. This probably explains why most ministers habitually referred to churchgoers interchangeably as *parishioners, members, auditors,* and *adherents.* In any case, we cannot restrict our consideration of "churched" Americans to communicants alone, since this not only contradicts eighteenth-century usage but excludes from consideration the majority of colonial churchgoers.

The clergymen have left a good deal of information about local church-going practice, the best of it for many denominations coming from the S.P.G. [Society for the Propagation of the Gospel, an Anglican missionary society] correspondence. In describing the religious complexion of their territory, the missionaries had little difficulty identifying most inhabitants with a specific denomination or sect. One writes that of several hundred white people inhabiting a North Carolina parish in 1710, only "five or six [were] of no professed religion"; among 1750 whites in Sussex County, Pennsylvania, a minister reported that 1075 were Anglicans, 600 Presbyterians, and 75 Quakers. . . .

New England was universally regarded as the best churched section. Visitors marveled at the regularity of religious practice in a land where "every five Miles, or perhaps less, you have a Meeting-House." Boston, a city of 15,000 inhabitants, had eighteen churches by 1750—ten of them representing the Congregational establishment. Large church buildings were needed to accommodate city congregations that ranged up to 1500 persons and more by mid-century. Indeed, as early as the 1720s Cotton Mather of Second Church scorned a congregation of a thousand as "Thinner . . . than Ordinary."

Middle-colony church life, though reflecting the rapid changes overtaking that section in the eighteenth century, was anything but moribund. New York, New Jersey, Pennsylvania, and Delaware were collectively subject to a 530-percent white population growth between 1710 and 1760 (nearly double the rate in either New England or the South), which added disproportionately large communities of Germans and Scots to the initial Swedish, Dutch, and English populations. Churches, like other middle-colony institutions, experienced strain as new congregations and sects proliferated in the hothouse environment generated by the fierce competition for adherents. By 1750, the middle region had more congregations per capita than any other section, though with the shortage of clergymen many of them were served by itinerant preachers. Philadelphia had twenty principal churches by the 1760s, and New York City eighteen. . . .

The Anglican Church in the Chesapeake was settled on a sufficiently solid foundation by 1701 that the newly organized S.P.G. could direct its resources to the needier Carolinas and later Georgia, where dissenters abounded. Religious competition once again stimulated growth in all denominations; by 1750 South Carolina, for example, had almost twice as many churches per capita as did either Virginia or Maryland. Charleston, the South's only city—with a population of around 12,000—boasted a number of fine churches including Anglican St. Philip's, described by one admirer as "the most elegant Religious Edifice in British America." Though one hundred feet long and sixty wide, its congregation was so numerous that a second large church. St. Michael's, was built in 1761. Nonetheless, by mid-century the South as a whole lagged behind the North in congregation formation, opening opportunities for the evangelical Presbyterian and Baptist preachers who appeared in increasing numbers from that time forward. . . .

"Daughters of Zion"

By the second half of the eighteenth century mothers were becoming the primary custodians of the family's religious heritage, and in genteel households they took significant responsibility for the children's religious education, often in conjunction with a private tutor. A number of wealthy women also left substantial legacies to their churches. . . .

Besides spiritual refreshment, religion offered women of energy and intellect an outlet to the wider world, as well as opportunities for self-expression, personal growth, and even leadership. Many women spoke with authority about complex theological issues. William Byrd II recorded that his wife and sister-in-law spent one evening at Westover [his home] in "fierce dispute about the infallibility of the Bible." Frances Carter of Nomini Hall discussed with her daughter the question of whether women had souls, and she conversed "with great propriety" about religion to tutor Philip Fithian, demonstrating "a very extensive knowledge." Devereux Jarratt was instructed in vital religion by the New Light wife of the planter whose children he tutored. In New England the religious writings of such pious matrons as Elizabeth Cotton and Jerusha Mather Oliver were incorporated into sermons or published for the enlightenment of a wider audience.

Women of middle and lower status also found that religious activity offered them a wider stage. The Society of Friends in America defined women and men as equal in the sight of God, opening to females a prominent role in their public ministry. . . . A number of them gained approval from their meetings to leave home and family for extended periods in the eighteenth century to spread the Quaker message. For those at home the Women's

Meeting in each congregation exercised significant powers, disciplining female members, regulating marriages, and overseeing church attendance by both men and women. No other denomination matched the Friends in opening opportunities to women, though New Light and especially Baptist meetings sometimes allowed them a voice in church government and a vote on new members.

Occasionally a woman appeared with sufficient self-confidence to test the boundaries of women's religious sphere. . . . [S]uch a one was an elderly parishioner of [Lutheran clergyman] Henry Muhlenberg in mid-eighteenth-century Pennsylvania. This unnamed woman did not shrink from challenging Muhlenberg on such theological points as original sin and conversion, and was much distressed at his seeming to teach that the Jews were under sentence of damnation. Muhlenberg clearly found her conversation edifying, and used her as a "bellwether" of the congregation. Another was the Congregationalist Sarah Haggar Osborne of Newport, Rhode Island. Mrs. Osborne started conventionally enough as leader of a young women's prayer society, following the scriptural rule that older women might instruct the younger. But for some reason this modest venture began to take on the most gratifying momentum. Slaves, male and female, took to attending the Sunday evening prayer meetings; on other evenings came "Little white Lads" and girls from the neighborhood; and during the revival of 1766–1767 between 300 and 500 persons were crowding into the Osborne house every week. For Sarah Osborne it was all wonderfully inspiriting. Languor and sick spells faded away; she now slept well, had a good appetite, and knew "nothing about weariness." . . .

The relief that religion brought to the ordinary colonial woman's life of toil, especially on the frontier, is frequently noted in Henry Muhlenberg's record of his pastoral encounters. Muhlenberg tells of aged and ill women who found their only solace in God, of widows with large families rising above adversity through Christian faith, and of women afflicted with melancholia who found surcease from it in religion. One Pennsylvania frontierswoman gave her husband some concern from the frequency with which she would go off to sit in the woods by herself, and he spoke to the pastor about it. But the reason should have been obvious. She was "somewhat weak physically and always had a flock of children around her"; she was not really "melancholy," just worn out—and when things got too much, the best restorative she could think of was a session of solitary prayer.

The sisterhood of the Ephrata cloister at Lancaster, Pennsylvania, offers the most striking case of an institutional haven for women who believed themselves, from whatever causes, to have reached the end of their earthly tether. This Seventh Day Baptist community—which had male as well as female houses—was headed by Conrad Beissel, who believed in a life of celibacy and regarded marriage as the penitentiary of carnal man. A number of women joined the Ephrata cloister when they were quite young. Life in the Saron, or sisterhouse, took many of its features from the nunneries of Europe, a circumstance that provided a satiric foil for Ephrata's critics. The sisters' habit consisted of a vest and long skirt, belted at the waist and covered with a large apron that resembled a monk's scapulary. Their heads were covered by a rounded hood. The sisters' dedication to a "modest, quiet, tranquil and retired" life was regulated by a hierarchy of overseers, sub-prioress, and prioress. Whereas some young women found the regimen too harsh or finally rejected the celibate life, a number of others remained in the Saron, some for forty or fifty years. . . .

The Ephrata experience represents an extreme of female piety in colonial America. Most women followed the more orthodox path of participation with their families in local religious institutions. Yet the rising proportion of women associated with a number of churches and sects suggests that religion offered them satisfactions that nothing else in their existence could provide. Starting from their customary if circumscribed role as guardians of family piety and teachers of the young, many women sought and found in religious life a larger scope for their energy and talents. . . .

Young and Old

Churchgoing was largely an adult activity in colonial America, especially where homesteads were widely scattered. Parents simply would not expose small children to the long journeys and extreme temperatures that churchgoing entailed in rural areas. Anglican parish reports indicate that older youths concentrated their attendance in the Lenten period when rectors gave instruction in the catechism, though schoolmasters regularly catechized young people and parents also were encouraged to do so. Devereux Jarratt recalled that his parents taught their children short prayers and "made us very perfect in repeating the Church Catechism." With no bishop resident in the colonies confirmation in accordance with church canons was impossible, but ministers apparently examined youths at about age sixteen or older and, when satisfied with their level of understanding, admitted them to communion. The sons of Robert Carter III, eighteen-year-old Ben and sixteen-year-old Bob, often "begged" Philip Fithian to let them go to church despite poor weather, and occasionally the boys attended even when their parents would not venture forth. This along with similar evidence from William Byrd's diaries suggests that Sunday was an important day on the social calendar of Virginia's young people.

Middle-colony Lutherans and German Reformed often traveled ten or fifteen miles to worship, which generally restricted churchgoing to adults. The Presbytery of Hanover County, Virginia, noted as late as 1775 that its boundaries were so extensive that "women, children, and servants" often could not attend church. One consequence was that baptism of colonial children was often delayed, less through parental neglect—though that was sometimes a factor—than the inaccessibility of churches and ministers.

When clergymen traveled out to such areas, children were brought to them by the score, even by the hundreds, to be baptized. "Baptized Children till was weary" was a familiar comment from frontier itinerants.

In the towns and cities youths participated more regularly in church life. The Anglican rector at Philadelphia, for example, organized a society of young men which met on Sunday evenings to hear sermons, read Scripture, and sing psalms. Henry Muhlenberg provides an unusually full picture of the religious training given children at the Philadelphia Lutheran church. Sunday morning catechism classes, or *Kinderlehre,* were held in the school-house adjacent to the church. (Muhlenberg's notation of a three-year-old child who got lost on her way to *Kinderlehre* suggests that instruction began at an early age.) Muhlenberg often undertook that catechizing himself, leaving morning church service to an assistant pastor. He advocated that children be confirmed by age fourteen, observing that some German and English sects were "sharply critical of us because they consider that we take them too young." Though a few Lutheran children were confirmed at fourteen, or even thirteen in a case or two, admission was more commonly delayed until age sixteen and seventeen and many persons were confirmed only after marriage. Owing to the paucity of Lutheran clergy in the early eighteenth century, Muhlenberg frequently found himself instructing both young and old. During a 1752 sojourn in New York City—where the Lutheran church was often bereft of a regular minister and many adults never had received instruction—Muhlenberg reported that "a number of young people and at least as many adults, some sixty, seventy, and more years of age, came to *Kinderlehre.*"

New England children below the age of seven or eight rarely attended the Congregational churches, though religious education certainly went on at home. Churchgoing boys in the mischievous pre-adolescent years were herded into "boys pews" or ranged along the gallery stairs where appointed monitors watched over them, dealing out "raps and blows" to those making "Indecent Gestures and Wry Faces" during service. The more decorous girls sat on little stools in the pews or aisles. Judging from the diary of eleven-year-old Anna Green Winslow, the religious training of young females was well advanced by eleven or twelve. Anna solemnly recorded the biblical texts and applications of the Reverend Mr. Beacon's sermons at Boston's Old South Church, especially those directed to "the young people." She also read daily from the Bible and regularly attended Thursday lecture and catechism. . . .

Congregationalists became formal church members at a later age than did Anglicans, Lutherans, and most others, perhaps because of stricter admission standards. In the early eighteenth century, Andover females and males joined as half-way members around ages twenty and twenty-four, respectively. Before 1730, Andover women delayed entry into full communion until ages twenty-six to twenty-eight, while men did not become full members until their middle to late 30s. At Norton and Middleborough, and in the Connecticut town of Milford, males admitted to full communion before 1740 averaged between twenty-eight and thirty-nine years of age. At Woodbury, Connecticut, where admission policies were quite lenient, women joined the church in their early to middle twenties whereas men were about five years older.

Thus in most denominations prior to the Great Awakening maximum involvement in the church's life was delayed until late adolescence or young adulthood, when religious matters might, presumably, be approached with greater maturity.

If churches were not the terrain of the very young they were certainly familiar ground to the aged. Sermons were regularly directed to elderly churchgoers, and ministers spent a large part of their time visiting aged parishioners who were too feeble to travel to church. In both North and South piety was expected to intensify as men and women moved into old age. Being closer to the eternal resolution, the elderly were presumed to possess a sharpened religious sensibility. . . .

The aged appear to have been disproportionately represented in the congregations of colonial America—a fact of religious sociology that is evident in all faiths and times.

Blacks, Indians, and Indentured Servants

Blacks, Indians, and white servants could also be found at church, though their involvement, subject to some regional and denominational variation, was for the most part quite restricted. The Church of England encouraged its ministers throughout the eighteenth century to convert the "infidels"— the term commonly applied to Negroes and Indians—and many took the charge seriously. The Reverend Anthony Gavin, who believed that slavery was "unlawfull for any Christian," baptized almost as many blacks as whites on his first tour of the South Carolina backcountry in 1738. Slave owners often resisted missionary efforts out of fear that Christianity would make their slaves prideful and rebellious, even though many clergymen took care to preach up humility and obedience to their black converts. What conversion to Christianity actually did for them under such circumstances is difficult to judge. Nevertheless when slaves ran away or were suspected of plotting rebellion, local authorities were quick to accuse Christian missionaries of fomenting disorder.

White resistance to slave conversion appears to have fluctuated according to the proportion of blacks in the population. Thus early support for S.P.G. missionaries' work in baptizing and catechizing slaves in South Carolina declined as blacks came to outnumber whites in the colony after about 1708. Virginia rectors reported occasional success in Christianizing slaves, but as blacks rose from less than 10 percent of the population in 1680 to around one-third by 1740 white resistance stiffened. Maryland's population was only 12 to 18 percent black in the first third of the century, which may account for the greater willingness of white masters there to allow slaves to be baptized and catechized.

This shading of attitudes is apparent in the responses of southern rectors to the bishop of London's 1724 questionnaire on the state of the colonial church. All nine respondents from South Carolina reported little or no success in converting Negroes, typically because "their Masters will not consent to Have them Instructed." About half of the twenty-eight Virginia respondents had managed to baptize "several," and in rarer cases "many," Negroes, though only three or four noted that some blacks actually came to church. But in Maryland nearly a third of the rectors had baptized "many" slaves, some of whom attended church and took communion. Though a number of ministers had to "press" masters to instruct their slaves, the tone of the Maryland responses is more sanguine, and one rector stated that slaves in his parish had "free liberty from their masters to attend divine service & other means of instruction." Yet if black conversions were more numerous in Maryland, there is no reason to question the conventional view that the overwhelming majority of southern blacks remained unchurched. As one writer summed it up in 1705: "Talk to a *Planter* of the *Soul of a Negro* . . . [and he will respond that whereas the body is worth £20] the souls of an hundred of them would not yield him one farthing."

Masters were undoubtedly the primary obstacle to slave conversions, but language was a further barrier among first-generation Afro-Americans. Moreover, since Sunday was the slaves' only day off, many spent it cultivating their own garden plots and a few "work[ed] for themselves on hire." Thus, as a rule, southern blacks figured no more than marginally in church life during the first half of the eighteenth century. Even fewer Indians were converted to the white people's religion in the South, most likely because the tribes had a strong religion of their own. Southern ministers, already overtaxed by the demands of their white parishioners, reported uniformly that Indians were averse to the Christian religion.

The lower number of blacks in the North suggests that the white population there should have been more receptive to missionary efforts. And, indeed, only New York and New Jersey, which along with Rhode Island contained the largest proportion of blacks, passed laws stipulating that baptism did not alter the slaves' condition of servitude. Conversion did little to ease the burden of slavery in any northern colony, but it appears that more slaves became church adherents there than in the South. . . .

As was the case in the South, Indians proved more resistant than blacks to the S.P.G.'s attempts to convert them, though one missionary successfully formed a congregation of them at Albany. . . .

In Boston, Cotton Mather organized a Society of Negroes which met on Sunday evenings for religious instruction. That blacks attended Mather's church is evident from the remarks he addressed to them in his printed sermons. Mather's deepest concern for blacks, as for whites, was to get them to Christ. "Oh! That more pains were taken, to show the *Ethiopians,* their *Sin,* which renders them so much *Blacker* than their *Skin!*" exhorted Mather. Would that he could "lead them unto the Saviour, who will bestow upon them a *Change* of *Soul,* which is much better than a *Change* of *Skin!*" Participation of blacks at other Congregational churches was probably quite limited, though some church records of the pre-Awakening years indicate that a few slaves, and even an occasional Indian "servant," owned the covenant [had been converted]. Still, these converts were barred from most church activities; they sat in the rear of meetinghouses, and their burial plots were segregated from those of white parishioners.

Though the public attitude of the Society of Friends toward both blacks and Indians was remarkably enlightened for the eighteenth century, the number of either group embraced by Quaker meetings was very small. Nor are Negroes often mentioned in Presbyterian, Lutheran, or Reformed records. Thus even in the North only a few Negroes, and even fewer Indians, were brought within the fold of the early eighteenth-century Christian churches.

White servants too were less likely to partake of religious instruction and Sabbath activities, especially in rural sections. . . .

In Congregational New England white servants were catechized along with children during family worship, and they went to church with the family unless the care of small children kept them at home. In the Middle Colonies, where many indentured servants settled after 1720, the picture is more blurred. Lutheran and Reformed ministers expressed much concern about the souls of German servants in the region, especially those placed in English families where their native religion was neglected. Still, servants regularly appear on Henry Muhlenberg's list of confirmands. A Quaker family in Pennsylvania encouraged a devout young woman in its employ to pursue the role of "speaker" in the Society of Friends. And Quakers were expected to include their servants as part of the family when attending meeting. Nonetheless, it seems likely that in America, as in England at this time, servants and the poor made up a disproportionately high percentage of those outside the embrace of some religious community.

The Great Awakening and Church Membership

The Great Awakening of 1739–1745 temporarily altered the pattern of church adherence described above. Indeed this foremost revival, as well as periodic and more localized quickenings, can be defined in part not only by surging church admissions but by heavier concentrations than usual from two constituencies: men and young people. A typical report came from the Reverend Peter Thacher of Middleborough, Massachusetts: "the Grace of God has surprisingly seized and subdued the hardiest men, and more Males have been added here than the tenderer sex." In addition, many youths were "crying and wringing their hands, and bewailing their Frolicking and Dancing." At Woodbury, Connecticut, between 1740 and 1742, First Church added fifty-nine male to forty-six female members. The awakened flocked to their minister in Wrentham, Massachusetts, "especially young People, under Soul Distress." From Natick came word that "Indians and English, Young and Old, Male and Female" had been called to Christ. In New England those who joined the churches during the revival were on average six years younger than members affiliating before the Awakening, a pattern that pertained also in the Middle Colonies. Considering the ministers' perennial concern for the rising generation, this melting of young hearts was especially gratifying. The addition of larger numbers of men also tended, at least temporarily, to slow the feminization of churches.

Women nonetheless continued to be drawn into the churches during the Great Awakening, where they spoke up more confidently than ever before. Boston's anti-revivalist minister Charles Chauncy, alarmed when "FEMALE EXHORTERS" began to appear, declared that "encouraging WOMEN, yea, GIRLS to speak in the assemblies for religious worship" was a clear breach of the Lord's commandment. One Old Light explained the peculiar susceptibility of women and youths to the emotionalism of the revival as follows: "The aptness of Children and Women to weep . . . in greater Abundance than grown Persons and Men is a plain proof . . . that their Fluids are more numerous in Proportion to their Solids, and their Nerves are weak."

The revival's emphasis on the spoken rather than the written word, and its concern for reaching out to new constituencies, gave it a broad social base. Blacks and Indians, groups with an oral tradition, frequently attended revival meetings in the North. George Whitefield, finding that Negroes could be "effectually wrought upon, and in an uncommon manner," developed "a most winning way of addressing them." In New England, blacks and Indians drawn to the Awakening were sometimes brought directly into the body of the church. Plymouth New Lights had among their members at least "a Negro or two who were directed to invite others to come to Christ," and at Gloucester, where a number of blacks joined the church, there was "a society of negroes, who in their meetings behave very seriously and decently." When the New Light preacher Eleazer Wheelock visited Taunton, Massachusetts, in 1741, he left "almost all the negroes in town wounded: three or four converted." And Wheelock's work among the Indians led, of course, to the founding of a school that later became Dartmouth College. David Brainerd gained a number of converts to Christianity among the Indians of New Jersey. James Davenport was responsible for the conversion of Samson Occum, an eighteen-year-old Mohegan from Connecticut. Occum attended Wheelock's school at Lebanon, Connecticut, for four years, was ordained by the Presbyterian Church in 1759, and carried the message of the revival to many of his brethren in Connecticut and New York. Scattered evidence suggests that the Awakening may have had a more significant and long-range impact on blacks than on any other northern group. . . .

Nor can it be doubted that the revival reached out to servants and laborers among the white population. As Dr. Alexander Hamilton commented with typical astringency during a 1744 trip throughout the North, even "the lower class of people here . . . talk . . . about justification, sanctification, adoption, regeneration, repentance, free grace, reprobation, original sin, and a thousand other such pritty, chimerical knick knacks as if they had done nothing but studied divinity all their life time." Still, the lowly origins of the awakened can easily be overstated. It is quite possible that the likeliest prospects for conversion came, after all, from the growing and varied ranks of the middle class, people who counted just a bit less than they felt they should in church and town, and for whom the revival opened up new possibilities and uncertainties—great hopes, great fears, great expectations.

Religious awakening came later to the colonial South, starting in the mid-1740s with Presbyterian itinerants and reaching full pitch in the 1760s and 1770s with the Baptist and Methodist revivals. How churchgoing was affected by these revivals remained to be explored, though long-standing regional characteristics probably shaped the southerners' response. Men and women may have continued to participate in church life in relatively equal numbers, whereas young people and Indians, pending new evidence, appear to have been only marginally affected by the revival. Negroes were another matter, however, for all evangelical denominations reported growing numbers of blacks among their adherents. Presbyterian Samuel Davies counted several hundred Negroes in his New Side [evangelical, revivalist] congregations in Virginia. The added dimension that religion gave to black lives is implicit in Davies's comment about the slaves' delight in psalmody: "Whenever they could get an hour's leisure from their masters, [they] would hurry away to my house . . . to gratify their peculiar taste for Psalmody. Sundry of them have lodged all night in my kitchen; and, sometimes, when I have awaked about two or three a-clock in the morning, a torrent of sacred harmony poured into my chamber, and carried my mind away to Heaven. In this seraphic exercise, some of them spend almost the whole night." . . .

To be sure, only a tiny proportion of blacks were active Christians before the Revolution. Yet great changes were in the making. In religion the implied promise of some small measure of fulfillment, in a life that otherwise had little of it, was considerable, and a foundation was being laid upon which future generations would construct the central institution of Afro-American culture.

The Great Awakening caused a visible warp in the configuration of colonial church adherence. True, for most groups the change was no more than temporary, as pre-Awakening patterns reemerged once the revival subsided. One continuing legacy of the Awakening, however, was that it stimulated a rise in the number of preachers, especially lay preachers, thereby facilitating the extension of religion to the frontier and other under-served sections. Individuals who had been beyond the reach of ministers and churches—owing more to circumstances than choice—were now brought within the purview of a structured religious community. That this previously isolated constituency tended to have a higher proportion of young people, immigrants, and economically marginal persons than were located in the longer settled towns and cities goes far to explain the popular overtones of the revival. The growth of religious institutions was not dependent, of course, on the Great Awakening or any other revival. Far from reviving a languishing church life, the Awakening bespoke the vitality and widening reach of an expanding religious culture. . . .

DOCUMENTS

A New York Act to Encourage the Baptizing of Negro, Indian, and Mulatto Slaves, 1706

Whereas divers of her Majesty's good Subjects, Inhabitants of this Colony now are and have been willing that such Negro, Indian and Mulatto Slaves who belong to them and desire the same, should be Baptized, but are deterr'd and hindered therefrom by reason of a Groundless opinion that hath spread itself in this Colony, that by the Baptizing of such Negro, Indian or Mulatto slave they would become free and ought to be sett at Liberty. In order therefore to put an end to all such Doubts and Scruples as have or hereafter at any time may arise about the same. Be it Enacted by the Governor Councill and Assembly and it is hereby Enacted by the authority of the same, That the Baptizing of any Negro, Indian or Mulatto Slave shall not be any Cause or reason for the setting them or any of them at Liberty.

And be it declared and Enacted by the Governor Councill & Assembly and by the Authority of the same, That all and every Negro, Indian, Mulatto and Mestee* and Bastard Child & Children who is, are, and shall be born of any Negro, Indian, Mulatto or Mestee, shall follow ye State and Condition of the Mother & be esteemed reputed taken & adjudged a Slave & Slaves to all intents & purposes whatsoever.

SOURCE: Hugh Hastings, ed., *Ecclesiastical Records of the State of New York 3* (Albany: State of New York, 1902): 1673.

*A *Mestee* is a person of mixed European and Indian ancestry. (Eds.)

Provided, always & be it declared & Enacted by ye said Authority That no slave whatsoever in this Colony shall Att any time be admitted as a witness for, or against, any Freeman, in any Case matter or Cause, Civill or Criminal whatsoever.

The Great Awakening in Connecticut, 1740

Now it pleased God to send Mr. Whitefield into this land; and my hearing of his preaching at Philadelphia, like one of the old apostles, and many thousands flocking to hear him preach the Gospel, and great numbers were converted to Christ, I felt the Spirit of God drawing me by conviction; I longed to see and hear him and wished he would come this way. I heard he was come to New York and the Jerseys and great multitudes flocking after him under great concern for their souls which brought on my concern more and more, hoping soon to see him; but next I heard he was at Long Island, then at Boston, and next at Northampton. Then on a sudden, in the morning about 8 or 9 of the clock there came a messenger and said Mr. Whitefield preached at Hartford and Wethersfield yesterday and is to preach at Middletown this morning at ten of the clock. I was in my field at work. I dropped my tool that I had in my hand and ran home to my wife, telling her to make ready quickly to go and hear Mr. Whitefield preach at Middletown, then ran to my pasture for my horse with all my might, fearing that I should be too late. Having my horse, I with my wife soon mounted the horse and went forward as fast as I thought the horse could bear; and when my horse got much out of breath, I would get down and put my wife on the saddle and bid her ride as fast as she could and not stop or slack for me except I bade her, and so I would run until I was much out of breath and then mount my horse again, and so I did several times to favour my horse. We improved every moment to get along as if we were fleeing for our lives, all the while fearing we should be too late to hear the sermon, for we had twelve miles to ride double in little more than an hour and we went round by the upper housen parish. And when we came within about half a mile or a mile of the road that comes down from Hartford, Wethersfield, and Stepney to Middletown, on high land I saw before me a cloud of fog arising. I first thought it came from the great river, but as I came nearer the road I heard a noise of horses' feet coming down the road, and this cloud was a cloud of dust made by the horses' feet. It arose some rods into the air over the tops of hills and trees; and when I came within about 20 rods of the road, I could see men and horses slipping along in the cloud like shadows, and as I drew nearer

SOURCE: Nathan Cole, ms. cited in Leonard W. Labaree, "George Whitefield Comes to Middletown," *William and Mary Quarterly*, 3d ser. 7 (1950): 590–591.

it seemed like a steady stream of horses and their riders, scarcely a horse more than his length behind another, all of a lather and foam with sweat, their breath rolling out of their nostrils every jump. Every horse seemed to go with all his might to carry his rider to hear news from heaven for the saving of souls. It made me tremble to see the sight, how the world was in a struggle. I found a vacancy between two horses to slip in mine and my wife said "Law, our clothes will be all spoiled, see how they look," for they were so covered with dust that they looked almost all of a colour, coats, hats, shirts, and horse. We went down in the stream but heard no man speak a word all the way for 3 miles but every one pressing forward in great haste; and when we got to Middletown old meeting house, there was a great multitude, it was said to be 3 or 4,000 or people, assembled together. We dismounted and shook off our dust, and the ministers were then coming to the meeting house. I turned and looked towards the Great River and saw the ferry boats running swift backward and forward bringing over loads of people, and the oars rowed nimble and quick. Everything, men, horses, and boats seemed to be struggling for life. The land and banks over the river looked black with people and horses; all along the 12 miles I saw no man at work in his field, but all seemed to be gone. When I saw Mr. Whitefield come upon the scaffold, he looked almost angelical; a young, slim, slender youth, before some thousands of people with bold undaunted countenance. And my hearing how God was with him everywhere as he came along, it solemnized my mind and put me into a trembling fear before he began to preach; for he looked as if he was clothed with authority from the Great God, and a sweet solemn solemnity sat upon his brow, and my hearing him preach gave me a heart wound. By God's blessing, my old foundation was broken up, and I saw that my righteousness would not save me.

"Sinners in the Hands of an Angry God," 1741

The God that holds you over the pit of hell, much as one holds a spider or some loathsome insect over the fire, abhors you, and is dreadfully provoked. His wrath towards you burns like fire; he looks upon you as worthy of nothing else but to be cast into the fire. He is of purer eyes than to bear you in his sight; you are ten thousand times as abominable in his eyes as the most hateful, venomous serpent is in ours.

You have offended him infinitely more than ever a stubborn rebel did his prince, and yet it is nothing but his hand that holds you from falling into the fire every moment. It is to be ascribed to nothing else that you did not go to hell last night; that you were suffered to awake again in this world, after

SOURCE: Jonathan Edwards, *Works* 2 (1840): 10–11.

you closed your eyes to sleep. And there is no other reason to be given why you have not dropped into hell since you arose in the morning, but that God's hand has held you up. There is no other reason to be given why you have not gone to hell since you have sat here in the house of God provoking his pure eye by your sinful, wicked manner of attending his solemn worship. Yea, there is nothing else that is to be given as a reason why you do not this very moment drop down into hell.

O sinner! consider the fearful danger you are in! It is a great furnace of wrath, a wide and bottomless pit, full of the fire of wrath that you are held over in the hand of that God whose wrath is provoked and incensed as much against you as against many of the damned in hell. You hang by a slender thread, with the flames of Divine wrath flashing about it, and ready every moment to singe it and burn it asunder. . . .

It would be dreadful to suffer this fierceness and wrath of Almighty God one moment; but you must suffer it to all eternity. There will be no end to this exquisite, horrible misery. When you look forward, you shall see along forever a boundless duration before you, which will swallow up your thoughts, and amaze your soul. And you will absolutely despair of ever having any deliverance, any end, any mitigation, any rest at all. You will know certainly that you must wear out long ages, millions of millions of ages in wrestling and conflicting with this Almighty, merciless vengeance. And then when you have so done, when so many ages have actually been spent by you in this manner, you will know that all is but a point [dot] to what remains. So that your punishment will indeed be infinite.

Oh! who can express what the state of a soul in such circumstances is! All that we can possibly say about it gives but a very feeble, faint representation of it. It is inexpressible and inconceivable: for "who knows the power of God's anger"!

How dreadful is the state of those that are daily and hourly in danger of this great wrath and infinite misery! But this is the dismal case of every soul in this congregation that has not been born again, however moral and strict, sober and religious, they may otherwise be. Oh! that you would consider it, whether you be young or old!

There is reason to think that there are many in this congregation, now hearing this discourse, that will actually be the subjects of this very misery to all eternity. We know not who they are, or in what seats they sit, or what thoughts they now have. It may be they are now at ease, and hear all these things without much disturbance, and are now flattering themselves that they are not the persons, promising themselves that they shall escape.

If we knew that there was one person, and but one in the whole congregation, that was to be the subject of this misery, what an awful thing it would be to think of! If we knew who it was, what an awful sight would it be to see such a person! How might all the rest of the congregation lift up a lamentable and bitter cry over him!

But, alas! instead of one, how many is it likely will remember this discourse in hell! And it would be a wonder, if some that are now present should not be in hell in a very short time before this year is out. And it would be no wonder if some persons that now sit here in some seats of this meeting-house, in health, and quiet and secure, should be there before to-morrow morning!

Chapter 6

Urban Life in the Eighteenth Century

Colonial American society was overwhelmingly agrarian—throughout the eighteenth century, farmers and their families represented over 90 percent of the population—but cities also prospered during this period. The very success of agriculture ensured their growth, for the primary function of Boston, Newport, New York, Philadelphia, Baltimore, and Charleston was to gather for export the surplus products of the farms and forests and to import and market manufactured goods. As centers of commerce and political, social, and cultural life, cities played a crucial role in shaping the character of the emerging nation.

In her essay "Boston and New York in the Eighteenth Century," Pauline Maier discusses the functions and characteristics common to American colonial cities. She describes and explains what made New York and Boston unique and very different from one another by the end of the eighteenth century. As you read, observe how the different reasons for the founding of these two cities exerted a lasting influence on them. Notice in each case the impact of geography, war, social class, and political structure. How does Maier's essay help to explain why Boston, America's third city in population and prosperity by 1775, stood in the forefront of events leading to the Revolutionary War?

The documents following the essay provide a view of another colonial city. By the outbreak of the Revolution, Philadelphia had become colonial America's largest city and within the British Empire was second only to London in population and prestige. In cities as on the frontier, colonial Americans learned the value of cooperative effort; voluntary militias, barn raisings, and husking bees provide apt examples. One of the chief advocates of cooperative ventures in an urban setting was Benjamin Franklin. He is credited with organizing America's first cooperative lending library, the first adult self-improvement group (the Junto), and, described in the initial document, the first adult volunteer fire department.

Visitors to Philadelphia found qualities to admire other than the city's cooperative spirit. The second document gives the impressions of Swedish botanist Peter Kalm during his 1748 visit to Philadelphia. What factors did Kalm deem most significant in accounting for Philadelphia's rapid rise to prominence?

Philadelphia also illustrates a fact of early American urban life that often goes unnoticed. City dwellers had to overcome numerous hazards: fires, street crime, primitive sanitary facilities, and epidemics of cholera, malaria, and yellow fever. The final document describes the yellow-fever epidemic that struck Philadelphia in 1793, causing the deaths of more than 5,000 of the city's approximately 55,000 inhabitants. What does the document reveal about the state of medical knowledge in the late eighteenth century?

ESSAY

Boston and New York in the Eighteenth Century

Pauline Maier

My title was inspired by George Rudé's *Paris and London in the Eighteenth Century,* though my concerns were not his. In the course of working on urban politics in the Revolutionary period I became aware of how remarkably different were Boston and New York—different not just in their people and politics but in feeling, in character, in that wonderfully all-encompassing thing called culture. Their differences were neither incidental nor ephemeral: to a remarkable extent the distinctive traits each city had developed by the end of the eighteenth century survived into the nineteenth and even the twentieth century. And so I propose to consider those differences, how they began and persisted over time, and their more general importance in American history.

SOURCE: Pauline Maier, "Boston and New York in the Eighteenth Century," *Proceedings of the American Antiquarian Society,* 91, Part 2 (Oct. 21, 1981): 177–195.

Any such exercise assumes that the subjects of inquiry were comparable, that is, that they had some essential identity in common upon which distinctions were grafted. The existence of such a common identity for two early American ports on the Atlantic seaboard is in part obvious. But there remains a problem relevant to their comparability that is worth beginning with, one that has troubled me and, I suppose, other students of the period since first encountering Carl Bridenbaugh's path-breaking books *Cities in the Wilderness* and *Cities in Revolt.* That is, by what right do we classify together Boston, New York, and similar communities as "cities" before 1800?

Consider the gulf between Rudé's subjects and mine. He wrote about two of the greatest cities in the Western world, population centers that no one hesitates to call urban. Paris already had over a half million people in 1700. It grew only modestly over the next century, while London expanded at a quick pace—from 575,000 people in 1750 to almost 900,000 fifty years later. By contrast Boston's population stood at 6,700, New York's nearer 5,000 when the eighteenth century began. One hundred years later New York had over 60,000 and Boston almost 25,000 people. It takes no very sophisticated statistical analysis to suggest that a "city" of 6,700 was something very different from one of a half million, that New York at its eighteenth-century peak was still in many ways distinct from London, whose population was some fifteen times greater. If "city" denotes a community's size, Boston and New York would not qualify.

The word "city" has not, however, distinguished places by size so much as by function. Historically it designated independent communities that served as centers for a surrounding countryside and as points of contact with the outside world. The word derives from the Latin word *civitas,* which the Romans used, as it happens, for a colonial situation—for the separate states or tribes of Gaul, and then for their most important towns. They were also *civitates* in Roman Britain, but the Angles and Saxons used instead the word *burh* or *borough,* adopting *city* in the thirteenth century for foreign or ancient cities, for large indigenous communities such as London, and later for the chief boroughs of a diocese, those that became cathedral towns.

Cities perform their centralizing function in many ways, most of which were exercised by Boston and New York. Like other major colonial cities, they were provincial capitals as well as important cultural centers where newspapers and pamphlets were published, discussed, and distributed. But above all they were commercial centers, Atlantic coastal ports where the produce of the countryside was collected and shipped to the West Indies, Africa, or Europe and exchanged for products or credits that could in turn be exchanged for goods of foreign origin needed by colonists in both city and country. Later cities became the merchandising centers for manufactures of either rural or urban origin, whose "reach" and therefore whose volume of business grew with the development of more advanced transportation systems; they became the homes of banks, of insurance companies, of stock exchanges. As they did so, they drew upon the efforts of increasing numbers of people. But it was not the size of their populations that made them cities so much as the functions Boston and New York shared with Paris and London even when their people were counted in thousands, not tens or hundreds of thousands.

From the beginning, moreover, colonial cities had a cosmopolitan character that distinguished them from more rural towns, of whose people it could be said, as [historian] George Homans wrote of thirteenth-century English villagers, that they "had upon the whole more contact with one another than they had with outsiders." While their ships traded at ports-of-call in the Caribbean and the larger Atlantic world, the cities played host to numbers of transients or "strangers," whether in the laboring force or among the more substantial persons of affairs who found business to transact at Boston or New York. Already in the seventeenth century Boston merchants found themselves in conflict with their colony's Puritan leaders, whose effort to isolate Massachusetts from Old World contamination proved incompatible with the demands of commerce. "The well-being of trade," [historian] Bernard Bailyn has observed, "demanded the free movement of people and goods." In the end the merchants won, but their victory was never such as made Boston altogether hospitable to new immigrants, particularly those of non-English origin. Only the French Huguenots—the Faneuils, Bowdoins, Rivoires, and their like—found a welcome there and were easily assimilated.

New York's population was more diverse in origin, including persons of Dutch as well as of French and English origin along with lesser numbers of Germans, Irishmen, Jews, and other Europeans as well as substantial numbers of Africans. Manhattan and the nearby counties of Long Island had the largest concentration of blacks anywhere in North America above the plantation colonies. The city also absorbed substantial numbers of migrants from New England.

The diversity of New York's peoples has, however, often been exaggerated, for they were, like Boston's people, predominantly Northern European Calvinists who shared, out of diverse historical experiences, a militant hostility to "papism" and to Catholic Absolutism in France and Spain. Even Manhattan's Sephardic [of Spanish or Portuguese origin] Jews shared in some measure this "Protestant" culture, for they had suffered from the same forces that the Dutch and fought in their long struggle for national independence—the Spanish monarchy and the Catholic Church. With people already so alike, the "melting pot" could melt: by the mid-eighteenth century . . . younger persons of Dutch descent, particularly on Manhattan, spoke mostly English, attended the English church, "and would even take it amiss if they were called Dutchmen and not Englishmen." French Huguenots [Protestants] who first arrived at New York in the seventeenth century also gradually became Anglicans, helping to make the city by the late eighteenth century far more culturally unified than it had been one hundred years earlier or would be a century later, when Italian Catholics, the Ashkenazic Jews of Eastern Europe, and other decidedly alien people were added in great numbers to the older "native stock."

In the course of the eighteenth century, Boston and New York also gave evidence of a new anonymity among their people that reflected the growth of their populations. That development was slow in coming. Certainly there remained much of the small town about Philadelphia, the largest of American cities in 1771 when Esther DeBerdt Reed reported to her father in London that "the people must either talk of their neighbors, of whom they know every particular of what they both do and say, or else of marketing. . . . We hardly dare tell one another our thoughts," she added, "lest it should spread all over town; so, if anybody asks you how we like Philadelphia, you must say very well." The newspapers published in colonial cities in their very dearth of local news also testify to the way eighteenth-century urban people knew their news without reading about it. There were, however, signs of change. [Historian] Thomas Bender cites the appearance of craftsmen's ads in New York newspapers of the 1750s as evidence that artisans were finding it necessary to announce their existence to townsmen who might in an earlier day have known of it without such formal notice. The publication of city directories at New York in 1786 and Boston in 1789 attests again to an increasing unfamiliarity of city people with each other. Soon thereafter authorities addressed themselves to the problem of locating people within the increasingly anonymous urban masses. In 1793 New York's Common Council ordered that buildings along the streets be numbered according to a prescribed method. From that regulation it was but a short step to the 1811 report of a New York commission that surveyed the island and planned the expanse of practical if monotonously regular numbered streets that would in time stretch from the old and irregular colonial city on the lower tip of Manhattan up toward the Harlem River, and which has been logically taken as the beginning of New York's emergence as a "modern" city.

In all these ways—in the functions that marked them as cities, in their relative cosmopolitanism and common Protestant culture, in the gradual development by the late eighteenth century of a social anonymity that has since become so much a part of urban life—Boston and New York were almost interchangeable. And yet they had acquired, like children, distinctive traits that they would carry with them into later life. The appearance of differences early in the cities' histories is striking, their persistence over time the more so. Both need to be explained. Their reasons lie, I suggest, in the ideals or purposes of the cities' founders, and in the peculiar, unpredictable way those early traditions were reinforced by eighteenth-century circumstances.

Boston's Puritan fathers came to America with a mission defined against the avarice and corruption of contemporary England. They sought

99

to establish close-knit communities where love of God and concern for neighbor took precedence over selfish gain. Their ideology proved well suited to the business of colonizing. Because the Puritans sought to found permanent homes in America, whole families migrated, not the men alone. The population of New England therefore grew naturally at a far faster rate than elsewhere in seventeenth-century North America. The Puritans' commitment to their "callings" and their emphasis on industry also contributed to the cause of success in this world as much as in the next, and Boston became the premier city of British North America.

Its early achievement proved impossible to sustain, however, and as the eighteenth century proceeded Boston gradually yielded its leadership to Philadelphia and New York. It is commonplace to say that geography determined Boston's destiny: the proximity of the Appalachian mountains to the Atlantic coast in New England, the rocky quality of soil along the coastal belt, the course of its rivers, which too often ran on a north-south axis and so provided no ready path to the interior, all these limited the extent and the richness of that hinterland upon which Boston's importance depended. But its fate, we now know, is not so simply explained. An "almost biblical series of misfortunes" afflicted Boston in the mid-eighteenth century, most of which were related to the series of colonial wars [with France] that brought disaster to Boston even as they blessed with prosperity the artisans and merchants of New York and Philadelphia. The city contributed heavily to imperial armies, and therefore to the casualty lists, which cut deeply into its male population and so into its tax base. Meanwhile taxes rose to finance the expeditions to Canada and to support the widows and orphans left behind, making Boston (then as now) a particularly expensive place to live, even in comparison to neighboring towns. Its shipbuilding industry dispersed to Marblehead, Salem, and Newport, and fear of impressment [seizure of sailors for service in the British navy] disrupted its trade. The results could be read in Boston's population figures, which reached 17,000 in 1740, then dropped, and failed to recover completely until after independence; in the striking excess of white adult females to males among Bostonians of 1764 (3,612 to 2,941); in the dense occupancy of Boston's houses, which included about half again as many people as those of New York and Philadelphia at mid-century, a difference [historian] Gary Nash attributes to the practice of taking in boarders by hard-pressed Boston widows; in the emergence of poverty as a serious social problem well before it reached such importance in other colonial ports.

It is too much to say that Boston never recovered, but its record in the late colonial period was overall one of decline. And hard times served the cause of tradition, for the Spartan ideal of the founders could ennoble necessity by calling it virtue. New England's ministers continued to cite the first generation of settlers as a model of achievement, as they had done from the late seventeenth century, and to chastise the children for failing to take up their fathers' "Errand into the Wilderness," explaining the calamities that fell upon them as punishments for the sinful shortcomings of those who had inherited that New World Israel. The ideals of the fathers provided, in short, a way of understanding and of organizing experience, of ordering history, and so continued to influence the life of the region and of its major city.

New York was founded instead as an outpost of the Dutch West India Company in its search for profit. No greater mission brought the Dutch from Holland: indeed, the Dutch were on the whole unwilling to migrate, finding their homeland hospitable as the English Puritans did not. The Dutch West India Company therefore turned elsewhere for settlers—to the oppressed Protestants of France, to Africa—in the hope that they might help make New Netherland economically viable. The commitment to material gain that marked Company rule continued after the British conquest. The financial needs of the later Stuart kings, the hopes of greater fortunes that motivated the governors appointed by them and their successors, the ambitions of colonists who flattered royal officials in a quest for land grants, contracts, or lucrative appointments, all these only enhanced New York's materialistic bent. The city became a nest of those after profit however won—of pirates and privateers, of slave traders and smugglers—a community whose spokesmen on into the Revolutionary era emphasized interest while those of Boston cultivated virtue.

New Yorkers did well—and then did better. The city sat at the mouth of the great Hudson River, which, with the Mohawk, provided ready access to a rich and extensive market even before the canal era added the trans-Appalachian West to Manhattan's "back yard." It benefited also from wartime contracts and privateering returns, and except for occasional years of recession continued the ascent that would in time make it the foremost American city. The results there could be seen in a sense of widespread opportunity such as possessed the immigrant James Murray in 1737, when he advised a clergyman in his native Northern Ireland to "tell aw the poor Folk of your place, tha God has open'd a Door for their Deliverance." In New York there was "no Scant of Breed"; and it was, "in short, . . . a bonny Country" where a man could readily make a good life for himself. In his *History of the Province of New-York,* first published in 1757, a more established New Yorker, William Smith, Junior, made much the same point. "Every man of industry and integrity has it in his power to live well," he wrote, and many who arrived "distressed by their poverty . . . now enjoy easy and plentiful fortunes."

Smith also claimed that there was "not so great an inequality" of riches among New Yorkers "as is common in Boston and some other places," but there he was almost certainly incorrect. The rich of Manhattan combined mercantile wealth with great landed estates in the Hudson Valley in a way unknown among Bostonians. The city's people shared a sense of social distance that also distinguished it from its urban neighbor to the northeast. Some of the most memorable expressions of class consciousness that the Revolutionary era produced came from New York—as in Gouverneur Morris's arrogant description of local mechanics and seamen as "poor reptiles . . . struggling to cast off their winter slough" who "bask in the sunshine, and ere noon . . . will bite." As for Morris's "riotous mob," it was characterized by deferential habits such as shocked John Hancock when he visited New York on his way to the Continental Congress. On his arrival there Hancock learned that the city's people intended to remove the horses from his carriage and pull it through the streets themselves, a ritual common enough in the Old World. But Hancock, no modest man but a Bostonian nonetheless, "would not have had [that] taken place upon any Consideration, not being fond of such Parade." His efforts to dissuade the crowd were unsuccessful, and he was saved from that "disagreeable occurrence" only by the intercession of some local gentlemen whose wishes the people of New York were more accustomed to honoring.

Politics moderated the distance between rich and poor in Boston. There the governing town meeting brought together persons of different station and blessed men with power for their eloquence, reason, and character as well as their wealth. Boston had a board of selectmen and a series of other municipal officers who were chosen by the town meeting, and those who sought such preferment learned, if they did not instinctively know, that respect was a prerequisite of political support. New York was governed differently. By the terms of the Montgomery Charter of 1731, the governor and provincial council named the city's mayor, recorder, clerk, and the treasurer. Municipal ordinances were passed by a Common Council that consisted of the mayor and recorder along with the city's aldermen, who were elected by voice vote within the several wards into which New York had been divided. Qualified voters also chose a set of assistants, several minor officials, and the vestrymen who cared for the poor. But they had no continuing, direct voice in governing the city as in Boston, where "the meanest citizen ratable at £20 beside the poll, may deliver his sentiments and give his suffrage in very important matters, as freely as the greatest Lord in the Land," according to the reports of Dr. Thomas Young, a native of the Hudson Valley who migrated to Boston in the mid-1760s. Political opportunities compensated in some measure for Boston's unpromising economy: "elevated stations," Young claimed, were there open "to every one whose capacity, integrity and diligence in the affairs of his country attracts the public attention." Those avenues of advancement, he wrote correspondents in Manhattan, "I lament are shut to you. . . ."

The existence of a wealthy upper class with a taste for European ways had, however, some cultural advantages, for its patronage set eighteenth-century New York on its way toward becoming an American center for the performing arts. Manhattan claimed two playhouses in 1732; by the time of the Revolution it had as many as seven. Not that all New Yorkers were free from scruples born of their Protestant heritage. William Hallam's London Company of Comedians, which came to the city in 1753, was denied official permission to perform until after it issued assurances that its members were "not cast in the same Mould" as their "Theatrical Predecessors," that "in private Life" and "publick Occupation" they were of a different moral order. In retrospect, however, it seems more important that the company went to New York because people in Virginia predicted a "genteel and favourable Reception" in Manhattan, where "the Inhabitants were generous and polite, naturally fond of Diversions rational, particularly those of the Theatre," and that Hallam's company finally enjoyed a successful and profitable run in the city. New York also saw occasional musical performances, as in January 1737 when the *New-York Gazette* advertised a "consort . . . for the benefit of Mr. Pachebell, the harpsicord parts performed by himself." And two years later an advertisement announced "A New Pantomime Entertainment. . . . To which will be added an Optick," which was a primitive predecessor of motion pictures. Cock-fighting was also popular, as was horse-racing, with wagers part of the event—all of which remained far from Boston, a city less open to such forms of commercial entertainment. Indeed, theatre was introduced at Boston only during the 1790s, having been earlier outlawed by an act of 1750.

Boston was distinguished instead by its traditional respect for learning and for the printed word. Before the Puritan fathers were more than a decade in America they founded Harvard College and established a printing press in Cambridge. New York City was settled in 1626—four years before Boston—but had no press for almost seventy years, until William Bradford was lured to Manhattan in 1693. Even a casual survey of the Evans bibliography of early American imprints testifies to the immense and continuing superiority of eighteenth-century Boston as a place of publication. Few books and pamphlets came out of New York, and those were heavily weighted toward the official publications of the provincial government. As for newspapers, the first to be published on a continuous schedule in British North America was the *Boston News-Letter,* begun in 1704. And Boston had two other papers, the *Boston Gazette* (1719) and the *New-England Courant* (1721) before the *New-York Gazette* began publication in 1725.

New Yorkers' sense of a good education apparently differed from that of Bostonians: the City of New York was "so conveniently Situated for Trade and the Genius of the people so inclined to merchandise," wrote the Rev. John Sharpe in 1713 after some twelve years on Manhattan, "that they generally seek no other Education for their children than writing and Arithmetick. So that letters must be in a manner forced upon them not only without their seeking, but against their consent"—a proposal unlikely to meet with success. New Yorkers were in fact bizarrely innocent in the world of learning—or so James Murray suggested when he told of a fellow

Scots-Irish immigrant who "now gets ane Hundred Punds for ane year for teechin a Letin Skulle, and God kens, little he is skilled in Learning, and yet they think him a high learned Man. Ye kin I had but sma Learning when I left ye," he added—and his primitive phonetic spelling suggests he had accumulated little thereafter. Yet Murray reported that he kept a "Skulle for wee Weans." Two decades later William Smith, Junior, concluded that New York's schools were of "the lowest order" and that their "instructors want instruction." "Through a long shameful neglect of all the arts and sciences," he added, "our common speech is extremely corrupt, and the evidences of a bad taste, both as to thought and language, are visible in all our proceedings, publick and private."

New York was, quite simply, a different kind of place than Boston, shaped by different values that were sustained by economic success. The "Art of getting money" preoccupied its people and served, according to Cadwallader Colden, as "the only principle of life propagated among the young People." New Yorkers of both town and country were "sober, industrious and hospitable," Smith noted, "though intent upon gain." The city's contemporary reputation reflected those traits. "Our Neighbours have told us in an insulting Tone, that the Art of getting money is the highest Improvement we can pretend to," wrote a pamphleteer arguing in 1749 for "Erecting a College in the Province of New-York." They say "that the wisest Man among us without a Fortune, is neglected and despised; and the greatest Blockhead with one, caress'd and honour'd: That, for this Reason, a poor Man of the most shining Accomplishments, can never emerge out of his Obscurity; while every wealthy Dunce is loaded with Honours, and bears down all before him." Such accusations were made, he thought, out of envy over "the flourishing Circumstances of this City," and could be easily refuted. "But that Learning hath not been encourag'd as it ought, admits of no Controversy."

These distinctions were reflected in John Adams's perceptions of New York, which he visited on the way to the Continental Congress in Philadelphia, as did Hancock, with eyes fully open and with Boston as a constant standard of comparison. Like all travellers, Adams was impressed by New York's beauty, for it was in ways long since lost a garden city whose clean and spacious streets were lined with trees, and where the noise of frogs, especially on hot nights when rain was expected, provided a major annoyance. He remarked on the striking views or "prospects" the city offered of the Hudson and East Rivers, of Long Island and what he called the "Sound River," and of New Jersey. He found New York's streets "vastly more regular and elegant than those in Boston, and the houses are more grand, as well as neat." New Yorkers were as hospitable as Smith—and Madam Sarah Knight before him—indicated they would be, and Adams was struck, too, by the evidence of wealth, as in the costly accoutrements of John Morin Scott's breakfast table, which he inventoried lovingly ("rich plate, a very large silver coffee-pot, a very large silver tea-pot, napkins of the very finest materials"), or the "rich furniture" at the home of Isaac Low. Still, the continuous socializing he found "very disagreeable on some accounts." It seems never to have crossed the New Yorkers' minds that a Bostonian might be more anxious to see the twenty-year-old King's College, or the city's churches, printers' offices, and bookshops. And "with all the opulence and splendor of this city," Adams reported that there was "very little good breeding to be found. . . . I have not seen one real gentleman, one well-bred man, since I came to town." There was, moreover, "no conversation that is agreeable" at their "entertainments": there was "no modesty, no attention to one another," for the New Yorkers of that still-pastoral island had already acquired the conversational style of the modern metropolis. "They talk very loud, very fast, and altogether," Adams observed. "If they ask you a question, before you can utter three words of your answer, they will break out upon you again, and talk away."

There are in these observations testimony not merely to style, but to the pace, the bewildering restlessness that already possessed New Yorkers long before the nineteenth century. Even the sleighs they rode in the winter to friends' homes out of town or to "Houses of entertainment at a place called the Bowery . . . fly with great swiftness," Madam Knight noted on her visit there in 1704, "and some are so furious that they'll turn out of the path for none except a Loaden Cart." What was the hurry? And why were New Yorkers always building, tearing down, rearranging, reconstructing their city, leaving not even the bones of their ancestors in peace? They seem forever to have done things with what struck outsiders as excess: convinced that "merchandizing" was a good employment, they went into trade in such numbers, reported the visitor John Miller in 1695, "that whosoever looks on their shops would wonder"—like a modern stroller down Madison Avenue—"where there are so many to sell, there should be any to buy." The monumental energy of colonial New Yorkers prefigured that of later Americans, who within a century of winning independence built from thirteen modest colonies a nation whose western boundary had pushed from the Appalachians to the Pacific. The enterprise of New Yorkers contributed generously to that development. Indeed, the very physical circumstances of New Yorkers identified them with the nation in 1776: they were concentrated within the lowest mile of a thirteen-and-a-half-mile-long island much as their countrymen were settled along the eastern edge of a vast continent whose expanses of empty land invited and even demanded expansion. People such as these had no time to celebrate the past. They were too engrossed with inventing the future.

How different the situation of the Bostonians, housed on a modest peninsula already fully settled by the time of the Revolution, suffering from a generation of decline, a people convinced that the model of their future lay in the past. In fact, nineteenth-century Boston, true to its colonial origins, became the literary capital of the new nation and also a financial center whose importance yielded to New York only in the 1840s. Meanwhile New Englanders, fleeing the rural poverty of their native region, settled and populated much of the West. There remains considerable irony nonetheless in the fact that Boston served for the generation of 1776 as a model for the new republic. Its democratic politics, tradition of disinterested public service, and modest style, inculcated by Puritanism and continued through hardship, coincided neatly with the demands of classical republicanism—so much so that Samuel Adams could see in the United States a final realization of New England's historic mission. New York played a far more ambiguous role in the politics of the Revolution than did Boston, and the city never took on a similar symbolic importance—perhaps because infinite possibilities are more difficult to comprehend than the limited values of an established and well-defined historical tradition. New York has in fact remained difficult to grasp, to summarize. "By preference, but also in some degree by necessity," Nathan Glazer and Daniel Patrick Moynihan observed in *Beyond the Melting Pot,* "America has turned elsewhere for its images and traditions. Colonial America is preserved for us in terms of the Doric simplicity of New England, or the pastoral symmetry of the Virginia countryside. Even Philadelphia is manageable. But who can summon an image of eighteenth-century New York that will *hold still in the mind*?" And yet the importance of openness, optimism, opportunity, and energy, even of materialism and of visual over literary entertainments to the nation that emerged from the American eighteenth century is undeniable. . . .

DOCUMENTS

Benjamin Franklin's
Union Fire Company, 1738

About this time I wrote a paper . . . on the different accidents and carelessnesses by which houses were set on fire, with cautions against them and means proposed of avoiding them. This was much spoken of as a useful piece, and gave rise to a project which soon followed it of forming a company for the more ready extinguishing of fires, and mutual assistance in removing and securing of goods when in danger. Associates in this scheme were presently found amounting to thirty. Our articles of agreement obliged every member to keep always in good order and fit for use a certain

SOURCE: John Bigelow, ed., *Works of Benjamin Franklin* 1 (New York: G. P. Putnam's Sons, 1877): 204–205.

number of leather buckets with strong bags and baskets (for packing and transporting of goods) which were to be brought to every fire; and we agreed to meet once a month and spend a social evening together in discoursing and communicating such ideas as occurred to us upon the subject of fires as might be useful in our conduct on such occasions. The utility of this institution soon appeared, and many more desiring to be admitted than we thought convenient for one company, they were advised to form another, which was accordingly done. And this went on, one new company being formed after another till they became so numerous as to include most of the inhabitants who were men of property; and now at the time of my writing this [1788], tho' upwards of fifty years since its establishment, that which I first formed, called the Union Fire Company, still subsists and flourishes, tho' the first members are all deceased but myself and one, who is older by a year than I am. The small fines that have been paid by members for absence at the monthly meetings have been applied to the purchase of fire engines, ladders, firehooks, and other useful implements for each company, so that I question whether there is a city in the world better provided with the means of putting a stop to beginning conflagrations; and in fact since those institutions, the city has never lost by fire more than one or two houses at a time, and the flames have often been extinguished before the house in which they began has been half consumed.

Philadelphia, 1748

All the streets except two which are nearest to the river, run in a straight line, and make right angles at the intersections. Some are paved, others are not; and it seems less necessary, since the ground is sandy, and therefore soon absorbs the wet. But in most of the streets is a pavement of flags, a fathom or more broad, laid before the houses, and posts put on the outside three or four fathom asunder. Under the roofs are gutters which are carefully connected with pipes, and by this means, those who walk under them, when it rains, or when the snow melts, need not fear being wet by the dropping from the roofs.

The houses make a good appearance, are frequently several stories high, and built either of bricks or of stone; but the former are more commonly used, since bricks are made before the town, and are well burnt. The stone which has been employed in the building of other houses, is a mixture of black or grey *glimmer*, running in undulated veins, and of a loose, and quite small grained *limestone*, which runs scattered between the bendings of

SOURCE: Peter Kalm, *Travels in North America 1*, translated into English by John Reinhold Forester (London: Printed for editor, 1770): 34–45; 58–60.

the other veins, and are of a grey colour, excepting here and there some single grains of sand, of a paler hue. The glimmer makes the greatest part of the stone; but the mixture is sometimes of another kind. This stone is now got in great quantities in the country, is easily cut, and has the good quality of not attracting the moisture in a wet season. Very good lime is burnt every where hereabouts, for masonry.

Characteristics of Philadelphians

The town is now quite filled with inhabitants, which in regard to their country, religion, and trade, are very different from each other. You meet with excellent masters in all trades, and many things are made here full as well as in *England.* Yet no manufactures, especially for making fine cloth, are established. Perhaps the reason is, that it can be got with so little difficulty from *England,* and that the breed of sheep which is brought over, degenerates in process of time, and affords but a coarse wool.

Here is great plenty of provisions, and their prices are very moderate. There are no examples of an extraordinary dearth.

Every one who acknowledges God to be the Creator, preserver, and ruler of all things, and teaches or undertakes nothing against the state, or against the common peace, is at liberty to settle, stay, and carry on his trade here, be his religious principles ever so strange. No one is here molested on account of the erroneous principles of the doctrine which he follows, if he does not exceed the above-mentioned bounds. And he is so well secured by the laws in his person and property, and enjoys such liberties, that a citizen of *Phildelphia* may in a manner be said to live in his house like a king.

On a careful consideration of what I have already said, it will be easy to conceive how this city should rise so suddenly from nothing, into such grandeur and perfection, without supposing any powerful monarch's contributing to it, either by punishing the wicked, or by giving great supplies in money. And yet its fine appearance, good regulations, agreeable situation, natural advantages, trade, riches and power, are by no means inferior to those of any, even of the most ancient towns in *Europe.* It has not been necessary to force people to come and settle here; on the contrary, foreigners of different languages have left their country, houses, property, and relations, and ventured over wide and stormy seas, in order to come hither. Other countries, which have been peopled for a long space of time, complain of the small number of their inhabitants. But *Pennsylvania,* which was no better than a desert in the year 1681, and hardly contained five hundred people, now vies with several kingdoms in *Europe* in number of inhabitants. It has received numbers of people, which other countries, to their infinite loss, have either neglected or expelled.

The Scourge of Yellow Fever, Philadelphia, 1793

On the origin of the disorder [yellow fever], there prevails a very good diversity of opinion. Dr. Hutchinson maintained that it was not imported, and
stated, in a letter which he wrote on the subject to Captain Falconer, the
health officer of the port of Philadelphia, that "the general opinion was, that
the disorder originated from some damaged coffee, or other putrified vegetable and animal matters." . . .

Several persons were swept away before any great alarm was excited. . . . About this time began the removals from the city, which were for
some weeks so general, that almost every hour in the day, carts, wagons,
coaches, and chairs, were to be seen transporting families and furniture to
the country in every direction. Business then became extremely dull. Mechanics and artists were unemployed; and the streets wore the appearance
of gloom and melancholy.

The first official notice taken of the disorder, was on the 22d of August,
on which day, the mayor of Philadelphia, Matthew Clarkson, esq., wrote to
the city commissioners, and after acquainting them with the state of the city,
gave them the most peremptory orders, to have the streets properly
cleansed and purified by the scavengers, and all the filth immediately
hawled away. These orders were repeated on the 27th, and similar ones
given to the clerks of the market. The 29th the governor of the state, in his
address to the legislature, acquainted them, that a contagious disorder existed in the city; and that he had taken every proper measure to ascertain
the origin, nature, and extent of it. He likewise assured them that the health
officer and physician of the port, would take every precaution to allay and
remove the public inquietude.

The 26th of the same month, the college of physicians had a meeting, at
which they took into consideration the nature of the disorder, and the
means of prevention and of cure. They published an address to the citizens,
signed by the president and secretary, recommending to avoid all unnecessary intercourse with the infected; to place marks on the doors or windows
where they were; to pay great attention to cleanliness and airing the rooms
of the sick; to provide a large and airy hospital in the neighbourhood of the
city for their reception; to put a stop to the tolling of the bells; to bury those
who died of the disorder in carriages and as privately as possible; to keep
the streets and wharves clean; to avoid all fatigue of body and mind, and
standing or sitting in the sun, or in the open air; to accommodate the dress

SOURCE: Matthew Carey, *A Short Account of the Malignant Fever Lately Prevalent in Philadelphia* (Philadelphia, 1793), 16–17, 20–23, 60–63.

to the weather, and to exceed rather in warm than in cool clothing; and to avoid intemperance, but to use fermented liquors, such as wine, beer, and cider, with moderation. They likewise declared their opinion, that fires in the streets were very dangerous, if not ineffectual means of stopping the progress of the fever, and that they placed more dependence on the burning of gunpowder. The benefits of vinegar and camphor, they added, were confined chiefly to infected rooms, and could not be too often used on handkerchiefs, or in smelling bottles, by persons who attended the sick.

In consequence of this address, the bells were immediately stopped from tolling, which was a measure very expedient; as they had before been kept pretty constantly going the whole day, so as to terrify those in health, and drive the sick, as far as the influence of imagination could produce that effect, to their graves. An idea had gone abroad, that the burning of fires in the streets, would have a tendency to purify the air, and arrest the progress of the disorder. The people had, therefore, almost every night large fires lighted at the corners of the streets. The 29th, the mayor published a proclamation, forbidding this practice. As a substitute, many had recourse to the firing of guns, which they imagined was a certain preventative of the disorder. This was carried so far, and attended with such danger, that it was forbidden by the mayor's order, of the 4th of September. . . .

On the 16th, the managers of Bushhill [hospital], after personal inspection of the state of affairs there, made report of its situation, which was truly deplorable. It exhibited as wretched a picture of human misery as ever existed. A profligate, abandoned set of nurses and attendants (hardly any of good character could at that time be procured,) rioted on the provisions and comforts, prepared for the sick, who (unless at the hours when the doctors attended) were left almost entirely destitute of every assistance. The dying and dead were indiscriminately mingled together. The ordure and other evacuations of the sick, were allowed to remain in the most offensive state imaginable. Not the smallest appearance of order or regularity existed. It was, in fact, a great human slaughter house, where numerous victims were immolated at the altar of riot and intemperance. No wonder, then, that a general dread of the place prevailed through the city, and that a removal to it was considered as the seal of death. In consequence, there were various instances of sick persons locking their rooms, and resisting every attempt to carry them away. At length, the poor were so much afraid of being sent to Bushhill, that they would not acknowledge their illness, until it was no longer possible to conceal it. For it is to be observed, that the fear of the contagion was so prevalent, that as soon as any one was taken sick, an alarm was spread among the neighbours, and every effort was used to have the sick person hurried off to Bushhill, to avoid spreading the disorder. The cases of the persons forced in this way to that hospital, though labouring under only common colds, and common fall fevers, are numerous and afflicting. There were not wanting instances of persons, only slightly ill, being sent to Bushhill, by their panic-struck neighbours, and embracing the first opportunity of running back to Philadelphia. But the case was soon altered under the direction of the two managers, Girard and Helm. They introduced such order and regularity, and had the patients treated with so much care and tenderness, that they retrieved the character of the hospital; and in the course of a week or two, numbers of sick people, who had not at home proper persons to nurse them, applied to be sent to Bushhill. Indeed, in the end, so many people, who were afflicted with other disorders, procured admittance there, that it become necessary to pass a resolve, that before an order of admission should be granted, a certificate must be produced from a physician, that the patient laboured under the malignant fever.

The committee sat daily at the city hall, and engaged a number of carts to convey the dead to a place of interment, and the sick to the hospital. From their organization to the present time, they have most unremittingly attended to the discharge of the trust reposed in them. Neither the regular increase of deaths till towards the middle of October, nor the afflicting loss of four very active members, in quick succession, appalled them. That the mortality would have been incomparably greater, but for their active interposition, is beyond doubt; as most of those who went to Bushhill, and died there, would have otherwise died in the city, and spread the contagion: and the dead bodies would have remained putrifying in deserted houses in every part of the city, and operated as dreadfully as the plague itself. In fact, at the time they entered on the execution of the dangerous office they undertook, there were found several bodies that had lain in this state for two, three, and four days.

Chapter 7

People at War: Society During
the American Revolution

THE BRITISH TROOPS FIRING ON THE AMERICANS AT LEXINGTON.

The American Revolution marked the end of the colonial epoch and the beginning of nationhood. Most Americans are well aware of the momentous events of the Revolutionary era and their historical significance. What is less well known and appreciated are the roles played by ordinary citizens in the drama and the conflict's impact on their lives. In the essay that follows, "George Robert Twelves Hewes, A Patriot Shoemaker of Boston," by Alfred F. Young, we are provided an opportunity to view the coming of the war "at street level" through the eyes of an active participant. The essay is based largely on two memoirs of Hewes, one written by James Hawkes in 1833 and the other by Benjamin Thatcher in 1835. Both biographers held extensive interviews with Hewes and commented on his amazing memory.

As you read the essay, be aware of the growing spirit of rebellion that characterized Boston's citizenry in general, and George Hewes specifically, in the years following 1768. Note the changes in Hewes's social views as well as in his political outlook. To what does the author attribute the transformation in Hewes's perceptions of himself and of his status in society?

The story of George Robert Twelves Hewes vividly illustrates the existence of marked class distinctions at the outset of the American Revolution. That equally rigid lines kept women politically and socially subservient to men is revealed with a blend of seriousness and good humor in the first document, excerpts from three let-

ters between Abigail and John Adams. Among them is Abigail Adams's famous "Remember the Ladies" letter, which pleads the case for including rights for women among the laws of the emerging nation. How would you evaluate her arguments and her husband's rebuttals in the context of their own time? in the context of our own era? How do you account for the blank space in the last line of John Adams's letter of April 14, 1776? What word do you think belongs there?

Active loyalist opposition to the patriot cause was not as significant a factor in Boston or the rest of New England as it was farther south, but, as the essay reveals, it did exist. Indeed, one of George Hewes's brothers was a Tory. It is estimated that 80,000 loyalists fled the country under pressure. The second document is a letter written by Catherine Van Cortlandt, one of those Tories who would ultimately go into permanent exile in England. At the time of the writing, she was traveling with her children to join her husband in British-occupied New York. A safe-passage permit enabled her journey through patriot lines but not without considerable physical and emotional suffering. What evidence is offered in the letter to support the view that the American Revolution had elements of a civil war as well as a struggle for independence? Note that those who fought for independence referred to themselves as "Patriots" while their opponents termed them "Rebels." In like manner, those opposed to the cause of independence preferred to be called "Loyalists," but their enemies branded them "Tories" or worse.

Although war brought hostility to British sympathizers and sacrifice and deprivation to most citizens and soldiers, for some it offered opportunity for power or profit, and for others it held out the promise of adventure. The last document is excerpted from the memoirs of Andrew Sherburne, a New Hampshire boy who in 1779, at the age of thirteen and filled with the spirit of adventure and patriotism, left his family farm to enlist in the new United States Navy. What parallels can be drawn between the interests, attitudes, and behavior that Sherburne recalled from his youth and those of today's teenagers?

ESSAY

George Robert Twelves Hewes, A Patriot Shoemaker of Boston

Alfred F. Young

Late in 1762 or early in 1763, George Robert Twelves Hewes, a Boston shoemaker in the last year or so of his apprenticeship, repaired a shoe for John Hancock and delivered it to him at his uncle Thomas Hancock's store in

SOURCE: "George Robert Twelves Hewes (1742–1840) A Boston Shoemaker and the Memory of the American Revolution," *William and Mary Quarterly*, Third Series, 33 (October 1981): 561–562, 585–600. Copyright © 1981 Alfred Young. Reprinted by permission of the author.

Dock Square. Hancock was pleased and invited the young man to "come and see him on New Year's day, and bid him a happy New-Year," according to the custom of the day, a ritual of noblesse oblige on the part of the gentry. We know of the episode through Benjamin Bussey Thatcher, who interviewed Hewes and wrote it up for his *Memoir* of Hewes in 1835. On New Year's Day, as Thatcher tells the story, after some urging by his master,

> George washed his face, and put his best jacket on, and proceeded straightaway to the Hancock House (as it is still called). His heart was in his mouth, but assuming a cheerful courage, he knocked at the front door, and took his hat off. The servant came:
>
> "Is 'Squire Hancock at home, Sir?" enquired Hewes, making a bow.
>
> He was introduced directly to the *kitchen*, and requested to seat himself, while report should be made above stairs. The man came down directly, with a new varnish of civility suddenly spread over his face. He ushered him into the 'Squire's sitting-room, and left him to make his obeisance. Hancock remembered him, and addressed him kindly. George was anxious to get through, and he commenced a desperate speech—"as pretty a one," he says, "as he any way knew how,"—intended to announce the purpose of his visit, and to accomplish it, in the same breath.
>
> "Very well, my lad," said the 'Squire—"now take a chair, my lad."
>
> He sat down, scared all the while (as he now confesses) "almost to death," while Hancock put his hand into his breeches-pocket and pulled out a crown-piece, which he placed softly in his hand, thanking him at the same time for his punctual attendance, and his compliments. He then invited his young friend to drink his health—called for wine—poured it out for him—and ticked glasses with him,—a feat in which Hewes, though he had never seen it performed before, having acquitted himself with a creditable dexterity, hastened to make his bow again, and secure his retreat, though not till the 'Squire had extorted a sort of half promise from him to come the next New-Year's—which, for a rarity, he never discharged.

The episode is a demonstration of what the eighteenth century called deference.

Another episode catches the point at which Hewes had arrived a decade and a half later. In 1778 or 1779, after one stint in the war on board a privateer and another in the militia, he was ready to ship out again, from Boston. As Thatcher tells the story: "Here he enlisted, or engaged to enlist, on board the Hancock, a twenty-gun ship, but not liking the manners of the Lieutenant very well, who ordered him one day in the streets to take his hat off to him—which he refused to do for any man,—he went aboard the 'Defence,' Captain Smedley, of Fairfield Connecticut." This, with a vengeance, is the casting off to deference.

What had happened in the intervening years? What had turned the young shoemaker tongue-tied in the face of his betters into the defiant person who would not take his hat off for any man? . . .

Between 1768 and 1775, the shoemaker became a citizen — an active participant in the events that led to the Revolution, an angry, assertive man who won recognition as a patriot. What explains the transformation? We have enough evidence to take stock of Hewes's role in three major events of the decade: the Massacre (1770), the Tea Party (1773), and the tarring and feathering of John Malcolm (1774). . . .

The presence of British troops in Boston beginning in the summer of 1768—four thousand soldiers in a town of fewer than sixteen thousand inhabitants—touched Hewes personally. Anecdotes about soldiers flowed from him. He had seen them march off the transports at the Long Wharf; he had seen them every day occupying civilian buildings on Griffin's Wharf near his shop. He knew how irritating it was to be challenged by British sentries after curfew (his solution was to offer a swig of rum from the bottle he carried).

More important, he was personally cheated by a soldier. Sergeant Mark Burk ordered shoes allegedly for Captain Thomas Preston, picked them up, but never paid for them. Hewes complained to Preston, who made good and suggested he bring a complaint. A military hearing ensued, at which Hewes testified. The soldier, to Hewes's horror, was sentenced to three hundred fifty lashes. He "remarked to the court that if he had thought the fellow was to be punished so severely for such an offense, bad as he was, he would have said nothing about it." And he saw others victimized by soldiers. He witnessed an incident in which a soldier sneaked up behind a woman, felled her with his fist, and "stripped her of her bonnet, cardinal muff and tippet." He followed the man to his barracks, identified him (Hewes remembered him as Private Kilroy, who would appear later at the Massacre), and got him to give up the stolen goods, but decided this time not to press charges. Hewes was also keenly aware of grievances felt by the laboring men and youths who formed the bulk of the crowd—and the principal victims—at the Massacre. From [James] Hawkes and Thatcher three causes can be pieced together.

First in time, and vividly recalled by Hewes, was the murder of eleven-year-old Christopher Seider on February 23, [1770], ten days before the Massacre. Seider was one of a large crowd of schoolboys and apprentices picketing the shop of Theophilus Lilly, a merchant violating the anti-import resolutions. Ebenezer Richardson, a paid customs informer, shot into the throng and killed Seider. Richardson would have been tarred and feathered, or worse, had not whig leaders intervened to hustle him off to jail. At

Seider's funeral, only a week before the Massacre, five hundred boys marched two by two behind the coffin, followed by two thousand or more adults, "the largest [funeral] perhaps ever known in America," [Governor] Thomas Hutchinson thought.

Second, Hewes emphasized the bitter fight two days before the Massacre between soldiers and workers at Gray's ropewalk down the block from Hewes's shop. Off-duty soldiers were allowed to moonlight, taking work from civilians. On Friday, March 3, when one of them asked for work at Gray's, a battle ensued between a few score soldiers and ropewalk workers joined by others in the maritime trades. The soldiers were beaten and sought revenge. Consequently, in Thatcher's words, "quite a number of soldiers, in a word, were determined to have a row on the night of the 5th."

Third, the precipitating events on the night of the Massacre, by Hewes's account, were an attempt by a barber's apprentice to collect an overdue bill from a British officer, the sentry's abuse of the boy, and the subsequent harassment of the sentry by a small band of boys that led to the calling of the guard commanded by Captain Preston. Thatcher found this hard to swallow—"a dun from a greasy barber's boy is rather an extraordinary explanation of the origin, or one of the occasions, of the massacre of the 5th of March"—but at the trial the lawyers did not. They battled over defining "boys" and over the age, size, and degree of aggressiveness of the numerous apprentices on the scene.

Hewes viewed the civilians as essentially defensive. On the evening of the Massacre he appeared early on the scene at King Street, attracted by the clamor over the apprentice. "I was soon on the ground among them," he said, as if it were only natural that he should turn out in defense of fellow townsmen against what was assumed to be the danger of aggressive action by soldiers. He was not part of a conspiracy; neither was he there out of curiosity. He was unarmed, carrying neither club nor stave as some others did. He saw snow, ice, and "missiles" thrown at the soldiers. When the main guard rushed out in support of the sentry, Private Kilroy dealt Hewes a blow on his shoulder with his gun. Preston ordered the townspeople to disperse. Hewes believed they had a legal basis to refuse: "they were in the king's highway, and had as good a right to be there" as Preston.

The five men killed were all workingmen. Hewes claimed to know four: Samuel Gray, a ropewalk worker; Samuel Maverick, age seventeen, an apprentice to an ivory turner; Patrick Carr, an apprentice to a leather breeches worker; and James Caldwell, second mate on a ship—all but Christopher Attucks. Caldwell, "who was shot in the back was standing by the side of Hewes, and the latter caught him in his arms as he fell," helped carry him to Dr. Thomas Young in Prison Lane, then ran to Caldwell's ship captain on Cold Lane.

More than horror was burned into Hewes's memory. He remembered the political confrontation that followed the slaughter, when thousands of angry townspeople faced hundreds of British troops massed with ready rifles. "The people," Hewes recounted, "then immediately chose a committee to report to the governor the result of Captain Preston's conduct, and to demand of him satisfaction." Actually the "people" did not choose a committee "immediately." In the dark hours after the Massacre a self-appointed group of patriot leaders met with officials and forced Hutchinson to commit Preston and the soldiers to jail. Hewes was remembering the town meeting the next day, so huge that it had to adjourn from Fanueil Hall, the traditional meeting place that held only twelve hundred, to Old South Church, which had room for five to six thousand. This meeting approved a committee to wait on the officials and then adjourned, but met again the same day, received and voted down an offer to remove one regiment, then accepted another to remove two. This was one of the meetings at which property bars were let down.

What Hewes did not recount, but what he had promptly put down in a deposition the next day, was how militant he was after the Massacre. At 1:00 A.M., like many other enraged Bostonians, he went home to arm himself. On his way back to the Town House with a cane he had a defiant exchange with Sergeant Chambers of the 29th Regiment and eight or nine soldiers, "all with very large clubs or cutlasses." A soldier, Dobson, "ask'd him how he far'd; he told him very badly to see his townsmen shot in such a manner, and asked him if he did not think it was a dreadful thing." Dobson swore "it was a fine thing" and "you shall see more of it." Chambers "seized and forced" the cane from Hewes, "saying I had no right to carry it. I told him I had as good a right to carry a cane as they had to carry clubs."

The Massacre had stirred Hewes to political action. He was one of ninety-nine Bostonians who gave depositions for the prosecution that were published by the town in a pamphlet. Undoubtedly, he marched in the great funeral procession for the victims that brought the city to a standstill. He attended the tempestuous trial of Ebenezer Richardson, Seider's slayer, which was linked politically with the Massacre. ("He remembers to this moment, even the precise words of the Judge's sentence," wrote Thatcher.) He seems to have attended the trial of the soldiers or Preston or both. . . .

Four years later, at the Tea Party on the night of December 16, 1773, the citizen "volunteered" and became the kind of leader for whom most historians have never found a place. The Tea Party, unlike the Massacre, was organized by the radical whig leaders of Boston. They mapped the strategy, organized the public meetings, appointed the companies to guard the tea ships at Griffin's Wharf (among them Daniel Hewes, George's brother), and planned the official boarding parties. As in 1770, they converted the town meetings into meetings of "the whole body of the people," one of which Hutchinson found "consisted principally of the Lower ranks of the People & even Journeymen Tradesmen were brought in to increase the number & the Rabble were not excluded yet there were divers Gentlemen of good Fortunes among them."

The boarding parties showed this same combination of "ranks." Hawkes wrote:

> On my inquiring of Hewes if he knew who first proposed the project of destroying the tea, to prevent its being landed, he replied that he did not; neither did he know who or what number were to volunteer their services for that purpose. "But from the significant allusion of some persons in whom I had confidence, together with the knowledge I had of the spirit of those times, I had no doubt but that a sufficient number of associates would accompany me in that enterprise."

The recollection of Joshua Wyeth, a journeyman blacksmith, verified Hewes's story in explicit detail: "It was proposed that young men, not much known in town and not liable to be easily recognized should lead in the business." Wyeth believed that "most of the persons selected for the occasion were apprentices and journeymen, as was the case with myself, living with tory masters." Wyeth "had but a few hours warning of what was intended to be done." Those in the officially designated parties, about thirty men better known, appeared in well-prepared Indian disguises. As nobodies, the volunteers—anywhere from fifty to one hundred men—could get away with hastily improvised disguises. Hewes said he got himself up as an Indian and daubed his "face and hands with coal dust in the shop of a blacksmith." In the streets "I fell in with many who were dressed, equipped and painted as I was, and who fell in with me and marched in order to the place of our destination."

At Griffin's Wharf the volunteers were orderly, self-disciplined, and ready to accept leadership.

> When we arrived at the wharf, there were three of our number who assumed an authority to direct our operations, to which we readily submitted. They divided us into three parties, for the purpose of boarding the three ships which contained the tea at the same time. The name of him who commanded the division to which I was assigned was Leonard Pitt [Lendell Pitts]. The names of the other commanders I never knew. We were immediately ordered by the respective commanders to board all the ships at the same time, which we promptly obeyed.

But for Hewes there was something new: he was singled out of the rank and file and made an officer in the field.

> The commander of the division to which I belonged, as soon as we were on board the ship, appointed me boatswain, and ordered me to go to the captain and demand of him the keys to the hatches and a dozen candles. I made the demand accordingly, and the captain

promptly replied, and delivered the articles; but requested me at the same time to do no damage to the ship or rigging. We then were ordered by our commander to open the hatches, and take out all the chests of tea and throw them overboard, and we immediately proceeded to execute his orders; first cutting and splitting the chests with our tomahawks, so as thoroughly to expose them to the effects of the water. In about three hours from the time we went on board, we had thus broken and thrown overboard every tea chest to be found in the ship; while those in the other ships were disposing of the tea in the same way, at the same time. We were surrounded by British armed ships, but no attempt was made to resist us. We then quietly retired to our several places of residence, without having any conversation with each other, or taking any measures to discover who were our associates.

This was Hewes's story, via Hawkes. Thatcher, who knew a good deal more about the Tea Party from other sources, accepted it in its essentials as an accurate account. He also reported a new anecdote which he treated with skepticism, namely, that Hewes worked alongside John Hancock throwing tea overboard. And he added that Hewes, "whose whistling talent was a matter of public notoriety, acted as a boatswain," that is, as the officer whose duty it was to summon men with a whistle. That Hewes was a leader is confirmed by the reminiscence of Thompson Maxwell, a teamster from a neighboring town who was making a delivery to Hancock the day of the event. Hancock asked him to go to Griffin's Wharf. "I went accordingly, joined the band under one Captain Hewes; we mounted the ships and made tea in a trice; this done I took my team and went home as any honest man should."

A month later, at the third event for which we have full evidence, Hewes won public recognition for an act of courage that almost cost his life and precipitated the most publicized tarring and feathering of the Revolution. The incident that set it off would have been trivial at any other time. On Tuesday, January 25, 1774, at about two in the afternoon, the shoemaker was making his way back to his shop after his dinner. According to the very full account in the *Massachusetts Gazette*,

Mr. George-Robert-Twelves Hewes was coming along Fore-Street, near Captain Ridgway's, and found the redoubted John Malcolm, standing over a small boy, who was pushing a little sled before him, cursing, damning, threatening and shaking a very large cane with a very heavy ferril on it over his head. The boy at that time was perfectly quiet, notwithstanding which Malcolm continued his threats of striking him, which Mr. Hewes conceiving if he struck him with that weapon he must have killed him out-right, came up to him, and said to him, Mr. Malcolm I hope you are not going to strike this boy with that stick.

Malcolm had already acquired an odious reputation with patriots of the lower sort. A Bostonian, he had been a sea captain, an army officer, and recently an employee of the customs service. He was so strong a supporter of royal authority that he had traveled to North Carolina to fight the Regulators* and boasted of having a horse shot out from under him. He had a fiery temper. As a customs informer he was known to have turned in a vessel to punish sailors for petty smuggling, a custom of the sea. In November 1773, near Portsmouth, New Hampshire, a crowd of thirty sailors had "genteely tarr'd and feather'd" him, as the *Boston Gazette* put it: they did the job over his clothes. Back in Boston he made "frequent complaints" to Hutchinson of "being hooted at in the streets" for this by "tradesmen"; and the lieutenant governor cautioned him, "being a passionate man," not to reply in kind.

The exchange between Malcolm and Hewes resonated with class as well as political differences:

> Malcolm returned, you are an impertinent rascal, it is none of your business. Mr. Hewes then asked him, what had the child done to him. Malcolm damned him and asked him if he was going to take his part? Mr. Hewes answered no further than this, that he thought it was a shame for him to strike the child with such a club as that, if he intended to strike him. Malcolm on that damned Mr. Hewes, called him a vagabond, and said he would let him know he should not speak to a gentleman in the street. Mr. Hewes returned to that, he was neither a rascal nor vagabond, and though a poor man was in as good credit in town as he was. Malcolm called him a liar, and said he was not, nor ever would be. Mr. Hewes retorted, be that as it will, I never was tarred nor feathered any how. On this Malcolm struck him, and wounded him deeply on the forehead, so that Mr. Hewes for some time lost his senses. Capt. Godfrey, then present, interposed, and after some altercation, Malcolm went home.

Hewes was rushed to Joseph Warren, the patriot doctor, his distant relative. Malcolm's cane had almost penetrated his skull. Thatcher found "the indentation as plainly perceptible as it was sixty years ago." So did Hawkes. Warren dressed the wound, and Hewes was able to make his way to a magistrate to swear out a warrant for Malcolm's arrest "which he carried to a

---

Regulators were for the most part Scots-Irish backcountry settlers who took up arms in protest against inadequate political representation and against heavy taxation. They were routed by government forces in the Battle of Almanac River, May 16, 1771.

constable named Justice Hale." Malcolm, meanwhile, had retreated to his house, where he responded in white heat to taunts about the halfway tarring and feathering in Portsmouth with "damn you let me see the man that dare do it better."

In the evening a crowd took Malcolm from his house and dragged him on a sled into King Street "amidst the huzzas of thousands." . . .

> . . . [T]hey proceeded to elevate Mr. Malcolm from his sled into a cart, and stripping him to buff and breeches, gave him a modern jacket [a coat of tar and feathers] and hied him away to liberty-tree, where they proposed to him to renounce his present commission, and swear that he would never hold another inconsistent with the liberties of his country; but this he obstinately refusing, they then carted him to the gallows, passed a rope round his neck, and threw the other end over the beam as if they intended to hang him: But this manoeuvre he set at defiance. They then basted him for some time with a rope's end, and threatened to cut his ears off, and on this he complied, and they then brought him home.

Hewes had precipitated an electrifying event. It was part of the upsurge of spontaneous action in the wake of the Tea Party that prompted the Whig leaders to promote a "Committee for Tarring and Feathering" as an instrument of crowd control. The "Committee" made its appearance in broadsides signed by "Captain Joyce, Jun.," a sobriquet meant to invoke the bold cornet who had captured King Charles in 1647. The event was reported in the English newspapers, popularized in three or four satirical prints, and dramatized still further when Malcolm went to England, where he campaigned for a pension and ran for Parliament (without success) against John Wilkes, the leading champion of America. The event confirmed the British ministry in its punitive effort to bring rebellious Boston to heel.

What was lost to the public was that Hewes was at odds with the crowd. He wanted justice from the courts, not a mob; after all, he had sworn out a warrant against Malcolm. And he could not bear to see cruel punishment inflicted on a man, any more than on a boy. As he told the story to Thatcher, when he returned and saw Malcolm being carted away in tar and feathers, "his instant impulse was to push after the procession as fast as he could, with a blanket to put over his shoulders. He overtook them [the crowd] at his brother's [Shubael's] house and made an effort to relieve him; but the ruffians who now had the charge of him about the cart, pushed him aside, and warned him to keep off." This may have been the Good Samaritan of 1835, but the story rings true. While "the very excitement which the affront must have wrought upon him began to rekindle," Hewes conveyed no hatred for Malcolm.

The denouement of the affair was an incident several weeks later. "Malcolm recovered from his wounds and went about as usual. 'How do you do, Mr. Malcolm?' said Hewes, very civilly, the next time he met him. 'Your humble servant, Mr. George Robert Twelves Hewes,' quoth he,—touching his hat genteelly as he passed by. 'Thank ye,' thought Hewes, 'and I am glad you have learned *better manners at last.*'" Hewes's mood was one of triumph. Malcolm had been taught a lesson. The issue was respect for Hewes, a patriot, a poor man, an honest citizen, a decent man standing up for a child against an unspeakably arrogant "gentleman" who was an enemy of his country. . . .

What moved Hewes to action? It was not the written word; indeed there is no sign he was much of a reader until old age, and then it was the Bible he read. "My whole education," he told Hawkes, "consisted of only a moderate knowledge of reading and writing." He seems to have read one of the most sensational pamphlets of 1773, which he prized enough to hold onto for more than fifty years, but he was certainly not like Harbottle Dorr, the Boston shopkeeper who pored over every issue of every Boston newspaper, annotating Britain's crimes for posterity.

Hewes was moved to act by personal experiences that he shared with large numbers of other plebeian Bostonians. He seems to have been politicized, not by the Stamp Act, but by the coming of the troops after 1768, and then by things that happened to him, that he saw, or that happened to people he knew. Once aroused, he took action with others of his own rank and condition—the laboring classes who formed the bulk of the actors at the Massacre, the Tea Party, and the Malcolm affair—and with other members of his family: his uncle Robert, "known for a staunch Liberty Boy," and his brother Daniel, a guard at the tea ship. Shubael, alone among his brothers, became a Tory. These shared experiences were interpreted and focused more likely by the spoken than the written word and as much by his peers at taverns and crowd actions as by leaders in huge public meetings.

As he became active politically he may have had a growing awareness of his worth as a shoemaker. . . . In city after city, "cobblers" were singled out for derision by conservatives for leaving their lasts to engage in the body politic. Hewes could not have been unaware of all this; he was part of it.

He may also have responded to the rising demand among artisans for support of American manufacturers, whether or not it brought him immediate benefit. He most certainly subscribed to the secularized Puritan ethic—self-denial, industry, frugality—that made artisans take to the nonimportation agreement with its crusade against foreign luxury and its vision of American manufacturers. . . .

But what ideas did Hewes articulate? He spoke of what he did but very little of what he thought. In the brief statement he offered Hawkes about why he went off to war in 1776, he expressed a commitment to general principles as they had been brought home to him by his experiences. "I was continually reflecting upon the unwarrantable sufferings inflicted on the citizens of Boston by the usurpation and tyranny of Great Britain, and my mind was excited with an unextinguishable desire to aid in chastising them." When Hawkes expressed a doubt "as to the correctness of his conduct in absenting himself from his family," Hewes "emphatically reiterated" the same phrases, adding to a "desire to aid in chastising them" the phrase "and securing our independence." This was clearly not an afterthought; it probably reflected the way many others moved toward the goal of Independence, not as a matter of original intent, but as a step made necessary when all other resorts failed. Ideology thus did not set George Hewes apart from Samuel Adams or John Hancock. The difference lies in what the Revolution did to him as a person. His experiences transformed him, giving him a sense of citizenship and personal worth. Adams and Hancock began with both; Hewes had to arrive there, and in arriving he cast of the constraints of deference. . . .

This gives meaning to Hewes's tale of working beside Hancock at the Tea Party—"a curious reminiscence," Thatcher called it, "but we believe it a mistake." . . .

Thatcher was justifiably skeptical; it is very unlikely that Hancock was there. Participants swore themselves to secrecy; their identify was one of the best-kept secrets of the Revolution. In fact, in 1835 Thatcher published in an appendix the first list of those "more or less actively engaged" in the Tea Party as furnished by "an aged Bostonian," clearly not Hewes. Hancock was not named. More important, it was not part of the patriot plan for the well-known leaders to be present. When the all-day meeting that sanctioned the action adjourned, the leaders, including Hancock, stayed behind conspicuously in Old South. Still, there can be little question that Hewes was convinced at the time that Hancock was on the ship: some gentlemen were indeed present; it was reasonable to assume that Hancock, who had been so conspicuous on the tea issue, was there; Hewes knew what Hancock looked like; he was too insistent about details for his testimony to be dismissed as made up. And the way he recorded it in his mind at the time was the way he stored it in his memory.

Hewes in effect had brought Hancock down to his own level. The poor shoemaker had not toppled the wealthy merchant; he was no "leveller." But the rich and powerful—the men in "ruffles"—had become, in his revealing word, his "associates." John Hancock and George Hewes breaking open the same chest at the Tea Party remained for Hewes a symbol of a moment of equality. To the shoemaker, one suspects, this above all was what the Revolutionary events of Boston meant, as did the war that followed.

DOCUMENTS

"Remember the Ladies,"
Abigail and John Adams Exchange Views, 1776

ABIGAIL ADAMS TO JOHN ADAMS   MARCH 31, 1776

. . . I long to hear that you have declared an independancy—and by the way in the new Code of Laws which I suppose it will be necessary for you to make I desire you would Remember the Ladies, and be more generous and favourable to them than your ancestors. Do not put such unlimited power into the hands of the Husbands. Remember all Men would be tyrants if they could. If perticuliar care and attention is not paid to the Ladies we are determined to foment a Rebelion, and will not hold ourselves bound by any Laws in which we have no voice, or Representation.

That your Sex are Naturally Tyrannical is a Truth so thoroughly established as to admit of no dispute, but such of you as wish to be happy willingly give up the harsh title of Master for the more tender and endearing one of Friend. Why then, not put it out of the power of the vicious and the Lawless to use us with cruelty and indignity with impunity. Men of Sense in all Ages abhor those customs which treat us only as the vassals of your Sex. Regard us then as Beings placed by providence under your protection and in immitation of the Supreem Being make use of that power only for our happiness.

JOHN ADAMS TO ABIGAIL ADAMS   APRIL 14, 1776

. . . As to Declarations of Independency, be patient. Read our Privateering Laws, and our Commercial Laws. What signifies a Word.

As to your extraordinary Code of Laws, I cannot but laugh. We have been told that our Struggle has loosened the bands of Government every where. That Children and Apprentices were disobedient—that schools and Colledges were grown turbulent—that Indians slighted their Guardians and Negroes grew insolent to their Masters. But your Letter was the first Intimation that another Tribe more numerous and powerfull than all the rest were grown discontented.—This is rather too coarse a Compliment but you are so saucy, I wont blot it out.

Depend upon it, We know better than to repeal our Masculine systems. Altho they are in full Force, you know they are little more than Theory. We

SOURCE: Charles Francis Adams, *Familiar Letters of John Adams and His Wife Abigail During the Revolution* . . . (Boston: 1875), 149–150, 155, 169.

dare not exert our Power in its full Latitude. We are obliged to go fair, and softly, and in Practice you know We are the subjects. We have only the Name of Masters, and rather than give up this, which would compleatly subject Us to the Despotism of the Peticoat, I hope General Washington, and all our brave Heroes would fight. I am sure every good Politician would plot, as long as he would against Despotism, Empire, Monarchy, Aristocracy, Oligarchy, or Ochlocracy.—A fine Story indeed. I begin to think the Ministry as deep as they are wicked. After stirring up Tories, Landjobbers, Trimmers, Bigots, Canadians, Indians, Negroes, Hanoverians, Hessians, Russians, Irish Roman Catholicks, Scotch Renegadoes, at last they have stimulated the   to demand new Priviledges and threaten to rebell.

ABIGAIL ADAMS TO JOHN ADAMS   MAY 7, 1776

. . . I can not say that I think you very generous to the Ladies, for whilst you are proclaiming peace and good will to Men, Emancipating all Nations, you insist upon retaining an absolute power over Wives. But you must remember that Arbitrary power is like most other things which are very hard, very liable to be broken—and notwithstanding all your wise Laws and Maxims we have it in our power not only to free ourselves but to subdue our Masters, and without violence throw both your natural and legal authority at our feet—

> "Charm by accepting, by submitting sway
> Yet have our Humour most when we obey."

Travails of a Loyalist Wife and Mother, 1777

TO PHILLIP VAN CORTLANDT   FEBRUARY 19TH, 1777

My beloved husband,
      Doctor Bond succeeded and with orders for my removal brought me General Washington's pass which I now enclose.*
      To describe the scene at parting with our few though sincere friends, the destruction of our property, the insulting looks and behaviour of those

SOURCE: H.O.H. Vernon-Jackson, ed., "A Loyalist Wife: Letters of Mrs. Philip Van Cortlandt, December 1776–February 1777," *History Today*, 14 (1964), 580.

*General Washington's pass to Mrs. Philip Van Cortlandt: Mrs. Catharine Cortlandt, wife of Philip Cortlandt, Esq., now in New York or Long Island and to carry with her, her Servants, Furniture and Apparel.

Given under my Hand at Head Quarters at Morris town this 15th day of February 1777.
                                                                    G. Washington.

who had been accessory to our ruin, the situation of our beloved children and faithful servants on the day we were turned off from our once peaceful and happy cottage, in a cold snow storm, with my feelings on the occasion, is more than I dare attempt. At four in the afternoon, a cold, disagreeable day, we bid *adieu* to our home to make room for the sick of General Washington's Army and, after an unpleasant and fatiguing journey, arrived at twelve o'clock at night at the Fork of the Rivers Rockaway, Pompton and Haakinsack. A Young Woman, whose father and brother were both in the Rebel service, was much affected with my Situation and endeavoured to remove me into another room. The next evening, after a most distressing ride through snow and rain with much difficulty in changing Carriages for ourselves and baggage, we arrived at Campbell's Tavern at Haakinsack, the mistress of which refused me admittance when she was informed whose family it was, alleging as an excuse that she expected a number of Officers, and notwithstanding my earnest entreaties only to permit me to have shelter in one of her empty rooms for myself and children from the inclemency of the weather, as I could make use of my own beds though wet.

The town was filled with Soldiers and the night advancing. Whilst reflecting on my situation, a person came up to me, looked me in the face, and asked me to accompany him to his Uncle's house with my whole family. I did not thank him, though I attempted more than once; he read my gratitude in my countenance. On entering a room with a large fire, it had an effect on the children, whose stomachs had been empty the greatest part of the day, that caused instant puking, and was near proving fatal to them.

The next morning early, we again set off in a most uncomfortable sleet and snow, and rode until ten o'clock, when our youngest children could not pass a farm yard where they were milking cows without wishing for some. My little Willing was almost in agonies, springing in my Arms and calling for milk. I therefore rode up and requested the good man to let me have some from one of his pails. He partly advanced. My dear boy reached out his arms. The man stopped, asked who we were and, upon being informed by the driver, swore bitterly he would not give a drop to any Tory Bitch. I offered him money, my children screamed; and, as I could not prevail, I drove on.

On my arrival here, it was necessary for me to take some repose, after which my anxiety was considerable until the coming of the servants, who had been obliged to leave me soon after setting off from Haakinsack, on account of the baggage and the badness of the roads. About two hours ago, they come in and inform me that, crossing the river on the ice at the ferry, they were stopped and fired upon by a party of armed Rebels, nearly killing several of them (as a ball went through Old Sam's hat). Upon being shewn a copy of General Washington's pass, the original being with me, they damned the General 'for giving the mistress a pass,' and said they were sorry they had not come a little sooner as they would have stopped the whole, but swore they would make a prize of the three loads they had in their possession, and immediately fell to plundering chests, trunks, boxes, etc., throwing the heavy Articles into a hole in the ice, and breaking a barrel of old fashioned China into a thousand pieces. The Officers of this party are a Captain Dodd and Lieutenant Irvin. The former put on your new plaid Gown which he wore.

The small remains of our property is now here; and, after paying the drivers in hard money and expenses on the road, but little remains. With that little, let us now, my dear Philly, be content, and though fortune frowns we will still be happy, in each other. When we parted a few months ago, I was hearty and blooming; but be not surprised, my dear Pappa, if you see your Kitty altered. Indeed, I am much altered. But I know your heart, you will not love me less, but heal with redoubled affection and tenderness the wounds received in your behalf for those principles of loyalty which alone induced you to leave to the mercy of Rebels nine innocent children and your fond and ever affectionate Wife,

C.V.C.

A New Hampshire Boy Joins the Navy, 1779

Ships were building, prizes taken from the enemy unloading, privateers fitting out, standards waved on the forts and batteries, the exercising of soldiers, the roar of cannon, the sound of martial music and the call for volunteers so infatuated me, that I was filled with anxiety to become an actor in the scene of war. . . . Though not yet fourteen years of age, like other boys, I imagined myself almost a man. I had intimated to my sister, that if my father would not consent that I should go to sea, I would run away, and go on board a privateer. My mind became so infatuated with the subject, that I talked of it in my sleep, and was overhead by my mother. She communicated what she had heard to my father. —My parents were apprehensive that I might wander off and go on board some vessel without their consent. At this period it was not an uncommon thing for lads to come out of the country, step on board a privateer, make a cruise and return home, their friends remaining in entire ignorance of their fate, until they heard it from themselves. Others would pack up their clothes, take a cheese and a loaf of bread, and steer off for the army. There was a disposition in commanders of privateers and recruiting officers to encourage this spirit of

SOURCE: Andrew Sherburne, *Memoirs*, 2d ed. (Providence: H. H. Brown, 1831), 18–21.

enterprise in young men and boys. Though these rash young adventurers did not count the cost, or think of looking at the dark side of the picture, yet this spirit, amidst the despondency of many, enabled our country to maintain a successful struggle and finally achieve her independence.

The continental ship of war *Ranger*, of eighteen guns, commanded by Thomas Simpson, Esq., was at this time shipping a crew in Portsmouth. This ship had been ordered to join the Boston and Providence frigates and the *Queen of France* of twenty guns, upon an expedition directed by Congress. My father having consented that I should go to sea, preferred the service of Congress [the Continental Navy] to privateering. He was acquainted with Capt. Simpson. —On board this ship were my two half uncles, Timothy and James Weymouth. Accompanied by my father, I visited the rendezvous of the *Ranger* and shipped as one of her crew. There were probably thirty boys on board this ship. As most of our principal officers belonged to the town, parents preferred this ship as a station for their sons who were about to enter the naval service. Hence most of these boys were from Portsmouth. As privateering was the order of the day, vessels of every description were employed in the business. Men were not wanting who would hazard themselves in vessels of twenty tons or less, manned by ten or fifteen hands. Placing much dependence on the protection of my uncles, I was much elated with my supposed good fortune, which had at last made me a sailor.

I was not yet fourteen years of age. I had received some little moral and religious instruction, and was far from being accustomed to the habits of town boys, or the maxims or dialect of sailors. The town boys thought themselves vastly superior to country lads; and indeed in those days the distinction was much greater than at present. My diffidence and aversion to swearing, rendered me on object of ridicule to those little profane chaps. I was insulted, and frequently obliged to fight. In this I was sometimes victorious. My uncles, and others, prompted me to defend my rights. I soon began to improve in boxing, and to indulge in swearing. At first this practice occasioned some remorse of conscience. —I however endeavored to persuade myself that there was a necessity for it. I at length became a proficient in this abominable practice. To counterbalance my guilt in this, I at the same time became more constant in praying; heretofore I had only prayed occasionally; now I prayed continually when I turned in at night, and vainly imagined that I prayed enough by night to atone for the sins of the day. Believing that no other person on board prayed, I was filled with pride, concluding I had as much or more religion than the whole crew besides. The boys were employed in waiting on the officers, but in time of action a boy was quartered to each gun to carry cartridges. I was waiter to Mr. Charles Roberts, the boatswain, and was quartered at the third gun from the bow. Being ready for sea, we sailed to Boston, joined the Providence frigate, commanded by Commodore Whipple, the Boston frigate and the *Queen of France.* I believed that this small squadron composed nearly the entire navy of the United States. We proceeded to sea some time in June 1779. A considerable part of the crew of the *Ranger* being raw hands and the sea rough, especially in the gulf stream, many were exceedingly sick, and myself among the rest. We afforded a subject of constant ridicule to the old sailors.

PART I

Suggestions for Further Reading

For the racial and ethnic mix of the colonial American population, consult Gary Nash, *Red, White and Black: The Peoples of Early America* (1974). Three excellent books on Europeans and Indians are Francis Jennings, *Invasion of America* (1975), James Axtell, *The Invasion Within: The Contest of Cultures in Colonial North America* (1985), and Colin G. Calloway, *New Worlds for All: Indians, Europeans and the Remaking of Early America* (1997). Richard White, *The Middle Ground: Indians, Empires and Republicans in the Great Lakes Region, 1650–1815* (1991) deals with relations between Indians and white Americans throughout the colonial period and into the early years of the republic. For the impact of European colonization on Indian society and culture, see James H. Merrell, *The Indians' New World: Catawbas and Their Neighbors from European Contact Through the Era of Removal* (1989). A most thorough treatment of the Iroquois Confederation may be found in Francis Jennings, *The Ambiguous Iroquois Empire* (1984). On the Puritans and Indians, see Alden Vaughan, *New England Frontier: Puritans and Indians* (1965). On immigration, see Thomas Archdeacon, *Becoming American: An Ethnic History* (1983) and Maldwyn Jones, *American Immigration* (1992). For the Southwest, see Ramon Gutierrez, *When Jesus Came the Cornmothers Went Away: Marriage, Sexuality, and Power in New Mexico, 1500–1846* (1991). For New York, consult Joyce Goodfriend, *Before the Melting Pot: Society and Culture in New York City, 1664–1730* (1992). David Galenson, *White Servitude in Colonial America* (1982) and A. R. Ekirch, *Bound for America* (1987) discuss indentured servitude and convict labor. For colonial Germans, see Aaron Spencer Fogelman, *Hopeful Journeys: German Immigration, Settlement, and Political Culture in Colonial America, 1717–1775* (1997).

On African Americans, four books are outstanding: Peter Wood, *Black Majority: Negroes in Colonial South Carolina from 1676 Through the Stono Rebellion* (1974), Gerald Mullin, *Slave Resistance in Eighteenth Century Virginia* (1972), Donald R. Wright, *African Americans in the Colonial Era: From African Origins Through the American Revolution* (1990), and Philip D. Morgan, *Slave Counterpoint: Slave Culture in the Eighteenth Century Chesapeake and Lowcountry* (1998). A fine study of the development of a black urban community is Gary B. Nash, *Forging Freedom: The Formation of Philadelphia's Black Community, 1720–1840* (1988). On white racism, Winthrop Jordan, *White over Black: American Attitudes Toward the Negro, 1550–1812* (1968) is a classic.

Jack P. Greene, *Pursuit of Happiness: The Social Development of Early Modern British Colonies and the Formation of American Culture* (1988) provides an excellent one-volume synthesis of the colonial experience. David Hacker Fischer, *Albion's Seed: Four British Folkways in America* (1989) combines anthropology and history in a detailed study of the development of American colonial culture. On early developments in the colonies, see Clarence L. Ver Steeg, *The Formative Years, 1607–1763* (1965) and Daniel J. Boorstin, *The Americans: The Colonial Experience* (1958). On the northern colonies, there are a number of good books. Among them are John Demos, *A Little Commonwealth: Family Life in Plymouth Colony* (1970); Sumner Powell, *Puritan Village: The Formation of a New Town* (1963); Kenneth A. Lockridge, *A New England Town; The First Hundred Years, Dedham, Massachusetts, 1636–1736* (1970); Bernard Bailyn, *The New England Merchants in the Seventeenth Century* (1955); and T. H. Breen, *From Puritans and Adventurers: Change and Persistence in Early America* (1980).

On the southern colonies, see two works by Wesley Frank Craven: *The Southern Colonies in the Seventeenth Century, 1607–1689* (1949) and *White, Red, and Black: The Seventeenth Century Virginian* (1971). Edmund S. Morgan, *American Slavery, American Freedom: The Ordeal of Colonial Virginia* (1975) provides an exciting, readable treatment of developments in seventeenth-century Virginia. Also recommended are Clarence L. Ver Steeg, *Origin of the Southern Mosaic* (1975) and Carl Bridenbaugh, *Jamestown, 1544–1699* (1980).

On society in the eighteenth century, useful works are Richard Hofstadter, *America at 1750: A Social Portrait* (1971); Michael Zuckerman, *Peaceable Kingdoms: New England Towns in the Eighteenth Century* (1970); Gary Nash, *The Urban Crucible: Social Change, Political Consciousness, and the Origins of the American Revolution* (1979); Alan Kulikoff, *Tobacco and Slaves* (1986); T. H. Breen, *Tobacco Culture* (1987); Jackson Turner Main, *The Social Structure of Revolutionary America* (1965); and James Henretta, *The Evolution of American Society, 1700–1815: An Interdisciplinary Analysis* (1973).

A good general discussion of religion during the colonial period is found in George M. Marsden, *Religion in American Culture* (1990). On religious developments in the eighteenth century, refer to Carl Bridenbaugh, *Mitre and Sceptre: Trans-Atlantic Faiths, Ideas, Personalities, and Politics, 1689–1775* (1962). J. M. Bumstead and John E. Van de Wetering, *What Must I Do to Be Saved? The Great Awakening in Colonial America* (1976) provides an excellent introduction to the great revival movement of the colonial period. For the impact of the Great Awakening in Virginia, see Rhys Isaac, *The Transformation of Virginia, 1740–1790* (1982) and Richard Beeman, *The Evolution of the Southern Backcountry: A Case Study of Lunenburg County, Virginia, 1746–1832* (1984). See also Jon Butler, *Awash in a Sea of Faith: Christianizing the American People* (1990).

On women three general books are helpful: Laurel Ulrich, *A Midwife's Tale: The Life of Martha Ballard, Based on Her Diary* (1990); Nancy Woloch, *Women and the American Experience* (1984); and Mary Ryan, *Womanhood in America: From Colonial Times to the Present* (1975). For the colonial period, information about women can be found in Edmund Morgan, *The Puritan Family: Religion and Domestic Relations in Seventeenth-Century New England* (1966) and John Demos, *A Little Commonwealth: Family Life in Plymouth Colony*

(1970). On attitudes toward children, see Phillip Greven, *The Protestant Temperament: Patterns of Child-Rearing, Religious Experience and the Self in Early America* (1977). A general history of African-American women is Darlene Clark Hine and Kathleen Thompson, *A Shining Thread of Home: The History of Black Women in America* (1998). See also Carol Berkin, *First Generations: Women in Colonial America* (1998) and Mary Beth Norton, *Founding Mothers and Fathers: Gendered Power and the Forming of American Society* (1996). Women in port cities are covered in Elaine Crane, *Ebb Tide in New England* (1998).

A number of books explore the social history of the American Revolution. For a view that the Revolution was radical, see Gordon Wood, *The Radicalism of the American Revolution* (1991). For women, see Mary Beth Norton, *Liberty's Daughters: The Revolutionary Experience of American Women, 1750–1800* (1980); Linda Kerber, *Women of the Republic: Intellect and Ideology in Revolutionary America* (1980); and Phyllis Lee Levin, *Abigail Adams: A Biography* (1987). Among studies of the Loyalist side of the conflict are Bernard Bailyn, *The Ordeal of Thomas Hutchinson* (1975); Robert M. Calhoon, *The Loyalists in Revolutionary America, 1760–1781* (1973); and William H. Nelson, *The American Tory* (1961). Regional studies of the war include Robert Gross, *The Minutemen and Their World* (1976) and Robert J. Taylor, *Western Masschusetts in the Revolution* (1954). For the middle colonies Eric Foner, *Tom Paine and Revolutionary America* (1976) is useful. For a view of the war through the eyes of those who fought, see George F. Scheer and Hugh F. Rankin, *Rebels and Redcoats* (1957) and John Shy, *A People Numerous and Armed: Reflections on the Military for American Independence* (1976). The Revolution's impact on religion is the subject of John G. West Jr., *The Politics of Revolution and Reason: Religion and Civil Life in the New Nation* (1996).

Part II

Social Life in a New Nation
1784–1877

Chapter 8

The Onset of Industry: The Lowell Venture

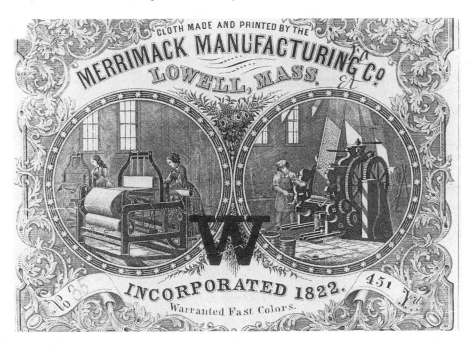

Urban centers in the new nation experienced dramatic growth and change during the first half of the nineteenth century. Established cities boomed and new ones sprang up, with industry and commerce the focus of endeavor. Canals, railroads, and steamboats linked city to city and town to countryside, facilitating the movement of people, products, and ideas within the United States as well as between the young nation and foreign lands.

The textile mill town of Lowell, Massachusetts, symbolized an evolving industrial order central to the dynamic new century. Its population of 200 in 1820 rose to 6,477 in 1830, 21,000 in 1840, and more than 33,000 by 1850. Most of the increase of these decades derived from an expanded workforce of predominantly young, single women drawn to Lowell from their rural farm homes. Mill owners energetically sought such workers, for Lowell's founders wanted not only to build factories but also to establish a model, ordered community under their benevolent control and direction.

Thomas Dublin's essay "Women, Work, and Protest in the Early Lowell Mills" describes the life and labor of Lowell's female operatives during the 1830s and 1840s. It details the emergence of a close-knit community of workers that not only rejected the subservient role envisioned by the founders but that, first through strikes and later through political action, protested against employer policies and working conditions. What does Dublin identify as the key factors contributing to a sense of community among the operatives? What does the author mean when he states that "The Lowell mills both exploited and liberated women in ways unknown to the pre-industrial economy"?

As a young girl, Harriet Hanson Robinson had worked in a Lowell mill. In 1898 she looked back over more than sixty years and told of her experiences in a book that she titled Loom and Spindle. *The first document contains an excerpt from this work in which she recalls her role in the mill workers' strike of 1836. How do you account for her pride, even after so many years, in having been associated with the action? Her reference to "the right of suffrage" should provide a clue to the answer.*

Regulations governing employees of the Hamilton Manufacturing Company of Lowell are set forth in the second document. In what ways do these rules reflect the social outlook of the owners?

As competition in the textile industry grew heated, working conditions deteriorated. During the 1840s, the mill workers turned to government for redress. The final document, from testimony before a Massachusetts legislative committee investigating workers' grievances, reveals those conditions and helps explain why the mills were losing their appeal for American farm women by the late 1840s and increasingly being staffed by immigrants.

ESSAY
•◆•

Women, Work, and Protest in the Early Lowell Mills
Thomas Dublin

In the years before 1850 the textile mills of Lowell, Massachusetts, were a celebrated economic and cultural attraction. Foreign visitors invariably included them on their American tours. Interest was prompted by the massive scale of the mills, the astonishing productivity of the power-driven machinery, and the fact that women comprised most of the workforce. Visitors were struck by the newness of both mills and city as well as by the culture of the female operatives. The scene stood in sharp contrast to the gloomy mill towns of the English Industrial Revolution.

Lowell, was, in fact, an impressive accomplishment. In 1820, there had been no city at all—only a dozen family farms along the Merrimack River in

SOURCE: "Women, Work, and Protest in the Early Lowell Mills" by Thomas Dublin. From *Labor History,* 16(1), pp. 99–112, 115–116. Reprinted by permission from Carfax Publishing Limited, P.O. Box 25, Abingdon, Oxfordshire OX143UE, United Kingdom.

East Chelmsford. In 1821, however, a group of Boston capitalists purchased land and water rights along the river and a nearby canal, and began to build a major textile manufacturing center. Opening two years later, the first factory employed Yankee women recruited from the nearby countryside. Additional mills were constructed until, by 1840, ten textile corporations with thirty-two mills valued at more than ten million dollars lined the banks of the river and nearby canals. Adjacent to the mills were rows of company boarding houses and tenements which accommodated most of the eight thousand factory operatives.

As Lowell expanded and became the nation's largest textile manufacturing center, the experiences of women operatives changed as well. The increasing number of firms in Lowell and in the other mill towns brought the pressure of competition. Overproduction became a problem, and the prices of finished cloth decreased. The high profits of the early years declined and so, too did conditions for the mill operatives. Wages were reduced and the pace of work within the mills was stepped up. Women operatives did not accept these changes without protest. In 1834 and 1836 they went on strike to protest wage cuts, and between 1843 and 1848 they mounted petition campaigns aimed at reducing the hours of labor in the mills.

These labor protests in early Lowell contribute to our understanding of the response of workers to the growth of industrial capitalism in the first half of the nineteenth century. They indicate the importance of values and attitudes dating back to an earlier period and also the transformation of these values in a new setting.

The major factor in the rise of a new consciousness among operatives in Lowell was the development of a close-knit community among women working in the mills. The structure of work and the nature of housing contributed to the growth of this community. The existence of community among women, in turn, was an important element in the repeated labor protests of the period. . . .

The mutual dependence among women in early Lowell was rooted in the structure of mill work itself. Newcomers to the mills were particularly dependent on their fellow operatives, but even experienced hands relied on one another for considerable support.

New operatives generally found their first experiences difficult, even harrowing, though they may have already done considerable hand-spinning and weaving in their own homes. The initiation of one of them is described in fiction in the *Lowell Offering*.*

> The next morning she went into the Mill; and at first the sight of so
> many bands, and wheels, and springs in constant motion, was very
> frightful. She felt afraid to touch the loom, and she was almost sure

*A publication produced by the mill workers with financial support from management. (Eds.)

she could never learn to weave . . . the shuttle flew out, and made a new bump on her head; and the first time she tried to spring the lathe, she broke out a quarter of the treads.

While other accounts present a somewhat less difficult picture, most indicate that women only became proficient and felt satisfaction in their work after several months at the mills.

The textile corporations made provisions to ease the adjustment of new operatives. Newcomers were not immediately expected to fit into the mill's regular work routine. They were first assigned work as sparehands and were paid a daily wage independent of the quantity of work they turned out. As a sparehand, the newcomer worked with an experienced hand who instructed her in the intricacies of the job. The sparehand spelled her partner for short stretches of time, and occasionally took the place of an absentee. One woman described the learning process in a letter reprinted in the *Offering:*

> Well, I went into the mill, and was put to learn with a very patient girl. . . . You cannot think how odd everything seems. . . . They set me to threading shuttles, and tying weaver's knots, and such things, and now I have improved so that I can take care of one loom. I could take care of two if only I had eyes in the back part of my head. . . .

After the passage of some weeks or months, when she could handle the normal complement of machinery—two looms for weavers during the 1830s—and when a regular operative departed, leaving an opening, the sparehand moved into a regular job.

Through this system of job training, the textile corporations contributed to the development of community among female operatives. During the most difficult period in an operative's career, the first months in the mill, she relied upon other women workers for training and support. And for every sparehand whose adjustment to mill work was aided in this process, there was an experienced operative whose work was also affected. Women were relating to one another during the work process and not simply tending their machinery. Given the high rate of turnover in the mill workforce, a large proportion of women operatives worked in pairs. At the Hamilton Company in July 1836, for example, more than a fifth of all females on the Company payroll were sparehands. Consequently, over forty percent of the females employed there in this month worked with one another. Nor was this interaction surreptitious, carried out only when the overseer looked elsewhere; rather, it was formally organized and sanctioned by the textile corporations themselves.

In addition to the integration of sparehands, informal sharing of work often went on among regular operatives. A women would occasionally take off a half or full day from work either to enjoy a brief vacation or to recover from illness, and fellow operatives would each take an extra loom or side of spindles so that she might continue to earn wages during her absence. Women were generally paid on a piece rate basis, their wages being determined by the total output of the machinery they tended during the payroll period. With friends helping out during her absence, making sure that her looms kept running, an operative could earn almost a full wage even though she was not physically present. Such informal work-sharing was another way in which mutual dependence developed among women operatives during their working hours.

Living conditions also contributed to the development of community among female operatives. Most women working in the Lowell mills of these years were housed in company boarding houses. In July 1836, for example, more than 73 percent of females employed by the Hamilton Company resided in company housing adjacent to the mills. Almost three-fourths of them, therefore, lived and worked with each other. Furthermore, the work schedule was such that women had little opportunity to interact with those not living in company dwellings. They worked, in these years, an average of 73 hours a week. Their workday ended at 7:00 or 7:30 P.M., and in the hours between supper and the 10:00 curfew imposed by management on residents of company boarding houses, there was little time to spend with friends living "off the corporation."

Women in the boarding houses lived in close quarters, a factor that also played a role in the growth of community. A typical boarding house accommodated twenty-five young women, generally crowded four to eight in a bedroom. There was little possibility of privacy within the dwelling, and pressure to conform to group standards was very strong. The community of operatives which developed in the mills, it follows, carried over into life at home as well.

The boarding house became a central institution in the lives of Lowell's female operatives in these years, but it was particularly important in the initial integration of newcomers into urban industrial life. Upon first leaving her rural home for work in Lowell, a woman entered a setting very different from anything she had previously known. . . .

In the boarding house, the newcomer took the first steps in the process which transformed her from an "outsider" into an accepted member of the community of women operatives.

Recruitment of newcomers into the mills and their initial hiring was mediated through the boarding house system. Women generally did not travel to Lowell for the first time entirely on their own. They usually came because they knew someone—an older sister, cousin, or friend—who had already worked in Lowell. . . . The Hamilton Company Register Books indicate that numerous pairs of operatives, having the same surname and coming from the same town in northern New England, lived in the same boarding houses. If the newcomer was not accompanied by a friend or rela-tive, she was usually directed to "Number 20, Hamilton Company," or to a similar address of one of the other corporations where her acquaintance lived. Her first contact with fellow operatives generally came in the board-ing houses and not the mills. Given the personal nature of recruitment in this period, therefore, newcomers usually had the company and support of a friend or relative in their first adjustment to Lowell.

Like recruitment, the initial hiring was a personal process. Once settled in the boarding house a newcomer had to find a job. She would generally go to the mills with her friend or with the boarding house keeper who would introduce her to an overseer in one of the rooms. If he had an opening, she might start work immediately. More likely, the overseer would know of an opening elsewhere in the mill, or would suggest that something would probably develop within a few days. . . .

The boarding houses were the centers of social life for women opera-tives after their long days in the mills. There they ate their meals, rested, talked, sewed, wrote letters, read books and magazines. From among fellow workers and boarders they found friends who accompanied them to shops, to Lyceum lectures, to church and church-sponsored events. On Sundays or holidays, they often took walks along the canals or out into the nearby countryside. The community of women operatives, in sum, developed in a setting where women worked and lived together, twenty-four hours a day.

Given the all-pervasiveness of this community, one would expect it to exert strong pressures on those who did not conform to group standards. Such appears to have been the case. The community influenced newcomers to adopt its patterns of speech and dress. . . . In addition, it enforced an un-written code of moral conduct. Henry Miles, a minister in Lowell, described the way in which the community pressured those who deviated from ac-cepted moral conduct:

> A girl, suspected of immoralities, or serious improprieties, at once loses caste. Her fellow boarders will at once leave the house, if the keeper does not dismiss the offender. In self-protection, therefore, the patron is obliged to put the offender away. Nor will her former companions walk with her, or work with her; till at length, finding herself everywhere talked about, and pointed at, and shunned, she is obliged to relieve her fellow-operatives of a presence which they feel brings disgrace.

The power of the peer group described by Miles may seem extreme, but there is evidence in the writing of women operatives to corroborate his account. Such group pressure is illustrated by a story (in the *Offering*)—in which operatives in a company boarding house begin to harbor suspicions about a fellow boarder, Hannah, who received repeated evening visits from a man whom she does not introduce to the other residents. Two boarders declare that they will leave if she is allowed to remain in the household. The house keeper finally informed Hannah that she must either depart or not see the man again. She does not accept the ultimatum, but is promptly discharged after the overseer is informed, by one of the boarders, about her conduct. And, only one of Hannah's former friends continues to remain on cordial terms.

One should not conclude, however, that women always enforced a moral code agreeable to Lowell's clergy, or to the mill agents and overseers for that matter. After all, the kind of peer pressure imposed on Hannah could be brought to bear on women in 1834 and 1836 who on their own would not have protested wage cuts. It was much harder to go to work when one's roommates were marching about town, attending rallies, circulating strike petitions. Similarly, the ten-hour petitions of the 1840s were certainly aided by the fact of a tight-knit community of operatives living in a dense neighborhood of boarding houses. To the extent that women could not have completely private lives in the boarding houses, they probably had to conform to group norms, whether these involved speech, clothing, relations with men, or attitudes toward the ten-hour day. Group pressure to conform, so important to the community of women in early Lowell, played a significant role in the collective response of women to changing conditions in the mills.

In addition to the structure of work and housing in Lowell, a third factor, the homogeneity of the mill workforce, contributed to the development of community among female operatives. In this period the mill workforce was homogeneous in terms of sex, nativity, and age. Payroll and other records of the Hamilton Company reveal that more than 85 percent of those employed in July 1836, were women and that over 96 percent were native-born. Furthermore, over 80 percent of the female workforce was between the ages of 15 and 30 years old; and only 10 percent was under 15 or over 40.

Workforce homogeneity takes on particular significance in the context of work structure and the nature of worker housing. These three factors combined mean that women operatives had little interaction with men during their daily lives. Men and women did not perform the same work in the mills, and generally did not even labor in the same rooms. Men worked in the picking and initial carding processes, in the repair shop and on the watchforce, and filled all supervisory positions in the mills. Women held all sparehand and regular operative jobs in drawing, speeding, spinning, weaving and dressing. A typical room in the mill employed eighty women tending machinery, with two men overseeing the work and two boys assisting them. Women had little contact with men other than their supervisors in the course of the working day. After work, women returned to their boarding houses, where once again there were few men. Women, then, worked and lived in a predominantly female setting.

Ethnically the workforce was also homogeneous. Immigrants formed only 3.4 percent of those employed at Hamilton in July 1836. In addition, they comprised only 3 percent of residents in Hamilton Company housing. The community of women operatives was composed of women of New England stock drawn from the hill-country farms surrounding Lowell. Consequently, when experienced hands made fun of the speech and dress of newcomers, it was understood that they, too, had been "rusty" or "rustic" upon first coming to Lowell. This common background was another element shared by women workers in early Lowell.

The work structure, the workers' housing, and workforce homogeneity were the major elements which contributed to the growth of community among Lowell's women operatives. To best understand the larger implications of community, it is necessary to examine the labor protests of this period. For in these struggles, the new values and attitudes which developed in the community of women operatives are most visible.

In February 1834, 800 of Lowell's women operatives "turned-out"— went on strike—to protest a proposed reduction in their wages. They marched to numerous mills in an effort to induce others to join them; and, at an outdoor rally, they petitioned others to "discontinue their labors until terms of reconciliation are made." Their petition concluded:

Resolved, That we will not go back into the mills to work unless our wages are continued . . . as they have been.

Resolved, That none of us will go back, unless they receive us all as one.

Resolved, That if any have not money enough to carry them home, they shall be supplied.

The strike proved to be brief and failed to reverse the proposed wage reductions. Turning-out on a Friday, the striking women were paid their back wages on Saturday, and by the middle of the next week had returned to work or left town. Within a week of the turn-out, the mills were running near capacity.

This first strike in Lowell is important not because it failed or succeeded, but simply because it took place. In an era in which women had to overcome opposition simply to work in the mills, it is remarkable that they would further overstep the accepted middle-class bounds of female propriety by participating in a public protest. The agents of the textile mills certainly considered the turn-out unfeminine. William Austin, agent of the Lawrence Company, described the operatives' procession as an "amizonian [sic] display." He wrote further, in a letter to his company treasurer in Boston: "This afternoon we have paid off several of these Amazons & presume that they will leave town on Monday." The turn-out was particularly offensive to the agents because of the relationship they thought they had with their operatives. William Austin probably expressed the feelings of other agents when he wrote: ". . . notwithstanding the friendly and disinterested advice which has been on all proper occassions [sic] communicated to the girls of the Lawrence mills a spirit of evil omen . . . has prevailed, and overcome the judgement and discretion of too many, and this morning a general turn-out from most of the rooms has been the consequence."

Mill agents assumed an attitude of benevolent paternalism toward their female operatives, and found it particularly disturbing that the women paid such little heed to their advice. The strikers were not merely unfeminine, they were ungrateful as well.

Such attitudes notwithstanding, women chose to turn-out. They did so for two principal reasons. First, the wage cuts undermined the sense of dignity and social equality which was an important element in their Yankee heritage. Second, these wage cuts were seen as an attack on their economic independence.

Certainly a prime motive for the strike was outrage at the social implications of the wage cuts. In a statement of principles accompanying the petition which was circulated among operatives, women expressed well the sense of themselves which prompted the protest of these wage cuts:

UNION IS POWER

Our present object is to have union and exertion, and we remain in possession of our unquestionable rights. We circulate this paper wishing to obtain the names of all who imbibe the spirit of our Patriotic Ancestors, who preferred privation to bondage, and parted with all that renders life desirable—and even life itself—to procure independence for their children. The oppressing hand of avarice would enslave us, and to gain their object, they gravely tell us of the pressure of the time, this we are already sensible of, and deplore it. If any are in want of assistance, the Ladies will be compassionate and assist them; but we prefer to have the disposing of our charities in our own hands; and as we are free, we would remain in possession of what kind Providence has bestowed upon us; and remain daughters of freemen still.

At several points in the proclamation the women drew on their Yankee heritage. Connecting their turn-out with the efforts of their "Patriotic Ancestors" to secure independence from England, they interpreted the wage cuts as an effort to "enslave" them—to deprive them of their independent status as "daughters of freemen." . . .

In point of fact, these Yankee operatives were subordinate in early Lowell's social and economic order, but they never consciously accepted this status. Their refusal to do so became evident whenever the mill owners attempted to exercise the power they possessed. This fundamental contradiction between the objective status of operatives and their consciousness of it was at the root of the 1834 turn-out and of subsequent labor protests in Lowell before 1850. The corporations could build mills, create thousands of jobs, and recruit women to fill them. Nevertheless, they bought only the workers' labor power, and then only for as long as these workers chose to stay. Women could always return to their rural homes, and they had a sense of their own worth and dignity, factors limiting the actions of management. . . .

While the women's traditional conception of themselves as independent daughters of freemen played a major role in the turn-out, this factor acting alone would not necessarily have triggered the 1834 strike. It would have led women as individuals to quit work and return to their rural homes. But the turn-out was a collective protest. When it was announced that wage reductions were being considered, women began to hold meetings in the mills during meal breaks in order to assess tactical possibilities. Their turn-out began at one mill when the agent discharged a woman who had presided at such a meeting. Their procession through the streets passed by other mills, expressing a conscious effort to enlist as much support as possible for their cause. At a mass meeting, the women drew up a resolution which insisted that none be discharged for their participation in the turn-out. This strike, then, was a collective response to the proposed wage cuts—made possible because women had come to form a "community" of operatives in the mill, rather than simply a group of individual workers. The existence of such a tight-knit community turned individual opposition of the wage cuts into a collective protest.

In October 1836, women again went on strike. This second turn-out was similar to the first in several respects. Its immediate cause was also a wage reduction; marches and a large outdoor rally were organized; again, like the earlier protest, the basic goal was not achieved; the corporations refused to restore wages; and operatives either left Lowell or returned to work at the new rates.

Despite these surface similarities between the turn-outs, there were some real differences. One involved scale: over 1500 operatives turned out in 1836, compared to only 800 earlier. Moreover, the second strike lasted much longer than the first. In 1834 operatives stayed out for only a few days; in 1836, the mills ran far below capacity for several months. . . .

Differences between the two turn-outs were not limited to the increased scale and duration of the later one. Women displayed a much higher degree of organization in 1836 than earlier. To co-ordinate strike activities, they formed a Factory Girls' Association. According to one historian, membership in the short-lived association reached 2,500 at its height. . . .

Now giving more thought than they had in 1834 to the specific tactics of the turn-out, the women made a deliberate effort to shut down the mills in order to win their demands. They attempted to persuade less committed operatives, concentrating on those in crucial departments within the mill. . . .

In their organization of a Factory Girls' Association and in their efforts to shut down the mills, the female operatives revealed that they had been changed by their industrial experience. Increasingly, they acted not simply as "daughters of freemen" offended by the impositions of the textile corporations, but also as industrial workers intent on improving their position within the mills.

There was a decline in protest among women in the Lowell mills following these early strike defeats. During the 1837–1843 depression, textile corporations twice reduced wages without evoking a collective response from operatives. Because of the frequency of production cutbacks and lay-offs in these years, workers probably accepted the mill agents' contention that they had to reduce wages or close entirely. But with the return of prosperity and the expansion of production in the mid-1840s, there were renewed labor protests among women. Their actions paralleled those of working men and reflected fluctuations in the business cycle. Prosperity itself did not prompt turn-outs, but it evidently facilitated collective actions by women operatives.

In contrast to the protests of the previous decade, the struggles now were primarily political. Women did not turn-out in the 1840s; rather, they mounted annual petition campaigns calling on the State legislature to limit the hours of labor within the mills. These campaigns reached their height in 1845 and 1846, when 2,000 and 5,000 operatives respectively signed petitions. Unable to curb the wage cuts, or the speed-up and stretch-out imposed by mill owners, operatives sought to mitigate the consequences of these changes by reducing the length of the working day. Having been defeated earlier in economic struggles, they now sought to achieve their new goal through political action. The Ten Hour Movement, seen in these terms, was a logical outgrowth of the unsuccessful turn-outs of the previous decade. Like the earlier struggles, the Ten Hour Movement was an assertion of the dignity of operatives and an attempt to maintain that dignity under the changing conditions of industrial capitalism. . . .

The women's Ten Hour Movement, like the earlier turn-outs, was based in part on the participants' sense of their own worth and dignity. . . . At the same time, however, [it] also indicted the growth of a new consciousness. It reflected a mounting feeling of community among women operatives and a realization that their interests and those of their employers were not identical, that they had to rely on themselves and not on corporate benevolence to achieve a reduction in the hours of labor. One woman, in an open letter to a State legislator, expressed this rejection of middle-class paternalism: "Bad as is the condition of so many women, it would be much worse if they had nothing but your boasted protection to rely upon; but they have at least learnt the lesson which a bitter experience teaches, that not to those who style themselves their 'natural protectors' are they to look for the needful help, but to the strong and resolute of their own sex." Such an attitude, underlying the self-organization of women in the ten-hour petition campaigns, was clearly the product of the industrial experience in Lowell.

Both the early turn-outs and the Ten Hour Movement were in large measure dependent upon the existence of a close-knit community of women operatives. Such a community was based on the work structure, the nature of worker housing, and workforce homogeneity. Women were drawn together by the initial job training of newcomers; by the informal work sharing among experienced hands, by living in company boarding houses, by sharing religious, educational, and social activities in their leisure hours. Working and living in a new and alien setting, they came to rely upon one another for friendship and support. Understandably, a community feeling developed among them.

This evolving community as well as the common cultural traditions which Yankee women carried into Lowell were major elements that governed their response to changing mill conditions. The pre-industrial tradition of independence and self-respect made them particularly sensitive to management labor policies. The sense of community enabled them to transform their individual opposition to wage cuts and to the increasing pace of work into public protest. In these labor struggles women operatives expressed a new consciousness of their rights both as workers and as women. Such a consciousness, like the community of women itself, was one product of Lowell's industrial revolution.

The experiences of Lowell women before 1850 present a fascinating picture of the contradictory impact of industrial capitalism. Repeated labor protests reveal that female operatives felt the demands of mill employment to be oppressive. At the same time, however, the mills provided women with work outside of the home and family, thereby offering them an unprecedented point of entry into the public realm. That they came to challenge employer paternalism was a direct consequence of the increasing opportunities offered them in these years. The Lowell mills both exploited and liberated women in ways unknown to the pre-industrial political economy.

DOCUMENTS

Recollections of a Strike (1836), 1898

One of the first strikes of cotton-factory operatives that ever took place in this country was that in Lowell, in October 1836. When it was announced that the wages were to be cut down, great indignation was felt, and it was

SOURCE: Harriet Hanson Robinson, *Loom and Spindle or Life Among the Early Mill Girls* (New York: T. Y. Crowell, 1898), 51–53.

decided to strike, *en masse*. This was done. The mills were shut down, and the girls went in procession from their several corporations to the "grove" on Chapel Hill, and listened to "incendiary" speeches from early labor reformers.

One of the girls stood on a pump, and gave vent to the feelings of her companions in a neat speech, declaring that it was their duty to resist all attempts at cutting down the wages. This was the first time a woman had spoken in public in Lowell, and the event caused surprise and consternation among her audience.

Cutting down the wages was not their only grievance, nor the only cause of this strike. Hitherto the corporations had paid twenty-five cents a week towards the board of each operative, and now it was their purpose to have the girls pay the sum; and this, in addition to the cut in wages, would make a difference of at least one dollar a week. It was estimated that as many as twelve or fifteen hundred girls turned out, and walked in procession through the streets. They had neither flags nor music, but sang songs, a favorite (but rather inappropriate) one being a parody on "I won't be a nun."

> "Oh! isn't it a pity, such a pretty girl as I—
>   Should be sent to the factory to pine away and die?
> Oh! I cannot be a slave,
>   I will not be a slave,
> For I'm so fond of liberty
>   That I cannot be a slave."

My own recollection of this first strike (or "turn out" as it was called) is very vivid.* I worked in a lower room, where I had heard the proposed strike fully, if not vehemently, discussed; I had been an ardent listener to what was said against this attempt at "oppression" on the part of the corporation, and naturally I took sides with the strikers. When the day came on which the girls were to turn out, those in the upper rooms started first, and so many of them left that our mill was at once shut down. Then, when the girls in my room stood irresolute, uncertain what to do, asking each other, "Would you?" or "Shall we turn out?" and not one of them having the courage to lead off, I, who began to think they would not go out, after all their talk, became impatient, and started on ahead, saying, with childish bravado, "I don't care what you do, *I* am going to turn out, whether any one else does or not;" and I marched out, and was followed by the others.[1]

As I looked back at the long line that followed me, I was more proud than I have ever been since at any success I may have achieved, and more

---

*As the Dublin essay reveals, there actually was a brief earlier strike in 1834. (Eds.)
[1] I was then eleven years and eight months old. H.H.R.

proud than I shall ever be again until my own beloved State gives to its women citizens the right of suffrage.

The agent of the corporation where I then worked took some small revenges on the supposed ringleaders; on the principle of sending the weaker to the wall, my mother was turned away from her boarding-house, that functionary saying, "Mrs. Hanson, you could not prevent the older girls from turning out, but your daughter is a child, and *her* you could control."

"Regulations to Be Observed," Hamilton Manufacturing Company, 1848

Regulations to be observed by all persons employed in the factories of the Hamilton Manufacturing Company. The overseers are to be always in their rooms at the starting of the mill, and not absent unnecessarily during working hours. They are to see that all those employed in their rooms, are in their places in due season, and keep a correct account of their time and work. They may grant leave of absence to those employed under them, when they have spare hands to supply their places, and not otherwise, except in cases of absolute necessity.

All persons in the employ of the Hamilton Manufacturing Company, are to observe the regulations of the room where they are employed. They are not to be absent from their work without the consent of the overseer, except in cases of sickness, and then they are to send him word of the cause of their absence. They are to board in one of the houses of the company and give information at the counting room, where they board, when they begin, or, whenever they change their boarding place; and are to observe the regulations of their boarding-house.

Those intending to leave the employment of the company, are to give at least two weeks' notice thereof to their overseer.

All persons entering into the employment of the company, are considered as engaged for twelve months, and those who leave sooner, or do not comply with all these regulations, will not be entitled to a regular discharge.

The company will not employ any one who is habitually absent from public worship on the Sabbath, or known to be guilty of immorality.

A physician will attend once in every month at the counting-room, to vaccinate all who may need it, free of expense.

Any one who shall take from the mills or the yard, any yarn, cloth or other article belonging to the company, will be considered guilty of stealing and be liable to prosecution.

SOURCE: John R. Commons (ed.), *A Documentary History of American Industrial Society* 3 (Cleveland: The Arthur H. Clark Co., 1910): 135–136.

Payment will be made monthly, including board and wages. The accounts will be made up to the last Saturday but one in every month, and paid in the course of the following week.

These regulations are considered part of the contract, with which all persons entering into the employment of the Hamilton Manufacturing Company, engage to comply.

JOHN AVERY, AGENT.

A Mill Worker's Grievances, 1845

The first petitioner who testified was *Eliza R. Hemmingway*. She had worked 2 years and 9 months in the Lowell Factories, 2 years in the Middlesex, and 9 months in the Hamilton Corporations. Her employment is weaving,—works by the piece. The Hamilton Mill manufactures cotton fabrics. The Middlesex, woollen fabrics. She is now at work in the Middlesex Mills, and attends one loom. Her wages average from $16 to $23 a month exclusive of board. She complained of the hours for labor being too many, and the time for meals too limited. In the summer season, the work is commenced at 5 o'clock, A.M., and continued till 7 o'clock, P.M., with half an hour for breakfast and three quarters of an hour for dinner. During eight months of the year, but half an hour is allowed for dinner. The air in the room she considered not to be wholesome. There were 293 small lamps and 61 large lamps lighted in the room in which she worked, when evening work is required. These lamps are also lighted sometimes in the morning. —About 130 females, 11 men, and 12 children (between the ages of 11 and 14) work in the room with her. She thought the children enjoyed about as good health as children generally do. The children work but 9 months out of 12. The other 3 months they must attend school. Thinks that there is no day when there are less than six of the females out of the mill from sickness. Has known as many as thirty. She, herself, is out quite often, on account of sickness. There was more sickness in the Summer than in the Winter months: though in the Summer, lamps are not lighted.

SOURCE: Massachusetts House of Representatives, "Report on Hours of Labor, 1845," Doc. 50, in *Documents, 1845* (Boston, 1845), 2–3.

Chapter 9

The Cherokee Removal:
An American Tragedy

Most people are aware of the fate of Native Americans as white settlement pushed ever westward. However, one episode in the history of white–Indian relations is in many ways unique and constitutes one of our nation's darkest moments: the forcible removal and transport in 1838–1839 of thousands of Cherokees from their ancestral homeland in the Southern uplands.

Ironically, no other Indian nation had responded so fully to Thomas Jefferson's urgings that they abandon their nomadic ways and pattern their lifestyle after that of the whites. Jefferson had told Congress in 1803, "In leading them [the Indians] thus to agriculture, to manufactures, and civilizations; in bringing together their and our sentiments, and in preparing them ultimately to participate in the benefits of our Government, I trust and believe we are acting for their greatest good." In 1806 Jefferson congratulated the Cherokee chiefs on the progress they had made in farming: "Go on, my children, in the same way and be assured the further you advance in it the happier and more respectable you will be. . . ."

Dee Brown's essay "The Trail of Tears" graphically describes the Cherokees' progress toward "civilization," and the betrayal by both state and federal govern-

ments of the assurances and promises made to the Cherokee nation by Jefferson and other national leaders. The Cherokees were not the only Native Americans removed forcibly from their ancestral lands, yet the large measure of sympathy and support on their behalf was atypical. How do you account for the apparent contradiction between the strong contemporary sentiment against the removal of the Cherokees and the failure to prevent it?

The three documents following the essay provide eloquent examples of the arguments presented on both sides of the removal controversy. The first is from the "Memorial of the Cherokee Nation" (July 1830), which sets forth the Cherokee view of the removal proposed by President Andrew Jackson. The second is from President Jackson's Second Annual Message to Congress (December 6, 1830). Contrast these two descriptions of the life awaiting the Indians in the new western territory. Whose argument do you find more convincing? How did Jackson respond to those who objected to white encroachment on Indian land?

The task of implementing Jackson's program to remove the Cherokees fell on his successor, President Martin Van Buren. The final document is a letter to Van Buren from Ralph Waldo Emerson, who rarely spoke out on political matters. The letter presents the legal and moral arguments against removal and reveals the mood of those opposed to that policy.

ESSAY
—— •◆• ——

The Trail of Tears

Dee Brown

In the spring of 1838, Brigadier General Winfield Scott with a regiment of artillery, a regiment of infantry, and six companies of dragoons marched unopposed into the Cherokee country of northern Georgia. On May 10 at New Echota, the capital of what had been one of the greatest Indian nations in eastern America, Scott issued a proclamation:

> The President of the United States sent me with a powerful army to cause you, in obedience to the treaty of 1835, to join that part of your people who are already established in prosperity on the other side of the Mississippi. . . . The emigration must be commenced in haste. . . . The full moon of May is already on the wane, and before another shall have passed away every Cherokee man, woman and child . . . must be in motion to join their brethren in the West. . . . My troops already occupy many positions . . . and thousands and

SOURCE: Dee Brown, "The Trail of Tears," *American History Illustrated*, 7 (June 1972): 30–39. Reprinted through the courtesy of Cowles Magazines, publisher of *American History Illustrated*.

thousands are approaching from every quarter to render resistance and escape alike hopeless. . . . Will you then by resistance compel us to resort to arms? Or will you by flight seek to hide yourselves in mountains and forests and thus oblige us to hunt you down? Remember that in pursuit it may be impossible to avoid conflicts. The blood of the white man or the blood of the red man may be spilt, and if spilt, however accidentally, it may be impossible for the discreet and humane among you, or among us, to prevent a general war and carnage.

For more than a century the Cherokees had been ceding their land, thousands of acres by thousands of acres. They had lost all of Kentucky and much of Tennessee, but after the last treaty of 1819 they still had remaining about 35,000 square miles of forested mountains, clean, swift-running rivers, and fine meadows. In this country which lay across parts of Georgia, North Carolina, and Tennessee, they cultivated fields, planted orchards, fenced pastures, and built roads, houses, and towns. Sequoya had invented a syllabary for the Cherokee language so that thousands of his tribesmen quickly learned to read and write. The Cherokees had adopted the white man's way—his clothing, his constitutional form of government, even his religion. But it had all been for nothing. Now these men who had come across the great ocean many years ago wanted all of the Cherokees' land. In exchange for their 35,000 square miles, the tribe was to receive five million dollars and another tract of land somewhere in the wilderness beyond the Mississippi River.

This was a crushing blow to a proud people. "They are extremely proud, despising the lower class of Europeans," said Henry Timberlake, who visited them before the Revolutionary War. William Bartram, the botanist, said the Cherokees were not only a handsome people, tall, graceful, and olive-skinned, but "their countenance and actions exhibit an air of magnanimity, superiority and independence."

Ever since the signing of the treaties of 1819, Major General Andrew Jackson, a man they once believed to be their friend, had been urging Cherokees to move beyond the Mississippi. Indians and white settlers, Jackson told them, could never get along together. Even if the government wanted to protect the Cherokees from harassment, he added, it would be unable to do so. "If you cannot protect us in Georgia," a chief retorted, "how can you protect us from similar evils in the West?"

During that period of polite urging, a few hundred Cherokee families did move west, but the tribe remained united and refused to give up any more territory. In fact, the council leaders passed a law forbidding any chief to sell or trade a single acre of Cherokee land on penalty of death.

In 1828, when Andrew Jackson was running for President, he knew that in order to win he must sweep the frontier states. Free land for the land-hungry settlers became Jackson's major policy. He hammered away at this theme especially hard in Georgia, where waves of settlers from the coastal lowlands were pushing into the highly desirable Cherokee country. He promised the Georgians that if they would help elect him President, he would lend his support to opening up the Cherokee lands for settlement. The Cherokees, of course, were not citizens and could not vote in opposition. To the Cherokees and their friends who protested this promise, Jackson justified his position by saying that the Cherokees had fought on the side of the British during the Revolutionary War. He conveniently forgot that the Cherokees had been his allies during the desperate War of 1812, and had saved the day for him in his decisive victory over the British-backed Creeks at Horseshoe Bend. (One of the Cherokee chiefs who aided Jackson was Junaluska. Said he afterward: "If I had known that Jackson would drive us from our homes I would have killed him that day at the Horseshoe.")

Three weeks after Jackson was elected President, the Georgia legislature passed a law annexing all the Cherokee country within that state's borders. As most of the Cherokee land was in Georgia and three-fourths of the tribe lived there, this meant an end to their independence as a nation. The Georgia legislature also abolished all Cherokee laws and customs and sent surveyors to map out land lots of 160 acres each. The 160-acre lots were to be distributed to white citizens of Georgia through public lotteries.

To add to the pressures on the Cherokees, gold was discovered near Dahlonega in the heart of their country. For many years the Cherokees had concealed the gold deposits, but now the secret was out and a rabble of gold-hungry prospectors descended upon them.

John Ross, the Cherokees' leader, hurried to Washington to protest the Georgia legislature's actions and to plead for justice. In that year Ross was 38 years old; he was well-educated and had been active in Cherokee government matters since he was 19. He was adjutant of the Cherokee regiment that served with Jackson at Horseshoe Bend. His father had been one of a group of Scottish emigrants who settled near the Cherokees and married into the tribe.

In Washington, Ross found sympathizers in Congress, but most of them were anti-Jackson men and the Cherokee case was thus drawn into the whirlpool of politics. When Ross called upon Andrew Jackson to request his aid, the President bluntly told him that "no protection could be afforded the Cherokees" unless they were willing to move west of the Mississippi.

While Ross was vainly seeking help in Washington, alarming messages reached him from Georgia. White citizens of that state were claiming the homes of Cherokees through the land lottery, seizing some of them by force. Joseph Vann, a hard-working half-breed, had carved out an 800-acre plantation at Spring Place and built a fine brick house for his residence. Two men arrived to claim it, dueled for it, and the winner drove Vann and his family into the hills. When John Ross rushed home he found that the same thing had happened to his family. A lottery claimant was living in his beautiful home on the Coosa River, and Ross had to turn north toward Tennessee to find his fleeing wife and children.

During all this turmoil, President Jackson and the governor of Georgia pressed the Cherokee leaders hard in attempts to persuade them to cede all their territory and move to the West. But the chiefs stood firm. Somehow they managed to hold the tribe together, and helped dispossessed families find new homes back in the wilderness areas. John Ross and his family lived in a one-room log cabin across the Tennessee line.

In 1834, the chiefs appealed to Congress with a memorial in which they stated that they would never voluntarily abandon their homeland, but proposed a compromise in which they agreed to cede the state of Georgia a part of their territory provided that they would be protected from invasion in the remainder. Furthermore, at the end of a definite period of years to be fixed by the United States, they would be willing to become citizens of the various states in which they resided.

"Cupidity has fastened its eye upon our lands and our homes," they said, "and is seeking by force and by every variety of oppression and wrong to expel us from our lands and our homes and to tear from us all that has become endeared to us. In our distress we have appealed to the judiciary of the United States, where our rights have been solemnly established. We have appealed to the Executive of the United States to protect those rights according to the obligation of treaties and the injunctions of the laws. But this appeal to the Executive has been made in vain."

This new petition to Congress was no more effectual than their appeals to President Jackson. Again they were told that their difficulties could be remedied only by their removal to the west of the Mississippi.

For the first time now, a serious split occurred among the Cherokees. A small group of subchiefs decided that further resistance to the demands of the Georgia and United States governments was futile. It would be better, they believed, to exchange their land and go west rather than risk bloodshed and the possible loss of everything. Leaders of this group were Major Ridge and Elias Boudinot. Ridge had adopted his first name after Andrew Jackson gave him that rank during the War of 1812. Boudinot was Ridge's nephew. Originally known as Buck Watie, he had taken the name of a New England philanthropist who sent him through a mission school in Connecticut. Stand Watie, who later became a Confederate general, was his brother. Upon Boudinot's return from school to Georgia, he founded the first tribal newspaper, the *Cherokee Phoenix,* in 1827, but during the turbulence following the Georgia land lotteries he was forced to suspend publication.

And so in February 1835 when John Ross journeyed to Washington to resume his campaign to save the Cherokee nation, a rival delegation headed by Ridge and Boudinot arrived there to seek terms for removal to the West. The pro-removal forces in the government leaped at this opportunity to by-pass Ross's authority, and within a few days drafted a preliminary treaty for the Ridge delegation. It was then announced that a council would be held later in the year at New Echota, Georgia, for the purpose of negotiating and agreeing upon final terms.

During the months that followed, bitterness increased between the two Cherokee factions. Ridge's group was a very small minority, but they had the full weight of the United Sates Government behind them, and threats and inducements were used to force a full attendance at the council which was set for December 22, 1835. Handbills were printed in Cherokee and distributed throughout the nation, informing the Indians that those who did not attend would be counted as assenting to any treaty that might be made.

During the seven days which followed the opening of the treaty council, fewer than five hundred Cherokees, or about 2 percent of the tribe, came to New Echota to participate in the discussions. Most of the other Cherokees were busy endorsing a petition to be sent to Congress stating their opposition to the treaty. But on December 29, Ridge, Boudinot and their followers signed away all the lands of the great Cherokee nation. Ironically, thirty years earlier Major Ridge had personally executed a Cherokee chief named Doublehead for committing one of the few capital crimes of the tribe. That crime was the signing of a treaty which gave away Cherokee lands.

Charges of bribery by the Ross forces were denied by government officials, but some years afterward it was discovered that the Secretary of War had sent secret agents into the Cherokee country with authority to expend money to bribe chiefs to support the treaty of cession and removal. And certainly the treaty signers were handsomely rewarded. In an era when a dollar would buy many times its worth today, Major Ridge was paid $30,000 and his followers received several thousand dollars each. Ostensibly they were being paid for their improved farmlands, but the amounts were far in excess of contemporary land values.

John Ross meanwhile completed gathering signatures of Cherokees who were opposed to the treaty. Early in the following spring, 1836, he took the petition to Washington. More than three-fourths of the tribe, 15,964, had signed in protest against the treaty.

When the governor of Georgia was informed of the overwhelming vote against the treaty, he replied: "Nineteen-twentieths of the Cherokees are too ignorant and depraved to entitle their opinions to any weight or consideration in such matters."

The Cherokees, however, did have friends in Congress. Representative Davy Crockett of Tennessee denounced the treatment of the Cherokees as unjust, dishonest, and cruel. He admitted that he represented a body of frontier constituents who would like to have the Cherokee lands opened for settlement, and he doubted if a single one of them would second what he was saying. Even though his support of the Cherokees might remove him from public life, he added, he could not do otherwise except at the expense of his honor and conscience. Daniel Webster, Henry Clay, Edward Everett, and other great orators of the Congress also spoke for the Cherokees.

When the treaty came to a final decision in the Senate, it passed by only one vote. On May 23, 1836, President Jackson signed the document. According to its terms, the Cherokees were allowed two years from that day in which to leave their homeland forever.

The few Cherokees who had favored the treaty now began making their final preparations for departure. About three hundred left during that year and then early in 1837 Major Ridge and 465 followers departed by boats for the new land in the West. About 17,000 others, ignoring the treaty, remained steadfast in their homeland with John Ross.

For a while it seemed that Ross might win his long fight, that perhaps the treaty might be declared void. After the Secretary of War, acting under instructions from President Jackson, sent Major William M. Davis to the Cherokee country to expedite removal to the West, Davis submitted a frank report: "That paper called a treaty is no treaty at all," he wrote, "because it is not sanctioned by the great body of the Cherokees and was made without their participation or assent. . . . The Cherokees are a peaceable, harmless people, but you may drive them to desperation, and this treaty cannot be carried into effect except by the strong arm of force."

In September 1836, Brigadier General Dunlap, who had been sent with a brigade of Tennessee volunteers to force the removal, indignantly disbanded his troops after making a strong speech in favor of the Indians: "I would never dishonor the Tennessee arms in a servile service by aiding to carry into execution at the point of the bayonet a treaty made by a lean minority against the will and authority of the Cherokee people."

Even Inspector General John E. Wool, commanding United States troops in the area, was impressed by the united Cherokee resistance, and warned the Secretary of War not to send any civilians who had any part in the making of the treaty back into the Cherokee country. During the summer of 1837, the Secretary of War sent a confidential agent, John Mason, Jr., to observe and report. "Opposition to the treaty is unanimous and irreconcilable," Mason wrote. "They say it cannot bind them because they did not make it; that it was made by a few unauthorized individuals; that the nation is not party to it."

The inexorable machinery of government was already in motion, however, and when the expiration date of the waiting period, May 23, 1838, came near, Winfield Scott was ordered in with his army to force compliance. As already stated, Scott issued his proclamation on May 10. His soldiers were already building thirteen stockaded forts—six in North Carolina, five in Georgia, one in Tennessee, and one in Alabama. At these points the Cherokees would be concentrated to await transportation to the West. Scott then ordered the roundup started, instructing his officers not to fire on the Cherokees except in case of resistance. "If we get possession of the women and children first," he said, "or first capture the men, the other members of the same family will readily come in."

James Mooney, an ethnologist who afterwards talked with Cherokees who endured this ordeal, said that squads of troops moved into the forested mountains to search out every small cabin and make prisoners of all the occupants however or wherever they might be found. "Families at dinner were startled by the sudden gleam of bayonets in the doorway and rose up to be driven with blows and oaths along the weary miles of trail that led to the stockades. Men were seized in their fields or going along the road, women were taken from their spinning wheels and children from their play. In many cases, on turning for one last look as they crossed a ridge, they saw their homes in flames, fired by the lawless rabble that followed on the heels of the soldiers to loot and pillage. So keen were these outlaws on the scent that in some instances they were driving off the cattle and other stock of the Indians almost before the soldiers had fairly started their owners in the other direction."

Long afterward one of the Georgia militiamen who participated in the roundup said: "I fought through the Civil War and have seen men shot to pieces and slaughtered by thousands, but the Cherokee removal was the cruelest work I ever knew."

Knowing that resistance was futile, most of the Cherokees surrendered quietly. Within a month, thousands were enclosed in the stockades. On June 6 at Ross's Landing near the site of present-day Chattanooga, the first of many departures began. Eight hundred Cherokees were forcibly crowded onto a flotilla of six flatboats lashed to the side of a steamboat. After surviving a passage over rough rapids which smashed the sides of the flatboats, they landed at Decatur, Alabama, boarded a railroad train (which was a new and terrifying experience for most of them), and after reaching Tuscumbia were crowded upon a Tennessee River steamboat again.

Throughout June and July similar shipments of several hundred Cherokees were transported by this long water route—north on the Tennessee River to the Ohio and then down the Mississippi and up the Arkansas to their new homeland. A few managed to escape and make their way back to the Cherokee country, but most of them were eventually recaptured. Along the route of travel of this forced migration, the summer was hot and dry. Drinking water and food were often contaminated. First the young children would die, then the older people, and sometimes as many as half the adults were stricken with dysentery and other ailments. On each boat deaths ran as high as five per day. On one of the first boats to reach Little Rock, Arkansas, at least a hundred had died. A compassionate lieutenant who was with the military escort recorded in his diary for August 1: "My blood chills as I write at the remembrance of the scenes I have gone through."

When John Ross and other Cherokee leaders back in the concentration camps learned of the high mortality among those who had gone ahead, they petitioned General Scott to postpone further departures until autumn. Although only three thousand Cherokees had been removed, Scott agreed to wait until the summer drought was broken, or no later than October. The Cherokees in turn agreed to organize and manage the migration themselves. After a lengthy council, they asked and received permission to travel overland in wagons, hoping that by camping along the way they would not suffer as many deaths as occurred among those who had gone on the river boats.

During this waiting period, Scott's soldiers continued their searches for more than a thousand Cherokees known to be still hiding out in the deep wildernesses of the Great Smoky Mountains. These Cherokees had organized themselves under the leadership of a chief named Utsala, and had developed warning systems to prevent captures by the bands of soldiers. Occasionally, however, some of the fugitives were caught and herded back to the nearest stockade.

One of the fugitive families was that of Tsali, an aging Cherokee. With his wife, his brother, three sons and their families, Tsali had built a hideout somewhere on the border between North Carolina and Tennessee. Soldiers surrounded their shelters one day, and the Cherokees surrendered without resistance. As they were being taken back toward Fort Cass (Calhoun, Tennessee), a soldier prodded Tsali's wife sharply with a bayonet, ordering her to walk faster. Angered by the brutality, Tsali grappled with the soldier, tore away his rifle, and bayoneted him to the ground. At the same time, Tsali's brother leaped upon another soldier and bayoneted him. Before the remainder of the military detachment could act, the Cherokees fled, vanishing back into the Smokies where they sought refuge with Chief Utsala. Both bayoneted soldiers died.

Upon learning of the incident, Scott immediately ordered that Tsali must be brought in and punished. Because some of his regiments were being transferred elsewhere for other duties, however, the general realized that his reduced force might be occupied for months in hunting down and capturing the escaped Cherokee. He would have to use guile to accomplish the capture of Tsali.

Scott therefore dispatched a messenger—a white man who had been adopted as a child by the Cherokees—to find Chief Utsala. The messenger was instructed to inform Utsala that if he would surrender Tsali to General Scott, the Army would withdraw from the Smokies and leave the remaining fugitives alone.

When Chief Utsala received the message, he was suspicious of Scott's sincerity, but he considered the general's offer as an opportunity to gain time. Perhaps with the passage of time, the few Cherokees remaining in the Smokies might be forgotten and left alone forever. Utsala put the proposition to Tsali: If he went in and surrendered, he would probably be put to death, but his death might insure the freedom of a thousand fugitive Cherokees.

Tsali did not hesitate. He announced that he would go and surrender to General Scott. To make certain that he was treated well, several members of Tsali's band went with him.

When the Cherokees reached Scott's headquarters, the general ordered Tsali, his brother, and three sons arrested, and then condemned them all to be shot to death. To impress upon the tribe their utter helplessness before the might of the government, Scott selected the firing squad from Cherokee prisoners in one of the stockades. At the last moment, the general spared Tsali's youngest son because he was only a child.

(By this sacrifice, however, Tsali and his family gave the Smoky Mountain Cherokees a chance at survival in their homeland. Time was on their side, as Chief Utsala had hoped, and that is why today there is a small Cherokee reservation on the North Carolina slope of the Great Smoky Mountains.)

With the ending of the drought of 1838, John Ross and the 13,000 stockaded Cherokees began preparing for their long overland journey to the West. They assembled several hundred wagons, filled them with blankets, cooking pots, their old people and small children, and moved out in separate contingents along a trail that followed the Hiwassee River. The first party of 1,103 started on October 1.

"At noon all was in readiness for moving," said an observer of the departure. "The teams were stretched out in a line along the road through a heavy forest, groups of persons formed about each wagon. The day was bright and beautiful, but a gloomy thoughtfulness was depicted in the lineaments of every face. In all the bustle of preparation there was a silence and stillness of the voice that betrayed the sadness of the heart. At length the word was given to move on. Going Snake, an aged and respected chief whose head eighty summers had whitened, mounted on his favorite pony and led the way in silence, followed by a number of younger men on horseback. At this very moment a low sound of distant thunder fell upon my ear . . . a voice of divine indignation for the wrong of my poor and unhappy countrymen, driven by brutal power from all they loved and cherished in the land of their fathers to gratify the cravings of avarice. The sun was unclouded—no rain fell—the thunder rolled away and seemed hushed in the distance."

Throughout October, eleven wagon trains departed and then on November 4, the last Cherokee exiles moved out for the West. The overland route for these endless lines of wagons, horsemen, and people on foot ran from the mouth of the Hiwassee in Tennessee across the Cumberland plateau to McMinnville and then north to Nashville where they crossed the Cumberland River. From there they followed an old trail to Hopkinsville, Kentucky, and continued northwestward to the Ohio River, crossing into southern Illinois near the mouth of the Cumberland. Moving straight westward they passed through Jonesboro and crossed the Mississippi at Cape Girardeau, Missouri. Some of the first parties turned southward through Arkansas; the later ones continued westward through Springfield, Missouri, and on to Indian Territory.

A New Englander traveling eastward across Kentucky in November and December met several contingents, each a day apart from the others. "Many of the aged Indians were suffering extremely from the fatigue of the journey," he said, "and several were quite ill. Even aged females, apparently nearly ready to drop into the grave, were traveling with heavy burdens attached to their backs—on the sometimes frozen ground, and sometimes muddy streets, with no covering for the feet except what nature had given them. . . . We learned from the inhabitants on the road where the Indians passed, that they buried fourteen or fifteen at every stopping place, and they make a journey of ten miles per day only on an average. They will not travel on the Sabbath . . . they must stop, and not merely stop—they must worship the Great Spirit, too; for they had divine service on the Sabbath—a camp meeting in truth."

Autumn rains softened the roads, and the hundreds of wagons and horses cut them into morasses, slowing movement to a crawl. To add to their difficulties, tollgate operators overcharged them for passage. Their horses were stolen or seized on pretext of unpaid debts, and they had no recourse to the law. With the coming of cold damp weather, measles and whooping cough became epidemic. Supplies had to be dumped to make room for the sick in the jolting wagons.

By the time the last detachments reached the Mississippi at Cape Girardeau it was January, with the river running full of ice so that several thousand had to wait on the east bank almost a month before the channel cleared. James Mooney, who later heard the story from survivors, said that "the lapse of over half of century had not sufficed to wipe out the memory of the miseries of that halt beside the frozen river, with hundreds of sick and

160

dying penned up in wagons or stretched upon the ground, with only a blanket overhead to keep out the January blast."

Meanwhile the parties that left early in October were beginning to reach Indian Territory. (The first arrived on January 4, 1839). Each group had lost from thirty to forty members by death. The later detachments suffered much heavier losses, especially toward the end of their journey. Among the victims was the wife of John Ross.

Not until March 1839 did the last of the Cherokees reach their new home in the West. Counts were made of the survivors and balanced against the counts made at the beginning of the removal. As well as could be estimated, the Cherokees had lost about four thousand by deaths—or one out of every four members of the tribe—most of the deaths brought about as the direct result of the enforced removal. From that day to this the Cherokees remember it as "the trail where they cried," or the Trail of Tears.

DOCUMENTS

Memorial of the Cherokee Nation, 1830

We are aware, that some persons suppose it will be for our advantage to remove beyond the Mississippi. We think otherwise. Our people universally think otherwise. Thinking that it would be fatal to their interests, they have almost to a man sent their memorial to congress, deprecating the necessity of a removal. This question was distinctly before their minds when they signed their memorial. Not an adult person can be found, who has not an opinion on the subject, and if the people were to understand distinctly, that they could be protected against the laws of the neighboring states, there is probably not an adult person in the nation, who would think it best to remove; though possibly a few might emigrate individually. There are doubtless many, who would flee to an unknown country, however beset with dangers, privations and sufferings, rather than be sentenced to spend six years in a Georgia prison for advising one of their neighbors not to betray his country. And there are others who could not think of living as outlaws in their native land, exposed to numberless vexations, and excluded from being parties or witnesses in a court of justice. It is incredible that Georgia should ever have enacted the oppressive laws to which reference is here made, unless she had supposed that something extremely terrific in its character was necessary in order to make the Cherokees willing to remove. We are not willing to remove; and if we could be brought to this extremity, it

SOURCE: *Nile's Weekly Register*, 38 (August 21, 1830): 454–457.

would be not by argument, not because our judgment was satisfied, not because our condition will be improved; but only because we cannot endure to be deprived of our national and individual rights and subjected to a process of intolerable oppression.

We wish to remain on the land of our fathers. We have a perfect and original right to remain without interruption or molestation. The treaties with us, and laws of the United States made in pursuance of treaties, guaranty our residence and our privileges, and secure us against intruders. Our only request is, that these treaties may be fulfilled, and these laws executed.

But if we are compelled to leave our country, we see nothing but ruin before us. The country west of the Arkansas territory is unknown to us. From what we can learn of it, we have no prepossessions in its favor. All the inviting parts of it, as we believe, are preoccupied by various Indian nations, to which it has been assigned. They would regard us as intruders, and look upon us with an evil eye. The far greater part of that region is, beyond all controversy, badly supplied with wood and water; and no Indian tribe can live as agriculturists without these articles. All our neighbors, in case of our removal, though crowded into our near vicinity, would speak a language totally different from ours, and practice different customs. The original possessors of that region are now wandering savages lurking for prey in the neighborhood. They have always been at war, and would be easily tempted to turn their arms against peaceful emigrants. Were the country to which we are urged much better than it is represented to be, and were it free from the objections which we have made to it, still it is not the land of our birth, nor of our affections. It contains neither the scenes of our childhood, nor the graves of our fathers.

The removal of families to a new country, even under the most favorable auspices, and when the spirits are sustained by pleasing visions of the future, is attended with much depression of mind and sinking of heart. This is the case, when the removal is a matter of decided preference, and when the persons concerned are in early youth or vigorous manhood. Judge, then, what must be the circumstances of a removal, when a whole community, embracing persons of all classes and every description, from the infant to the man of extreme old age, the sick, the blind, the lame, the improvident, the reckless, the desperate, as well as the prudent, the considerate, the industrious, are compelled to remove by odious and intolerable vexations and persecutions, brought upon them in the forms of law, when all will agree only in this, that they have been cruelly robbed of their country, in violation of the most solemn compacts, which it is possible for communities to form with each other; and that, if they should make themselves comfortable in their new residence, they have nothing to expect hereafter but to be the victims of a future legalized robbery!

Such we deem, and are absolutely certain, will be the feelings of the whole Cherokee people, if they are forcibly compelled, by the laws of Georgia, to remove; and with these feelings, how is it possible that we should pursue our present course of improvement, or avoid sinking into utter despondency? We have been called a poor, ignorant, and degraded people. We certainly are not rich; nor have we ever boasted of our knowledge, or our moral or intellectual elevation. But there is not a man within our limits so ignorant as not to know that he has a right to live on the land of his fathers, in the possession of his immemorial privileges, and that this right has been acknowledged and guaranteed by the United States; nor is there a man so degraded as not to feel a keen sense of injury, on being deprived of this right and driven into exile. . . .

Removal Defended, 1830

It gives me pleasure to announce to Congress that the benevolent policy of the Government, steadily pursued for nearly thirty years, in relation to the removal of the Indians beyond the white settlements is approaching to a happy consummation. Two important tribes [the Choctaws and the Chickasaws] have accepted the provision made for their removal at the last session of Congress, and it is believed that their example will induce the remaining tribes also to seek the same obvious advantages.

The consequences of a speedy removal will be important to the United States, to individual States, and to the Indians themselves. The pecuniary advantages which it promises to the Government are the least of its recommendations. It puts an end to all possible danger of collision between the authorities of the General and State Governments on account of the Indians. It will place a dense and civilized population in large tracts of country now occupied by a few savage hunters. By opening the whole territory between Tennessee on the north and Louisiana on the south to the settlement of the whites, it will incalculably strengthen the southwestern frontier and render the adjacent States strong enough to repel future invasions without remote aid. It will relieve the whole State of Mississippi and the western part of Alabama of Indian occupancy, and enable those States to advance rapidly in population, wealth, and power. It will separate the Indians from immediate contact with settlements of whites; free them from the power of the States; enable them to pursue happiness in their own way and under their own rude institutions; will retard the progress of decay, which is lessening their numbers, and perhaps cause them gradually, under the protection of the Government and through the influence of good counsels, to cast off their savage habits and become an interesting, civilized, and Christian

SOURCE: Andrew Jackson, "Second Annual Message to Congress" (December 6, 1830), in J. D. Richardson, ed., *A Compilation of the Messages and Papers of the Presidents*, 2 (Washington, D.C.: Government Printing Office, 1896): 519–522.

community. These consequences, some of them so certain and the rest so probable, make the complete execution of the plan sanctioned by Congress at their last session an object of much solicitude.

Toward the aborigines of the country no one can indulge a more friendly feeling than myself, or would go further in attempting to reclaim them from their wandering habits and make them a happy, prosperous people. I have endeavored to impress upon them my own solemn convictions of the duties and powers of the General Government in relation to the State authorities. For the justice of the laws passed by the States within the scope of their reserved powers, they are not responsible to this Government. As individuals we may entertain and express our opinions of their acts, but as a Government we have as little right to control them as we have to prescribe laws for other nations.

With a full understanding of the subject, the Choctaw and the Chickasaw tribes have with great unanimity determined to avail themselves of the liberal offers presented by the act of Congress, and have agreed to remove beyond the Mississippi River. Treaties have been made with them, which in due season will be submitted for consideration. In negotiating these treaties they were made to understand their true condition, and they have preferred maintaining their independence in the Western forests to submitting to the laws of the States in which they now reside. These treaties, being probably the last which will ever be made with them, are characterized by great liberality on the part of the Government. They give the Indians a liberal sum in consideration of their removal, and comfortable subsistence on their arrival at their new homes. If it be their real interest to maintain a separate existence, they will there be at liberty to do so without the inconveniences and vexations to which they would unavoidably have been subject in Alabama and Mississippi.

Humanity has often wept over the fate of the aborigines of this country, and Philanthropy has been long busily employed in devising means to avert it, but its progress has never for a moment been arrested, and one by one have many powerful tribes disappeared from the earth. To follow to the tomb the last of his race and to tread on the graves of extinct nations excite melancholy reflections. But true Philanthropy reconciles the mind to these vicissitudes as it does to the extinction of one generation to make room for another. In the monuments and fortresses of an unknown people, spread over the extensive regions of the West, we behold the memorials of a once powerful race, which was exterminated or has disappeared to make room for the existing savage tribes. Nor is there anything in this which, upon a comprehensive view of the general interests of the human race, is to be regretted. Philanthropy could not wish to see this continent restored to the condition in which it was found by our forefathers. What good man would prefer a country covered with forests and ranged by a few thousand savages to our extensive Republic, studded with cities, towns, and prosperous farms, embellished with all the improvements which art can devise or industry execute, occupied by more than 12,000,000 happy people, and filled with all the blessings of liberty, civilization, and religion?

The present policy of the Government is but a continuation of the same progressive change by a milder process. The tribes which occupied the countries now constituting the Eastern States were annihilated or have melted away to make room for the whites. The waves of population and civilization are rolling to the westward, and we now propose to acquire the countries occupied by the red men of the South and West by a fair exchange, and, at the expense of the United States, to send them to a land where their existence may be prolonged and perhaps made perpetual. Doubtless it will be painful to leave the graves of their fathers; but what do they more than our ancestors did or than our children are now doing? To better their condition in an unknown land our forefathers left all that was dear in earthly objects. Our children by thousands yearly leave the land of their birth to seek new homes in distant regions. Does Humanity weep at these painful separations from everything, animate and inanimate, with which the young heart has become entwined? Far from it. It is rather a source of joy that our country affords scope where our young population may range unconstrained in body or in mind, developing the power and faculties of man in their highest perfection. These remove hundreds and almost thousands of miles at their own expense, purchase the lands they occupy, and support themselves at their new homes from the moment of their arrival. Can it be cruel in this Government when, by events which it can not control, the Indian is made discontented in his ancient home to purchase his lands, to give him a new and extensive territory, to pay the expense of his removal, and support him a year in his new abode? How many thousands of our own people would gladly embrace the opportunity of removing to the West on such conditions! If the offers made to the Indians were extended to them, they would be hailed with gratitude and joy.

And is it supposed that the wandering savage has a stronger attachment to his home than the settled, civilized Christian? Is it more afflicting to him to leave the graves of his fathers than it is to our brothers and children? Rightly considered, the policy of the General Government toward the red man is not only liberal, but generous. He is unwilling to submit to the laws of the States and mingle with their population. To save him from this alternative, or perhaps utter annihilation, the General Government kindly offers him a new home, and proposes to pay the whole expense of his removal and settlement.

In the consummation of a policy originating at an early period, and steadily pursued by every Administration within the present century—so just to the States and so generous to the Indians—the Executive feels it has a right to expect the cooperation of Congress and of all good and disinterested men. . . .

The "Crime" of Removal, 1838

Sir, [President Van Buren] my communication respects the sinister rumors that fill this part of the country [New England] concerning the Cherokee people. The interest always felt in the aboriginal population—an interest naturally growing as that decays—has been heightened in regard to this tribe. Even in our distant State [Massachusetts] some good rumor of their worth and civility has arrived. We have learned with joy their improvement in the social arts. We have read their newspapers. We have seen some of them in our schools and colleges. In common with the great body of the American people, we have witnessed with sympathy the painful labors of these red men to redeem their own race from the doom of eternal inferiority, and to borrow and domesticate in the tribe the arts and customs of the Caucasian race. And notwithstanding the unaccountable apathy with which of late years the Indians have been sometimes abandoned to their enemies, it is not to be doubted that it is the good pleasure and the understanding of all humane persons in the Republic, of the men and the matrons sitting in the thriving independent families all over the land, that they shall be duly cared for; that they shall taste justice and love from all to whom we have delegated the office of dealing with them.

The newspapers now inform us that, in December, 1835, a treaty contracting for the exchange of all the Cherokee territory was pretended to be made by an agent on the part of the United States with some persons appearing on the part of the Cherokees; that the fact afterwards transpired that these deputies did by no means represent the will of the nation; and that, out of eighteen thousand souls composing the nation, fifteen thousand six hundred and sixty-eight have protested against the so-called treaty. It now appears that the government of the United States choose to hold the Cherokees to this sham treaty, and are proceeding to execute the same. Almost the entire Cherokee Nation stand up and say, "This is not our act. Behold us. Here are we. Do not mistake that handful of deserters for us"; and the American President and the Cabinet, the Senate and the House of Representatives, neither hear these men nor see them, and are contracting to put this active nation into carts and boats, and to drag them over mountains and rivers to a wilderness at a vast distance beyond the Mississippi. And a paper purporting to be an army order fixes a month from this day as the hour for this doleful removal.

In the name of God, sir, we ask you if this be so. Do the newspapers rightly inform us? Men and women with pale and perplexed faces meet one another in the streets and churches here, and ask if this be so. We have inquired if this be a gross misrepresentation from the party opposed to the

SOURCE: Ralph Waldo Emerson, "Letter to President Van Buren," in Ralph Waldo Emerson, *Complete Works* 11 (Boston: Houghton Mifflin, 1903–1904): 89–96.

government and anxious to blacken it with the people. We have looked at the newspapers of different parties and find a horrid confirmation of the tale. We are slow to believe it. We hoped the Indians were misinformed, and that their remonstrance was premature, and will turn out to be a needless act of terror.

The piety, the principle that is left in the United States, if only in its coarsest form, a regard to the speech of men, forbid us to entertain it as a fact. Such a dereliction of all faith and virtue, such a denial of justice, and such deafness to screams for mercy were never heard of in times of peace and in the dealing of a nation with its own allies and wards, since the earth was made. Sir, does this government think that the people of the United States are become savage and mad? From their mind are the sentiments of love and a good nature wiped clean out? The soul of man, the justice, the mercy that is the heart's heart in all men, from Maine to Georgia, does abhor this business.

In speaking thus the sentiments of my neighbors and my own, perhaps I overstep the bounds of decorum. But would it not be a higher indecorum coldly to argue a matter like this? We only state the fact that a crime is projected that confounds our understandings by its magnitude, a crime that really deprives us as well as the Cherokees of a country for how could we call the conspiracy that should crush these poor Indians our government, or the land that was cursed by their parting and dying imprecations our country, any more? You, sir, will bring down that renowned chair in which you sit into infamy if your seal is set to this instrument of perfidy; and the name of this nation, hitherto the sweet omen of religion and liberty, will stink to the world.

You will not do us the injustice of connecting this remonstrance with any sectional and party feeling. It is in our hearts the simplest commandment of brotherly love. We will not have this great and solemn claim upon national and human justice huddled aside under the flimsy plea of its being a party act. Sir, to us the questions upon which the government and the people have been agitated during the past year, touching the prostration of the currency and of trade, seem but motes in comparison. These hard times, it is true, have brought the discussion home to every farmhouse and poor man's house in this town; but it is the chirping of grasshoppers beside the immortal question whether justice shall be done by the race of civilized to the race of savage man, whether all the attributes of reason, of civility, of justice, and even of mercy, shall be put off by the American people, and so vast an outrage upon the Cherokee Nation and upon human nature shall be consummated.

One circumstance lessens the reluctance with which I intrude at this time on your attention, my conviction that the government ought to be admonished of a new historical fact, which the discussion of this question has disclosed, namely, that there exists in a great part of the Northern people a gloomy diffidence in the *moral* character of the government.

On the broaching of this question, a general expression of despondency, of disbelief that any good will accrue from a remonstrance on an act of fraud and robbery, appeared in those men to whom we naturally turn for aid and counsel. Will the American government steal? Will it lie? Will it kill?—We ask triumphantly. Our counsellors and old statesmen here say that ten years ago they would have staked their lives on the affirmation that the proposed Indian measures could not be executed; that the unanimous country would put them down. And now the steps of this crime follow each other so fast, at such fatally quick time, that the millions of virtuous citizens, whose agents the government are, have no place to interpose, and must shut their eyes until the last howl and wailing of these tormented villages and tribes shall afflict the ear of the world.

I will not hide from you, as an indication of the alarming distrust, that a letter addressed as mine is, and suggesting to the mind of the Executive the plain obligations of man, has a burlesque character in the apprehensions of some of my friends. I, sir, will not beforehand treat you with the contumely of this distrust. I will at least state to you this fact, and show you how plain and humane people, whose love would be honor, regard the policy of the government, and what injurious inferences they draw as to the minds of the governors. A man with your experience in affairs must have seen cause to appreciate the futility of opposition to the moral sentiment. However feeble the sufferer and however great the oppressor, it is in the nature of things that the blow should recoil upon the aggressor. For God is in the sentiment, and it cannot be withstood. The potentate and the people perish before it; but with it, and its executor, they are omnipotent.

I write thus, sir, to inform you of the state of mind these Indian tidings have awakened here, and to pray with one voice more that you, whose hands are strong with the delegated power of fifteen millions of men, will avert with that might the terrific injury which threatens the Cherokee tribe.

With great respect, sir, I am your fellow citizen.

RALPH WALDO EMERSON.

Chapter 10

Moving West

The westward movement of American settlement, which spanned a large part of the nineteenth century, to this day continues to stir the imagination. Covered wagons by the hundreds have crossed motion picture and television screens and the dust jackets of books. Frontier heroes Daniel Boone, Kit Carson, and Buffalo Bill have become widely recognized names. Even so, the popular media have not revealed much about the personal dimension of the families in those wagons.

Those who made the decision to take the journey did so for a variety of reasons: the promise of new and fertile land to farm, like that which attracted settlers to Oregon; the search for a place to practice their religion without interference, such as led the Mormons to Utah; the dream of wealth inspired by discoveries of gold or silver, like that which drew thousands by land and sea to the California goldfields beginning in the winter of 1848–1849. Whatever their motives and wherever their destination, they all shared the wrenching experience of leaving home, friends, and families, as well as the drama and difficulties of the long journey west. The essay that follows, from Malcom J. Rohrbough's Days of Gold: The California Gold Rush and the American Nation, *presents in very real terms the experiences of the gold-seeking 49ers, or "Argonauts" as they were called, as they traveled west. In what significant ways were the experiences of those who traveled by sea different from those who took the overland route? In what respects were they similar? How would you describe the travelers' attitudes toward the people they encountered from different regions and countries during their journey?*

The contrast between romantic views of westward migration and actual experiences on the trail is apparent in the first two documents. The first is a description by the editor of the Missouri Expositor *(May 3, 1845) of the wagon trains passing through Independence, Missouri, a jumping-off point for the long journey to Oregon. Next is an excerpt from Frederick Law Olmsted's* A Journey Through Texas *(1857), in which the author describes caravans of Southerners emigrating to Texas. (Olmsted, a famous landscape architect, wrote a number of works describing his extensive travels throughout the South.) How do you account for the striking differences between the two descriptions? Is one view more accurate than the other?*

The visions that inspired thousands to leave homes, families, and friends and head west were shaped in large measure by accounts in travel journals, newspapers, and letters from those already arrived in the new territories. Examples of such writing are found in the final documents of this chapter, a piece from the Monterey Californian *and a letter from an Oregon settler to a friend in Illinois. Identify the elements in each that would most likely attract potential emigrants. To what extent has the Monterey newspaper's prediction of California's agricultural future been realized?*

ESSAY

To California by Sea and by Land

Malcolm J. Rorbough

Annually, beginning in the winter of 1848–1849 and for the next decade, Americans journeyed to California by sea and by land. The journey by sea could be begun at any season, anywhere along the Atlantic coast, and could follow either the long route around Cape Horn or the shorter route across Panama. The trek overland began in mid-May from the edge of the prairies outside St. Joseph or Independence, Missouri, and concluded in Placerville, in the foothills of the Sierra, after a journey of twenty-two hundred miles.

Even as they moved in response to economic opportunity, Americans remained a local people, accustomed to the supportive surroundings of their families, friends, and communities. This encounter with exotic peoples on a long ocean voyage or with the western half of the continent by travel overland was something they always remembered. Many kept journals and diaries to mark the occasion; others wrote voluminous letters to their relatives and friends, filled with minute descriptions of the dangers and won-

SOURCE: From *Days of Gold: The California Gold Rush and the American Nation* by Malcolm J. Rorbough, pp. 55–66. Copyright © 1997 by The Regents of the University of California Press. Reprinted with permission.

ders of the trip. Their accounts, whether to family members, friends, or editors, and whether private or public, conveyed astonishment at a series of new worlds encountered and a sense of wonder that was often mixed with uneasiness and sometimes hostility. The new people, customs, and values that awaited them in California were equally striking and disturbing. They were also part of a new and different world with which they all had to come to terms.

Seagoing Argonauts

For many Americans—especially New Englanders, but also for others on the Atlantic coast, from New York and Pennsylvania through the Carolinas to New Orleans—a voyage by sea was the sensible way to go to California. The voyage itself began with weeks of preparation, and ... the myriad duties for planning and departure found scores of willing hands to carry them out. Young men who had recently been clerks or apprenticed tradesmen, farm laborers, or students found themselves officers in a company bound for California. Company officers and company committees crisscrossed port cities in search of a ship, then laid in provisions for the voyage and supplies and equipment for the mines, and finally tended to the thousand details that led to a prompt departure. The prospective 49ers found a sense of independence and importance in their tasks that signaled a transition from their families to a new community of like-minded Argonauts.

The departed Argonauts now encountered for the first time their diverse companions. Lafayette Fish left his home in Jackson, Michigan, and went down the Mississippi River to New Orleans, where he took a steamer to Panama. Of the other travelers, he wrote, "We have 200 passengers which puts us pretty close together. They comprise every grade and condition in life, and nearly if not all the States are represented." The vessels from Boston and New York were largely filled with New Englanders and New Yorkers, but one 49er who sailed from Boston in May 1849 described his companions as "Yankees from Cape Cod, Western men, New Yorkers, an old man of sixty, all alone, a one-eyed Baptist preacher about forty-five, who is the butt of all, more especial on account of his having brought a formidable looking revolver with him, but forgot to bring any powder."

Some 49ers expressed unhappiness about their companions on the voyage. One wrote of the voyage up the Pacific coast in 1850 that he had been thrown together with several Southerners, "nearly all of whom were excessively addicted to swearing and many of them, to gambling." Among the passengers were two "fine men" from Michigan who also had left families behind, and with whom the Argonaut passed his time. William P. Daingerfield sketched the origins of his fellow passengers in these terms: "Virginia sends four representatives, Baltimore four, Ohio one, and where the rest hail from the Lord only knows and I don't care." He observed of his companions, "Our party is composed of very ordinary materials, there are more good clothes than brains in it, more affectation than politeness, more cowardice than courage, more deceit than good feeling." Many felt this sense of superiority on meeting 49ers from other states and distant sections of the nation.

The length of the voyage and the ensuing idleness associated with it soon generated internal conflicts as companies of 49ers split into factions and bickered among themselves. "Nothing can be more dull and monotonous than a calm at sea," observed one Argonaut. "A kind of uneasy restlessness creeps over a person which he has not the power to repress. So much of his time seems lost and thrown away." Enoch Jacobs, a 49er who took passage on the *Edward Everett,* wrote six weeks out of Boston, "I observe Cliques forming which seem to bode anything but good." His apprehensions were well founded, and the listless wind that delayed the passage increased internal acrimony. "God Grant us a breeze soon for these long Calms are fruitful in producing dissension and disaffections," he continued. And later, he commented of his company, "this is truly a jealous people, Strangely given to fault finding."

Variations in acommodations and services increased the divisions. Those who could afford to do so sometimes brought along special food and drink for themselves and their friends. Edward P. Abbe, a Bostonian with aristocratic airs, sailed on the *Edward Everett,* along with 150 members of the New England Mining and Trading Company. On board, he dined with his friends. They ate well, supplementing the ship's dining arrangements, or "mess," with their own "picknicks" of delicacies. Others referred to them as "the aristocratic mess," a term that Abbe embraced with satisfaction because, he wrote, "we have generally speaking the most gentlemanly & polished & educated men in our mess."

As a way of reducing the tension and boredom, many companies organized activities of an entertaining and practical nature. The entertainments included amateur theatricals, military drills on the deck, and improvised music performances. Some companies sponsored lectures ranging from the geology of California to customs of the peoples in the ports of call. And from the beginning, companies laid plans for what they would do on arrival, establishing a command structure (would the elected officers continue to exercise authority once the party reached California?), organizing the company into squads of miners, and making plans to distribute equipment and to parcel out the resources of the company. These projects testified to their leisure and boredom, their images of the gold country, and the serious nature of their enterprise.

The idleness associated with a long sea voyage soon led to other recreational outlets, notably gambling and card playing. Both these exercises were among the vices that ministers, editors, officials, relatives, and friends had held up to scorn in public and private partings, and now they quickly became the most popular recreations. John J. Craven wrote after a scant five weeks at sea, "I am out of all patience and never was so heartily sick of cards in my life for it is nothing else from morning til night." Another 49er commented,

> All kinds of amusements have become stale except that gambling, which is carried to the greatest excess. I counted today, no less than seven companies on the deck, of from four to six persons each, with a pile of coin before him which is lessening or increasing every moment. . . . Several of those who have learned to play since leaving New York have rushed into it with the greatest rashness.

Cards and gambling not only drew veteran players, but also rapidly seduced those heretofore innocent of such vices.

Into the boredom and routine of shipboard activity intruded at irregular intervals an astonishing array of new sights, sounds, tastes, and smells that alternately astonished, confused, and dismayed. The voyage to California provided most seagoing 49ers with their first contact with the Tropics, new cultures, and new values. The revelations included flying fish, swarms of birds, strange aromas, and brilliant sunsets and sunrises. Rinaldo Taylor from Boston wrote to his wife of his ship's passing Savannah, "The night was bright & clear, and as warm as we could wish, while the air came from off shore absolutely loaded with perfume. It was like nothing I ever experienced at the north." Neither was the slave sale that he visited in New Orleans. Like many Northerners on the way to California, Taylor had his first direct contact with the institution of slavery, and he had strongly negative reactions.

The largest group of seagoing 49ers sailed down the coast—sometimes calling at Charleston or New Orleans—to Panama, where passengers disembarked for a trip across the peninsula to the Pacific. The stopover in Panama—sometimes extended to several weeks by bad weather and the scarcity of vessels on the Pacific side—gave the 49ers a look at a new tropical world that simultaneously captivated and appalled them. It was the first experience for most with a Spanish and Catholic culture. The transient Americans called the tropical landscape exciting beyond words and the native peoples heathen (which for them was synonymous with Catholic) and lazy. "It appears to me as fine a country as one could wish, but it is cursed with the most lazy indolent population that breathes," ran a characteristic observation. "They cultivate nothing whatever. The finest land in the world lies just as nature made it, at the very gates of Panama."

Most of the 49ers sharply criticized Panamanian customs. J. E. Clayton called a "fandango" dance "the most vulgar thing I ever saw. They seem to have no sense of shame about them." James Barnes from upstate New York expressed shock at the vigorous social activity on the Sabbath, with music and dancing, and he wrote of it, "Sunday is no more respected here than any other day. Gambling and drinking is carried on here to a great extent. I have seen thousands of dollars piled on gaming tables all in gold and silver." Like other 49ers, Barnes did not know whether to be shocked at the desecration of the Sabbath or impressed by the large quantities of hard currency in plain view. Milo Goss shared this low opinion of Panamanians, and he wrote, "Rivoting, debauchery in all its different form, prevails here, in all its deformity. The Sabbath day is a day of revelry among the Spanish and of drinking and gambling with the Americans, and all kinds of sin is committed with more boldness than one performs a good act." He was also astonished to see Spanish ladies smoking. Once again, what seemed disturbing was the degree to which Americans were vulnerable to such blandishments. Of their experiences, one wrote, "Many an American who never thought of such a thing at home, gets carried away by the general excitement & gets his pockets emptied 'presto.'"

Many Americans found the Catholic churches old and impressive, the services ranging from "very solemn and imposing" to "pompous." Christian Miller wrote of Rio de Janeiro, "the riches and beauty of the interiors of these churches I cant describe." The 49ers, especially Yankees from New England, showed no inclination to join the services, but their reactions suggested a sense of awe and respect, if not sympathy for this alien church.

The trip across the isthmus by canoe and mule took three days, and the jungle landscape evoked wonder and admiration. J. E. Clayton summed up the river trip inland with the comment, "For me to attempt to describe the scenery on this river would be to overrate my powers of description. It is so different from anything I ever saw that I am lost in admiration and wonder." S. Schufelt loved the "howling of the monkeys & chattering of parrots" that formed a chorus for the 49ers across the isthmus. The capacity of Panamanians to carry heavy loads and maneuver the loaded canoes evoked much admiration. The tropical downpours on the trails and on the rivers produced resignation and humor. One 49er wrote to his wife, "If you could have looked upon me then, groping through the forest, with my red shirt, straw hat & linen pants, the only clothing I had on, covered with mud, with the rain pouring down on me, you would have thought I was the most miserable being imaginable."

The pungent smells and rich foods were also reminders of a different world. Jacob Townsend, who shipped as a member of the crew from Nantucket for fifteen dollars a month in order to get to the gold fields, loved the oranges of the Tropics, "some of them sweet as my wife's kisses." William A. Brown of Toledo, Ohio, was fascinated by the variety of foods served in Panama, and he wrote his parents elaborate descriptions of the meals.

A second group of seagoing 49ers sailed down the coast, around the Horn, and up the Pacific side, calling at ports along the way. For these Argonauts, being certain of the accommodations, costs, and traveling conditions they would encounter more than compensated for greater distance and a longer time at sea. The ports of call for these 49ers had their own surprises, however. William F. Denniston expressed shock that men and women bathed together on Grenada. John Stone considered Rio de Janeiro "a disgusting filthy city." He thought only slightly better of Callao and Lima, Peru. Enoch Jacobs found the character of Chileans wanting ("a very indolent and idle class of People possessing but little enterprise"), while at the same time he was enormously impressed by the natural beauty of Valparaiso harbor. "The dawn of this morning disclosed one of the most splendid views I ever beheld. The Towering Andes extended north and south as far as I could see," he confided to his journal.

The long periods of idleness that were a dominant feature of the voyages by sea, and that followed the hectic physical activity of preparation and the emotional stress of parting, led frequently to intensive introspection. As the Argonauts stared out at the wide expanses of water, they had time to consider their ties to their families and their motives for making the voyage to California. Some tried to come to terms with the sense of selfishness that seemed to lie at the root of the search for gold. William DeCosta was more frank and introspective than most in his analysis of his motives. His companions, he confided to his journal, were "bound by bands of gold," slaves to the search for the precious metal. As for himself, "I will not say that gold is not my god, for it is, and further that it is the god of almost every man, though there are few that will acknowledge it." But DeCosta was ultimately persuaded of the uprightness of the enterprise, and he continued, "I look upon it as a good god and great operator in human affairs. Gold is charity and makes love, it produces smiling faces, relieves the sick and afflicted, and, in fact, does everything great and good." Therefore, he was engaged in a search for an instrument that would do enormous good in the world. Indeed, he concluded, "Let us call it good, looking for no evil, and leave it, the mighty engine, to revolve around everything save the great wheel of time." His Biblical allusions echoed American values and language at midcentury. Perhaps such arguments provided the Argonauts with an armor against the shocks of California and the gold fields and their continued sense of guilt at leaving home and family.

Interspersed with the leisure and boredom of the long voyages were experiences of otherness that many of the voyagers found disturbing. The 49ers were struck by how rapidly they were cast into a new world. William Elder wrote to his wife, "Although it is less than six weeks since we parted it seems to be more than so many months; so many new and strange scenes have continually passed before. Scenes so unlike anything I have before seen that it all most seems like a dream." He was delighted when the voyage was at last over. Aside from boredom and monotonous food and cramped quarters, he loved the "American" character of San Francisco, where "I seemed to feel quite at home among the good honest Saxon countenances [that] are everywhere to be seen contrasting favorably with the sallow narrow visaged Spaniards." The sense of relief on reaching California extended beyond the gold of their dreams and the boredom of the voyage to a comfort in finding a familiar culture and familiar ways of doing things. In many respects, the voyage to California by sea might be thought of as a dress rehearsal for the placers* in California. Men jostled one another in close quarters, competed for space, for sustenance, and for services, paid a high price for everything, and above all, focused on the same objective.

The voyages of the 49ers to California placed in sharp relief the wide range of individuals and groups set in motion to the gold fields. More than other routes to the California gold fields, the sea voyages confirmed social and economic distinctions within the passengers. Some could afford superior accommodations and food; others had to settle for primitive quarters and plain subsistence. Some went to San Francisco with the leisure and resources to speculate and to spy out the main chance; others had to trek to the mines immediately to support themselves and to make good on the promises to their families and relatives. These distinctions might enlarge over time in California, but they were already clear and sharp on the voyage there, as explicit as the traditional American reaction to new cultures and values in foreign lands.

Overland Argonauts

The overland 49ers faced a formidable journey across half the continent. Some voyages from Atlantic ports were accustomed to long sea journeys, but almost no one among the Argonauts who chose the overland route had made such a journey before. A few thousand pioneers already had made the transcontinental migration to Oregon, but these had been farm families headed west in search of land. Never in the history of the Republic had there been a mass migration of tens of thousands overland to the West Coast. The voyage of the overland Argonauts was all the more striking because these pilgrims included city dwellers, along with people from small towns and farms, who now found themselves caught up in the greatest pioneering challenge of the day. The great distances and monotonous character of the landscape, together with towering mountain ranges and deserts, posed dramatic obstacles. Added to these physical challenges were fears of the Plains Indian tribes to heighten apprehensions.

Like their seagoing counterparts, these 49ers also joined together for purposes of travel. From the earliest creation of companies in home communities to the great campouts in Independence and St. Joseph, groups of men sought out others with similar origins and values. Beginning with family groups, these associations extended out to include those from the immediate community, nearby villages, and regions or sections, as New Englanders and Southerners sought their own kind for traveling companions. Those with special concerns formed their own companies. The Sabbath keepers

*A *placer* refers to someone who pans for gold in a stream. (Eds.)

joined in groups that would observe a Sunday of rest, and temperance men often banded together. There were also exercises in the random selection of traveling companions. A St. Louis company, the "Pioneer Line," offered freight wagons, wagonmasters, teamsters, and guides to transport 49ers to California at a cost of two hundred dollars each; the Argonauts would furnish their own tents, cooking gear, and rations. For many, joining a traveling company involved coming to terms, at least temporarily, with new kinds of people—new kinds of Americans to be sure, but still different peoples.

The Argonauts soon came to view the overland expedition as a competition, as well as an exercise in cooperation. Tens of thousands of men were on the same trail to California, narrowly intent on the same objective. The sense of rivalry was the stronger because the Argonauts could literally see the competitors everywhere around them, ahead, behind, and even alongside. "There are thousands of men going along the road; in fact, it looks like the wagons hauling cotton to Macon just after a rise in the staple," wrote John Milner of Alabama to his family. "I believe there are wagons stretched in sight of one another for 500 miles."

Of the notable differences from the sea voyage, the most significant was the enormous amount of work on the trip itself. Whereas seagoing 49ers suffered from boredom once underway, those on the California Trail coped with endless daily chores. Henry Packer's observation on the daily duties on the trail was repeated in a hundred letters to family and friends:

> When traveling, we are up at day break; and by the time the horses are fed, curried and harnessed, the breakfast is ready; as soon as that is dispatched, we hitch up and away. At noon—heretofore we have spent no longer time than is just necessary for the horses and ourselves to eat; but when we get to feeding them on grass, a little longer time will be required. In the evening, after stopping, the horses are to offgear, tie up, currey, and feed and water; the tent is to put up—bed clothes to arrange, supper to prepare and eat—which last is not hard to do—by this time it is bed time, and we "turn in." Then again, each member of the company comes upon guard duty once every fourth or fifth night.

These were familiar routines for men from rural areas, but other kinds of tasks emerged for which the 49ers had little or no preparation. Thousands of men had their first experiences with sewing, washing, and cooking, and in company with the other duties on the trail, they found these burdensome. Little did the overland travelers realize that domestic work on the overland trail was only the beginning of a new range of chores that would confront 49ers in the gold fields.

Along with the combination of exhilaration and danger in the West went encounters with new people and new places on a more familiar scale.

Like those who went to California by sea, the overland 49ers admired the scenery and generally disliked the new peoples they encountered. Indeed, their experiences seemed to confirm the provincial views of Americans at midcentury. Southerners despised Northerners as reformist fanatics and grasping merchants, interested only in cheating their fellow travelers. Men from Massachusetts clustered together in self-admiration; others disdained emigrants from the Bay State as coming from a place "where the majority are in favor of amalgamation." Everyone castigated the Missourians as crude, a miserable, impoverished group of pioneers "on the extreme border of civilization." One 49er characterized them as "nasty, dirty looking whelps and all Hogs or most of them." The new state of Iowa, by contrast, drew praise for its rich lands and industrious population, but widespread condemnation for its terrible roads and gouging prices.

The overland route west was more than a test of physical strength and endurance. Those who went to California in the summer of '49 and in subsequent annual migrations saw the challenges of an overland journey as a test of their character and of their capacity to maintain their standards of conduct surrounded by strangers and a new landscape. The trip across the plains was the first test of their traditional standards of behavior and conduct in a world without institutional force to ensure compliance. This struggle to preserve individual character appeared on two different levels throughout the journey: in setting and fulfilling the contractual arrangements to which so many men had agreed prior to setting forth and in coming to terms with the question of identity.

Almost everyone going overland to California joined a company. The company's arrangements were democratic in the sense that participants signed a document (generally referred to as a constitution) that spelled out rules of conduct, especially with respect to participation and sharing of duties. Deviations from these agreements began with the first turn of the road beyond the farm or the village, for no sooner had the trip begun than some men left to return to their farms, their parents, their wives, and their children. The situation was sometimes awkward. These men were now returning to the very farms and villages from which they had departed only a few days or weeks earlier with so much emotional outpouring. The term "backed-out Californians," always spoken with contempt, quickly came into use to describe those who turned back. Continuing 49ers were sometimes at pains to assure those at home that the Argonauts continuing to California held no hard feelings against the returning individual and that he should be welcomed back into the family as a member in good standing. William Rothwell saw the defection of his brother-in-law, Pemberton Gibbs, with regret, but he assured his father that all had parted on most amicable terms.

The overland Argonauts also confronted the question of the identity of their fellow travelers, an issue that would carry over into the placers in California. From the intimate world of family, relatives, and friends, the 49ers entered increasingly into an anonymous condition in which one's identity might with little effort be hidden or changed. A striking quality of the mining camps in California was the anonymity of the individuals who lived there. Part of the unsettling experience of meeting new people, and in the gold fields, of having to place trust in strangers on short acquaintance, lay in confronting a world in which people were not always what they seemed. Except for a circle of close friends, in the case of those who had gone together, these were gatherings of strangers. Those so inclined could create an entirely new identity. The only connections with the past were friends, who were easily evaded, and mail from home, which could be left unclaimed or ignored. Some women complained that men along the trail and in California hid the fact that they were married. In this transient world, where men had come temporarily in pursuit of wealth in a separate chapter of their lives, no one cared to inquire too closely into the past. This anonymity became more faceless as men moved west.

One of the astonishing features of the overland trail to California was the enormous waste of goods. Argonauts who went to California by sea took more of everything, but ships carried the weight effortlessly. Draft animals demanded more personal attention, and parties of 49ers shared a common characteristic in casting aside supplies and possessions to lighten the load. The 49ers littered the California Trail with discarded food supplies and heavy gold-mining equipment, often fancy gold-washing machines. They began to throw things away at the beginning of the journey, littering the trail for a thousand miles to and past Fort Laramie. Commenting on this array of discarded supplies, one Argonaut noted, "there has been enough thrown away on this trip to make a man rich." At the beginning of the final stage on the Humboldt River, many 49ers left their wagons and proceeded on foot, using as pack animals the stock horses they had brought for breeding. Horace Ballew described his astonishment at the sight of hundreds of abandoned wagons in the Humboldt River valley.

Almost all the overland Argonauts wrote of their journey as characterized by hard work and danger, an odyssey to the farthest reaches of the new American Empire in which they triumphantly reached California against great odds. John Gish of Logan County, Ohio, compared crossing the plains to the hardest physical labor of his own work experience when he wrote, "I would rather tend a threshing machine than take a trip a cross the plains." And Joshua Sullivan commented that "nothing but poverty would induce me to go any further."

The 49ers who went overland celebrated their participation in a triumphal march, a voyage whose successful completion welcomed them to membership in the club of American pioneers. It was not an exclusive club, certainly not by the early 1850s, but still, to cross the plains at midcentury was the great American pioneering experience. In their eyes, it forever conferred on those who made the journey a special status, different from those who went by sea at the start of the Gold Rush or by the railroad in the next generation. This journey by land with draft animals was a final large-scale reenactment of America's pioneering pattern, which had been largely unchanged for a century. It brought them into contact with what would become the fabled icons of the American West: the huge herds of buffalo, the dangerous Plains Indian tribes (sensed rather than seen), the towering peaks of the Rockies and the deserts of Nevada, and the great monuments of American expansion—Chimney Rock, Fort Laramie, the Great Salt Lake, and the desert reaching to the eastern foothills of the Sierra. These varied peoples, geography, and experiences seemed to provide a suitable introduction to the infinite varieties of California.

DOCUMENTS

Oregon Fever, 1845

Even while we write, we see a long train of wagons coming through our busy streets; they are hailed with shouts of welcome by their fellow voyagers, and, to judge from the pleased expression on every face, it "all goes merry as a marriage bell." On looking out at the passing train, we see among the foremost a very comfortably covered wagon, one of the sheets drawn aside, and an extremely nice looking lady seated inside very quietly sewing; the bottom of the wagon is carpeted; there are two or three chairs, and at one end there is a bureau, surmounted by a mirror; various articles of ornament and convenience hang around the sides—a perfect prairie boudoir. Blessed be woman! Shedding light and happiness where'er she goes; with her the wild prairie will be a paradise! Blessed be him who gave us this connecting link between heaven and man to win us from our wilder ways. Hold on there; this is getting entirely too sentimental; but we don't care who laughs, we felt better and happier when we looked on this picture than we may express. That fine manly fellow riding along by the side of the wagon, and looking in so pleasantly, is doubtless the lady's husband; we almost envy him. But they are past, and now comes team after team, each drawn by six or eight stout oxen, and such drivers! positively sons of Anak! not one of them less than six feet two in his stockings. Whoo ha! Go it boys! We're in perfect *Oregon fever*. Now comes on a stock of every description, children, niggers, horses, mules, cows, oxen; and there seems to be no end of them. From present evidences, we suppose that not less than two or three

SOURCE: *Nile's National Register* (May 21, 1845), quoting the *Missouri Expositor* (May 3, 1845), 203.

180

thousand people are congregating at this point previous to their start upon the broad prairie, which will be on or about the 10th of May.

Emigrants to Texas, c. 1857

We overtook, several times in the course of each day, the slow emigrant trains, for which this road, though less frequented than years ago, is still a chief thoroughfare. Inexorable destiny it seems that drags or drives on, always Westward, these toil-worn people. Several families were frequently moving together, coming from the same district, or chance met and joined, for company, on the long road from Alabama, Georgia, or the Carolinas. Before you come upon them you hear, ringing through the woods, the fierce cries and blows with which they urge on their jaded cattle. Then the stragglers appear, lean dogs or fainting negroes, ragged and spiritless. An old granny, holding on, by the hand, a weak boy—too old to ride and too young to keep up. An old man, heavily loaded, with a rifle. Then the white covers of the wagons, jerking up and down as they mount over a root or plunge into a rut, disappearing, one after another, where the road descends. Then the active and cheery prime negroes, not yet exhausted, with a joke and a suggestion about tobacco. Then the black pickininnies, staring, in a confused heap, out at the back of the wagon, more and more of their eyes to be made out among the table legs and bedding as you get near; behind them, further in, the old people and young mothers, whose turn it is to ride. As you get by, the white mother and babies, and the tall, frequently ill-humored master, on horseback, or walking with his gun, urging up the black driver and his oxen. As a scout ahead is a brother, or an intelligent slave, with the best gun, on the look-out for a deer or a turkey. We passed in the day perhaps one hundred persons attached to these trains, probably an unusual number; but the immigration this year had been retarded and condensed by the fear of yellow fever, the last case of which, at Natchitoches, had indeed begun only the night before our arrival. Our chances of danger were considered small, however, as the hard frosts had already come. One of these trains was made up of three large wagons, loaded with furniture, babies, and invalids, two or three light wagons, and a gang of twenty able field hands. They travel ten or fifteen miles a day, stopping wherever night overtakes them. The masters are plainly dressed, often in home-spun, keeping their eyes about them, noticing the soil, sometimes making a remark on the crops by the roadside; but, generally, dogged, surly, and silent. The women are silent, too, frequently walking, to relieve the teams, and weary,

SOURCE: Frederick Law Olmsted, *A Journey Through Texas* (New York: Dix, Edwards & Co., 1857), 55–57.

haggard, mud-bedraggled, forlorn, and disconsolate, yet hopeful and careful. The negroes, mud-incrusted, wrapped in old blankets or gunny-bags, suffering from cold, plod on, aimless, hopeless, thoughtless, more indifferent than the oxen to all about them.

The Promise of California, 1846

EMIGRATION.—Emigrants from the United States are daily flocking into California, their landmark, after crossing the Rocky Mountains, is the Sacramento valley, amongst them are mechanics and labourers of all descriptions, and altho' they invariably strike for the Sacramento valley, still not one half of them will settle there, they will, as soon as they get acquainted with the country, and the winter season is over, spread all over California, and as many of these are people, who understand agriculture in all its branches, they will undoubtedly spy out thousands of acres of land, which are now considered as useless, except for grazing, and will in a short time prove to the old inhabitants that there is more land fit for cultivation in California, than ever has been imagined, by the natives; and many vegetable substances will be planted, and brought to maturity, which heretofore have never had a fair trail.

We have already had sufficient proof in various instances that the grape vine flourishes, in California, to the northward of San Luis Obispo, if not in an equal degree to that of the Angeles, at most, very little inferior, and there can be little doubt, that the industry, and intelligence of the agriculturists, which are daily emigrating to this country, will improve the nature of the soil to such a degree, as to greatly augment both the produce, and improve the flavour of this most delicious fruit, and the same may be said of all the other production of this country.

A Letter from Oregon Territory, 1847

APRIL 6, 1847

We arrived safe in Oregon City on the 12th of September last. We reached Fort Laramie in 42 days from Independence; Fort Hall in 33 days more; the Dalles in 37 days more; and Oregon City in 16 days more—making in all 128 days. Our journey was two weeks longer than necessary had we lost no time. We met with no serious obstructions on our journey. We had to raise

SOURCE: Monterey *Californian*, November 7, 1846.
SOURCE: Letter from Richard R. Howard, dated April 6, 1847, and published in the [Springfield] *Illinois Journal*, November 11, 1847.

the front of our wagon beds two or three inches in crossing the Larimie Fork to keep the water out; sometimes we had long drives to find a good place for camping, with water and grass. . . . No single man should come to this country. One third of the men in Oregon at this time are without wives. Nothing but men of families are wanted here to till the soil, to make this one of the greatest countries in the world. This country does not get so muddy as Illinois. There is no dust in summer here. The good land in this country is more extensive than I expected to find it. The hills are not so high as represented. From the Cascade mountains to the Pacific, the whole country can be cultivated. The natural soil of the country, especially in the bottoms, is a black loam, mixed with gravel and clay. We have good timber; but there appears to be a scarcity of good building rock. The small streams furnish us with trout the year round.

My wife to the old lady—Greeting; says she was never more satisfied with a move in her life before; that she is fast recovering her health; and she hopes you will come to Oregon, where you can enjoy what little time you have remaining in health.

The roads to Oregon are not as bad as represented. Hastings in his history speaks of the Falls of Columbia being 50 feet and roaring loud, making the earth tremble, &c. The falls are about like that of a mill-dam. Everything in this country now is high, except molasses, sugar and salt; but when we raise our wheat crop to trade on, we will make them pay for their high charges. I think no place where a living is to be made out of the earth can be preferable to Oregon for that purpose—and let people say what they may— all agree that it is healthy. It is certainly the healthiest country in the world, disease is scarcely known here, except among the late emigrants, ninety-nine out of a hundred of them get well the first season. I have heard of only two deaths since I have been in Oregon; one of them was a man who came here diseased and in one year died; the other was a woman who it is said was near dead ten years before she came here.

RICHARD R. HOWARD

Chapter 11

Paths to Salvation:
Revivalism and Communitarianism

During the first decades of the nineteenth century, a wave of evangelical revivalism began in upstate New York, western New England, and frontier Kentucky and Tennessee. Ultimately, this Second Great Awakening swept the nation. Like its mid-eighteenth-century predecessor, the revival was initiated by clergymen concerned with what they perceived to be a climate of moral laxity and religious decline. America, as they viewed it, had paid a price for its rapid growth and expansion: rootlessness, Godlessness, and drunkenness, which too often afflicted both frontier settlements and urban centers. They believed that the intellectualism and mechanistic view of the universe spawned by the Enlightenment philosophy of the Revolutionary era had contributed to these conditions. What the country needed was a return to spiritual values, to faith in God's guiding hand.

In many respects similar in style to the first Great Awakening, the nineteenth-century revival was even less constrained by theological orthodoxy. Its clergy placed less emphasis on threats of damnation for sin, and more on preaching a message of God's love, which, if freely accepted, offered both a better life on earth and *eternal salvation. Appealing to the emotions of their listeners, using words all could understand, revivalist preachers found enthusiastic audiences.*

The essay that follows, from Paul E. Johnson's A Shopkeepers Millennium, *provides a detailed picture of one of the era's most famous revivals, that in Rochester, New York. The completion of the Erie Canal had transformed the once placid town into the fastest growing city in the nation. Economic expansion brought prosperity to many members of the business and professional classes, but it also brought concerns over an influx of laborers and boatmen who frequented a waterfront district of taverns, flophouses, and often riotous disturbances. The fears and anxieties caused by rapid social and economic changes and the arrival in 1830 of the nation's most outstanding revivalist preacher, Charles Grandison Finney, combined to make Rochester the ideal setting for a great evangelical awakening, one that would have consequences far beyond the city's borders. As described in the essay, what revival techniques did Finney consider essential for success? In what respect was Finney's revival highly individualistic while at the same time being an "intensely social event"? How did he perceive the coming millennium?*

Charles Finney's employment of highly emotional sermons was, as he reveals in the first document, the result of thoughtful planning. Indeed, as you read, note his keen insight into patterns of human behavior decades before the rise of modern psychological study.

Evangelical revivalism was not everyone's cup of tea. The second document presents a most unflattering view of an Indiana camp meeting in 1829, witnessed by an English visitor, Mrs. Frances Trollope, and described in her book Domestic Manners of the Americans. *What would draw European travelers in America to revivalist camp meetings?*

Some Americans of this period believed that they could create the ideal community only by removing themselves from society and building anew. Prominent among several religious communitarian sects were the Shakers. By 1830, they had gathered themselves into more than twenty communities throughout the East and Midwest to await what they believed would be Christ's imminent return and rule on earth, a view of the millennium quite different from that of Charles Finney. In anticipation of this event, they forsook private ownership of property and practiced celibacy. The third document provides a view of this sect by a Lowell mill girl who paid two visits to a New York Shaker community. Does your previous reading about Lowell suggest why this young woman initially found Shaker village life so appealing?

From the 1820s through the 1840s, a number of predominantly secular utopian experiments in communal living were initiated, with the goal of serving as models of nobler, purer ways of life. One of the most famous was the Brook Farm community established in West Roxbury, Massachusetts, under the leadership of George Ripley, a New England Transcendentalist. Its participants included some of the leading New England intellectuals, among them Nathaniel Hawthorne, Margaret Fuller, and Charles A. Dana. The final document is from a letter that Hawthorne wrote to his sister Louisa a few weeks after he arrived at Brook Farm in April 1841.

185

How do you account for his enthusiasm for the agrarian, communitarian life? Despite his initial sentiments, six months later Hawthorne left the community after deciding that he could not be both farmer and writer. Other members made similar decisions. In 1847, after six years of existence, the Brook Farm experiment ended. The farm's short life was a fate shared by most other utopian communities.

ESSAY
•◆•

Charles Finney's Rochester Revival
Paul E. Johnson

Charles Grandison Finney came to Rochester in September 1830. For six months he preached in Presbyterian churches nearly every night and three times on Sunday, and his audience included members of every sect. During the day he prayed with individuals and led an almost continuous series of prayer meetings. Soon there were simultaneous meetings in churches and homes throughout the village. Pious women went door-to-door praying for troubled souls. The high school stopped classes and prayed. Businessmen closed their doors early and prayed with their families. "You could not go upon the streets," recalled one convert, "and hear any conversation, except upon religion." By early spring the churches faced the world with a militance and unity that had been unthinkable only months before, and with a boundless and urgent sense of their ability to change society. In the words of its closest student, "... no more impressive revival has occurred in American history."

New Measures

First, a word on the evangelical plan of salvation. Man is innately evil and can overcome his corrupt nature only through faith in Christ the redeemer—that much is common to Christianity in all its forms. Institutional and theological differences among Christians trace ultimately to varying means of attaining that faith. The Reformation abolished sacred beings, places, and institutions that had eased the path between the natural and supernatural worlds. Without ritual, without priest-magicians, without divine immanence in an institutional church, Protestants face God across infinite lonely space. They bridge that space through prayer—through the state of absolute selflessness and submission known generally as transcendence. The experience of transcending oneself and this world through prayer is for Protestants direct experience of the Holy Ghost, and it constitutes assurance of salvation, sanctification, and new life.

SOURCE: Paul E. Johnson, *A Shopkeepers Millenium: Society and Revivals in Rochester, New York, 1815–1837.* (New York: Hill and Wang, 1978), 95–102, 109–115.

Prayer, then, is the one means by which a Protestant establishes his relation with God and his assurance that he is one of God's people. Prayer is a personal relationship between God and man, and the decision whether that relationship is established belongs to God. No Protestants dispute that. But they have argued endlessly on man's ability to influence the decision. The evangelical position was phrased (and it was understood by its detractors) as an increase in human ability so great that prayer and individual salvation were ultimately voluntary. Hurried notes to Charles Finney's Rochester sermons insisted: "It should in all cases be required now to repent, now to give themselves up to God, now to say and feel Lord here I am take me, it's all I can do. And when the sinner can do that . . . his conversion is attained." "The truth," he explained, "is employed to influence men, prayer to move God . . . I do not mean that God's mind is changed by prayer . . . But prayer produces such a change *in us* as renders it consistent for him to do otherwise." To hyper-Calvinists who protested that this filled helpless man with false confidence, Finney shouted, "What is that but telling them to hold on to their rebellion against God? . . . as though God was to blame for not converting them." The only thing preventing individual conversion was the individual himself.

This reevaluation of human ability caught the evangelicals in a dilemma. But it was a dilemma they had already solved in practice. Finney and his friends insisted that God granted new life in answer to faithful prayer. But the ability to pray with faith was itself experimental proof of conversion. By definition, the unregenerate could not pray. For Finney there was a clear and obvious way out, a way that he and Rochester Protestants witnessed hundreds of times during the revival winter: "Nothing is more calculated to beget a spirit of prayer, than to unite in social prayer with one who has the spirit himself." That simple mechanism is at the heart of evangelical Protestantism.

Conversion had always ended in prayer and humiliation before God. But ministers had explained the terms of salvation and left terrified sinners to wrestle with it alone. Prayer was transacted in private between a man and his God, and most middle-class Protestants were uncomfortable with public displays of humiliation. As late as 1829, Rochester Presbyterians had scandalized the village when they began to kneel rather than stand at prayer. More than their theological implications, Finney's revival techniques aroused controversy because they transformed conversion from a private to a public and intensely social event. The door-to-door canvass, the intensification of family devotions, prayer meetings that lasted till dawn, the open humiliation of sinners on the anxious bench: all of these transformed prayer and conversion from private communion into spectacular public events.

What gave these events their peculiar force was the immediatist corollary to voluntary conversion. The Reverend Whitehouse of St. Luke's Church (yes, the Episcopalians too) explained it in quiet terms:

Appeals are addressed to the heart and the appeals are in reference to the present time. And each time the unconverted sinner leaves the house of God without having closed with the terms of the Gospel he rejects the offer of mercy. Had some future time been specified as that in which we were to make a decision we might listen time after time to the invitations and reject them. But it is expressly said today and now is the accepted time.

Initially, these pressures fell on the already converted. It was the prayers of Christians that led others to Christ, and it was their failure to pray that sent untold millions into hell. Lay evangelicals seldom explained the terms of salvation in the language of a Reverend Whitehouse—or even of a Charles Finney. But with the fate of their children and neighbors at stake, they carried their awful responsibility to the point of emotional terrorism. Finney tells the story of a woman who prayed while her son-in-law attended an anxious meeting. He came home converted, and she thanked God and fell dead on the spot. Everard Peck reported the death of his wife to an unregenerate father-in-law, and told the old man that his dead daughter's last wish was to see him converted. "We are either marching towards heaven or towards hell," wrote one convert to his sister. "How is it with you?"

The new measures brought sinners into intense and public contact with praying Christians. Conversion hinged not on private prayer, arbitrary grace, or intellectual choice, but on purposive encounters between people. The secret of the Rochester revival and of the attendant transformation of society lay ultimately in the strategy of those encounters.

While Finney led morning prayer meetings, pious women visited families. Reputedly they went door-to-door. But the visits were far from random. Visitors paid special attention to the homes of sinners who had Christian wives, and they arrived in the morning hours when husbands were at work. Finney himself found time to pray with Melania Smith, wife of a young physician. The doctor was anxious for his soul, but sickness in the village kept him busy and he was both unable to pray and unwilling to try. But his wife prayed and tormented him constantly, reminding him of "the woe which is denounced against the families which call not on the Name of the Lord." Soon his pride broke and he joined her as a member of Brick Presbyterian Church. Finney's wife, Lydia, made a bolder intrusion into the home of James Buchan, a merchant-tailor and a Roman Catholic whose wife, Caroline, was a Presbyterian. Buchan, with what must have been enormous self-restraint, apologized for having been out of the house, thanked Finney for the tract, and invited him and his wife to tea. (It is not known whether Finney accepted the invitation, but this was one bit of family meddling which may have backfired. In 1833 Caroline Buchan withdrew from the Presbyterian Church and converted to Catholicism.) In hundreds of cases the strategy of family visits worked. As the first converts fell, the

Observer announced with satisfaction that the largest group among them was "young heads of families."

Revival enthusiasm began with the rededication of church members and spread to the people closest to them. Inevitably, much of it flowed through family channels. Finney claimed Samuel D. Porter, for instance, as a personal conquest. But clearly he had help. Porter was an infidel, but his sister in Connecticut and his brother-in-law Everard Peck were committed evangelicals. Porter came under a barrage of family exhortation, and in January Peck wrote home that "Samuel is indulging a trembling hope . . ." He remained the object of family prayer for eight more months before hope turned into assurance. Then he joined his sister and brother-in-law in praying for the soul of their freethinking father. The realtor Bradford King left another record of evangelism within and between related households. After weeks of social prayer and private agony, he awoke and heard himself singing, *"I am going to the Kingdom will you come along with me."* He testified at meeting the next day, but did not gain assurance until he returned home and for the first time prayed with his family. He rose and "decided that as for me & my house we would serve the Lord." Immediately King turned newfound powers on his brother's house in nearby Bloomfield. After two months of visiting and prayer he announced, "We had a little pentecost at brothers . . . all were praising and glorifying God in one United Voice." The revival made an evangelist of every convert, and most turned their power on family members.

Charles Finney's revival was based on group prayer. It was a simple, urgent activity that created new hearts in hundreds of men and women, and it generated—indeed it relied upon—a sense of absolute trust and common purpose among participants. The strengthening of family ties that attended the revival cannot be overestimated. But it was in prayer meetings and evening services that evangelism spilled outside old social channels, laying the basis for a transformed and united Protestant community.

Bradford King had no patience for "Old Church Hipocrites who think more of their particular denomination than Christ Church," and his sentiments were rooted in an astonishing resolution of old difficulties. Presbyterians stopped fighting during the first few days, and peace soon extended to the other denominations. Before the first month was out, Finney marveled that "Christians of every denomination generally seemed to make common cause, and went to work with a will, to pull sinners out of the fire." The most unexpected portent came in October, when the weight of a crowded gallery spread the walls and damaged the building at First Church. Vestrymen at St. Paul's—most of them former Masons and bitter enemies of the Presbyterians—let that homeless congregation into their church. But it was in prayer meetings and formal services that the collective regeneration of a fragmented churchgoing community took place, for it was there that "Christians of different denominations are seen mingled together in the sanctuary on the Sabbath, and bowing at the same altar in the social prayer meeting."

Crowded prayer meetings were held almost every night from September until early March, and each of them was managed carefully. When everyone was seated the leader read a short verse dealing with the object of prayer. Satisfied that everyone understood and could participate, he called on those closest to the spirit. These prayed aloud, and within minutes all worldly thoughts were chased from the room. (Finney knew that the chemistry of prayer worked only when everyone shared in it, and he discouraged attendance by scoffers, cranks, and the merely curious.) Soon sinners grew anxious; some of them broke into tears, and Christians came close to pray with them. Then followed the emotional displays that timid ministers had feared, but which they accepted without a whimper during the revival winter. In October Artemissia Perkins prayed with her fiancé in Brick Church. Suddenly her voice rose above the others, and over and over she prayed, "Blessed be the Name of Jesus," while her future husband, her neighbors, and people who never again could be strangers watched and participated in the awesome work. It was in hundreds of encounters such as this that the revival shattered old divisions and laid the foundation for moral community among persons who had been strangers or enemies. "I know this is all algebra to those who have never felt it," Finney explained. "But to those who have experienced the agony of wrestling, prevailing prayer, for the conversion of a soul, you may depend on it, that soul . . . appears as dear as a child is to the mother who brought it forth with pain."

At formal services this mechanism took on massive proportions. During services Christians gathered in other churches and nearby homes to pray for the evangelist's success. Sometimes crowds of people who could not find seats in the house prayed outside in the snow. Downstairs the session room was packed, and every break in the lecture was punctuated by the rise and fall of prayer.

Inside, every seat was filled. People knelt in the aisles and doorways. Finney reserved seats near the pulpit for anxious sinners—not random volunteers, but prominent citizens who had spoken with him privately. None sat on the anxious bench who was not almost certain to fall. Separated from the regenerate and from hardened sinners, their conversions became grand public spectacles. In the pulpit, Finney preached with enormous power, but with none of the excesses some people expected. He had dropped a promising legal career to enter the ministry, and his preaching demonstrated formidable courtroom skills, not cheap theatrics. True, he took examples from everyday experience and spoke in folksy, colloquial terms. (With what may have been characteristic modesty, he reminded his listeners that Jesus had done the same.) Most of his lectures lasted an hour, but it was not uncommon for a packed church to listen twice that long "without the movement of a foot." When he gestured at the room, people ducked as if he were throwing things. In describing the fall of sinners he pointed to the ceiling, and as he let his finger drop people in the rear seats stood to watch the final entry into hell. Finney spoke directly to the anxious bench in front of him, and at the close of the lecture he demanded immediate repentance and prayer. Some of Rochester's first citizens humbled themselves on the anxious bench, sweating their way into heaven surrounded by praying neighbors. It was the most spectacular of the evangelist's techniques, and the most unabashedly communal. . . .

A Shopkeeper's Millennium

Charles Finney's revival enlarged every Protestant church, broke down sectarian boundaries, and mobilized a religious community that had at its disposal enormous economic power. Motives which determined the use of that power derived from the revival, and they were frankly millenarian.

As Rochester Protestants looked beyond their community in 1831, they saw something awesome. For news of Finney's revival had helped touch off a wave of religious enthusiasm throughout much of the northern United States. The revival moved west into Ohio and Michigan, east into Utica, Albany, and the market towns of inland New England. Even Philadelphia and New York City felt its power. Vermont's congregational churches grew by 29 percent in 1831. During the same twelve months the churches of Connecticut swelled by over a third. After scanning reports from western New York, the Presbyterian General Assembly announced in wonder that "the work has been so general and thorough, that the whole customs of society have changed." Never before had so many Americans experienced religion in so short a time. Lyman Beecher, who watched the excitement from Boston, declared that the revival of 1831 was the greatest revival of religion that the world had ever seen.

Rochester Protestants saw conversions multiply and heard of powerful revivals throughout Yankee Christendom. They saw divisions among themselves melt away, and they began to sense that the pre-millennial unanimity was at hand—and that they and people like them were bringing it about. They had converted their families and neighbors through prayer. Through ceaseless effort they could use the same power to convert the world. It was Finney himself who told them that "if they were united all over the world the Millennium might be brought about in three months." He did not mean that Christ was coming to Rochester. The immediate and gory millennium predicted in Revelation had no place in evangelical thinking. Utopia would be realized on earth, and it would be made by God with the active and united collaboration of His people. It was not the physical reign of Christ that Finney predicted but the reign of Christianity. The millennium would be accomplished when sober, godly men—men whose every step was guided by a living faith in Jesus—exercised power in this world. Clearly, the revival of 1831 was a turning point in the long struggle to establish that state of affairs. American Protestants knew that, and John Humphrey Noyes later recalled that "in 1831, the whole orthodox church was in a state of ebullition in regard to the Millennium." Rochester evangelicals stood at the center of that excitement.

After 1831 the goal of revivals was the christianization of the world. With that at stake, membership in a Protestant church entailed new kinds of personal commitment. Newcomers to Brick Presbyterian Church in the 1820s had agreed to obey the laws of God and of the church, to treat fellow members as brothers, and "to live as an humble Christian." Each new convert was told that "renouncing all ungodliness and every worldly lust, you give up your all, soul and body, to be the Lord's, promising to walk before him in holiness and love all the days of your life." Not easy requirements, certainly, but in essence personal and passive. With the Finney revival, the ingrown piety of the 1820s turned outward and aggressive. In 1831 Brick Church rewrote its covenant, and every member signed this evangelical manifesto:

> We [note that the singular "you" has disappeared] do now, in the presence of the Eternal God, and these witnesses, covenant to be the Lord's. *We promise to renounce all the ways of sin, and to make it the business of our life to do good and promote the declarative glory of our heavenly Father.* We promise steadily and devoutly to attend upon the institutions and ordinances of Christ as administered in this church, and to submit ourselves to its direction and discipline, until our present relation shall be regularly dissolved. We promise to be kind and affectionate to all the members of this church, to be tender of their character, and to endeavor to the utmost of our ability, to promote their growth in grace. *We promise to make it the great business of our life to glorify God and build up the Redeemer's Kingdom in this fallen world,* and constantly to endeavor to present our bodies a living sacrifice, holy and acceptable to Him.

In that final passage, the congregation affirmed that its actions—both individually and in concert—were finally meaningful only in relation to the Coming Kingdom. Everything they did tended either to bring it closer or push it farther away.

Guiding the new activism was a revolution in ideas about human ability. The Reverend Williams James of Brick Church had insisted in 1828 that most men were innately sinful. Christians could not change them, but only govern their excesses through *"a system of moral regulations, founded upon the natural relations between moral beings, and having for its immediate end the happiness of the community."* We have seen, however, that certain of those "natural relations" were in disarray, and that the businessmen and master workmen who were expected to govern within them were the most active participants in the revival. Evangelical theology absolved them of responsibility by teaching that virtue and order were products not of external authority but of choices made by morally responsible individuals. Nowhere, perhaps, was this put more simply than in the Sunday schools. In the 1820s children had been taught to read and then forced to memorize huge parts of the Bible. (Thirteen-year-old Jane Wilson won a prize in 1823 when she committed a numbing 1,650 verses to memory.) After 1831 Sunday-school scholars stopped memorizing the Bible. The object now was to have them study a few verses a week and to come to an understanding of them, and thus to prepare themselves for conversion and for "an active and useful Christian life." Unregenerate persons were no longer to be disciplined by immutable authority and through fixed social relationships. They were free and redeemable moral agents, accountable for their actions, capable of accepting or rejecting God's promise. It was the duty of Christian gentlemen not to govern them and accept responsibility for their actions but to educate them and change their hearts.

William Wisner, pastor at Brick Church during these years, catalogued developments that were "indispensably necessary to the bringing of millennial glory." First, of course, was more revivals. Second, and tied directly to the first, was the return of God's people to the uncompromising personal standards of the primitive Christians and Protestant martyrs. For the public and private behavior of converts advertised what God had done for them. If a Christian drank or broke the Sabbath or cheated his customers or engaged in frivolous conversation, he weakened not only his own reputation but the awesome cause he represented. While Christian women were admonished to discourage flattery and idle talk and to bring every conversation onto the great subject, troubled businessmen were actually seen returning money to families they had cheated. Isaac Lyon, half-owner of the Rochester Woolen Mills, was seen riding a canal boat on Sunday in the fall of 1833. Immediately he was before the trustees of his church. Lyon was pardoned after writing a confession into the minutes and reading it to the full congregation. He confessed that he had broken the eighth commandment. But more serious, he admitted, was that his sin was witnessed by others who knew his standing in the church and in the community, and for whom the behavior of Isaac Lyon reflected directly on the evangelical cause. He had shamed Christ in public and given His enemies cause to celebrate.

Finney's revival had, however, centered among persons whose honesty and personal morals were beyond question before they converted. Personal piety and circumspect public behavior were at bottom means toward the furtherance of revivals. At the moment of rebirth, the question came to each of them: "Lord what wilt thou have me do?" The answer was obvious: unite with other Christians and convert the world. The world, however, contained bad habits, people, and institutions that inhibited revivals and whose removal must precede the millennium. Among church members who had lived in Rochester in the late 1820s, the right course of action was clear.

With one hand they evangelized among their own unchurched poor. With the other they waged an absolutist and savage war on strong drink.

On New Year's Eve of the revival winter, Finney's coworker Theodore Weld delivered a four-hour temperance lecture at First Presbyterian Church. Weld began by describing a huge open pit at his right hand, and thousands of the victims of drink at his left. First he isolated the most hopeless—the runaway fathers, paupers, criminals, and maniacs—and marched them into the grave. He moved higher and higher into society, until only a few well-dressed tipplers remained outside the grave. Not even these were spared. While the audience rose to its feet the most temperate drinkers, along with their wives and helpless children, were swallowed up and lost. Weld turned to the crowd and demanded that they not only abstain from drinking and encourage the reform of others but that they unite to stamp it out. They must not drink or sell liquor, rent to a grogshop, sell grain to distillers, or patronize merchants who continued to trade in ardent spirits. They must, in short, utterly disengage from the traffic in liquor and use whatever power they had to make others do the same. A packed house stood silent.

The Reverend Penney rose from his seat beside the Methodist and Baptist preachers and demanded that vendors in the audience stop selling liquor immediately. Eight or ten did so on the spot, and the wholesale grocers retired to hold a meeting of their own. The next day Elijah and Albert Smith, Baptists who owned the largest grocery and provisions warehouse in the city, rolled their stock of whiskey out onto the sidewalk. While cheering Christians and awestruck sinners looked on, they smashed the barrels and let thousands of gallons of liquid poison run out onto Exchange Street.

Within a week, Everard Peck wrote home that "the principal merchants who have traded largely in ardent spirits are about abandoning this unholy traffic & we almost hope to see this deadly poison expelled from our village." The performance of the Smith brothers was being repeated throughout Rochester. Sometimes wealthy converts walked into groceries, bought up all the liquor, and threw it away. A few grocers with a fine taste for symbolism poured their whiskey into the Canal. Even grocers who stayed outside the churches found that whiskey on their shelves was bad for business. The firm of Rossiter and Knox announced that it was discontinuing the sale of whiskey, but "not thinking it a duty to 'feed the Erie Canal' with their property, offer to sell at cost their whole stock of liquors . . ." Those who resisted were refused advertising space in some newspapers, and in denying the power of a united evangelical community they toyed with economic ruin. S. P. Needham held out for three years, but in 1834 he announced that he planned to liquidate his stock of groceries, provisions, and liquors and leave Rochester. "Church Dominancy," he explained, "has such influence over this community that no honest man can do his own business in his own way . . ."

Almost immediately, Weld's absolutist temperance pledge became a condition of conversion—the most visible symbol of individual rebirth. The teetotal pledge was only the most forceful indication of church members' willingness to use whatever power they had to coerce others into being good, or at least to deny them the means of being bad. While whiskey ran into the gutters, two other symbols of the riotous twenties disappeared. John and Joseph Christopher, both of them new Episcopalians, bought the theater next door to their hotel, closed it, and had it reopened as a livery stable. The Presbyterian Sprague brothers bought the circus building and turned it into a soap factory. Increasingly, the wicked had no place to go.

These were open and forceful attacks on the leisure activities of the new working class, something very much like class violence. But Christians waged war on sin, not workingmen. Alcohol, the circus, the theater, and other workingmen's entertainments were evil because they wasted men's time and clouded their minds and thus blocked the millennium. Evangelicals fought these evils in order to prepare society for new revivals. It was missionary work, little more. And in the winter following Finney's departure, it began to bear fruit.

DOCUMENTS

Religious Excitability, 1835

A "Revival of Religion" presupposes a declension. Almost all the religion in the world has been produced by revivals. God has found it necessary to take advantage of the excitability there is in mankind, to produce powerful excitements among them, before he can lead them to obey. Men are so spiritually sluggish, there are so many things to lead their minds off from religion, and to oppose the influence of the Gospel, that it is necessary to raise an excitement among them, till the tide rises so high as to sweep away the opposing obstacles. They must be so excited that they will break over these counteracting influences, before they will obey God. Not that excited feeling is religion, for it is not; but it is excited desire, appetite and feeling that prevents religion. The will is, in a sense, enslaved by the carnal and worldly desires. Hence it is necessary to awaken men to a sense of guilt and danger, and thus produce an excitement of counter feeling and desire which will break the power of carnal and worldly desire and leave the will free to obey God. . . .

SOURCE: Charles G. Finney, *Lectures on Revivals of Religion* (New York: Fleming H. Revell Co., n.d.), 9–11.

There is so little *principle* in the church, so little firmness and stability of purpose, that unless the religious feelings are awakened and kept excited, counter worldly feeling and excitement will prevail, and men will not obey God. They have so little knowledge, and their principles are so weak, that unless they are excited, they will go back from the path of duty, and do nothing to promote the glory of God. The state of the world is still such, and probably will be till the millennium is fully come, that religion must be mainly promoted by means of revivals. How long and how often has the experiment been tried, to bring the church to act steadily for God, without these periodical excitements? Many good men have supposed, and still suppose, that the best way to promote religion, is to go along *uniformly,* and gather in the ungodly gradually, and without excitement. But however sound such reasoning may appear in the abstract, *facts* demonstrate its futility. If the church were far enough advanced in knowledge, and had stability of principle enough to *keep awake,* such a course would do; but the church is so little enlightened, and there are so many counteracting causes, that she will not go steadily to work without a special interest being awakened. As the millennium advances, it is probable that these periodical excitements will be unknown. Then the church will be enlightened, and the counteracting causes removed, and the entire church will be in a state of habitual and steady obedience to God. The entire church will stand and take the infant mind, and cultivate it for God. Children will be trained up in the way they should go, and there will be no such torrents of worldliness, and fashion, and covetousness, to bear away the piety of the church, as soon as the excitement of a revival is withdrawn.

It is very desirable it should be so. It is very desirable that the church should go on steadily in a course of obedience without these excitements. Such excitements are liable to injure the health. Our nervous system is so strung that any powerful excitement, if long continued, injures our health and unfits us for duty. If religion is ever to have a pervading influence in the world, it cannot be so; this spasmodic religion must be done away. Then it will be uncalled for. . . . Then there will be no need that ministers should wear themselves out, and kill themselves, by their efforts to roll back the flood of worldly influence that sets in upon the church. But as yet the state of the Christian world is such, that to expect to promote religion without excitements is unphilosophical and absurd. The great political, and otherworldly excitements that agitate Christendom, are all unfriendly to religion, and divert the mind from the interests of the soul. Now these excitements can only be counteracted by *religious* excitements. And until there is religious principle in the world to put down irreligious excitements, it is vain to try to promote religion, except by counteracting excitements. This is true in philosophy, and it is a historical fact.

A Camp Meeting, 1829

It was in the course of this summer that I found the opportunity I had long wished for, of attending a camp-meeting, and I gladly accepted the invitation of an English lady and gentleman to accompany them in their carriage to the spot where it is held; this was in a wild district in the confines of Indiana.

The prospect of passing a night in the back woods of Indiana was by no means agreeable, but I screwed my courage to the proper pitch, and set forth determined to see with my own eyes, and hear with my own ears, what a camp-meeting really was. I had heart it said that being at a camp-meeting was like standing at the gate of heaven, and seeing it opening before you; I had heard it said that being at a camp-meeting was like finding yourself within the gates of hell; in either case there must be something to gratify curiosity, and compensate one for the fatigue of a long rumbling ride and a sleepless night.

We reached the ground about an hour before midnight, and the approach to it was highly picturesque. The spot chosen was the verge of an unbroken forest, where a space of about twenty acres appeared to have been partially cleared for the purpose. Tents of different sizes were pitched very near together in a circle round the cleared space; behind them were ranged an exterior circle of carriages of every description, and at the back of each were fastened the horses which had drawn them thither. Through this triple circle of defence we distinguished numerous fires burning brightly within it; and still more numerous lights flickering from the trees that were left in the enclosure. The moon was in meridian splendour above our heads. . . .

When we arrived, the preachers were silent; but we heard issuing from nearly every tent mingled sounds of praying, preaching, singing, and lamentation. . . .

We made the circuit of the tents, pausing where attention was particularly excited by sounds more vehement than ordinary. We contrived to look into many; all were strewed with straw, and the distorted figures that we saw kneeling, sitting, and lying amongst it, joined to the woeful and convulsive cries, gave to each, the air of a cell in Bedlam [Bethlehem Hospital, an insane asylum in London]. . . .

At midnight a horn sounded through the camp, which, we were told, was to call the people from private to public worship; and we presently saw them flocking from all sides to the front of the preachers' stand. Mrs. B. and I contrived to place ourselves with our backs supported against the lower

SOURCE: Frances Trollope, *Domestic Manners of the Americans* (London: Whittaker, Treacher & Co., 1832), 229–241.

part of this structure, and we were thus enabled to witness the scene which followed without personal danger. There were about two thousand persons assembled.

One of the preachers began in a low nasal tone, and, like all other Methodist preachers, assured us of the enormous depravity of man as he comes from the hands of his Maker, and of his perfect sanctification after he had wrestled sufficiently with the Lord to get hold of him, *et caetera*. The admiration of the crowd was evinced by almost constant cries of "Amen! Amen!" "Jesus! Jesus!" "Glory! Glory!" and the like. But this comparative tranquility did not last long: the preacher told them that "this night was the time fixed upon for anxious sinners to wrestle with the Lord"; that he and his brethren "were at hand to help them," and that such as needed their help were to come forward into "the pen." . . . "The pen" was the space immediately below the preachers' stand; we were therefore placed on the edge of it, and were enabled to see and hear all that took place in the very centre of this extraordinary exhibition.

The crowd fell back at the mention of the *pen*, and for some minutes there was a vacant space before us. The preachers came down from their stand and placed themselves in the midst of it, beginning to sing a hymn, calling upon the penitents to come forth. As they sang they kept turning themselves round to every part of the crowd, and, by degrees, the voices of the whole multitude joined in chorus. This was the only moment at which I perceived any thing like the solemn and beautiful effect, which I had heard ascribed to this woodland worship. It is certain that the combined voices of such a multitude, heard at dead of night, from the depths of their eternal forests, the many fair young faces turned upward, and looking paler and lovelier as they met the moon-beams, the dark figures of the officials in the middle of the circle, the lurid glare thrown by the altar-fires on the woods beyond, did altogether produce a fine and solemn effect, that I shall not easily forget; but ere I had well enjoyed it, the scene changed, and sublimity gave place to horror and disgust. . . .

. . . Above a hundred persons, nearly all females, came forward, uttering howlings and groans, so terrible that I shall never cease to shudder when I recall them. They appeared to drag each other forward, and on the word being given, "let us pray," they all fell on their knees; but this posture was soon changed for others that permitted greater scope for the convulsive movements of their limbs; and they were soon all lying on the ground in an indescribable confusion of heads and legs. They threw about their limbs with such incessant and violent motion, that I was every instant expecting some serious accident to occur.

But how am I to describe the sounds that proceeded from this strange mass of human beings? I know no words which can convey an idea of it. Hysterical sobbings, convulsive groans, shrieks and screams the most appalling, burst forth on all sides. I felt sick with horror. As if their hoarse and overstrained voices failed to make noise enough, they soon began to clap their hands violently. . . .

One woman near us continued to "call on the Lord," as it is termed, in the loudest possible tone, and without a moment's interval, for the two hours that we kept our dreadful station. She became frightfully hoarse, and her face so red as to make me expect she would burst a blood-vessel. Among the rest of her rant, she said, "I will hold fast to Jesus, I never will let him go; if they take me to hell, I will still hold him fast, fast, fast!" . . .

Visiting the Shakers, c. 1841

Sometime in the summer of 18—, I paid a visit to one of the Shaker villages in the State of New York. Previously to this, many times and oft had I (when tired of the noise and contention of the world, its erroneous opinions, and its wrong practices) longed for some retreat, where, with a few chosen friends, I could enjoy the present, forget the past, and be free from all anxiety respecting any future portion of time. And often had I pictured, in imagination, a state of happy society, where one common interest pre-vailed—where kindness and brotherly love were manifested in all of the every-day affairs of life—where liberty and equality would live, not in name, but in very deed—where idleness in no shape whatever would be tolerated—and where vice of every description would be banished, and neatness, with order, would be manifested in all things.

Actually to witness such a state of society, was a happiness which I never expected. I thought it to be only a thing among the airy castles which it has ever been my delight to build. But with this unostentatious and truly kind-hearted people, the Shakers, I found it; and the reality, in beauty and harmony, exceeded even the picturings of imagination.

No unprejudiced mind could, for a single moment, resist the conviction that this singular people, with regard to their worldly possessions, lived in strict conformity to the teachings of Jesus of Nazareth. There were men in this society who had added to the common stock thousands and tens of thousands of dollars; they nevertheless labored, dressed, and esteemed themselves as no better and fared in all respects, like those who had never owned, neither added to the society, any worldly goods whatever. The cheerfulness with which they bore one another's burdens, made even the temporal calamities, so unavoidable among the inhabitants of the earth, to be felt but lightly. . . .

In whatever light it may appear to others, to me it appears beautiful in-deed, to see a just and an impartial equality reign, so that the rich and the

SOURCE: "Visit to the Shakers," *Lowell Offering* (1841), 279–281, and "A Second Visit to the Shakers," *Lowell Offering* (1841), 337–340.

poor may share an equal privilege, and have all their wants supplied. That the Shakers are in reality what they profess to be, I doubt not. Neither do I doubt that many, very many lessons of wisdom might be learned of them, by those who profess to be wiser. And to all who wish to know if "any good thing can come out of Nazareth," I would say, you had better "go and see."

I was so well pleased with the appearances of the Shakers, and the prospect of quietness and happiness among them, that I visited them a second time. I went with a determination to ascertain as much as I possibly could of their forms and customs of worship, the every-day duties devolving on the members, &c.; and having enjoyed excellent opportunities for acquiring the desired information, I wish to present a brief account of what "I verily do know" in relation to several particulars.

First of all, justice will not permit me to retract a word in relation to the industry, neatness, order, and general good behavior, in the Shaker settlement which I visited. In these respects, that singular people are worthy of all commendation—yea, they set an example for the imitation of Christians every-where. Justice requires me to say, also, that their hospitality is proverbial, and deservedly so. They received and entertained me kindly, and (hoping perhaps that I might be induced to join them) they extended extra-civilities to me. I have occasion to modify the expression of my gratitude in only one particular—and that is, one of the female elders made statements to me concerning the requisite confessions to be made, and the forms of admission to their society, which statements she afterwards denied, under circumstances that rendered her denial a most aggravated insult. Declining further notice of this matter, because of the indelicacy of the confessions alluded to, I pass to notice,

1st. The domestic arrangements of the Shakers. However strange the remark may seem, it is nevertheless true, that our factory population work fewer hours out of every twenty-four, than are required by the Shakers, whose bell to call them from their slumbers, and also to warn them that it is time to commence the labors of the day, rings much earlier than our factory bells; and its calls were obeyed, in the family where I was entertained, with more punctuality than I ever knew the greatest "workey" among my numerous acquaintances (during the fourteen years in which I have been employed in different manufacturing establishments) to obey the calls of the factory-bell. And not until nine o'clock in the evening were the labors of the day closed, and the people assembled at their religious meetings.

Whoever joins the Shakers with the expectation of relaxation from toil, will be greatly mistaken, since they deem it an indispensable duty to have every moment of time profitably employed. The little portions of leisure which the females have, are spent in knitting—each one having a basket of knitting-work for a constant companion.

Their habits of order are, in many things, carried to the extreme. The first bell for their meals rings for all to repair to their chambers, from which, at the ringing of the second bell, they descend to the eating-room. Here, all take their appropriate places at the tables, and after locking their hands on their breasts, they drop on their knees, close their eyes, and remain in this position about two minutes. Then they rise, seat themselves, and with all expedition swallow their food; then rise on their feet, again lock their hands, drop on their knees, close their eyes, and in about two minutes rise and re-tire. Their meals are taken in silence, conversation being prohibited.

Those whose chambers are in the fourth story of one building, and whose work-shops are in the third story of another building, have a daily task in climbing stairs, which is more oppressive than any of the rules of a manufacturing establishment.

2d. With all deference, I beg leave to introduce some of the religious views and ceremonies of the Shakers.

From the conversation of the elders, I learned that they considered it doing God service, to sever the sacred ties of husband and wife, parent and child—the relationship existing between them being contrary to their re-ligious views—views which they believe were revealed from heaven to "Mother Ann Lee," the founder of their sect, and through whom they pro-fess to have frequent revelations from the spiritual world. These communi-cations, they say, are often written on gold leaves, and sent down from heaven to instruct the poor, simple Shakers in some new duty. They are copied, and perused, and preserved with great care. I one day heard quite a number of them read from a book, in which they were recorded, and the names of several of the brethren and sisters to whom they were given by the angels, were told me. One written on a gold leaf, was (as I was told) pre-sented to Proctor Sampson by an angel, so late as the summer of 1841. These "revelations" are written partly in English, and partly in some unintelligible jargon, or unknown tongue, having a spiritual meaning, which can be un-derstood only by those who possess the spirit in an eminent degree. They consist principally of songs, which they sing at their devotional meetings, and which are accompanied with dancing, and many unbecoming gestures and noises.

Often in the midst of a religious march, all stop, and with all their might set to stamping with both feet. And it is no uncommon thing for many of the worshipping assembly to crow like a parcel of young chanticleers, while other imitate the barking of dogs; and many of the young women set to whirling round and round—while the old men shake and clap their hands; the whole making a scene of noise and confusion, which can be better imag-ined than described. The elders seriously told me that these things were the outward manifestations of the spirit of God.

Apart from their religious meetings, the Shakers have what they call "union meetings." These are for social converse, and for the purpose of making the people acquainted with each other. During the day, the elders tell who may visit such and such chambers. A few minutes past nine, work is laid aside; the females change, or adjust, as best suits their fancy, their caps, handkerchiefs, and pinners, with a precision which indicates that they are not *altogether* free from vanity. The chairs, perhaps to the number of a dozen, are set in two rows, in such a manner that those who occupy them may face each other. At the ringing of a bell, each one goes to the chamber where either he or she has been directed by the elders, or remains at home to receive company, as the case may be. They enter the chambers *sans ceremonie,* and seat themselves—the men occupying one row of chairs, the women the other. Here, with their clean, checked, home-made pocket-handkerchiefs spread in their laps, and their spitboxes standing in a row between them, they converse about raising sheep and kine, herbs and vegetables, building wall and raising corn, heating the oven and paring apples, killing rats and gathering nuts, spinning tow and weaving sieves, making preserves and mending the brethren's clothes—in short, everything they do will afford some little conversation. But beyond their own little world, they do not appear to extend scarcely a thought. And why should they? Having so few sources of information, they know not what is passing beyond them. They however make the most of their own affairs, and seem to regret that they can converse no longer, when, after sitting together from half to three-quarters of an hour, the bell warns them that it is time to separate, which they do by rising up, locking their hands across their breasts, and bowing. Each one then goes silently to his own chamber.

It will readily be perceived, that they have no access to libraries, no books, excepting school-books, and a few relating to their own particular views; no periodicals, and attend no lectures, debates, Lyceums, &c. They have none of the many privileges of manufacturing districts—consequently their information is so very limited, that their conversation is, as a thing in course, quite insipid. The manner of their life seems to be a check to the march of mind and a desire for improvement; and while the moral and perceptive faculties are tolerably developed, the intellectual, with a very few exceptions, seem to be below the average.

A Letter from Brook Farm, 1841

As the weather precludes all possibility of ploughing, hoeing, sowing and other such operations, I bethink me that you may have no objection to hear something of my whereabout and whatabout. You are to know then, that I

SOURCE: Nathaniel Hawthorne to Louisa Hawthorne, cited by Richard B. Morris and James Woodress, eds., *Voices from America's Past* 2 (New York: E. P. Dutton & Co., 1961, 1962, 1963): 46–47.

took up my abode here on the 12th ultimo, in the midst of a snowstorm, which kept us all idle for a day or two. At the first glimpse of fair weather, Mr. Ripley summoned us into the cowyard and introduced me to an instrument with four prongs, commonly called a dung-fork. With this tool, I have already assisted to load twenty or thirty carts of manure, and shall take part in loading nearly three hundred more. Besides, I have planted potatoes and peas, cut straw and hay for the cattle, and done various other mighty works. This very morning, I milked three cows; and I milk two or three every night and morning. The weather has been so unfavorable, that we have worked comparatively little in the fields; but, nevertheless, I have gained strength wonderfully—grown quite a giant, in fact—and can do a day's work without the slightest inconvenience. In short, I am transformed into a complete farmer.

This is one of the most beautiful places I ever saw in my life, and as secluded as if it were a hundred miles from any city or village. There are woods, in which we can ramble all day, without meeting anybody, or scarcely seeing a house. Our house stands apart from the main road; so that we are not troubled even with passengers looking at us. Once in a while, we have a transcendental visitor, such as Mr. [Bronson] Alcott; but, generally, we pass whole days without seeing a single face, save those of the brethren. At this present time, our effective force consists of Mr. Ripley, Mr. Farley (a farmer from the far west), Rev. Warren Burton (author of various celebrated works), three young men and boys, who are under Mr. Ripley's care, and William Allen, his hired man, who has the chief direction of our agricultural labors. In the female part of the establishment there is Mrs. Ripley and two women folks. The whole fraternity eat together; and such a delectable way of life has never been seen on earth, since the days of the early Christians. We get up at half-past four, breakfast at half-past six, dine at half-past twelve, and go to bed at nine.

The thin frock, which you made for me, is considered a most splendid article; and I should not wonder if it were to become the summer uniform of the community. I have a thick frock, likewise; but it is rather deficient in grace, though extremely warm and comfortable. I wear a tremendous pair of cow-hide boots, with soles two inches thick. Of course, when I come to see you, I shall wear my farmer's dress.

We shall be very much occupied during most of this month, ploughing and planting; so that I doubt whether you will see me for two or three weeks. You have the portrait by this time, I suppose; so you can very well dispense with the original. When you write to me (which I beg you will do soon) direct your letter to West Roxbury, as there are two post offices in the town. I would write more; but William Allen is going to the village, and must have this letter; so good-bye.

NATH HAWTHORNE
PLOUGHMAN

Chapter 12

New People in a New Land

The influx of people from abroad played a central role in the story of America's growth from the seventeenth century forward. In the 1830s, 1840s, and 1850s, this immigration reached massive proportions: more than 4.5 million people arrived from the Old World. They sought a better life and escape from economic deprivation, religious persecution, and political oppression. The overwhelming majority of these newcomers were non-English in origin; approximately one-third came from Germany, and 40 percent were Irish Catholics. The Germans, like their predecessors in eighteenth-century Pennsylvania, met with some prejudice, but, as in the past, their ability to settle quickly and prosper as farmers, merchants, and craftsmen helped to curtail nativist (antiforeign) attacks. The Irish experience was quite different; they were desperately poor; they settled mostly in cities, although they were not accustomed to urban living; and they were steadfastly Catholic in a land overwhelmingly Protestant. As a result, they suffered as no prior immigrants had in the land of promise.

Peter Quinn's essay, "The Tragedy of Bridget Such-A-One," portrays the full scope of the Irish drama: the conditions that drove them from their homeland, the perils of the transatlantic journey, their struggle to survive and prosper in America in the face of virulent nativist prejudice. The author writes that the Irish migration had "profound" effects on both Ireland and the United States. What key points does the essay present in support of this? In what ways is the adherence of the Irish immigrants to their Roman Catholic faith both a cause of the prejudice they suffer and a most significant factor in enabling them "to survive, progress, and eventually reach undreamed-of levels of success"?

The first two documents depict divergent attitudes toward the Irish. The most destitute of all immigrant groups, the Irish took up pick and shovel and performed the miserable, backbreaking work of building the nation's canals, railroads, and urban structures. When the famous Irish actor Tyrone Power toured the South in the 1830s, he came upon a workforce of Irish immigrants engaged in digging a canal that would connect Lake Ponchatrain and New Orleans. The first document reveals Power's positive and sympathetic view of the laborers. Unfortunately, as Peter Quinn's essay reveals, some of America's most prominent figures of the day were outspoken nativists and anti-Catholic bigots. Prominent among them was artist and inventor Samuel F. B. Morse. The second document is an excerpt from his tract Imminent Dangers to the United States Through Foreign Immigration. *What was the basis of Morse's hostility toward the Irish? In what ways are the arguments of today's advocates of immigration restriction similar or different from those put forth in Morse's day?*

The horrors of the sea voyage depicted in Quinn's essay were experienced to a greater or lesser degree by most immigrants—so too were the difficulties encountered at the ports of debarkation and inland railroad stations. To alleviate these conditions and to assist their fellow countrymen in their struggle to adapt to a new and strange land, immigrants who had arrived earlier established immigrant aid societies along ethnic lines. The third document is an excerpt from the annual report of the German Society in Chicago for the period April 1857 to April 1858. What were among the most serious problems facing the newly arrived immigrants, and what steps did the society take to help relieve them?

ESSAY

The Tragedy of Bridget Such-A-One

Peter Quinn

Walking through the woods outside Concord, Massachusetts, in the spring of 1846, amid his solitary experiment in living close to nature, Henry David Thoreau was driven by a sudden storm to find shelter in what he thought

SOURCE: Peter Quinn, "The Tragedy of Bridget Such-A-One," *American Heritage,* Vol. 48(8), 37–51. Reprinted by permission of *American Heritage* magazine, a division of Forbes, Inc. © Forbes, Inc., December 1997.

was an uninhabited hut. "But therein," Thoreau recounts in *Walden*, he found living "John Field, an Irishman, and his wife, and several children," and he sat with them "under that part of the roof which leaked the least, while it showered and thundered without."

Thoreau pitied this "honest, hard-working, but shiftless man," a laborer probably drawn to the area to lay track for the railroad and now reduced to clearing bogs for a local farmer. He also "purposely talked to him as if he were a philosopher, or desired to be one." "But alas," Thoreau lamented, "the culture of an Irishman is an enterprise to be undertaken with a sort of moral bog hoe."

Field "heaved a sigh" at Thoreau's suggestion that "if he and his family would live simply, they might go a-huckleberrying in the summer for their amusement." Field's wife neither sighed nor spoke. A woman of "round greasy face," her breast exposed to suckle an infant, she "stared with arms a-kimbo" at the Yankee in their midst. The Fields left no account of this visit. Yet along with weighing the bewildering improbability of Thoreau's suggestion, it is probable that there were other matters on their minds.

By the spring of 1846 the condition of Ireland was well known. The country was on the edge. Hunger was widespread, and though the Fields may well have been illiterate, they must have shared with fellow immigrants a growing fear of what might happen if the potato failed again, as it had in 1845. Perhaps they had already received pleas from relatives still in Ireland who had sold their livestock or fishing nets to buy the American corn the government had imported. "For the honour of our lord Jasus christ and his Blessed mother," one contemporary letter writer to America cried, "hurry and take us out of this."

The Fields themselves were part of a steady stream of Irish who had been heading to North America for more than a century. The so-called Scotch-Irish—mostly Presbyterians from Ulster—were the first to come. They settled in large numbers in Canada and the American South, especially on the westward-moving edge of settlement, away from the low country with its established churches and plantation economy. By 1790 there were at least 250,000 Scotch-Irish in the United States.

After 1815 and the conclusion of the Napoleonic Wars, a steep fall in prices caused an agricultural depression in Ireland. At the same time, the start of widespread canal building in the United States (the Erie Canal was begun in 1817) and the laying of the groundwork for the country's industrial emergence drew more Irish Catholics, men whose sole marketable skill was their ability to wield a spade and whose religion, poverty, and numbers made them immediately suspect. The rough, brute work of canal building presaged the role that unskilled Irish labor would play in railroad construction, road building, and mining. Subject to cyclical employment and low wages, often living in shanties, the Irish were prized for their hard work and resented for what was seen as their proclivity to rowdiness and labor militancy.

The numbers of unskilled Irish in the cities along the Eastern seaboard grew. They lived where they worked, near the docks, foundries, and warehouses, in decaying housing that the former residents had fled or in flimsy, crowded structures erected to bring a maximum profit to their owners. By the early 1840s the increasing presence of the Catholic Irish helped prompt such prominent Americans as Samuel F. B. Morse, the inventor of the telegraph, and Lyman Beecher, progenitor of Harriet Beecher Stowe, to sound the tocsin against a supposed Catholic plot to subvert the liberties of native (i.e., white Protestant) Americans. A Boston mob attacked and burned a Catholic convent in Charlestown in 1834. In the spring of 1844 a nativist rally in Philadelphia ended in a three-day riot in which two Catholic churches, a convent, and a library were torched and a dozen people were left dead.

All this was prelude to the transformation that the Irish Famine brought. The famine represented the greatest concentration of civilian suffering and death in Western Europe between the Thirty Years' War and World War II. It rearranged the physical and mental landscape of Ireland, sweeping away a language and a way of life, and within a generation made a people steeped in rural traditions into the most urbanized ethnic group in North America.

Of the eight and a half million people in Ireland in 1845, a million perished from hunger and the fever and disease that stalked, jackal-like, in its wake. Between 1845 and 1855, in an unprecedented movement of people that was often less an organized migration than a panic, a mass unraveling, more than two million people left, for England and Australia and the great majority for North America.

It was part of the continuum of the transatlantic movement of people, but the famine migration was also different and extraordinary. Particularly in the densely populated townlands of the south and west of Ireland, where the bonds of culture and community went deep, the famine broke the traditional ties of Irish society. More people left Ireland in the decade of the famine than had in the previous 250 years. The exodus from Cork, Tipperary, Kerry, Galway, Clare, Mayo, and Donegal became a self-perpetuating process of removal. It swept aside all the old reluctance of the people to let go of their one hope for survival—the land—and made emigration an expectation rather than an exception.

Just as the mass flight of the famine years dissolved the underpinnings of the Irish countryside, its impact on America was profound. From independence to 1845 the Republic had absorbed about 1.6 million immigrants, the great majority Protestants looking to settle on the land. The annual number of Irish arriving in the United States tripled between 1843 and 1846, from 23,000 to 70,000. By 1851 it had reached a peak of 219,000, almost ten times what it had been less than a decade before.

Between 1845 and 1855 Irish Catholic immigration approached that of all groups over the previous seventy years, and the condition of these Irish sometimes bore more resemblance to modern-day "boat people" than to the immigrants arriving from Germany and Scandinavia. In an 1855 address to the Massachusetts legislature, Gov. Henry J. Gardner went back to classical history to find a comparable event. The scale of Irish immigration and the inmates it had deposited in the commonwealth's prisons and asylums called to mind, the governor said, the "horde of foreign barbarians" that had overthrown the Roman Empire.

The cause of this influx was the blight that attacked the potatoes of Ireland in the late summer of 1845. It is estimated that the potato crop represented about 60 percent of Ireland's annual food supply. Almost three and a half million people relied on it for the greatest part of their diet. The dreadful implications of a sudden and universal threat to the potato, which were instantaneously clear to Irish laborers and government officials alike, threw into dramatic relief the precarious condition of large parts of the population even in the best of times.

A decade earlier, in 1835, Alexis de Tocqueville had made a tour of Ireland. "You cannot imagine," he wrote his father soon after landing, "what a complexity of miseries five centuries of oppression, civil disorder, and religious hostility have piled on this poor people." The poverty he subsequently witnessed was, he recorded, "such as I did not imagine existed in this world. It is a frightening thing, I assure you, to see a whole population reduced to fasting like Trappists, and not being sure of surviving to the next harvest, which is still not expected for another ten days." The same year as Tocqueville's visit, a German traveler in Kilkenny, in the relatively prosperous eastern part of the country, watched as a mother collected the skins of gooseberries that had been spit on the ground and fed them to her child.

Among the more unusual witnesses to the extent of Irish poverty was Asenath Nicholson, a widowed American temperance crusader and Protestant evangelist, who arrived from New York on the eve of the famine to distribute Bibles among the Catholic poor and stayed to become a one-woman relief expedition. Mrs. Nicholson told of giving a "sweet biscuit" to an obviously famished child, who held it in her hand and stared at it. "How is it," Mrs. Nicholson asked the child's mother, "she cannot be hungry?" The mother replied that the child had never seen such a delicacy before and "cannot think of parting with it." Mrs. Nicholson marveled that "such self-denial in a child was quite beyond my comprehension, but so inured are these people to want, that their endurance and self-control are almost beyond belief."

The anecdotes of visitors were confirmed by a commission of inquiry formed to study the extent of Irish poverty. Reporting in 1835, the commission noted that two-fifths of the population lived in "fourth-class accommodations"—one-room windowless mud cabins—and at least two and a half million people annually required some assistance in order to avoid starvation.

Although central to Irish life, the potato was a relatively recent ecological interloper. It is said to have been introduced in Cork in the 1580s by Sir Walter Raleigh, a principal in the plantation of both Ireland and the New World. Until the potato arrived, cattle and oats were the Irish mainstays. The land itself was divided among an amalgam of Gaelic and Norman-Gaelic lords, who were often feuding with one another. In the east a wedge of English-controlled territory—the Pale—had variously expanded and contracted since its conquest by the Normans.

The Atlantic explorations, the contest for overseas empire, and the bitter ideological divisions that accompanied the Reformation conferred on Ireland a new strategic importance. Beginning in the 1540s and extending through a long series of bloody wars and rebellions that ended in the defeat of the Catholic forces in 1691, Ireland was brought under the control of the English crown. Political power and ownership of the land were relentlessly concentrated in the hands of a Protestant ascendancy. The widespread dislocation caused by the long struggle for mastery of Ireland opened the way for the spread of the hardy, reliable, nutritionally rich potato, which not only thrived in the cool, damp climate but yielded, per acre, three times the calories of grain.

Between 1700 and 1845, thanks in large part to the potato, a populace of less than three million grew to almost eight and a half million, to the point where Disraeli pronounced Ireland the most thickly peopled country in Europe. However, the population distribution was uneven. In pre-famine Ireland the general rule was: The worse the land, the more people on it. The greatest growth was in reclaimed bogs and on mountainsides. The number of small tenant farmers and laborers soared, particularly in the west, where the scramble for land drove an intense process of reclamation and subdivision.

The unit of Irish settlement was the *clachan* or *baile,* a cluster of cabins unlike the neatly laid-out village of school, shop, and church found throughout most of the British Isles. The *clachan* was a collection of families, often tied by friendship or blood, organized around a communal system of agriculture designed to ensure a fair distribution of the best land for tillage. The usually Irish-speaking culture of the *clachan* was carried on in the lives of the people, in storytelling, music, and dance, and in wakes, religious devotions, and fairs.

Like the potato, the fungus that destroyed it came from the Americas. In 1843 potato crops in the eastern United States were largely ruined by a mysterious blight. In June of 1845 the blight was reported in the Low Countries. In mid-September an English journal announced "with very great regret" that the blight had "unequivocally declared itself" in Ireland, then posed the question that anyone even passingly acquainted with the country knew must be faced: "Where will *Ireland* be, in the event of a universal potato rot?" The speed of the blight bewildered observers. Over and over they expressed amazement at how fields lush with potato plants could the next day be putrid wastelands. It was a generation before the agent of destruction was fingered as a spore-spreading fungus, *Phytophthora infestans,* and a generation after that before an antidote was devised.

Without prospect of a cure, Sir Robert Peel, the Tory prime minister, faced a crisis in Ireland. The appearance of the blight in late summer meant two-thirds of the potatoes had already been harvested, yet the near-total reliance of a sizable part of the population on a single crop left no doubt that extraordinary measures would have to be taken. Peel was an able administrator, knowledgeable about Ireland and its discontents. Responding quickly to the impending food crisis, he ordered the secret purchase of a hundred thousand pounds' worth of American corn to be held in reserve and released into the market when demand threatened to drive food prices out of control. This same supply was to be available for purchase, at cost, by local relief committees. Landlord-directed committees were set up to cooperate with the Board of Works in funding work schemes. The aim was to provide tenants and laborers with the chance to earn the money they needed to buy imported food and avoid direct government handouts that would encourage what was seen as the congenital laziness of the Irish.

In December 1845, in order to lower grain prices, Peel proposed repeal of the Corn Laws, import duties that protected British agriculture from foreign competition. He was convinced that increased competition would result in lowering the price of food for the British working classes, which it did. Cheap imports would not only lessen the immediate threat of mass hunger but help wean the poor from reliance on the potato and transform small tenants into landless, wage-earning laborers. As a result of Peel's relief measures, Ireland averted the worst consequences of the blight through the winter of 1845–46. The weather was unusually cold. The poorhouses began to fill up. The poor exhausted whatever reserves they may have had. But starvation was held at bay.

The repeal of the Corn Laws in June 1846 quickly precipitated the fall of Peel's government. Lord Russell, the new Whig prime minister, faced a more daunting challenge than had Peel. The return of the blight for a second year, and the devastation of three-quarters of the potato crop, drove thousands more on to the public works. In August 1846 the works were temporarily halted and overhauled along lines set down by Charles Trevelyan, the head permanent civil servant in the Treasury. The rules of employment were made stricter, and more of the cost was put on local landlords. By October the public works employed 114,000; three months later, in January 1847, more than 500,000; by March, 750,000. Reports of extreme suffering and death began to pour in from different parts of the country. In Skibbereen, County Cork, an artist sent by the *Illustrated London News* testified that neither pictures nor words could capture the horror of "the dying, the living, and the dead, lying indiscriminately upon the same floor, without anything between them and the cold earth, save a few miserable rags upon them."

The American temperance worker Asenath Nicholson got her first view of the worsening condition of Ireland in the outskirts of Dublin. In December 1846 a servant in a house where she was staying implored her to see a man nearby, the father of seven, who, though sick with fever and "in an actual state of starvation," had "staggered with his spade" to the public works. The servant brought in a human skeleton "emaciated to the last degree." Horrified as she was, Mrs. Nicholson would remember this as only "the *first* and the beginning of . . . dreadful days yet in reserve."

Daunted by the expense of the public works, the government decided to switch to soup kitchens, a form of relief introduced by the Quakers. The public works began to close in March. By midsummer of 1847 three million men, women, and children were being fed with soup. An indication of the government's capacity to restrain the ravages of hunger, the soup kitchens were the apogee of the relief effort—and its effective end.

Writing in *Blackwood's Magazine* in April 1847, a commentator complained of the expense being incurred to help the Irish. The famine was not an English problem, he wrote, and there was no need for wasting another shilling on a disaster "which the heedlessness and indolence of the Irish had brought upon themselves." A month earlier the *Times* of London had expressed a similar sense of the widespread frustration with the Irish, again connecting Ireland's agony to the innate defects of its people: "The Celt is less energetic, less independent, less industrious than the Saxon. This is the archaic condition of his race. . . . [England] can, therefore, afford to look with contemptuous pity on the Celtic cottier suckled in poverty which he is too callous to feel, and too supine to mend."

Since the abolition of the Dublin parliament in 1801, Ireland had theoretically been an integral part of the United Kingdom, its people entitled to the same protections and considerations as those of English shires. But as the famine made inexorably clear, Ireland remained a colony, one usually viewed as a turbulent, perplexing, intractable anomaly.

During the period immediately preceding the famine, Daniel O'Connell, who had led the agitation in the 1820s that won Catholics the right to sit in Parliament, had headed a movement to repeal the union with Britain and return a measure of self-rule to Dublin. The union was maintained, but now, in the face of Ireland's continuing distress, a tired, broken O'Connell told the House of Commons: "Ireland is in your hands. If you do not save her, she cannot save herself." His plea went unheeded. As framed by Sir Charles Wood, the chancellor of the exchequer, the challenge was no longer to help feed the Irish but "to force them into self-government . . . our song . . . must be—'It is your concern, not ours.'"

The potato didn't fail in the summer of 1847, yet the distress of the past two seasons had seriously curtailed the scale of plantings. Trevelyan, however, convinced that Ireland's problem wasn't inadequate food supplies but "the selfish, perverse and turbulent character of the people," pronounced the famine over. There would be no more extraordinary measures by the Treasury, not even when the potato failed again in 1848, 1849, and into the early 1850s. Irish needs would be met out of Irish resources.

The government's change of direction went beyond the withdrawal of desperately needed assistance. The passage in June 1847 of the Irish Poor Law Extension Act married racial contempt and providentialism—the prevalent conviction among the British elite of God's judgment having been delivered on the Irish—with political economy. According to the theorists of the iron laws of economics, the great deficiencies of Ireland were a want of capital accumulation—the result of the maze of small tenancies—and the incurable lethargy of a people inured to indolent reliance on an inferior food. The famine provided an opportunity to sweep away the root causes of Ireland's economic backwardness.

The amendment of the Irish Poor Law made landlords responsible for the rates (taxes collected to support the workhouses) on all holdings valued under four pounds per year. Another provision—the Gregory Clause—denied relief to anyone holding more than a quarter-acre of land. This left many tenants with the choice of abandoning their holdings or condemning their families to starvation. Together these clauses were a mandate to clear the land of the poorest and most vulnerable. Entire villages were "tumbled." In one instance a newspaper reported that some of the evicted were found dead along the roadsides, "emitting green froth from their mouths, as if masticating soft grass." On the Mullet Peninsula in Mayo, James Hack Tuke, a Quaker involved in the intensive relief effort undertaken by the Society of Friends, witnessed an entire settlement being razed: "Six or seven hundred people were evicted; young and old, mother and babe, were alike cast forth, without shelter and without means of subsistence! A fountain of ink (as one of them said) would not write half our misfortunes."

Asenath Nicholson traveled some of the same territory as Tuke and was horrified by the sheer scale of what she witnessed: "Village upon village, and company after company, have I seen; and one magistrate who was travelling informed me that at nightfall the preceding day, he found a company who had gathered a few sticks and fastened them into a ditch, and spread over what miserable rags they could collect . . . under these more than two hundred men, women, and children, were to crawl for the night . . . and not *one* pound of any kind of food was in the whole encampment."

Across much of Ireland the purgatory of the first two years of famine became a living hell. The workhouses, which the people had once done their best to avoid, were besieged by mobs clamoring to get in. The dead were buried coffinless in mass graves. The Reverend Francis Webb, a Church of Ireland rector in West Cork, published an account of dead children being left unburied and asked in anger and disbelief, "Are we living in a portion of the United Kingdom?" Asiatic cholera, carried from India in the bowels of British soldiers, eventually arrived and cut down thousands of those already weakened by hunger.

Emigration from Ireland became a torrent, no longer a quest for new opportunities but a question of life or death. The ports filled with people. Most sought passage to Liverpool, the former capital of the slave trade and now the entrepôt of emigration. From there they hoped to find a cheap fare to America. Jammed in the holds of coal barges and on the decks of cattle boats, three hundred thousand Irish sailed to Liverpool in 1847 alone.

The government made a pretense of enforcing regulations that prescribed medical inspection of all passengers and minimum space and rations for each. In reality emigrants, having scrambled however they could to put together the four pounds that passage to America typically cost, were at the mercy of a laissez-faire system that treated them more like ballast than like human beings. Dr. J. Custis, who served as a ship's surgeon on half a dozen emigrant vessels, published a series of articles that described their sailings: "I have been engaged during the worst years of famine in Ireland; I have witnessed the deaths of hundreds from want; I have seen the inmates of a workhouse carried by the hundreds weekly through its gates to be thrown unshrouded and coffinless into a pit with quicklime . . . and revolting to the feelings as all this was, it was not half so shocking as what I subsequently witnessed on board the very first emigrant ship I ever sailed on."

During a journey in steerage of anywhere from three to seven weeks, disease, seasickness, spoiled rations, hostile crews, and a lack of space and air—an experience one observer compared to "entering a crowded jail"— eroded whatever differences of region or accent or status once had divided the emigrants. By the time they landed, it was easy for nativists to lump them together as a race of feckless Paddies destined to be a permanent drain on American resources.

The reaction to the arrival of growing numbers of impoverished, famished immigrants wasn't long in coming. Congress tightened the regulations that governed passenger ships entering American ports and raised the fines on violators. Massachusetts began to enforce a law requiring that before any pauper or sick person was landed on its shores, the ship's master had to post a bond for every passenger. New York also required a bond and leveled a per person tax to cover the cost of those who became public charges. The net effect was that in the spring of 1847 a significant portion of the first wave of famine migrants left not for the United States but for British North America.

The demand for passage resulted in a hodgepodge of vessels being pressed into service. Poorly provisioned, devoid of medicines or sanitary facilities, crowded with hungry, fever-ridden passengers, they quickly developed a well-earned reputation as "coffin ships." In May 1847 the first of them arrived at a quarantine station, with a small hospital that had been set up on Grosse Île, in the St. Lawrence, thirty miles below Quebec. Out of a company of 240 passengers, 80 were down with typhus, and 9 already dead. By June nearly forty vessels were backed up for miles along the river, and 14,000 people awaited quarantine. The dead were buried in mass graves. By the end of the sailing season, the British government's conservative estimate was that of the 107,000 who had left for Canada from British ports, 17,500— one out of every six—had died.

Despite the barriers raised by American ports, the overwhelming majority of famine emigrants sought passage to the United States, for few wished to remain under British dominion. Even in 1847, as many as 25,000 immigrants arrived in Boston from British ports, and at least another 5,000 managed to find their way down from Canada. New York received the greatest number. Between 1845 and 1855, a million Irish—one-eighth of the country's population—landed on the wharves and piers around Manhattan. Many moved on. But many stayed, helping swell the city's population from 370,000 to 630,000 in a single decade.

The voyage to the United States wasn't characterized by the same catalogue of horrors as the emigration to Canada in 1847, but it was ordeal enough. Stephen de Vere, an Anglo-Irish gentleman with an interest in emigration, sailed to New York aboard the *Washington,* a well-built ship, in 1847. He watched the passengers in steerage being physically abused and denied the rations they were supposedly due. When he protested, the first mate knocked him to the deck. Taking his complaint to the captain, de Vere was threatened with the brig. Dysentery was rampant on the ship; a dozen children died from it. On landing, de Vere collected accounts of similar abuse aboard other ships and wrote a complaint to the emigration commissioners in London. In the end nothing was done.

One of the most compelling renderings of the emigrant trade in the famine era was by an American whose introduction to the sea was aboard a packet ship between Liverpool and New York. Herman Melville was nineteen when he made the voyage out and back in 1839. Ten years later, in 1849, he published *Redburn,* an account of his journey that is part fiction, part memoir, and part meditation on the changes that the mass descent of strangers was bringing to America. Though a novel, the book is alive with a real sense of the grandeur and misery of Liverpool and of the unromantic business of hauling five hundred emigrants across the Atlantic in a creaking, swaying, wind-driven ship.

The emigrants aboard Melville's fictional ship, the *Highlander*, were mostly Irish, and like many real emigrant ships, the *Highlander* wasn't built for passengers but was converted to that purpose. Triple tiers of bunks jerry-built along the ship's sides "looked more like dog-kennels than anything else" and soon smelled little different. "We had not been at sea one week," the protagonist, Wellingborough Redburn, observed, "when to hold your head down the fore hatchway was like holding it down a suddenly opened cesspool." Driven by hunger, some of the passengers stole a small pig, and "*him* they devoured raw, not venturing to make an incognito of his carcass." Fever struck. Emigrants began to die. Venturing down into steerage, Redburn encountered "rows of rude bunks, hundreds of meager, begrimed faces were turned upon us. . . . the native air of the place . . . was foetid in the extreme."

Docked at last on South Street, crew and passengers dispersed. As they left, young Redburn wondered at the fate of those who had survived the gantlet of hunger and emigration but now seemed exhausted and broken: "How, then, with these emigrants, who, three thousand miles from home, suddenly found themselves, deprived of brothers and husbands, with but a few pounds, or perhaps but a few shillings, to buy food in a strange land?"

Other Americans shared such doubts, and for many the answer was that the Catholic Irish were a threat to the country's prosperity and liberty. Nativists focused on Irish poverty as a function of Irish character, a result of their addiction to "rum and Romanism." When the Irish banded together to form religious, fraternal, and labor organizations aimed at improving their lot, this was taken as proof of their conspiratorial clannishness. Near the end of the famine decade, in 1854, the American party, which was formed to halt the incursion of foreigners and Catholics, controlled the legislatures of most New England states as well as those of Maryland, Delaware, Kentucky, New Jersey, Pennsylvania, and California. For a time it was the most successful third-party movement in American history.

The poverty of the Irish, while only a part of the famine story, was not merely a figment of the nativist imagination. The cities of the Northeast faced problems of public order that wouldn't be repeated until after World War II. The newcomers didn't invent street gangs or rioting or machine politics—all pre-dated the arrival of the famine Irish—but the deluge of masses of disoriented, disorganized, unskilled alien labor raised an unprecedented sense of alarm. In 1851 it was estimated that one out of every six New Yorkers was a pauper. Of the 113,000 people residing in jails, workhouses, hospitals, or asylums or receiving public or private charity, three-quarters were foreign-born, the bulk of them Irish.

New York State formally opened its first immigrant depot in 1855 at Castle Garden, its purpose to bring order to the process of arrival. Three decades later, under federal control, the depot was moved to Ellis Island. Golden or not, the door America erected at its entryway was a legacy of the famine.

By the autumn of 1849, when Melville wrote of the travails of his company of tired and poor Irish immigrants, Asiatic cholera had arrived in New York. It spread as far west as St. Louis and took thousands of lives. At that same moment, two real-life immigrants reached American shores, and, for all their differences—one was an ex-policeman fleeing arrest, the other a young woman seeking work—they embodied much of the pain and the promise of the famine years.

Michael Corcoran was the son of an Irishman who had made a career in the Royal Army. In 1845, at the age of eighteen, Corcoran joined the Revenue Police, which, along with the Irish Constabulary, was organized along military lines. He was posted to Donegal to help suppress the trade in illicit liquor. The advent of the famine heightened the role of the constabulary and the army in Ireland, already the most policed and garrisoned part of the British Isles. By 1848 their combined total was at an all-time high of forty thousand—almost twice the size of the expeditionary force that the British government would soon send to the Crimea at a cost nine times what it spent on famine relief in Ireland.

Whether Corcoran, as a member of the Revenue Police, was called to the support of the army or constabulary is unknown. Both forces were active during the famine, especially in areas like Donegal. They helped distribute relief as well as guarantee the all-important rights of property. In the latter capacity they not only assisted in mass clearances but guarded the convoys that carried grain and beef to England throughout the famine. The image of those convoys became a touchstone of Irish bitterness in later years, alleged proof of the charge leveled by the Irish nationalist John Mitchel that "the Almighty indeed sent the potato blight, but the English created the Famine."

Over the course of the famine, more grain may have entered Ireland than left. But often the imports didn't reach the most distressed parts of the country, or were spoiled by the time they did. Unfamiliar with processing or cooking the yellow corn imported from America, people were made sick by it. The memory of soldiers and police guarding precious stores of food from the starving wasn't an invention. Mrs. Nicholson testified to the sight of well-fed, well-armed soldiers and "haggard, meagre, squalid skeletons ... grouped in starving multitudes around them." In 1847—"Black '47," the Irish called it—two thousand people were transported to Australia for cattle stealing. On Spike Island, in Cork Harbor, three hundred adolescents were imprisoned for "taking bread while starving."

Whatever Corcoran witnessed or took part in as a policeman may have been part of what led him to break his oath to the Crown. In August 1849 he was "relinquished" from his duties on suspicion of belonging to one of the secret agrarian societies that were violently resisting evictions. Before he could be arrested, he slipped aboard an emigrant ship and escaped to New York. There was little to distinguish him from his fellow immigrants when he landed in October 1849. But he quickly made a name for himself. He got work in a tavern and became a district leader for Tammany Hall, which was just awakening to the potential of the Irish vote, and he was an early member of the Fenian Brotherhood, the secret Irish revolutionary society fueled by the burning intent to revenge the famine and overthrow British rule in Ireland.

Five years after he arrived, Corcoran was elected a captain in a heavily Irish militia unit, the 69th New York. Not long afterward he was commended for helping defend the quarantine station on Staten Island, which a mob had attempted to burn. In 1860 the Prince of Wales (the future Edward VII) paid the first visit by a member of the royal family to the Unites States. The militia was ordered to parade in the prince's honor; Corcoran, now the colonel of the 69th, refused to march his men for someone they called the "Famine Prince." He was court-martialed for what in many eyes confirmed the worst suspicions of Irish disloyalty to American institutions.

The outbreak of the Civil War saved Corcoran from being cashiered. He returned to his regiment, which he commanded at Bull Run, where he was badly wounded and captured. Freed a year later in a prisoner exchange, he returned to service as head of his own "Irish Legion." He again fell under an official cloud when he shot and killed an officer who had not only assaulted him, Corcoran said, but had called him "a damned Irish son of a bitch." Before any official judgment could be reached, Corcoran died—partly as the result of his wounds—and was given a hero's funeral in New York.

As with generations of immigrants to come, Irish and otherwise, Corcoran was eager for the opportunities that America had to offer and grateful when they proved real. He readily took on American citizenship and showed no hesitation about defending the Union. Yet he was equally unwilling to turn his back on the culture and people that had formed him. Fiercely loyal to his new homeland, he had no intention of abandoning his religion, disguising his ancestry, or detaching himself from the struggles of his native land. No one who observed Michael Corcoran could doubt that a powerful new element had been added to the American mix.

The month Michael Corcoran landed in New York, October 1849, Henry David Thoreau traveled to Cohasset, Massachusetts, to see the wreck of the *St. John,* a Boston-bound brig that had set sail from Ireland "laden with emigrants." It was one of sixty emigrant ships lost between 1847 an 1853. Thoreau walked the beach and inspected the bodies collected there: "I saw many marble feet and matted heads as the cloths were raised, and one livid, swollen and mangled body of a drowned girl,—who probably had intended to go out to service in some American family. . . . Sometimes there were two or more children, or a parent and child, in the same box, and on the lid would perhaps be written with red chalk, 'Bridget such-a-one, and sister's child.'"

Besides what Thoreau tells us of the drowned girl, we know only that she sailed from Galway, part of a legion of Bridget such-a-ones. It's possible that coming from the west, she was an Irish speaker; more than a third of the famine emigrants were. Perhaps she had relatives waiting for her. Perhaps not. Yet her corpse points to a larger story than the perils of the Atlantic crossing or the travails of a single season of immigrants. The dissolution of Irish rural life resulted in a bleak, narrow society of late marriage and of dowries carefully passed to single heirs, encouraging the young, especially girls, to emigrate. No other group of nineteenth-century immigrants had nearly the proportion of women as the Irish reached in the aftermath of the famine: more than 50 percent.

Encouraged, even expected, to make a contribution to the welfare of the parents and siblings they had left behind, Irishwomen worked in factories and mills. Irish maids became a fixture of bourgeois American life. Domestic service became so associated with the Irish that maids were often referred to generically as "Kathleens" or "Bridgets." The work could be demeaning as well as demanding. In 1845 the antislavery crusader Abby Kelley visited fellow abolitionists in Pennsylvania. Her hosts' Irish servant girl came to her in private and catalogued the work she had to perform for a dollar a week. "When I tried to console her and told her that we were trying to bring about a better state of things," Kelley wrote, "a state in which she would be regarded as an equal, she wept like a child."

Female employment was a source of independence and adaptation to American life, but above all, it was a wellspring of the money that poured back into Ireland, rescuing families from starvation and financing a self-perpetuating chain of emigration that would stretch across generations. At the height of the famine, Mrs. Nicholson marveled that "the Irish in America, and in all other countries where they are scattered, were sending one continued train of remittances, to the utter astonishment of the Postmasters." In the famine decade more than £8.4 million was remitted for passage out of the British Isles. The British colonial secretary was delighted that the outflow of Irish was being funded at no expense to the government and surprised to discover that "such feelings of family affection, and such fidelity and firmness of purpose, should exist so generally among the lower classes." In Massachusetts, Edward Everett Hale was struck by the generosity of the Irish but worried that their "clannish" spirit of sharing might drag them down together. "For example," he wrote, "it is within my own observation, that in the winter of 1850 to 1851, fourteen persons, fresh from Ireland, came in on the cabin hospitality of a woman in Worcester, because she was the cousin of one of the party."

The strains of adjustment to America were enormous. The itinerant work of railroad building, which many took part in, and high rates of disease, accidental death, and alcohol abuse put tremendous pressure on families. Irishwomen were more likely to be widowed or deserted than their American counterparts. But amid the epic transformation of potato-growing tenants into urban laborers, moving from the tightly woven fabric of Irish townlands to the freewheeling environment of American cities, what was most remarkable of all was the speed and scope with which the Irish reorganized themselves. Within little more than a generation they translated their numbers into control of the Democratic party in the major cities and turned municipal patronage into an immediate and pragmatic method for softening the ravages of boom-and-bust capitalism. Barred from the privileged circle of high finance, equipped with few entrepreneurial skills, suspicious through experience of theories that made capital accumulation a supreme good, the Irish spearheaded the rise of organized labor.

The greatest manifestation of their effort to regroup was the Catholic Church, which was elevated from an ingredient in Irish life to its center, the bulwark of a culture that had lost its language and almost disintegrated beneath the catastrophe of the famine. In America as well as Ireland, vocations to the priesthood and sisterhood soared. Catholic parishes became the defining institution of Irish neighborhoods. Catholic schools, hospitals, and asylums created a vast social welfare network. Catholic nuns founded protectories and orphanages that countered the placing-out system, which took hundreds of thousands of immigrant children and shipped them west to "Christian" (Protestant) homes. Eventually these institutions were influential in establishing the obligation of the state to the support of dependent children.

The Catholic Church was the strongest institutional link in the exodus from Ireland and adjustment to America. It was *the* enduring monument to the effects of the famine: to the sexual repression and religious devotionalism that followed it; to the quest for respectability amid jarring dislocation and pervasive discrimination; and to the discipline, cohesion, and solidarity that allowed the Irish to survive, progress, and eventually reach undreamed-of levels of success. Only after a century and a half, when the Irish had erased almost every trace of their once seemingly ineradicable status as outsiders, would the power of the church begin to wane.

For Irish Catholics in America, the famine was the forge of their identity, fire and anvil, the scattering time of flight and dissolution, and the moment of regathering that would one day make them an influential part of the world's most powerful democracy. The famine was rarely recalled in its specifics. There was no record made of its horrors or complexities. The blistering humiliations it inflicted and the divisions it exacerbated—the way it fell hardest on the landless Irish-speaking poor—were subsumed in a bitter and near-universal detestation of British rule in Ireland. Yet, unspoken,

nined, largely lost to conscious memory, the famine was threaded
rish America's attitudes, expectations, and institutions. The Irish-
rican film director John Ford said that he was drawn to making the
rie version of *The Grapes of Wrath* because in the Depression-era saga of
Okies evicted from the land and left to wander and starve he recognized the
story of his own ancestors.

For America as well the famine was a time of testing. As Herman
Melville saw it, the immigrants arriving unchecked on the docks of New
York were a sign that America would be "not a nation, so much as a world."
The greatness and genius of America wasn't in reproducing the ethnic
sameness of Britain or France, he wrote. The world had no need of more
pure-blooded tribes or xenophobic nationalities. Bereft of wealth or education or Anglo-Saxon pedigree, what Bridget such-a-one and all the other
nameless, tired, hope-filled immigrants carried with them was the opportunity for America to affirm its destiny: "We are the heirs of all time, and with
all nations we divide our inheritance. On this Western Hemisphere all tribes
and people are forming into federated whole; and there is a future which
shall see the estranged children of Adam restored as to the old hearth-stone
in Eden."

DOCUMENTS

Irish Immigrants: A Sympathetic View, c. 1833

One of the greatest works now in progress here, is the canal planned to connect Lac Pontchartrain with the city [New Orleans]. In the month of February it was completed to within three miles of the lake; and as it was a
pleasant ride to the point where the digging was in progress, I two or three
times visited the scene, after its bearings had been explained by the two intelligent persons under whose guidance I first penetrated the swamp.

I only wish that the wise men at home who coolly charge the present
condition of Ireland upon the inherent laziness of her population, could be
transported to this spot, to look upon the hundreds of fine fellows labouring
here beneath a sun that at this winter season was at times insufferably
fierce, and amidst a pestilential swamp whose exhalations were foetid to a
degree scarcely endurable even for a few moments; wading amongst
stumps of trees, mid-deep in black mud, clearing the spaces pumped out by
powerful steam-engines; wheeling, digging, hewing, or bearing burdens it

SOURCE: Tyrone Power, *Impressions of America During the Years 1833, 1834, and 1835* 2 (London: R. Bentley, 1836): 238–244.

made one's shoulders ache to look upon; exposed meantime to every change of temperature, in log-huts, laid down in the very swamp, on a foundation of newly-felled trees, having the water lying stagnant between the floor-logs, whose interstices, together with those of the side-walls, are open, pervious alike to sun or wind, or snow. Here they subsist on the coarsest fare, holding life on a tenure as uncertain as does the leader of a forlorn hope; excluded from all the advantages of civilization; often at the mercy of a hard contractor, who wrings his profits from their blood; and all this for a pittance that merely enables them to exist, with little power to save, or a hope beyond the continuance of the like exertion.

Such are the labourers I have seen here, and have still found them civil and courteous, with a ready greeting for the stranger inquiring into their condition, and a quick jest on their own equipment, which is frequently, it must be admitted, of a whimsical kind.

Here too were many poor women with their husbands; and when I contemplated their wasted forms and haggard sickly looks, together with the close swamp whose stagnant air they were doomed to breathe, whose aspect changeless and deathlike alone met their eyes, and fancied them, in some hour of leisure, calling to memory the green valley and the pure river, or the rocky glen and sparkling brook of their distant home, with all the warmth of colouring the imaginative spirit of the Irish peasant can so well supply, my heart has swelled and my eyes have filled with tears.

I cannot hope to inspire the reader with my feelings upon a mere sketch like this; but if I could set the scene of these poor labourers' exile fairly forth, with all the sad accompaniments detailed; could I show the course of the hardy, healthy pair, just landed, to seek fortune on these long-sighed-for shores, with spirits newly lifted by hope and brighter prospects from the apathy into which compulsory idleness and consequent recklessness had reduced them at home; and then paint the spirit-sinking felt on a first view of the scene of their future labour,—paint the wild revel designed to drown remembrance, and give heart to the newcomers; describe the nature of the toil where exertion is taxed to the uttermost, and the weary frame stimulated by the worst alcohol, supplied by the contractor, at a cheap rate for the purpose of exciting a rivalry of exertion amongst these simple men.

Next comes disease, either a sweeping pestilence that deals, wholesale on its victims, or else a gradual sinking of mind and body; finally, the abode in the hospital, if any comrade is interested enough for the sufferer to bear him to it; else, the solitary log-hut and quicker death. Could these things with their true colours be set forth in detail before the veriest grinder of the poor that ever drove the peasant to curse and quit the soil of his birth, he would cover his eyes from the light of heaven, and feel that he yet possessed a heart and human sympathy.

At such works all over this continent the Irish are the labourers chiefly employed, and the mortality amongst them is enormous,—a mortality I feel certain might be vastly lessened by a little consideration being given to their condition by those who employ them. At present they are, where I have seen them working here, worse lodged than the cattle of the field; in fact, the only thought bestowed upon them appears to be, by what expedient the greatest quantity of labour may be extracted from them at the cheapest rate to the contractor. I think, however, that a better spirit is in progress amongst the companies requiring this class of labourers; in fact it becomes necessary this should be so, since, prolific as is the country from whence they are drawn, the supply would in a little time cease to keep pace with the demand, and slave labour cannot be substituted to any extent, being much too expensive; a good slave costs at this time two hundred pounds sterling, and to have a thousand such swept off a line of canal in one season, would call for prompt consideration.

Independent of interest, Christian charity and justice should alike suggest that the labourers ought to be provided with decent quarters, that sufficient medical aid should always be at hand, and above all, that the brutalizing, accursed practice of extorting extra labour by the stimulus of corn spirit should be wholly forbidden.

Let it be remembered that, although rude and ignorant, these men are not insensible to good impressions, or incapable of distinguishing between a kindly and paternal care of their well-doing, and the mercenary cold-blooded bargain which exacts the last scruple of flesh it has paid for. . . .

At present the priest is the only stay and comfort of these men; the occasional presence of the minister of God alone reminds them that they are not forgotten of their kind: and but for this interference, they would grow in a short time wholly abandoned and become uncontrollable; unfortunately of these men, who conscientiously fulfill their holy functions, there are but too few,—the climate, and fatigue, soon incapacitates all but the very robust. Those who follow the ministry of God in the swamp and in the forest must have cast the pride of flesh indeed out from them, since they brave the martyr's fate without a martyr's triumph. . . .

The gloomy picture of the labourer's condition, which my mention of this canal has drawn from me, may by some be considered overcharged; but I protest I have, on the contrary, withheld details of suffering from heat, and cold, and sickness, which my heart at this moment aches when I recall. . . .

Imminent Dangers, 1835

I have shown what are the *Foreign materials* imported into the country, with which the Jesuits can work to accomplish their designs. Let us examine this point a little more minutely. These materials are the *varieties of Foreigners* of the same Creed, the Roman Catholic, over all of whom the Bishops or Vicars General hold, as a matter of course, ecclesiastical rule; and we well know what is the nature of Roman Catholic ecclesiastical rule,—it is the double refined spirit of despotism, which, after arrogating to itself the prerogatives of Deity, and so claiming to bind or loose the *soul* eternally, makes it, in the comparison, but a mere trifle to exercise absolute sway in all that relates to the body. The notorious ignorance in which the great mass of these emigrants have been all their lives sunk, until their minds are dead, makes them but senseless machines; they obey orders mechanically, for it is the habit of their education, in the despotic countries of their birth. And can it be for a moment supposed by any one that by the act of coming to this country, and being naturalized, their darkened intellects can suddenly be illuminated to discern the nice boundary where their *ecclesiastical obedience* to their priests *ends,* and their *civil independence* of them *begins?* The very supposition is absurd. They obey their priests as demigods, from the habit of their whole lives; they have been taught from infancy that their priests are infallible in the greatest matters, and can they, by mere importation to this country, be suddenly imbued with the knowledge that in civil matters their priests may err, and that they are not in these also their infallible guides? ... Must not the priests, as a matter almost of *certainty,* control the opinions of their ignorant flock in civil as well as religious matters? and do they not do it? ...

That a change of some kind in the Naturalization Laws is required, seems to be conceded on all sides, but the nature and extent of this change are strangely opposite in character. While some, and doubtless the greater part of the American population, would have them changed with the view of *discouraging* immigration, and of guarding our institutions from foreign interference, at the point where they are not only assailable, but where they are at this moment actually assailed and greatly endangered; others would have them changed so as to throw down all the barriers which protect us as an independent nation, and extend the right of suffrage, strange as it may seem, with such an unheard of universality of application, as no advocate of the proper and just principles of universal suffrage ever before ventured to dream of; to the extent, in fact, virtually of giving the administration of our government to any and all nations of the world, no matter how barbarous, who choose to take the trouble to exercise it. Instead of guarding with

SOURCE: Samuel F.B. Morse, *Imminent Dangers to the United States Through Foreign Immigration.* Document from Bibliobase®, edited by Micheal Bellesiles. Copyright © Houghton Mifflin Company. Reprinted by permission.

greater vigilance and care our institutions, when attacked, by new defences, these patriots would not only make no resistance, but would actually invite the enemy, by demolishing the fortresses already existing, and yield up the country into his uncontrolled possession.

Coming to the Aid of Immigrants, 1857–1858

Annual Report of the Officials of the German Society in Chicago for the year from April 1857 to April 1858

Our attention has been focused on preventing the swindling of immigrants by innkeepers and their runners* in and around the train stations. We had presented the city council with recommendations for laws to this effect and obtained their passage. One ordinance enacted in June requires that a licensed German innkeeper or runner present a business card when recommending his inn to arriving passengers. The card must give the following information in both English and German: name of the innkeeper, name of the inn and the street where it is located, the cost of meals per day, the cost of a room per night and per week, and whether he transports his guests with or without charge to and from his inn.

In order to see if and how the police were enforcing the new ordinances, the agent and I made an inspection of the various train stations, during which we were insulted by the runners in the most vile manner; the police captain was at a loss and could only suggest that we too be deputized. In this new capacity we brought about the arrests of several transgressors of the above-mentioned ordinance, and this had the desired effect.

Each day, however, we were unpleasantly reminded that our effectiveness would have to remain one-sided and insufficient as long as we did not have access to financial resources. Many families arriving from New York had been forced to ask for advances in Castle Garden using their baggage as collateral, and they subsequently pestered us with requests to retrieve their baggage for them. But this could only be done by paying the freight and the outstanding debt in New York. Similarly, there were people who were still in possession of their baggage and wanted to continue on their way but had no more money to do so; many of them wanted to deposit their bags with us instead of with an immigrant innkeeper. Our means were unfortunately in-

SOURCE: "Annual Report of the German Society for April, 1857–58," (Chicago: Chg. Sonne, 1858) in Hartmut Keil and John B. Jentz (eds.), *German Workers in Chicago: A Documentary History of Working-Class Culture from 1850 to World War I* (Urbana and Chicago: University of Illinois Press, 1988), 35–39.

Runners were agents of boarding house operators. Their goal was to win the migrants' trust, and then proceed to bilk them of as much cash and property as possible in return for overpriced travel tickets, baggage transport at exorbitant rates, and boarding house accommodations at highly unfair prices. (Eds.)

sufficient to aid each person in this manner, and it is possible that this led to frequent and considerable losses at the hands of the innkeepers. . . .

As mentioned above, since last summer, together with the agent, I have taken over the surveillance of the train stations to see that the city ordinances are being enforced. But even if they had sufficient time, two officials would still be too few. I would therefore recommend that the president and agent be assigned to a committee of six to be elected for this purpose and to be called the Train Station Surveillance Committee.

These officials would likewise have to have police authorization. Their duty would not only entail being frequently present at the arrival of immigrant trains, but also at their departure. Here they would ask their departing countrymen whether they were satisfied with the food, living conditions, and treatment at the inn where they stayed; in the case of complaints or accusations, the officials would either take notes or detain the people until the case could be looked into by the proper legal authorities.

After having collected information of this kind for a few months, this committee would be in a position to draw up a list of those immigrant inns which are of good repute in our city. This list would then be sent to those German Societies in eastern port cities which could best make use of it. On the other hand, it would also be the duty of this committee to present the mayor with a list of those inns which have proven detrimental to the interests of immigrants, and to petition for the revocation of their licenses. Here, too, the character of our highest municipal authorities guarantees us the necessary support. . . .

Last winter some honest, upright craftsmen and their families, who were reluctant to ask strangers for help, were forced to bring beds, clothes, and household goods to the pawnbroker. For many, the payment or foreclosure date is at the door, and most of them still have neither work to earn the money nor friends from whom to borrow it. Several such families have turned to me in the past few days to advance them the interest for one or two months in order to put off the due date. They all hope to thus redeem their hard-earned possessions. I would like to recommend lending good families the interest needed to prolong foreclosure, while holding their pawn tickets as security. . . .

I still hear it said that the agent's wages are too high and that he has too little to do, that people would of course like to support the society, but that they don't want their entire contribution going to the preservation of the agent.

I am convinced that these people have not gone to the trouble to investigate what they maintain, and if they had, they would have found that the activities of this official fulfill the most important objectives of the German Society as it has existed to date. These people have not been to the society's office, they haven't seen the throngs—often uninterrupted—of people coming and going. The one asks the agent to find relatives or friends, the agent sees to the relevant notice in the newspapers; the other has lost his baggage on the way from New York to Chicago, the agent writes off to Detroit and Dunkirk;* a third would like to send money—safely and without cost—to a relative living somewhere or other, the agent takes care of this, too. Now immigrants come who want advances against their baggage so they can continue their trip; the agent accompanies them to the train station or to the inn, estimates the value of the baggage, pays the advances and has the things brought back to the office. On the way he picks up five letters, all addressed to the same person. The first is not very flattering; "Mr. Agent, I've been waiting so long for my two suitcases, and you said you would see to them immediately. Send the checks back to me so I'll know what's going on!" The good man is of the opinion that the lost things must still be where he last saw them on his trip. His bags, in the meantime, were either pilfered by corrupt railroad officials or have been sent on a grand tour without their owner, but the latter suspects the agent of negligence or even deceit. Next comes an entire family of immigrants, freshly arrived. They have lost one of their suitcases in the train station or have been cheated by an innkeeper; the agent goes along with them so that they, too, will be content. A local citizen wants to bring over a relative from his hometown in Germany. He requests a travel guide with exact directions for getting from his hometown to Chicago, as well as sure means of alerting the cousin of swindlers along the way; the agent, to the best of his ability, also tries to satisfy this request. News is received from an immigrant inn that the proprietor wants to throw out a sick immigrant. The agent goes to see the sick person, gets medical assistance, calms the innkeeper or sees to it that the sick person is brought to a hospital. The agent is once again busy trying to finish a letter to somewhere or other when a man comes in and interrupts him with the words: "Listen, the guy you sent me last time was even worse than the others. I told him to go to the devil! Do you have anyone good today?" Two years ago this same man with the charming manners—always on the lookout for slave labor—was a dues-paying member of the German Society; now, however, he'll not hear of supporting the society because he had the misfortune of having been dissatisfied with the workers referred to him free of charge.

But what the agent has to suffer when he has evoked the righteous anger of a patroness by having secured her a good-for-nothing maid—it would be better if he told you himself. No one, in any case, would envy him this pleasure.

I will not tax your patience any longer. But I would again like to strongly recommend that each member try to introduce at least one of his friends to the society; membership is so easily acquired, as the minimum annual contribution is only $1, and from then on up, absolutely no limits are imposed on generosity.

*A railroad junction in western New York State. (Eds.)

Chapter 13

The Age of Reform

Economic growth, territorial expansion, and a spirit of democracy characterized the second quarter of the nineteenth century, a time of great national optimism. Americans believed that their institutions, know-how, and values could overcome all problems. Revivalism and the founding of utopian communities were manifestations of this seemingly boundless perfectionist faith, and so too were the great reform movements that began to emerge after the War of 1812. These movements reached their peak during the 1830s and 1840s before gradually declining in the 1850s. Wherever people perceived problems, they organized to do battle. They formed societies to promote such ideas as temperance, world peace, the abolition of slavery, women's rights, and prison reform, as well as to support such public institutions as libraries, hospitals for the mentally ill, and schools.

The subject of Margaret Hope Bacon's essay "Lucretia Mott: Pioneer for Peace" was one of the foremost figures of the era, certainly one of the most courageous. Although the author calls particular attention to Mott's role in the peace movement and to her advocacy of nonviolent, direct action on behalf of reform, clearly she also involved herself in a variety of causes seeking to improve society, most notably antislavery and women's rights. What evidence can you find to illustrate that many of the reform movements were interrelated? Note that although reformers generally agreed as to ends, they often disagreed over means or tactics. Can you identify areas of disagreement that persist to our own day?

The three documents reflect the scope of causes promoted during the great era and the fervent dedication of their adherents. One of the most eloquent and courageous spokesmen for the cause of the abolition of slavery was Frederick Douglass, former slave, newspaper editor, and political activist. The first document, Douglass's 1852 Independence Day address delivered in Rochester, New York, readily reveals his eloquence. Once you identify the theme of his address, the courage he displayed becomes apparent. This speech not only antagonized the foes of abolition but also shocked many of the supporters of the cause. Can you understand why?

The temperance movement, like all reform causes, blended concern with optimism. However, it outdistanced the others in longevity and wide appeal. Some idea of the fervor of the attacks on drunkenness is revealed in the second document, "Songs of the Temperance Movement." These tunes were included in The Mountain Minstrel, *compiled and edited in 1847 by T. D. Bonner, an agent of the New Hampshire Temperance Society. What evils attributed to alcohol are revealed in the songs' lyrics?*

Horace Mann, foremost leader of the movement for universal, free, public schools, had been a successful politician-reformer in Massachusetts before being appointed secretary of the Massachusetts Board of Education. He had also spoken out and legislated on behalf of temperance, civil rights for blacks, prison reform, the prevention of pauperism, and better care of the mentally ill. The third document is a selection from Mann's twelfth, and final, Annual Report *as secretary. How does the document explain why Mann viewed public education as the hub of all reform?*

ESSAY

•◆•

Lucretia Mott: Pioneer for Peace

Margaret Hope Bacon

So much has been written about Lucretia Mott's contribution to the antislavery and women's rights movement of the nineteenth century that an equally significant aspect of her public career has been lost sight of. No other nineteenth century American woman did as much to forward the cause of peace, to involve women in the peace movement, and to establish the links between women's rights and nonresistance, as did this small but dynamic Quaker minister. . . .

SOURCE: Margaret Hope Bacon, "Lucretia Mott: Pioneer for Peace," *Quaker History*, 82 (Fall 1993), 63–78. Reprinted by permission of the Friends Historical Society.

228

Speaking at an 1860 meeting of the Pennsylvania Anti-Slavery Society she laid out her creed:

> Robert Purvis has said that I was "the most belligerent Non-Resistant" he ever saw. I accept the character he gives me; and I glory in it. I have no idea, because I am a Non-Resistant, of submitting tamely to injustice inflicted either on me or on the slave. I will oppose it with all the moral powers with which I am endowed. I am no advocate of passivity. Quakerism, as I understand it, does not mean quietism. The early Friends were agitators; disturbers of the peace; and were more obnoxious in their days to charges which are now so freely made than we are.

As a . . . Quaker, Lucretia had grown up believing that war was wrong. On Nantucket, where she was born, the largely Quaker populace had suffered hunger from blockades inflicted by both the British and the Americans because of the islanders' neutrality during the Revolutionary War. Again, during the War of 1812, Lucretia experienced war personally when the cotton mill run by James Mott's uncle, Richard Mott, was forced to close because of the British blockade, and James lost his job.

The Mott family into which Lucretia had married were, like the Coffins, strong pacifists. James Mott's brother, Richard, who was a printer for a short time in his career, and published an almanac, enclosed small peace pamphlets in each one he sold, a task at which Lucretia assisted.

It was, however, in a time of comparative peace that Lucretia and James Mott began to develop their concepts of nonresistance. When the American Anti-Slavery Society was formed in Philadelphia in 1833 they were pleased that the constitution pledged its members to work against slavery by moral means alone. The Philadelphia Female Anti-Slavery Society, organized by Lucretia and others four days later, echoed these sentiments. The Motts supported their friend and fellow abolitionist William Lloyd Garrison as he began to unfold his commitment to nonresistance in his paper *The Liberator*. And they supported another friend, Henry C. Wright, also an early advocate of turning the other cheek.

The Motts themselves had been for some time involved in the Free Produce movement: an effort to permit those who felt conscientious scruples against buying products grown by slave labor to obtain them in small Free Produce shops. The supporters of Free Produce did not explicitly see their movement as a form of boycott, or an effort to place the burden or moral suasion on the merchant of slave-made produce, as it would have been seen in 20th-century nonviolent theory, but rather as answering a Christian need to keep oneself free of complicity. James Mott ran such a shop in 1829, himself in transition from the trade of cotton merchant to that of wool merchant. He was also president of the Free Produce Society. Lucretia supported him in these moves, and she used free produce religiously. She often exhorted others to do the same, as at the 1837 Anti-Slavery Convention of American Women, when she introduced a resolution.

> That the support of the iniquitous system of slavery at the South is dependent on the co-operation of the North, by commerce and manufactures, as well as by the consumption of its products—therefore that, despising the gain of oppression we recommend to our friends, by a candid and prayerful examination of the subject, to ascertain if it be not a duty to cleanse our hands from this unrighteous participation, by no longer indulging in the luxuries which come through this polluted channel; and in the supply of the necessary articles of food and clothing, &., that we "provide things honest in the sight of all men," by giving preference to goods which come through requited labor.

In addition, Lucretia Mott began advocating nonresistance explicitly. In November of 1837 when an abolitionist editor in Alton, Illinois, Elijah Lovejoy, defended his presses by force when he was attacked by a proslavery mob, and was himself shot and killed, abolitionists were divided between those who viewed his action as heroic, and those who considered his resort to the use of force as weakening the moral principles of their position. Lucretia Mott felt the latter rather strongly. The Philadelphia Female Anti-Slavery Society, under her leadership, decided to hold a public meeting for the support of Lovejoy's widow, but stated that they regretted that he took up arms, not "the proper means" to pursue the antislavery crusade.

At first antislavery sentiment was respectable in the North. In Philadelphia, a number of prominent citizens had joined to form in 1775 the Pennsylvania Society for Promoting the Abolition of Slavery; the Relief of Negroes Unlawfully Held in Bondage; and For Improving the Condition of the African Race. Reorganized in 1784, it lobbied diligently to persuade the infant Congress to ban slavery. But as the years passed and slavery became more deeply entrenched in the South after the invention of the cotton gin, Northern businessmen began to feel that the antislavery movement was a danger, threatening to interrupt business connections up and down the Eastern seaboard, while Northern white laborers, especially the newly arrived Irish immigrants, saw free black labor as possible competition for jobs. Antislavery spokespersons were frequently booed by angry mobs, and even the churches began to refuse the use of their buildings for antislavery meetings. Although the Society of Friends had a traditional concern against slavery, even the Quakers began to fear the secular antislavery movement as disruptive, and to bar such gatherings in the meeting houses.

After several years of frustration, the reformers in Philadelphia decided to raise money for a structure of their own in which to hold antislavery and related meetings. By selling shares at twenty dollars apiece to some 2000 sympathetic persons, they were able to raise a sum of $40,000. Both James and Lucretia Mott started working on fundraising in 1836. In the early months of 1838 a beautiful new building, Pennsylvania Hall, began to take shape on Sixth Street between Mulberry and Sassafras. It had the pillared facade of a Greek temple. Its first floor contained a small auditorium, committee rooms, and a free produce store; the second floor consisted of a large hall with galleries. The whole was lit with modern gas, and there were ventilators in the ceiling to permit a flow of fresh air, all new inventions. By early May it was ready for use.

The dedication ceremonies were set for May 14. There were many speeches and a special poem written by John Greenleaf Whittier for the occasion. On Tuesday the 15th, the Second Annual Meeting of the Anti-Slavery Convention of American Women opened its sessions in the new hall. The women agreed upon resolutions calling for the boycotting of slave produce and for an end to slavery in the District of Columbia. They could not, however, agree on the question of the right or duty of antislavery women to speak to mixed or promiscuous audiences. This issue, which had been brought to the fore by the speaking tour of Angelina and Sarah Grimke, was proving divisive in the Boston Female Anti-Slavery Society, where some women attached to Garrison, under the leadership of Maria Weston Chapman and her sisters, Caroline, Anne and Deborah Weston, were in favor of "promiscuous" speaking, and others, influenced by the more conservative, clerical wing of the movement, were opposed. Many of the New York women were close to the clerical wing and therefore also opposed antislavery women speaking to mixed audiences, while the Philadelphia Female Antislavery Society . . . supported public speaking for women. It was finally decided that a meeting would be held on Wednesday evening not under the formal sponsorship of the Convention, at which those who believed in woman's duty to speak to a mixed audience might be heard.

A mob had formed around the Hall on May 14, and each day it had become larger and uglier. When it was discovered that blacks and whites, men and women, were going to meet together at the hall, public prejudice against racial "amalgamation" flared. Each day the crowd grew a little more threatening, and the feminist-abolitionists had to learn to walk through it, heads held high, in order to attend their meetings.

Word about the promiscuous meeting on Wednesday night had gotten out, and the mob which gathered was larger and uglier than at any time before. Much of the anger was directed against the black delegates. It was estimated that 10,000 persons, primarily men, surrounded Pennsylvania Hall, and threats to break in and stop proceedings were widespread. The few policemen present made no secret that their sympathies lay with the mob and made no effort to restrain it. When William Lloyd Garrison, the very symbol of antislavery, rose to speak, some of the men surged into the hall, shouting catcalls. Unperturbed, Maria Chapman made a ten-minute speech, followed by Angelina Grimke Weld. The day before, Grimke had married abolitionist Theodore Weld in a ceremony in which they pledged themselves to equality in marriage, and had asked black friends as well as white to witness their union. Word of this affair, with its aspect of "social amalgamation," had spread through the city and led to further fury. When Angelina Weld spoke, telling of her first-hand experience with slavery as a Southerner, the mob began to shout again and to throw brickbats. This incensed a young admirer, Abby Kelley of Worcester, Massachusetts, who made an impassioned maiden speech as an antislavery orator. Lucretia Mott closed the meeting, deploring the fact that the session had not been sponsored by the convention. "Let us hope that such false notions of delicacy and propriety will not long obtain in this enlightened country," she said.

That night someone posted notices in prominent places throughout Philadelphia, calling on all citizens with a due regard for property and the preservation of the Constitution to interfere "forcibly if they must," with the proceedings of the convention. The crowd that gathered Thursday outside the hall was huge and in an ugly mood. Daniel Neall, the president of Pennsylvania Hall, visited the mayor with a delegation and asked for protection. The mayor told them that the trouble was their own fault for holding an amalgamated convention in the first place. Unable to protect the delegates, Daniel Neall next asked Lucretia Mott to suggest that the black women stay away, since they seemed to be the most exposed to danger. Mott agreed to deliver the message Thursday afternoon, but said that she did not agree with it, and hoped that no one would act upon it, not be put off by a "little *appearance* of danger."

Undeterred, the delegates of the convention completed their regular business sessions throughout the day. When it was time to adjourn, the women went arm in arm, each white delegate protecting a black woman, maintaining their dignity despite the outrageous words shouted and stones thrown by the mob. This technique, which had first been tried in Boston, again worked, and with no armor other than their own sense of moral purpose the women passed through the angry mob unharmed.

As soon as the hall was emptied, the mayor stepped forward and locked the door, then made a speech in which he told the mob that they must serve as his police. As for himself, he proposed to go home. After he had left, members of the mob burst the doors down, collected all the books and benches, and started a huge fire, breaking the gas pipes to increase the conflagration. After a while fire companies arrived and played their hoses on the adjacent buildings, while the new hall burned to the ground.

William Lloyd Garrison, Maria Chapman and Anne Weston were staying at the Motts' house at 148 North Ninth Street, a few blocks from Pennsylvania Hall. When friends came by to report that the mob might attack the Motts' house after the hall was consumed, these visitors thought it prudent to leave town. Local abolitionists however gathered at the Motts, who themselves had decided that nonresistance principles demanded that they not flee. One friend moved some furniture and clothes to a neighbor's, while another volunteered to spend the evening next door at the home of Maria Davis, where two younger Mott daughters as well as Lucretia's mother, Anna Coffin, had taken refuge.

At the Mott house, Lucretia and James and their guests tried to talk as though nothing was happening, while young Thomas Mott ran in and out to find out what was going on. By nine o'clock they learned that Pennsylvania Hall was consumed, and shortly afterwards, that a leader of the mob had shouted "On to the Motts" and started up Race Street toward the house on Ninth. But a friend of the Motts intervened. Shouting "On to the Motts" he turned the mob south, not north at the corner of Ninth and Race. Their anger unquenched, the members of the mob next attacked and burned Mother Bethel Church, then the nearby Shelter for Colored Orphans.

Undeterred by the burning of Pennsylvania Hall, the feminist-abolitionists met the next morning at the school house of Sarah Pugh to complete their convention, condemned the brutal actions of racial violence, and pledged themselves to "*expand*, not contract their social relations with their colored friends." Speaking to her fellow delegates, Lucretia Mott confessed she had found the occasion "a searching time."

> I had often thought how I should sustain myself if called to pass such an ordeal. I hope I speak it not in the spirit of boasting when I tell you, my sisters, I believe I was strengthened by God. I felt at the moment that I was willing to suffer whatever the cause required. My best feelings acquit me of shrinking back in the hour of danger. But the mob was not suffered to molest us, and I feel thankful that we slept a few hours in tranquility and peace.

The next year the Anti-Slavery Convention of American Women again planned to meet in Philadelphia. After the mob scenes around Pennsylvania Hall the year before, Philadelphian reformers were frightened about the approaching convention. Lucretia Mott requested space to hold the convention from all the Quaker meetings, including her own Cherry Street Meeting, and was refused. Only the small Universalist Church was willing, but their space was much too small. The convention was finally forced to meet in a stable, the hall of the Pennsylvania Riding School.

City officials were also frightened of the approaching convention. Several days before it was scheduled, Mayor Isaac Roach called on Mott at her home on North Ninth Street. He told her that he wanted to prevent the troubles that had occurred last year, and that he had some questions and some suggestions. Was the meeting to be confined only to women? He would suggest Clarkson Hall, the property of the Pennsylvania Abolition Society which was already guarded by his officers. If the women would not meet in the evening, if they would avoid "unnecessary walking with colored people," he thought he could guarantee to prevent mob violence.

Lucretia Mott was furious. She regarded Mayor Roach's suggestions as disrespectful to all women and especially demeaning to black women, and let him know of her displeasure. . . .

The Convention assembled on May 1, 1839. Soon however a messenger arrived from Mayor Roach and called Lucretia Mott out of the meeting. The mayor wanted to know what time the Convention would close, since he had several officers in waiting whom he would like to discharge. According to the account of this interchange she gave to the convention, she had replied "that she could not tell when our business would be finished, but that we had not asked, and, she presumed, did not wish his aid."

Whether because of the firmness of their principles, or whether because they were not meeting at night, the convention passed without incident. For Lucretia Mott and those around her, the experience cemented their belief that turning to the corrupt power of the state in the form of police protection to guard their meetings was inconsistent with the moral nature of their crusade, and ineffectual as well, since the police often had the point of view of the mob. Thereafter, at their antislavery fairs and the women's rights conventions which were held following the Seneca Falls meeting of 1848, they generally refused to turn to the police to deal with the mob.

On one occasion in 1853, when Lucretia Mott was chairing a women's rights meeting in New York City which was beset by a mob organized by Tammany Hall boss Isaiah Rynders, she vacated the chair so that Ernestine Rose, who did not share her scruples, could call for police protection. Before the police could arrive however, the mob burst into the hall, and Lucretia Mott organized her colleagues to walk two by two through the angry crowd, choosing Rynders himself as her escort. To everyone's amazement, he complied.

The experience of the women also fed into the developing nonresistance movement. Henry C. Wright, agent of the New England Non-Resistance Society, wrote about the 1839 Convention in the *Non-Resistant:*

> The Mayor of the city went to the Convention and proffered the power at his command, to protect them from the violence of those who might be disposed to molest them. But the women, as I am told, gave him to understand that their confidence was in a higher power, that they dared not put themselves under the protection of clubs, swords and guns, and that their quiet and safety would be too dearly purchased by the destruction of those who might wish to disturb them. Half a day was spent in discussing what notice of the Mayor's offered protection should be entered in the minutes of the Convention or whether any notice should be taken of it.

Lucretia Mott was not present when the New England Non-Resistance Society was formed in the fall of 1838, after the clergymen present at a Peace Convention called by Garrison walked out over the issue of women's right to serve on a committee. In the fall of 1839, however, she attended the First Annual Meeting of the new society September 25–27 in Boston and was elected to the business committee. In a debate over what views could be expressed at the meetings, she insisted on freedom of expression, "the right we cannot deny and ought to respect though the opinion may be such as we disapprove." When a resolution calling on members of the Society to apply the principles of nonresistance to family life, Henry Wright said he thought some physical restraint might be necessary for infants incapable of reason. Lucretia Mott said she believed that in family life all penalties were ineffective:

> My conviction is that penalty is ineffectual, and that there is a readier and better way of securing a willing obedience than by resorting to it. Some little incident in our own family will often illustrate the truth to us, in a way nothing else could do. One of our little girls when told to go to bed felt disinclined to obey, and some time after she was discovered hid under the table, thinking it a good piece of fun. No notice was taken of it, and she took her own time. We had forgotten the affair, when she came running downstairs with her little bare feet, saying "do mother forgive me!" It was abundantly more efficacious than the theory of penalty called into practice could have been. I would wish this resolution would pass if we are prepared for it.

In the discussion that followed, Stephen S. Foster suggested that in some extreme cases punishment might be necessary. Lucretia argued:

> The extreme cases which may be brought to demand corporal punishment are like the extreme cases brought to nullify so many other arguments. The reason why such extreme cases occur is, I believe, because parents are not prepared. They overlook the fact that a child, like all human beings, has inalienable rights. It is the master that is not prepared for emancipation, and it is the parent that is not prepared to give up punishment.

In the spring of 1840 Lucretia Mott traveled in Delaware with Daniel Neall, the chair of Pennsylvania Hall, and his new wife, a cousin of hers, Rebecca Bunker Neall. Word that some abolitionists were speaking in this border state spread to proslavery forces. Near Smyrna, Delaware, some men gathered to throw stones at their carriage. Rebecca Neall, who was new to antislavery actions, was frightened but Lucretia quieted her fears, and they went on to the home of a local antislavery Friend. They were just having tea when some of the proslavery mob men came to the door, and demanded that Daniel Neall be turned over to them. When the host refused, the men shoved him aside and forced their way into the house. Lucretia Mott described what happened next in a letter to Maria Chapman:

I pled hard with them to take me as I was the offender if offense had been committed and give him up to his wife—but they declining said "you are a woman and we have nothing to do with you"—to which I answered, "I ask no courtesy at your hands on account of my sex."

The men took Neall away, intending to tar and feather him. Lucretia Mott followed the party, continuing to offer herself as victim in place of Neall. Discomfited by her pursuit, the men finally gave way, having first smeared a bit of tar on Neall, and attached a few feathers, before shamefacedly turning him over to her. This story became famous in antislavery and nonresistance circles. . . .

In 1840, Lucretia and James Mott went to England to attend the World's Anti-Slavery Convention. The British hosts of this gathering were not prepared to accept women as delegates, and Lucretia and several other American women were denied seats on the floor of the convention, an action which had historic consequences. Elizabeth Cady Stanton, attending not as delegate but as the bride of her delegate husband, Henry Stanton, was so moved by Lucretia's handling of herself in reaction to this snub that she determined to do something for women. The Seneca Falls Convention of 1848, called by Lucretia Mott and Elizabeth Stanton, was the result. . . .

Throughout the 1840s, James and Lucretia Mott were occasionally involved in a form of nonviolent direct action, that of moving escaped slaves from safe house to safe house which was known as the underground railroad. Their friend Miller McKim, clerk of the Pennsylvania Anti-Slavery Society, and his black colleague, William Still, were central to this effort in Pennsylvania, and they occasionally called upon the Motts for help, as in the cases of Henry "Box" Brown and Jane Johnson, both escaped slaves who were briefly sheltered at the Motts.

With the passage of the Fugitive Slave Law in 1851, in an effort on the part of the U.S. Government to prevent this movement, and some forceful actions on the part of antislavery groups to prevent the recapture of slaves, some members of the antislavery movement began to believe that force was necessary to protect the fleeing slaves. Ultimately the connection between antislavery and nonresistance was broken.

In the Pennsylvania Anti-Slavery Society the issue came to the surface in 1851 when debate arose over the actions of William Parker and several other blacks in the town of Christiana, in Lancaster County, who had organized a mutual-protection group against slave hunters. When a slave master came to Christiana looking for four escaped slaves, an armed conflict arose, and the slaveowner was killed and his son wounded. Parker escaped to Canada, but a large number of blacks were arrested and charged with treason. So were three white farmers who had driven up but had refused to obey the marshal's order to help capture the slaves.

Lucretia Mott and the Female Anti-Slavery Society made warm clothes for the prisoners, who had been captured in early September in the clothes they were wearing, and held until their trial in late November in unheated prison cells at Moyamensing Prison. The women also attended the trial, which ended in acquittal. Lucretia Mott, however, was not convinced that the bloodshed at Christiana had been necessary. In 1852, when a report of the affair was made to the Pennsylvania Anti-Slavery Society, claiming that the results of the Christiana riot had been good, Lucretia Mott responded that good could never come from evil means. When Charles Burleigh argued that Harriet Beecher Stowe had been moved by the Fugitive Slave Law to write *Uncle Tom's Cabin*, recently serialized in the *National Era*, Lucretia Mott objected:

> We should attribute all good to the Infinite Source of Good. The evils of the Fugitive Law are infinite. Ask the colored people, whom it has scattered like sheep upon the mountains, what can compensate them for their sufferings and terrors and losses. See how it has corrupted the Northern people and how easily men, at first shocked at it, have become reconciled to it. This speculation is incapable of demonstration. It opens a controversy without end. Is it not better to speak of evil as evil, not deducing from it any consequences which do not strictly belong to it? Does it not tend to weaken our abhorrence of wrong? There is nothing easier than to quote texts of Scripture in favor of any theory, as every sect supports its faith by texts. I am not willing to admit that Harriet Beecher Stowe was moved to write *Uncle Tom's Cabin* by that law; if she says so, I think she mistakes the influences which have moved her. I believe, rather, that it has been the moral sentiments and truths promulgated by the *Liberator*, the *National Era*, and the public discussion of the subject, upon her pure mind, exciting it to feel for the oppressed. If you point to the progress of our cause, through persecution, as evidence that the efforts of its enemies have helped it on, I have as good a right to say that but for those impediments, Slavery would have been abolished before now.

Throughout the 1850s, as slave rescues increased, and the actions of John Brown in Kansas caused many persons in the antislavery movement to reconsider their commitment to nonresistance, Lucretia Mott remained steadfast in her belief that moral force alone could be relied on to resist slave catchers, and to bring an eventual end to slavery. When John Brown was hanged at Harper's Ferry, and became a martyr in the eyes of many,

Lucretia Mott was still careful to make a distinction between Brown's work against slavery, and his resort to violence:

> For it is not John Brown the soldier we praise, it is John Brown the moral hero; John Brown the noble confessor and patient martyr we honor, and whom we think it proper to honor in this day when men are carried away by the corrupt and proslavery clamour against him. Our weapons are drawn only from the armory of Truth; they are those of faith and love. They were those of moral indignation, strongly expressed against any wrong.

It was in this same speech that Lucretia Mott called herself "no advocate of passivity." Her belief that moral weapons were the only effective means with which to change institutions such as slavery did not abate with the coming of the Civil War. She regarded the resort to arms as a tragic error in the march toward justice. She was quick to point out, however, that the nation had not been at peace before Fort Sumter was fired upon; that there had been for years an "unequal, cruel war on the rights and liberties of millions of our unoffending fellow beings, a war waged from generation to generation with all the physical force of our government and our commander-in-chief." She was pointing out the violence of the status quo, not to excuse the resort to war but to clarify what real peace might mean. . . .

Prior to the war James and Lucretia Mott had attended several meetings of a group called the Pennsylvania Peace Society, which met sporadically. After the war they took part in forming a new organization, the Universal Peace Union, with a revived Pennsylvania Peace Society as its local affiliate. James Mott became president of the latter organization, serving until his death in 1868; Lucretia Mott was then president from 1870 until 1880, when she died. She was also for many years vice president of the Universal Peace Union. Into both these organizations she poured the fire of her remaining decades. Her sermons, which had previously focused largely on slavery and sometimes women's rights, now were often on the subject of peace. "Even the woman question, as far as voting goes, does not take hold of my every feeling as does war," she wrote a friend.

Lucretia Mott never conceded that the Civil War should have been fought with arms. It was moral warfare that had led to the abolition of slavery. The resort to arms had been a breakdown of that moral campaign:

> I regard the abolition of slavery as being much more the result of this moral warfare which was waged against the great crime of our nation than coming from the battlefield. It is true the Government had not risen to the high moral point which was required to accomplish this great object and [felt] it must use the weapons it was accustomed to employ.

In the same vein, she argued that it was possible to advocate nonresistance in a world where not everyone was yet converted to the use of moral force. We do not need to wait until everyone is converted to pure nonresistance, she argued, any more than we had to wait until everyone was converted to antislavery principles. It was possible to banish war and oppression without waiting for universal conversion. As she put it, "We are not to wait until there is no disposition to take revenge, but to declare that revenge shall not be acted out in the barbarous ways of the present."

The issues which Lucretia Mott supported through the peace societies were manifold. She campaigned to get military training out of the public schools, and continued to advocate the use of persuasion rather than punishment in raising children. She objected to capital punishment and insisted on the sacredness of human life. She argued for the arbitration of international disputes and the rights of the Native Americans, who were being driven ever further from their homes as the European Americans expanded the frontier westward. . . .

As she grew older, Lucretia Mott made peace the cornerstone of more and more of her sermons. She said she felt that peace was the natural instinct of humans, and that little children in particular grew up seeking peace. To turn from this instinctive support of peace to support of war required a high degree of miseducation. Jesus had taught peace, and so had many of the Old Testament prophets. It was not enough for members of the Religious Society of Friends to refuse to bear arms; they must actively work for peace with the "firmness and combativeness that marked us in the antislavery warfare."

The faith and optimism that had carried her through so many years of campaigning against slavery and for women's rights now made Lucretia Mott sure that the efforts to obtain world peace would be successful:

> When we see that the great mountain of slavery is cast down, we
> have great reason to believe that war also will be removed, for there
> are none but have a natural love of peace.

Modern advocates of nonviolence may not have quite the same faith in the goodness of human beings or the inevitability of progress which sustained Lucretia Mott through her many decades of struggle. Nevertheless they will find in her understanding of what we call the violence of the status quo: the need to couple peace with justice, and the need to pursue peace with "combativeness," concepts which have a modern ring. . . .

DOCUMENTS

An Abolitionist's Fourth of July, 1852

Fellow-Citizens—Pardon me, and allow me to ask, why am I called upon to speak here to-day? What have I, or those I represent, to do with your national independence? Are the great principles of political freedom and of natural justice, embodied in that Declaration of Independence, extended to us? And am I, therefore, called upon to bring our humble offering to the national altar, and to confess the benefits, and express devout gratitude for the blessings, resulting from your independence, to us?

Would to God, both for your sakes and ours, that an affirmative answer could be truthfully returned to these questions! Then would my task be light, and my burden easy and delightful. For who is there so cold that a nation's sympathy could not warm him? Who so obdurate and dead to the claims of gratitude, that would not thankfully acknowledge such priceless benefits? Who so stolid and selfish, that would not give his voice to swell the hallelujahs of a nation's jubilee, when the chains of servitude had been torn from his limbs? I am not that man. In a case like that, the dumb might eloquently speak, and the "lame man leap as an hart."

But, such is not the state of the case. I say it with a sad sense of the disparity between us. I am not included within the pale of this glorious anniversary! Your high independence only reveals the immeasurable distance between us. The blessings in which you this day rejoice, are not enjoyed in common. The rich inheritance of justice, liberty, prosperity, and independence, bequeathed by your fathers, is shared by you, not by me. The sunlight that brought life and healing to you, has brought stripes and death to me. This Fourth of July is yours, not mine. You may rejoice, I must mourn. To drag a man in fetters into the grand illuminated temple of liberty, and call upon him to join you in joyous anthems, were inhuman mockery and sacrilegious irony. Do you mean, citizens, to mock me, by asking me to speak to-day? If so, there is a parallel to your conduct.

And let me warn you that it is dangerous to copy the example of a nation whose crimes, towering up to heaven, were thrown down by the breath of the Almighty, burying that nation in irrecoverable ruin! I can to-day take up the plaintive lament of a peeled and woe-smitten people.

"By the rivers of Babylon, there we sat down. Yea! we wept when we remembered Zion. We hanged our harps upon the willows in the midst thereof. For there, they that carried us away captive, required of us a song; and they who wasted us required of us mirth, saying, Sing us one of the

SOURCE: Frederick Douglass, *My Bondage and My Freedom*. Document from Bibliobase®, edited by Micheal Bellesiles. Copyright © Houghton Mifflin Company. Reprinted by permission.

songs of Zion. How can we sing the Lord's song in a strange land? If I forget thee, O Jerusalem, let my right hand forget her cunning. If I do not remember thee, let my tongue cleave to the roof of my mouth."

Fellow-citizens, above your national, tumultuous joy, I hear the mournful wail of millions, whose chains, heavy and grievous yesterday, are to-day rendered more intolerable by the jubilant shouts that reach them. If I do forget, if I do not faithfully remember those bleeding children of sorrow this day, "may my right hand forget her cunning, and may my tongue cleave to the roof of my mouth!" To forget them, to pass lightly over their wrongs, and to chime in with the popular theme, would be treason most scandalous and shocking, and would make me a reproach before God and the world. My subject, then, fellow-citizens, is AMERICAN SLAVERY. I shall see this day and its popular characteristics from the slave's point of view. Standing there, identified with the American bondman, making his wrongs mine, I do not hesitate to declare, with all my soul, that the character and conduct of this nation never looked blacker to me than on this Fourth of July. Whether we turn to the declarations of the past, or to the professions of the present, the conduct of the nation seems equally hideous and revolting. America is false to the past, false to the present, and solemnly binds herself to be false to the future. Standing with God and the crushed and bleeding slave on this occasion, I will, in the name of humanity which is outraged, in the name of liberty which is fettered, in the name of the constitution and the bible, which are disregarded and trampled upon, dare to call in question and to denounce, with all the emphasis I can command, everything that serves to perpetuate slavery—the great sin and shame of America! "I will not equivocate; I will not excuse"; I will use the severest language I can command; and yet not one word shall escape me that any man, whose judgment is not blinded by prejudice, or who is not at heart a slaveholder, shall not confess to be right and just.

But I fancy I hear some one of my audience say, it is just in this circumstance that you and your brother abolitionists fail to make a favorable impression on the public mind. Would you argue more, and denounce less, would you persuade more and rebuke less, your cause would be much more likely to succeed. But, I submit, where all is plain there is nothing to be argued. What point in the anti-slavery creed would you have me argue? On what branch of the subject do the people of this country need light? Must I undertake to prove that the slave is a man? That point is conceded already. Nobody doubts it. The slaveholders themselves acknowledge it in the enactment of laws for their government. They acknowledge it when they punish disobedience on the part of the slave. There are seventy-two crimes in the state of Virginia, which, if committed by a black man (no matter how ignorant he be), subject him to the punishment of death; while only two of these same crimes will subject a white man to the like punishment. What is this but the acknowledgment that the slave is a moral, intellectual, and responsible being. The manhood of the slave is conceded. It is admitted in the fact that southern statute books are covered with enactments forbidding, under severe fines and penalties, the teaching of the slave to read or write. When you can point to any such laws, in reference to the beasts of the field, then I may consent to argue the manhood of the slave. When the dogs in your streets, when the fowls of the air, when the cattle on your hills, when the fish of the sea, and the reptiles that crawl, shall be unable to distinguish the slave from a brute, then will I argue with you that the slave is a man!

For the present, it is enough to affirm the equal manhood of the Negro race. Is it not astonishing that, while we are plowing, planting, and reaping, using all kinds of mechanical tools, erecting houses, constructing bridges, building ships, working in metals of brass, iron, copper, silver, and gold; that, while we are reading, writing, and cyphering, acting as clerks, merchants, and secretaries, having among us lawyers, doctors, ministers, poets, authors, editors, orators, and teachers; that, while we are engaged in all manner of enterprises common to other men—digging gold in California, capturing the whale in the Pacific, feeding sheep and cattle on the hillside, living, moving, acting, thinking, planning, living in families as husbands, wives, and children, and above all, confessing and worshipping the Christian's God, and looking hopefully for life and immortality beyond the grave—we are called upon to prove that we are men! Would you have me argue that man is entitled to liberty? that he is the rightful owner of his own body? You have already declared it. Must I argue the wrongfulness of slavery? Is that a question for republicans? Is it to be settled by the rules of logic and argumentation, as a matter beset with great difficulty, involving a doubtful application of the principle of justice, hard to be understood? How should I look to-day in the presence of Americans, dividing and subdividing a discourse, to show that men have a natural right to freedom, speaking of it relatively and positively, negatively and affirmatively? To do so, would be to make myself ridiculous, and to offer an insult to your understanding. There is not a man beneath the canopy of heaven that does not know that slavery is wrong for him.

What! Am I to argue that it is wrong to make men brutes, to rob them of their liberty, to work them without wages, to keep them ignorant of their relations to their fellow-men, to beat them with sticks, to flay their flesh with the lash, to load their limbs with irons, to hunt them with dogs, to sell them at auction, to sunder their families, to knock out their teeth, to burn their flesh, to starve them into obedience and submission to their masters? Must I argue that a system, thus marked with blood and stained with pollution, is wrong? No; I will not. I have better employment for my time and strength than such arguments would imply.

What, then, remains to be argued? Is it that slavery is not divine; that God did not establish it; that our doctors of divinity are mistaken? There is blasphemy in the thought. That which is inhuman cannot be divine. Who can reason on such a proposition! They that can, may! I cannot. The time for such argument is past. At a time like this, scorching irony, not convincing argument, is needed. Oh! Had I the ability, and could I reach the nation's ear, I would today pour out a fiery stream of biting ridicule, blasting reproach, withering sarcasm, and stern rebuke. For it is not light that is needed, but fire; it is not the gentle shower, but thunder. We need the storm, the whirlwind, and the earthquake. The feeling of the nation must be quickened; the conscience of the nation must be roused; the propriety of the nation must be startled; the hypocrisy of the nation must be exposed; and its crimes against God and man must be proclaimed and denounced.

What to the American slave is your Fourth of July? I answer, a day that reveals to him, more than all other days in the year, the gross injustice and cruelty to which he is the constant victim. To him, your celebration is a sham; your boasted liberty, an unholy license; your national greatness, swelling vanity; your sounds of rejoicing are empty and heartless; your denunciations of tyrants, brass-fronted impudence; your shouts of liberty and equality, hollow mockery; your prayers and hymns, your sermons and thanksgivings, with all your religious parade and solemnity, are to him mere bombast, fraud, deception, impiety, and hypocrisy—a thin veil to cover up crimes which would disgrace a nation of savages. There is not a nation on the earth guilty of practices more shocking and bloody, than are the people of these United States, at this very hour.

Go where you may, search where you will, roam through all the monarchies and despotisms of the old world, travel through South America, search out every abuse, and when you have found the last, lay your facts by the side of the every-day practices of this nation, and you will say with me, that, for revolting barbarity and shameless hypocrisy, America reigns without a rival.

Songs of the Temperance Movement, 1847

Take Courage
Tune—*Calvary*

From the mountain top and valley,
See! the banner streaming high!
While the sons of freedom rally
To the widow's lonely cry,
Sisters weeping,
Bid us to the rescue fly.

SOURCE: Willard Thorp, Merle Curti, Carlos Baker, eds., *American Issues* (Chicago: J. B. Lippincott Co., 1944), I, 475–476.

Could we hear the mother pleading,
Heaven relief will quickly send;
Can we see our country bleeding,
Still refuse our aid to lend?
No! dread monster,
Here thy triumph soon shall end.

Must we see the drunkard reeling
(Void of reason) to the grave?
Where's the heart so dead to feeling,
Who would not the wanderer save?
God of mercy,
'Tis thy blessing now we crave.

Dearest Savior, O, relieve us.
Unto thee we humbly bow,
Let that fiend no more deceive us,
Grant thy loving favor now;
While against him,
Here we pledge a sacred vow.

Now the trump of Temperance sounding,
Rouse! ye freemen! why delay?
Let your voices all resounding,
Welcome on the happy day,
When that tyrant
Must resign his cruel sway.

One Glass More

Stay, mortal, stay! nor heedless thus
Thy sure destruction seal;
Within that cup there lurks a curse,
Which all who drink shall feel.
Disease and death forever nigh,
Stand ready at the door,
And eager wait to hear the cry—
"O give me one glass more!"

Go, view that prison's gloomy cells—
Their pallid tenants scan;
Gaze—gaze upon these earthly hells,
Ask when they began:
Had these a tongue—oh, man! thy cheek
Would burn with crimson o'er—
Had these a tongue they'd to thee speak,
Oh take not *"one glass more."*

Behold that wretched female form,
An outcast from her home;
Crushed by affliction's blighting storm,
And doom'd in want to roam:
Behold her! ask that prattler dear,
Why mother is so poor,
He'll whisper in thy startled ear,
'Twas father's *"one glass more."*

Stay, mortal stay, repent, return!
Reflect upon thy fate;
The poisonous draught indignant spurn,
Spurn—spurn it ere too late.
Oh, fly thee ale-house's horrid din,
Nor linger at the door,
Lest thou perchance, should sip again
The treacherous *"one glass more."*

The *"Reformatory and Elevating Influences"* of the Public Schools, 1848

Under the Providence of God, our means of education are the grand machinery by which the "raw material" of human nature can be worked up into inventors and discoverers, into skilled artisans and scientific farmers, into scholars and jurists, into the founders of benevolent institutions, and the great expounders of ethical and theological science. By means of early education, those embryos of talent may be quickened, which will solve the difficult problems of political and economical law; and by them, too, the genius may be kindled which will blaze forth in the Poets of Humanity. Our schools, far more than they have done, may supply the Presidents and Professors of Colleges, and Superintendents of Public Instruction, all over the land; and send, not only into our sister states, but across the Atlantic, the men of practical science, to superintend the construction of the great works of art. Here, too, may those judicial powers be developed and invigorated, which will make legal principles so clear and convincing as to prevent appeals to force; and, should the clouds of war ever lower over our country, some hero may be found,—the nursling of our schools, and ready to become the leader of our armies,—the best of all heroes, who will secure the glories of a peace, unstained by the magnificent murders of the battle-field. . . .

SOURCE: [Horace Mann], Massachusetts Board of Education, *Twelfth Annual Report of . . . the Secretary of the Board* (Boston, 1849): 32, 37.

Without undervaluing any other human agency, it may be safely affirmed that the Common School, improved and energized, as it can easily be, may become the most effective and benignant of all the forces of civilization. Two reasons sustain this position. In the first place, there is a universality in its operation, which can be affirmed of no other institution whatever. If administered in the spirit of justice and conciliation, all the rising generation may be brought within the circle of its reformatory and elevating influences. And, in the second place, the materials upon which it operates are so pliant and ductile as to be susceptible of assuming a greater variety of forms than any other earthly work of the Creator. The inflexibility and ruggedness of the oak, when compared with the lithe sapling or the tender germ, are but feeble emblems to typify the docility of childhood, when contrasted with the obduracy and intractableness of man. It is these inherent advantages of the Common School, which, in our own State, have produced results so striking, from a system so imperfect, and an administration so feeble. In teaching the blind, and the deaf and dumb, in kindling the latent spark of intelligence that lurks in an idiot's mind, and in the more holy work of reforming abandoned and outcast children, education has proved what it can do, by glorious experiments. These wonders, it has done in its infancy, and with the lights of a limited experience; but, when its faculties shall be fully developed, when it shall be trained to wield its mighty energies for the protection of society against the giant vices which now invade and torment it;—against intemperance, avarice, war, slavery, bigotry, the woes of want and the wickedness of waste,—then, there will not be a height to which these enemies of the race can escape, which it will not scale, nor a Titan among them all, whom it will not slay.

Chapter 14

Plantation Society in the Antebellum South

By 1850 participants in a number of reform movements could point to some notable achievements. Throughout the Northeast and Midwest, public schools had sprung up in towns in which none had previously existed, while older systems were receiving substantially greater financial support. The public-library movement enjoyed similar success, and the treatment of debtors, criminals, and the mentally ill improved. Despite these and other achievements, it is unlikely that any reform leader considered the goals of his or her movement attained by the beginning of the 1850s; much work remained. As the decade wore on, the spirit of perfectionism gradually gave way to the bitter divisiveness of sectionalism and slavery—issues that ultimately were resolved by neither moral suasion nor legislation, but by war.

During the American Revolution, a number of white Americans had seen the inconsistency of fighting Great Britain in the name of freedom while holding slaves in bondage. Virginia, North Carolina, and Maryland passed laws making it easier for masters to free their slaves. A few planters released their slaves outright, and some others, including George Washington, made provisions for manumission in their wills. Gradually the Northern states abolished slavery. With the expansion of the cotton kingdom, however, white Southerners became increasingly dependent on slave labor. Far from liberalizing their attitudes and practices toward slavery, after 1800 Southern legislatures passed new restrictions that made it extremely difficult for masters to emancipate their bondsmen. In response to abolitionist attacks, many Southerners shifted their public posture on slavery from defending it as a necessary evil to advocating it as a positive good. By the time of the Civil War, the South had some 4 million slaves, the vast majority of whom lived and worked on the cotton plantations.

In the eyes of the law, slaves were little more than property, with few legal rights. Yet their individual experiences could vary greatly. In recent years scholars have devoted considerable attention to how blacks survived and created their own distinctive culture within slavery. A vivid example of this is found in the essay "Culture, Conflict, and Community on an Antebellum Plantation" by Drew Gilpin Faust. As you read the story of Silver Bluff plantation, many of your previously held perceptions of the relationship between master and slaves will undoubtedly be challenged. Notice the limitations—not imposed by law but originating in the slaves' culture and society—on the master's ability to control his bondsmen totally, as well as the many factors contributing to a sense of community and autonomy among the slaves. How does the author explain the decision of the blacks of Silver Bluff to remain on the plantation at the close of the Civil War, even after their freedom was proclaimed?

As James Hammond struggled to manage Silver Bluff effectively, he likely turned to the advice columns found in Southern newspapers and journals. The first document, from the pages of the Farmers' Register, not only includes recommendations for managing slaves and their overseers, but also reveals a good deal about attitudes toward slavery and black racial characteristics commonly held by whites of the antebellum South. What is your response to the author's contention that well-treated slaves "are the happiest laboring class in the world"?

Faust's essay provides numerous examples of how slaves asserted themselves as individuals and as a community. The spirituals that make up the second document display still another means by which blacks expressed their attitudes toward slavery and their aspirations for the future. Notice that the lyrics of each song have two levels of meaning, one telling a purely Biblical story or delivering a religious message, the other applying that story or message to the slaves' own lives. These songs should help to explain why James Hammond sought repeatedly to "break up negro preaching & negro churches."

A description of life on a single plantation cannot, of course, provide a complete picture of slavery. Conditions varied from plantation to plantation, from master to master. One factor was constant, however. Slaves were considered the property of their owners and treated as such. The final document provides only an inkling of the horrors endured by slaves at the mercy of a brutal master. Most slave narratives were written by men and, naturally, present a male perspective on plantation life. Harriet Jacobs' account, published shortly before the outbreak of the Civil War, enables us to see an aspect of slavery all too common yet rarely acknowledged at the time: the sexual abuse of female slaves by their owners. Note Ms. Jacobs' comments *regarding the impact of the master's behavior on his wife's attitude toward the victims. In considering the descriptions of slavery in this chapter, bear in mind that slaves had no control over where and for whom they labored.*

ESSAY
——— •◆• ———

Culture, Conflict, and Community on an Antebellum Plantation
Drew Gilpin Faust

A dozen miles south of Augusta, Georgia, the Savannah River curves gently, creating two bends that were known to antebellum steamboat captains as Stingy Venus and Hog Crawl Round. Nearby, on the South Carolina shore, a cliff abruptly rises almost thirty feet above the water. Mineral deposits in the soil give the promontory a metallic tinge, and the bank and the plantation of which it was part came as early as colonial times to be called Silver Bluff.

In 1831, an opportune marriage placed this property in the hands of twenty-four-year-old James Henry Hammond. An upwardly mobile lawyer, erstwhile schoolmaster and newspaper editor, the young Carolinian had achieved through matrimony the status the Old South accorded to planters alone. When he arrived to take possession of his estate, he found and carefully listed in his diary 10,800 acres of land, a dwelling, assorted household effects, and 147 bondsmen. But along with these valued acquisitions, he was to receive a challenge he had not anticipated. As he sought to exert his mastery over the labor force on which the prosperity of his undertaking depended, he was to discover that his task entailed more than simply directing 147 individual lives. Hammond had to dominate a complex social order already in existence on the plantation and to struggle for the next three decades to control what he called a "system of roguery" amongst his slaves.

Hammond astutely recognized that black life on his plantation was structured and organized as a "system," the very existence of which seemed necessarily a challenge to his absolute control—and therefore, as he perceived it, a kind of "roguery." Because Hammond's mastery over his bondsmen depended upon his success at undermining slave society and culture, he established a carefully designed plan of physical and psychological domination in hopes of destroying the foundations of black solidarity. Until he

SOURCE: Drew Gilpin Faust, "Culture, Conflict, and Community: The Meaning of Power on an Antebellum Plantation," *Journal of Social History*, vol. 14, no. 1 (Fall 1980): 83–97. Reprinted by permission of *Journal of Social History*.

relinquished management of the estate to his sons in the late 1850s, Hammond kept extraordinarily detailed records. Including daily entries concerning the treatment, work patterns, and vital statistics of his slaves, they reveal a striking portrait of slave culture and resistance and of the highly structured efforts Hammond took to overpower it. The existence of such data about one master and one community of slaves over a considerable period of time makes possible a tracing of the dialectic of their interaction as one not so much among individuals, but between two loci of power and two opposing systems of belief. While Hammond sought to assert both dominance and legitimacy, the slaves at Silver Bluff strove to maintain networks of communication and community as the bases of their personal and cultural autonomy. This struggle, which constantly tested the ingenuity and strength of both the owner and his slaves, touched everything from religion to work routines to health, and even determined the complex pattern of unauthorized absences from the plantation. . . .

When Hammond took possession of Silver Bluff, he assumed a role and entered a world largely unfamiliar to him. His father had owned a few slaves and even deeded two to young James Henry. But Hammond was entirely inexperienced in the management of large numbers of agricultural and domestic workers. The blacks at Silver Bluff, for their part, confronted a new situation as well, for they had become accustomed to living without a master in permanent residence. Hammond's wife's father, Christopher Fitzsimons, had been a prominent Charleston merchant who visited this upcountry property only intermittently. Upon his death in 1825, the plantation was left to his daughter Catherine, and came under the desultory management of Fitzsimons' sons, who had far less interest than would their future brother-in-law in making it a profitable enterprise. In 1831, therefore, both Hammond and his slaves faced new circumstances. But it was Hammond who was the outsider, moving into a world of established patterns of behavior and interaction in the community at Silver Bluff. Although by law all power rested with Hammond, in reality the situation was rather different.

As a novice at masterhood, Hammond received advice and encouragement from his friends. "Be kind to them. Make them feel an obligation," one acquaintance counselled, " . . . and by all means keep all other negroes away from the place, and make yours stay at home—and Raze their church to the ground—keep them from fanaticism for God's sake as well as for your own. . . ." Hammond took this exhortation to heart, seeking within a week of his arrival at the Bluff to enhance his power by extending control over the very souls of his slaves. "Intend to break up negro preaching & negro churches," he proclaimed in his diary. "Refused to allow Ben Shubrick to join the Negro Church . . . but promised to have him taken in the church . . . I attended. . . . Ordered night meetings on the plantation to be discontinued."

The desire to control black religious life led Hammond to endeavor to replace independent black worship with devotions entirely under white direction. At first he tried to compel slaves into white churches simply by making black ones unavailable, and even sought to prevent his neighbors from permitting black churches on their own lands. But soon he took positive steps to provide the kind of religious environment he deemed appropriate for his slaves. For a number of years he hired itinerant ministers for Sunday afternoon slave services. By 1845, however, Hammond had constructed a Methodist Church for his plantation and named it St. Catherine's after his wife.

The piety of the Hammond slaves became a source of admiration even to visitors. A house guest on the plantation in the 1860s found the services at St. Catherine's "solemn and impressive," a tribute, she felt, to Hammond's beneficent control over his slaves. "There was a little company of white people," she recalled, "the flower of centuries of civilization, among hundreds of blacks but yesterday . . . in savagery, now peaceful, contented, respectful and comprehending the worship of God. . . . By reason of Senator Hammond's wise discipline," the visitor assured her readers, there was no evidence of "religious excesses," the usual "mixture of hysteria and conversion" that she believed characterized most black religion. These slaves, it appeared to an outsider, had abandoned religious ecstasy for the reverential passivity prescribed for them by white cultural norms.

Hammond had taken great pains to establish just such white standards amongst his slaves, and the visitor's description of the behavior he succeeded in eliciting from his bondsmen would undoubtedly have pleased him. But even Hammond recognized that the decorous behavior of his slaves within the walls of St. Catherine's was but an outward compliance with his directives. He seemed unable to eradicate black religious expression, evidences of which appeared to him like tips of an iceberg indicating an underlying pattern of independent belief and worship that persisted among his slaves. Twenty years after his original decision to eliminate the slave church, Hammond recorded in his plantation diary, "Have ordered all church meetings to be broken up except at the Church with a white preacher." Hammond's slaves had over the preceding decades tested their master's initial resolve, quietly asserting their right to their own religious life in face of his attempt to deny it to them.

In the course of these years, they had re-established their church, forcing Hammond to accept a level of black religious autonomy and to permit the slaves to hold as many as four different prayer meetings in the quarters each week. Hammond returned to his original commitment to "break up negro preaching" only when the intensity of black religious fervor seemed to threaten that compromise level of moderation he and his slaves had come tacitly to accept. "Religious troubles among the negroes"—as in 1851 he described his sense of the growing disorder—revived his determination to control the very emotional and ideational sources of unruliness among his slaves. "They are running the thing into the ground," he remarked, "by being allowed too much organization—too much power to the head men & too much praying and Church meeting on the plantation." Black religious life re-emerged as an insupportable threat when it assumed the characteristics of a formal system, with, as Hammond explicitly recognized, organization and leadership to challenge his own power. The recurrent need for Hammond to act against the expanding strength of the black church indicates his failure either to eliminate this organization or to control his slaves' belief and worship.

The struggle for power manifested in the conflict over religious autonomy was paralleled in other areas of slave life on the Hammond domain. Just as Hammond sought from the time of his arrival in 1831 to control religious behavior, so too he desired to supervise work patterns more closely. "When I first began to plant," he later reminisced, "I found my people in very bad subjection from the long want of a master and it required of me a year of severity which cost me infinite pain." The slaves, accustomed to a far less rigorous system of management, resented his attempts and tried to undermine his drive for efficiency. "The negroes are trying me," Hammond remarked in his diary on more than one occasion during the early months of his tenure. In response, he was firm, recording frequent floggings of slaves who refused to comply with his will. When several bondsmen sought to extend the Christmas holiday by declining to return to work as scheduled, Hammond was unyielding, forcing them back to the fields and whipping them as well.

As the weeks passed, the instances of beatings and overt insubordination noted in plantation records diminished; a more subtle form of conflict emerged. Over the next decade, this struggle over work patterns at Silver Bluff fixed on the issue of task versus gang labor. The slaves clearly preferred the independent management of their time offered by the task system, while Hammond feared the autonomy it provided the bondsmen. "They do much more" in a gang, Hammond noted, and "are not so apt to strain themselves." Task work, he found, encouraged the blacks to complete required chores too rapidly, with "no rest until 3 or 4 o'clock," and then gave them the opportunity for hours of unsupervised recreation. But despite what owners generally tended to see as its wholesomeness and security, gang work had the significant disadvantage of displeasing the laborers, who at Silver Bluff performed badly in a calculated effort to restore the task system. "Negroes dissatisfied to work in a gang & doing badly," Hammond observed in 1838. Almost exactly a year later he made a similar remark, noting that hoers were leaving "all the weeds and bunches of grass" growing around the cotton plants. "Evidently want to work task work which I will not do again."

Although at this time Hammond succeeded in establishing the gang as the predominant form of labor at Silver Bluff, the victory was apparently neither final nor total. Indeed, it may simply have served to regularize the pattern of poorly performed work Hammond had viewed as a form of resistance to the gang system. He continued to record hoeing that ignored weeds, picking that passed over bulging cotton bolls, and cultivating that destroyed both mule and plough. But eventually the slaves here too won a compromise. By 1850, Hammond was referring once again in his correspondence and in his plantation diary to task work, although he complained bitterly about continuing poor performance and the frequent departure of many bondsmen from the fields as early as midafternoon.

Hammond seemed not so much to master as to manipulate his slaves, offering a system not just of punishments, but of positive inducements, ranging from picking contests to single out the most diligent hands, to occasional rituals of rewards for all, such as Christmas holidays; rations of sugar, tobacco and coffee; midsummer barbecues; or even the pipes sent all adult slaves from Europe when Hammond departed on the Grand Tour. The slaves were more than just passive recipients of these sporadic benefits; they in turn manipulated their master for those payments and privileges they had come to see as their due. Hammond complained that his bondsmen's demands led him against his will to countenance a slave force "too well fed & otherwise well treated," but he nevertheless could not entirely resist their claims. When after a particularly poor record of work by slaves in the fall of 1847 Hammond sought to shorten the usual Christmas holiday, he ruefully recorded on December 26 that he had been "persuaded out of my decision by the Negroes."

Hammond and his slaves arrived at a sort of accommodation on the issue of work. But in this process, Hammond had to adjust his desires and expectations as significantly as did his bondsmen. His abstract notions of order and absolute control were never to be fully realized. He and his slaves reached a truce that permitted a level of production acceptable to Hammond and a level of endeavor tolerable to his slaves.

Like his use of rewards and punishments, Hammond's more general instructions for plantation management reveal his understanding of the process of mastery as consisting in large measure of symbolic and psychological control. The necessity of resorting to physical punishment, he maintained, indicated a failure in ideal management. Hammond constantly tried to encourage the bondsmen to internalize their master's definition of their inferiority and thus willingly come to acknowledge his legitimacy. Yet Hammond recognized that to succeed in this aim, he had necessarily to mask his own dependence upon them. Hammond was well aware that the black driver Tom Kollock was a far more experienced agriculturist than his master or than the plantation overseers. "I wish you to consult him [Tom],"

Hammond instructed a new overseer, "on all occasions & in all matters of doubt take his opinion wh. you will find supported by good reasons." But, he warned, Kollock must be kept "in ignorance of his influence. . . . I would not have Tom injured by the supposition that he was the head manager any more than I would have you mortified by such a state of things." Yet Kollock knew more than he showed, for Hammond found two decades later that the driver had long exploited the power of which the master had presumed him ignorant. While pretending to effective management of both crops and personnel, Kollock had instead worked to undermine productivity by demanding the minimum of his workers. Kollock had fooled Hammond, who in a fury of discovery proclaimed him a "humbug." "I now see," Hammond declared in 1854, "that in him rests the fault of my last . . . crops. He has trained his hands to do very little & that badly."

Unaware how transparent and easily manipulable he must have appeared to slaves, Hammond sought continually to refine and perfect his system of management. A devoted disciple of scientific agriculture and administration, he developed in the 1840s a formal set of rules for treatment and supervision of slaves, allocating carefully defined areas of responsibility to master, overseer, and driver.

Nearly every detail of these regulations indicates a conscious desire to impress the bondsmen with their total dependence upon their master, and, simultaneously, with the merciful beneficence of his absolute rule. Lest the overseer's power seem to diminish the master's own authority, Hammond defined the role of the black driver to serve as check upon him. Because he could only be whipped by the master, the driver was removed from the overseer's control and his status enhanced amongst his fellow slaves. In addition, the driver had the explicit right to by-pass the overseer and to appeal directly to the master with suggestions or complaints about plantation management—or the overseer's behavior. Hammond invested the driver with enough power to encourage the slaves to accept as their official voice the leader Hammond had chosen and, he hoped, co-opted. It was Hammond's specific intention, moreover, to use administrative arrangements to set the overseer and driver at odds and thus to limit the power of each in relation to his own. One of his greatest fears was that the two would co-operate to conspire against him.

Such divisions of authority were clearly designed to emphasize the master's power, but at the same time were meant to cast him as a somewhat distant arbiter of justice, one who did not involve himself in the sordidness of daily floggings. Instead, Hammond sought to portray himself as the dispenser of that mercy designed to win the grateful allegiance of the slave and to justify the plantation's social order. He constantly tried to make himself appear not so much the creator of rules—which of course in reality he was—but the grantor of exceptions and reprieves.

At Silver Bluff, the distribution of provisions was an occasion for Hammond to display this paternalistic conception. The event assumed the form and significance of a cultural ritual, a ceremony in which Hammond endeavored to present himself to his slaves as the source from whom all blessings flowed. Once a week, the bondsmen were required to put on clean clothes and appear before the master to receive their food allowance. "They should," he recorded in his plantation regulations, "be brought into that contact with the master at least once a week of receiving the means of subsistence from him." Although the overseer could perfectly well have executed such a task, the ceremonial importance of this moment demanded the master's direct participation. The special requirement for fresh apparel set the occasion off from the less sacred events of daily life, and underlined the symbolic character of this interaction between lord and bondsmen. The event illustrated Hammond's most idealized conception of the master-slave relationship and represented his effort to communicate this understanding to the slaves themselves, convincing them of his merciful generosity and of their own humble dependence and need. The interaction was a statement designed to help transform his power into legitimized authority.

But Hammond's slaves were not taken in by this ritual; they remained less dependent on his dispensations of food and far more active in procuring the necessary means of subsistence than their master cared to admit. Slaves tended their own garden plots and fished for the rich bounty of the Savannah River. And to Hammond's intense displeasure, they also stole delicacies out of his own larder. Pilfering of food and alcohol at Silver Bluff did not consist simply of a series of random acts by slaves seeking to alleviate hunger or compensate for deprivation. Instead, theft assumed the characteristics of a contest between master and slave. Indeed, the prospect of winning the competition may have provided the organized slaves with nearly as much satisfaction as did the actual material fruits of victory; it was clearly a battle over power as well as for the specific goods in question. Although Hammond began immediately in 1831 to try to reduce the level of depredations against his hogs, flogging suspected thieves made little impact. He could not prevent the disappearance of a sizeable portion of his pork or break what he saw as the "habit" of theft among his slaves. Over the years, his supply of livestock consequently diminished, and he found himself compelled to buy provisions to feed his slaves. Hammond recorded with grim satisfaction that the resulting reduction of the meat allowance would be just retribution for the slaves' conspiracy against his herds. Theirs would be, he consoled himself, a hollow victory. "The negroes," he noted in 1845, "have for years killed about half my shoats and must now suffer for it." But the impact of black theft was perhaps even greater on other plantation products. Hammond was resigned to never harvesting his potato crop at all, for the slaves stole the entire yield before it was even removed from the ground.

Alcohol, however, was the commodity that inspired the most carefully designed system of slave intrigue. When Hammond began to ferment wines from his own vineyards, slaves constantly tapped his bottles, then blamed the disappearance of the liquid on leaks due to miscorking. But the slave community's most elaborate assault on Hammond's supplies of alcohol went well beyond such crude tactics to call upon a unique conjunction of engineering skill with the power of voodoo. In 1835, Hammond found that several of his slaves had dug tunnels beneath his wine cellar. Other house servants had provided aid, including necessary keys and information and some spiritual assistance as well. A female domestic, Urana, Hammond recorded, used "'root work'" and thus "screened" the excavators by her "conjuration." Hammond determinedly "punished all who have had anything to do with the matter far or near." But his response could not replace the lost wine, nor compensate for the way the incident challenged the literal and figurative foundations of his plantation order. The force of voodoo lay entirely outside his system of domination and his efforts to establish cultural hegemony. The slaves were undermining his power as well as his house.

Fork beliefs flourished in other realms of slave life as well. Hammond's bondsmen succeeded in perpetuating African medical ideas and customs, even though their master's commitment to scientific plantation management necessarily included an effort to exercise close medical supervision over slave lives, in times of sickness and of health. The blacks of Silver Bluff may well have been encouraged in their resistance to Hammond's therapeutics by his record of dismal failure: he had great difficulty in achieving a slave population that reproduced itself. For the first twenty years of his management, slave deaths consistently exceeded slave births at the Bluff, despite Hammond's sincere and vigorous efforts to reverse these disheartening statistics. Hammond continually purchased new bondsmen, however, in order to offset a diminution in his labor supply probably caused as much by the low, damp and unhealthy location of much of his property as by any physical mistreatment or deprivation of his slaves.

In part, these difficulties arose from the shortcomings of medical knowledge in antebellum white America more generally. Initially, Hammond and the physicians he consulted employed a series of those heroic treatments that characterized accepted nineteenth-century medical practice—compelling the slaves to submit to disagreeable purges, bleedings and emetics. When these failed to cure, and seemed often to harm, Hammond gave up in disgust on conventional medicine and turned first to "Botanic Practice," then in 1854 to homeopathy, a medical fad that in its misguidedness at least had the virtue of advocating tiny dosages and thus minimizing the damage a practitioner might inflict.

Although Hammond never faltered in his certainty that Western science would eventually provide the solution to his dilemmas, his slaves retained an active skepticism, resisting his treatments by hiding illness and continuing to practice their own folk cures and remedies. In 1851, Hammond recognized that an entire alternative system of medical services thrived on his plantation. "Traced out the negro Doctors . . . who have been giving out medicine for years here & have killed I think most of those that have died. Punished them and also their patients very severely." Hammond was even able to use the existence of black medicine as a justification for the failures of his own methods. Although he did not refer to these doctors again, it seemed likely that he achieved no greater success in controlling them than in eliminating black preaching or voodoo.

For most of Hammond's slaves, insubordination served to establish cultural and personal autonomy within the framework of plantation demands. Resistance was a tool of negotiation, a means of extracting concessions from the master to reduce the extent of his claims over black bodies and souls. At Silver Bluff, such efforts often were directed more at securing necessary support for black community life than at totally overwhelming the master's power. Hammond learned that he could to a certain degree repress, but never eliminate black cultural patterns; his slaves in turn concealed much of their lives so as not to appear directly to challenge their master's hegemony.

For some Silver Bluff residents, however, there could be no such compromise. Instead of seeking indirectly to avoid the domination inherent to slavery, these individuals confronted it, turning to arson and escape as overt expressions of their rebelliousness. Throughout the period of his management, Hammond referred to mysterious fires that would break out in the gin house on one occasion, the mill house or the plantation hospital the next. While these depredations could not be linked to specific individuals and only minimally affected the operation of the plantation, running away offered the angry slave a potentially more effective means of immediate resistance to the master's control. Between 1831 and 1855, Hammond recorded fifty-three attempts at escape by his bondsmen. Because he was sometimes absent from the plantation for months at a time during these decades, serving in political office or travelling in Europe, it seems unlikely that this list is complete. Nevertheless, Hammond's slave records provide sufficient information about the personal attributes of the runaways, the circumstances of their departure, the length of their absence and the nature of their family ties to demonstrate the meaning and significance of the action within the wider context of plantation life.

The most striking—and depressing—fact about Silver Bluff's runaways is that Hammond records no instance of a successful escape. A total of thirty-seven different slaves were listed as endeavoring to leave the plantation. Thirty-five percent of these were repeaters, although no slave was recorded as making more than three attempts. Newly purchased slaves who made several efforts to escape were often sold; those with long-term ties to the Silver Bluff community eventually abandoned the endeavor.

Runaways were eighty-four percent male, averaged thirty-three years of age, and had been under Hammond's dominance for a median period of two years. Hammond's initial assumption of power precipitated a flurry of escapes, as did subsequent changes in management. When the owner departed for long summer holidays or for business elsewhere, notations of increased numbers of slave escapes appeared in plantation records. This pattern suggests that slavery was rendered minimally tolerable to its victims by the gradual negotiation between master and slave of the kinds of implicit compromises earlier discussed. A shift in responsibility from one master to another or from master to overseer threatened those understandings and therefore produced eruptions of overt rebelliousness.

While the decision to run away might appear to be a rejection of the ties of black community as well as the chains of bondage, the way in which escape functioned at Silver Bluff shows it usually to have operated somewhat differently. Because there were no runaways who achieved permanent freedom and because most escapees did not get far, they remained in a very real sense a part of the slave community they had seemingly fled. Forty-three percent of the runaways at the Bluff left with others. The small proportion—sixteen percent of the total—of females were almost without exception running with husbands or joining spouses who had already departed. Once slaves escaped, they succeeded in remaining at large an average of forty-nine days. Sixty-five percent were captured and the rest returned voluntarily. The distribution of compulsory and elective returns over the calendar year reveals that harsh weather was a significant factor in persuading slaves to give themselves up. Seventy-seven percent of those returning in the winter months did so voluntarily, while in the spring and summer eighty percent were brought back against their will. Weather and workload made summer the runaway season, and fifty-eight percent of all escape attempts occurred in June, July, and August.

While certain individuals—notably young males, particularly those without family ties—were most likely to become runaways, the slave community as a whole provided these individuals with assistance and support. Hammond himself recognized that runaways often went no farther than the nearby Savannah River swamps, where they survived on food provided by those remaining at home. The ties between the escapees and the community were sufficiently strong that Hammond endeavored to force runaways to return by disciplining the rest of the slave force. On at least one occasion Hammond determined to stop the meat allowance of the entire plantation until the runaways came in. In another instance, he severely flogged four slaves harboring two runaways, hoping thereby to break the personal and communal bonds that made prolonged absences possible.

In the isolation of Silver Bluff, real escape seemed all but hopeless. Some newly arrived slaves, perhaps with family from whom they had been separated, turned to flight as a rejection of these new surroundings and an effort permanently to escape them. Individuals of this sort were captured as far as a hundred miles away. The majority of runaways, however, were part of the established black community on Hammond's plantation. Recognizing the near certainty of failure to escape the chains of bondage forever, they ran either in pursuit of a brief respite from labor or in response to uncontrollable anger. One function of the black community was to support this outlet for frustration and rage by feeding and sheltering runaways either until they were captured or until they were once again able to operate within the system of compromise that provided the foundation for the survival of black culture and identity at Silver Bluff.

Two examples demonstrate the way runaways eventually became integrated into the plantation order. Cudjo was returned to the Bluff as a plough hand in 1833 after a year of being hired out in Augusta. Thirty-two years old, he perhaps missed urban life or had established personal relationships he could not bear to break. In any case, he began to run away soon after his return. He first succeeded in departing for two weeks, but was seized in Augusta and imprisoned. Hammond retrieved him and put him in irons, but within days he was off again with his fetters on. Captured soon on a nearby plantation, Cudjo tried again a few days later and remained at large for ten months. In March of 1834, Hammond recorded in his diary, "Cudjo came home. Just tired of running away." Although Cudjo was still on the plantation two decades later, there appeared no further mention of his attempting to escape.

Alonzo had been with Hammond only eight months when he first fled in 1843. Thirty-four years old, he had not yet developed settled family ties on the plantation, and he ran away alone. Captured in this first attempt, he escaped twice more within the year, disappearing, Hammond recorded, "without provocation." His second absence ended when he was caught in Savannah after thirty-two days and placed in irons. After less than two months at home, he was off again, but this time he returned voluntarily within two weeks. Reironed, Alonzo did not flee again. After 1851, Hammond recorded an ever-growing family born to Alonzo and another Silver Bluff slave named Abby. But while he stopped trying to run away and became increasingly tied to Silver Bluff, Alonzo was by no means broken of his independence. In 1864 he provoked Hammond with a final act of resistance, refusing to supply his master with any information about the pains that were to kill him within a month. "A hale hearty man," Hammond remarked with annoyance, "killed by the negro perversity."

In the initial part of his tenure at the Bluff, Hammond recorded efforts to round up runaway slaves by means of extensive searches through the swamps on horseback or with packs of dogs. After the first decade, how- ever, he made little mention of such vigorous measures and seems for the most part simply to have waited for his escapees to be captured by neigh- bors, turn up in nearby jails, or return home. In order to encourage volun- tary surrender, Hammond announced a policy of punishment for runaways that allotted ten lashes for each day absent to those recaptured by force and three lashes per day to those returning of their own will. The establishment of this standardized rule integrated the problem of runaways into the sys- tem of rewards and punishments at Silver Bluff and rendered it an aspect of the understanding existing between master and slaves. Since no one es- caped permanently, such a rule served to set forth the cost of unauthorized absence and encouraged those who had left in irrational rage to return as soon as their tempers had cooled. When the respected fifty-three-year-old driver John Shubrick was flogged for drunkenness, he fled in fury and mor- tification, but within a week was back exercising his customary responsibil- ity in plantation affairs.

For some, anger assumed a longer duration and significance. These in- dividuals, like Alonzo or Cudjo, ran repeatedly until greater age or changed circumstances made life at home more bearable. Occasionally Hammond found himself confronted with a slave whose rage seemed so deep-rooted as to be incurable. When Hudson escaped soon after his purchase in 1844, he was not heard of for seven months. At last, Hammond was notified that the slave was in Barnwell, on trial for arson. To protect his investment, Hammond hired a lawyer to defend him. But when Hudson was acquitted, Hammond sold him immediately, determining that this individual was an insupportable menace to plantation life.

While runaways disrupted routine and challenged Hammond's system of management, his greatest anxieties about loss of control arose from the fear that slave dissatisfaction would be exploited by external forces to threaten the fine balance of concession and oppression he had established. From the beginning of his tenure at the Bluff, he sought to isolate his bonds- men from outside influences, prohibiting their trading in local stores, selling produce to neighbors, marrying off the plantation or interacting too closely with hands on the steamboats that refuelled at the Bluff landing. Despite such efforts, however, Hammond perceived during the 1840s and 1850s an ever-growing threat to his power arising from challenges levelled at the pe- culiar institution as a whole. To Hammond's horror, it seemed impossible to keep information about growing abolition sentiment from the slaves. Such knowledge, Hammond feared, might provide the bondsmen with addi- tional bases for ideological autonomy and greater motivation to resist his control. In an 1844 letter to John C. Calhoun, Hammond declared himself "astonished and shocked to find that some of them are aware of the opin- ions of the Presidential candidates on the subject of slavery and doubtless most of what the abolitionists are doing & I am sure they know as little of what is done off my place as almost any set of Negroes in the State. I fancy . . . there is a growing spirit of insubordination among the slaves in this section. In the lower part of this district they have fired several houses recently. This is fearful—horrible. A quick and potent remedy must be applied. *Disunion* if *needs* be."

Yet when disunion came, it proved less a remedy than a further exacerbation of the problem. Both the possibility of emancipation by Union soldiers and the resort to slave impressment by the Confederates intervened to disrupt the established pattern of relationship between master and bondsmen. Hammond seemed almost as outraged by Southern as by Yankee challenges to his power. He actively endeavored to resist providing workers to the Confederate government and proclaimed the impressment system "wrong every way & odious."

At the beginning of the war, Hammond was uncertain about the sympathies of his slaves. In 1861, he noted that they appeared "anxious," but remarked "Can't tell which side." As the fighting grew closer, with the firing of large guns near the coast audible at Silver Bluff, Hammond began to sense growing disloyalty among his slaves, and to confront intensifying problems of control. "Negroes demoralized greatly. Stealing right and left," he recorded in 1863. By the middle of that year, it seemed certain that the slaves expected "some great change." Despite his efforts, they seemed at all times "well apprised" of war news, sinking into "heavy gloom" at any Union reverse. Hammond observed the appearance of "a peculiar furtive glance with which they regard me & a hanging off from me that I do not like." They seemed to "shut up their faces & cease their cheerful greetings." Hammond felt the war had rendered his control tenuous, and he believed that even though his slaves sought to appear "passive . . . the roar of a single cannon of the Federal's would make them frantic—savage cutthroats and incendiaries."

Hammond never witnessed the Union conquest of the South or the emancipation of his slaves, for he died in November of 1864. Despite his dire prophecies, however, the people of Silver Bluff did not rise in revolution against those who had oppressed them for so long. Unlike many slaves elsewhere who fled during the war itself, the Hammond bondsmen did not depart even when freedom was proclaimed. "We have not lost many negroes," Hammond's widow complained in September 1865 as she worried about having too many mouths to feed. "I wish we could get clear of many of the useless ones."

Given the turbulent nature of the interaction between Hammond and his slaves in the antebellum years, it would be misguided to regard the blacks' decision to remain on the plantation as evidence either of docility or of indifference about freedom. Instead, it might better be understood as final testimony to the importance of that solidarity we have seen among bondsmen on the

Hammond estate. These blacks were more concerned to continue together as a group than to flee Hammond's domination. In the preoccupation with the undeniable importance of the master-slave relationship, historians may have failed fully to recognize how for many bondsmen, the positive meaning of the web of slave interrelationships was a more central influence than were the oppressive intrusions of the power of the master. Silver Bluff had been home to many of these slaves before Hammond ever arrived; the community had preceded him, and now it had outlived him. Its maintenance and autonomy were of the highest priority to its members, keeping them at Silver Bluff even when any single freedman's desire for personal liberty might have best been realized in flight. The values central to this cultural group were more closely associated with the forces of tradition and community than with an individualistic revolutionary romanticism.

On South Carolina's Sea Islands, blacks whose masters had fled perpetuated plantation boundaries as geographic definitions of black communal identity that have persisted to the present day. Although the ex-slaves at Silver Bluff never gained the land titles that would have served as the legal basis for such long-lived solidarity, they, like their Sea Island counterparts, chose in 1865 to remain on the plantation that in a powerful emotional way they had come to regard as their own. These freedmen saw themselves and their aspirations defined less by the oppressions of slavery than by the positive accomplishments of autonomous black community that they had achieved even under the domain of the peculiar institution.

DOCUMENTS

Managing Slaves, 1837

When negroes are accustomed to an overseer, and you dispense with the services of one, they *must* be exposed to a great deal of temptation, far more than they can resist. An education has not taught them the difference between right and wrong; at any rate, their ideas on the subject must be confused. What they learn of the moral code, is gathered from observation, and the example of others, their superiors. How can any person, who has no overseer, be at all hours with his negroes, when he is delivering his grain for example? Let him turn his back, and a cunning fellow will help himself to a bushel of corn or wheat, and he will never be informed upon by his fellow laborers, though ever so honest; for an informer, in their eyes, is held in greater detestation than the most notorious thief.

SOURCE: *Farmers' Register* 5 (September 1837): 301–302.

I admit that many overseers are vain, weak tyrants, "dressed in a little brief authority," but probably a larger proportion of farmers of Virginia are indifferent cultivators of the soil. I regard an overseer as an indispensable agent, whose first qualities should be honesty and firmness, united with forbearance and good temper. Sobriety is a *sine qua non*. A written agreement should be drawn up between the employer and the employed, to be signed by both, setting forth the terms, and mentioning the most important requisitions, which will occur to every one. An overseer's wages should always be paid in money; for if you give him a part of the crops, your land will be worked to death, and never have a dozen loads of manure spread upon it. In addition to this, your views and his will frequently come into collision.

Your overseer should be treated with marked respect; for if you treat him contemptuously or familiarly, your authority and his are injured. He should not be allowed to strike a negro with his fist or a stick, nor ever to punish with severity; for it is not the severity, but certainty of punishment, that wins implicit obedience.

The subject before me turns my thoughts to the food, houses, and clothing of the negro. The master should ever bear in mind, that he is the guardian and protector of his slaves, who if well treated and used, are the happiest laboring class in the world. . . .

Liberally and plentifully fed, warmly clad and housed, your negroes work harder and more willingly, will be more healthy, and their moral character be improved, for they will not be urged, by a hungry longing for meat, to steal their masters' hogs, sheep, and poultry, or to make predatory excursions upon his neighbors. Your negroes will breed much faster when well clothed, fed and housed; which fact, offers an inducement to those slave owners, whose hearts do not overflow with feelings of humanity.

The character of the negro is much underrated. It is like the plastic clay, which may be molded into agreeable or disagreeable figures, according to the skill of the molder. The man who storms at, and curses his negroes, and who tells them they are a parcel of infernal rascals, not to be trusted, will surely make them just what he calls them; and so far from loving such a master, they will hate him. Now, if you be not suspicious, and induce them to think, by slight trusts, that they are not unworthy of some confidence, you will make them honest, useful, and affectionate creatures.

Songs of Freedom, c. 1820–1860

Go Down, Moses

Go down, Moses
'Way down in Egypt land,
Tell ole Pharaoh,
To let my people go.

Go down, Moses,
'Way down in Egypt land,
Tell ole Pharaoh,
To let my people go.

When Israel was in Egypt land,
Let my people go,
Oppressed so hard they could not stand,
Let my people go,
Thus spoke the Lord, bold Moses said,
Let my people go,
If not I'll smite your first-born dead,
Let my people go.

Go down, Moses,
'Way down in Egypt land,
Tell ole Pharaoh,
To let my people go.

Steal Away to Jesus

Steal away, steal away, steal away to Jesus!
Steal away, steal away home,
I ain't got long to stay here.

My Lord, He calls me, He calls me by the thunder,
The trumpet sounds within-a my soul,
I ain't got long to stay here.

Steal away, steal away, steal away to Jesus!
Steal away, steal away home,
I ain't got long to stay here.

Green trees a-bending, po' sinner stand a-trembling,
The trumpet sounds within-a my soul,
I ain't got long to stay here.

SOURCE: Thomas R. Frazier (ed.), *Afro-American History: Primary Sources* (New York: Harcourt, Brace, & World, Inc., 1970), 92–95.

Steal away, steal away, steal away to Jesus!
Steal away, steal away home,
I ain't got long to stay here.

Didn't My Lord Deliver Daniel

Didn't my Lord deliver Daniel,
   deliver Daniel, deliver Daniel,
Didn't my Lord deliver Daniel,
An' why not every man.

He delivered Daniel from the lion's den,
Jonah from the belly of the whale,
An' the Hebrew chillun from the fiery furnace,
An' why not every man.

Didn't my Lord deliver Daniel,
   deliver Daniel, deliver Daniel,
Didn't my Lord deliver Daniel,
An' why not every man.

The moon run down in a purple stream,
The sun forbear to shine,
An' every star disappear,
King Jesus shall-a be mine.

The win' blows eas' an' the win' blows wes',
It blows like the judg-a-ment day,
An' ev'ry po' soul that never did pray'll
Be glad to pray that day.

Didn't my Lord deliver Daniel,
   deliver Daniel, deliver Daniel,
Didn't my Lord deliver Daniel,
An' why not every man.

A Sad Epoch in the Life of a Slave Girl, 1861

During the first years of my service in Dr. Flint's family, I was accustomed to share some indulgences with the children of my mistress. Though this seemed to me no more than right, I was grateful for it, and tried to merit the kindness by the faithful discharge of my duties. But I now entered on my fifteenth year—a sad epoch in the life of a slave girl. My master began to

SOURCE: Harriet Jacobs with L. Maria Child, *Incidents in the Life of a Slave Girl*. Document from Bibliobase®, edited by Micheal Bellesiles. Copyright © Houghton Mifflin Company. Reprinted by permission.

whisper foul words in my ear. Young as I was, I could not remain ignorant of their import.

I tried to treat them with indifference or contempt. The master's age, my extreme youth, and the fear that his conduct would be reported to my grandmother, made him bear this treatment for many months. He was a crafty man, and resorted to many means to accomplish his purposes. Sometimes he had stormy, terrific ways, that made his victims tremble; sometimes he assumed a gentleness that he thought must surely subdue. Of the two, I preferred his stormy moods, although they left me trembling. He tried his utmost to corrupt the pure principles my grandmother had instilled. He peopled my young mind with unclean images, such as only a vile monster could think of. I turned from him with disgust and hatred.

But he was my master. I was compelled to live under the same roof with him—where I saw a man forty years my senior daily violating the most sacred commandments of nature. He told me I was his property; that I must be subject to his will in all things. My soul revolted against the mean tyranny. But where could I turn for protection? No matter whether the slave girl be as black as ebony or as fair as her mistress. In either case, there is no shadow of law to protect her from insult, from violence, or even from death; all these are inflicted by fiends who bear the shape of men. The mistress, who ought to protect the helpless victim, has no other feelings towards her but those of jealousy and rage. The degradation, the wrongs, the vices, that grow out of slavery, are more than I can describe. They are greater than you would willingly believe. Surely, if you credited one half the truths that are told you concerning the helpless millions suffering in this cruel bondage, you at the north would not help to tighten the yoke. You surely would refuse to do for the master, on your own soil, the mean and cruel work which trained bloodhounds and the lowest class of whites do for him at the south.

Everywhere the years bring to all enough of sin and sorrow; but in slavery the very dawn of life is darkened by these shadows. Even the little child, who is accustomed to wait on her mistress and her children, will learn, before she is twelve years old, why it is that her mistress hates such and such a one among the slaves. Perhaps the child's own mother is among those hated ones. She listens to violent outbreaks of jealous passion, and cannot help understanding what is the cause. She will become prematurely knowing in evil things. Soon she will learn to tremble when she hears her master's footfall. She will be compelled to realize that she is no longer a child. If God has bestowed beauty upon her, it will prove her greatest curse. That which commands admiration in the white woman only hastens the degradation of the female slave. I know that some are too much brutalized by slavery to feel the humiliation of their position; but many slaves feel it most acutely, and shrink from the memory of it. I cannot tell how much I suffered in the presence of these wrongs, nor how I am still pained by the retrospect.

My master met me at every turn, reminding me that I belonged to him, and swearing by heaven and earth that he would compel me to submit to him. If I went out for a breath of fresh air, after a day of unwearied toil, his footsteps dogged me. If I knelt by my mother's grave, his dark shadow fell on me even there. The light heart which nature had given me became heavy with sad forebodings. The other slaves in my master's house noticed the change. Many of them pitied me; but none dared to ask the cause. They had no need to inquire. They knew too well the guilty practices under that roof; and they were aware that to speak of them was an offense that never went unpunished. . . .

O, what days and nights of fear and sorrow that man caused me! Reader, it is not to awaken sympathy for myself that I am telling you truthfully what I suffered in slavery. I do it to kindle a flame of compassion in your hearts for my sisters who are still in bondage, suffering as I once suffered.

I once saw two beautiful children playing together. One was a fair white child; the other was her slave, and also her sister. When I saw them embracing each other, and heard their joyous laughter, I turned sadly away from the lovely sight. I foresaw the inevitable blight that would fall on the little slave's heart. I knew how soon her laughter would be changed to sighs. The fair child grew up to be a still fairer woman. From childhood to womanhood her pathway was blooming with flowers, and overarched by a sunny sky. Scarcely one day of her life had been clouded when the sun rose on her happy bridal morning.

How had those years dealt with her slave sister, the little playmate of her childhood? She, also, was very beautiful; but the flowers and sunshine of love were not for her. She drank the cup of Sin, and shame, and misery, whereof her persecuted race are compelled to drink.

In view of these things, why are ye silent, ye free men and women of the north? Why do your tongues falter in maintenance of the right? Would that I had more ability! But my heart is so full, and my pen is so weak! There are noble men and women who plead for us, striving to help those who cannot help themselves. God bless them! God give them strength and courage to go on! God bless those, every where, who are laboring to advance the cause of humanity!

Chapter 15

The Soldiers' Civil War

At its outset, the Civil War triggered romantic impulses. Colorful uniforms, martial and sentimental music, promises of adventure, and the certainty of quick victory stirred both sides of the conflict. Ultimately, however, the war produced death and destruction on a massive scale (about 1 million casualties including more than 600,000 dead), and its conclusion left a legacy of bitterness that lasted for generations.

James L. McDonough's essay "Glory Can Not Atone: Shiloh—April 6, 7, 1862" looks at battle from the perspective of the participants and considers examples of these romantic notions of war. Were there any significant differences between the Union and Confederate soldiers described in the essay in terms of their reasons for enlisting, their military skill, and their patriotism?

Blacks played more than a passive role in the Civil War; approximately 230,000 of them enlisted in the Union Army and Navy, and many others served the armed forces as laborers, nurses, scouts, cooks, and spies. The first document, a let-

ter from Corporal James Henry Gooding of the Fifty-fourth Massachusetts Infantry Regiment to President Abraham Lincoln, reveals the intense patriotism of many black volunteers and the continuing injustices that they suffered. Gooding refers to the Confederacy's position that captured black soldiers would be treated as slaves rather than as prisoners of war, and to the Union's policy of paying black troops less than it paid whites. White privates were paid $13 per month; black soldiers, regardless of rank, received $10, the remaining $3 being deducted for clothing. Congress ultimately voted to equalize the pay of white and black soldiers in July 1864, by chance the month in which Corporal Gooding died of battle wounds. Why do you think such a discriminatory salary policy was established in the first place?

The prisoner-of-war status, denied to captured black soldiers by the Confederates, was by no means enviable. Conditions in the prison camps of both armies were generally dreadful, but among them one earned a lasting reputation as the most horrible: Andersonville in Georgia, a twenty-six-acre stockade where thousands of Union soldiers suffered and died. The second document is a description of Andersonville by one of its former inmates, Charles Ferren Hopkins of the First New Jersey Volunteers, captured at the Battle of the Wilderness in May 1864. He was twenty years old at the time, a three-year veteran of the war.

The final document was written by the great American poet, Walt Whitman, who served as a nurse in Union Army hospitals. After reading the several descriptions of the Civil War, how do you account for the continuing romantic fascination with the conflict, manifested in yearly full-dress reenactments of its battles and a seemingly endless flow of books and documentaries concerned with its campaigns, leaders, and regiments?

ESSAY
— •◆• —

Glory Can Not Atone: Shiloh—April 6, 7, 1862

James L. McDonough

Will Pope was a young Confederate soldier who suffered a mortal wound at the Battle of Shiloh [Tennessee]. As his life was ebbing away he looked into the eyes of Johnnie Green, one of his comrades in arms from the border state of Kentucky, and earnestly asked the question: "Johnnie, if a boy dies for his country the glory is his forever isn't it?" Indeed it is manifest that the more than 600,000 who died in the most tragic of American wars, at least the most tragic until Viet Nam, have laid claim to a certain glory in the very heart of

SOURCE: James L. McDonough, "Glory Can Not Atone: Shiloh—April 6, 7, 1862," *Tennessee Historical Quarterly* 35 (Fall 1976): 179–195. Reprinted by permission.

the America over whose fields and plains they fought, a glory which will endure as long as the annals of America herself shall last. The Battle of Shiloh, in which Will Pope lost his life, was a great part of that tragic war. And the stories of the Will Popes are an indispensable segment in the recounting of that Battle.

Confederate General Basil Duke, who fought at Shiloh, recalled the struggle some years later, and said that "Two great battles of the Civil War seem to command an especial interest denied the others.... There yet lingers a wish to hear all that may be told of Shiloh and Gettysburg...." Otto Eisenchiml, newspaperman and Civil War scholar, after extensive study and visits to many of the battlefields of America, wrote of Shiloh: "No novelist could have packed into a space of two days more action, romance, and surprises than history did on that occasion. Of all the battlefields . . . I thought Shiloh the most intriguing."

Certainly Gettysburg has deservedly received widespread attention, but there is still much to be told about Shiloh. Somehow the Battle has been relegated in the literature of the present century to a second priority position. Even though it was the decisive engagement in the struggle for the Mississippi Valley, without which the Rebels could not realistically hope to win the war, and even though it was the biggest and bloodiest fight of the entire war west of the Appalachian Mountains, Shiloh has never received the attention which has often been accorded to lesser battles, some of which have had several books written about them. What has been written about Shiloh has usually dealt with the commanders such as Grant, Sherman, Johnston, Beauregard, etc. The blunders and the missed opportunities have been the focal points. But Shiloh is also intriguing because of the role played by some of the lesser known, even unknown figures; particularly by the common soldiers of both armies.

This article presents some of those little known, and sometimes previously unpublished, human interest occurrences. The Battle can only cease to seem like the movements on a chess board of war when one knows the tangible, flesh and blood characters, the common men of North and South, who fought, suffered, and died at Shiloh. To understand their emotions, and what happened to them, is a large part of understanding the Battle itself. Theirs are the stories which run the gauntlet of human emotions, from pathos to romance, but most of all reveal the tragedy of war.

Many diverse elements composed the Southern army. From New Orleans came the heralded "Crescent Regiment," composed of men 18 to 35 years of age, many of whom regarded themselves as the Bluebloods of Louisiana. Nicknamed the "Kid Glove" regiment, the unit was a colorful, well-drilled outfit, including many members who were equipped with "servants," and enamored with the glory of war. The command impressed a resident of Corinth as one of the finest regiments he ever saw. The Crescents would fight gallantly and be badly cut up at Shiloh. On the other hand there were units like the Sixth Mississippi, which was a ragtag regiment whose men were dressed and equipped with little or no regard for uniformity.

Great numbers of the Southerners who assembled at Corinth were very young. Henry Morton Stanley of the Sixth Arkansas Infantry, the "Dixie Grays," who was nineteen years old, recalled going into battle at Shiloh beside Henry Parker, a boy seventeen. W. E. Yeatman, who fought at Shiloh with the "Cumberland Rifles," Company C., Second Tennessee Infantry (a regiment organized at Nashville which fought at Manassas and claimed to be the first to reenlist for the duration of the war) wrote that his company "mustered with a roll of 80 men, or boys rather, as much the largest number were youths from 16 to 18 years of age."

Willie Forrest, the son of Nathan Bedford Forrest, fought at Shiloh although he was only 15 years old. His father spent part of the night of April 6 searching for Willie among the casualties. The boy later turned up safe, along with two young companions and some Yankee stragglers the three had captured. Brigadier General James R. Chalmers commended two seventeen-year-old boys, in his official report of the battle, who acted as staff officers for him. He wrote that one of them, Sergeant-major William A. Rains, deserved special notice for carrying an order on Sunday evening "under the heaviest fire that occurred during the whole engagement." Major General B. F. Cheatham told of "a noble boy," John Campbell, who "while acting as my aide-de-camp, fell dead, his entire head having been carried away by a cannon shot."

A colonel of the Fifth Tennessee Infantry was amazed at the "coolness and bravery throughout the entire Shiloh fight" of a Private John Roberts who, although knocked down twice by spent balls, and his gun shattered to pieces, continued to push on with his advancing company. He was fifteen years old.

Not all of them were young, or even middle age, however. One man of about 60, who lived near Corinth, came to see his two sons who were in the army. He happened to arrive on the very day their unit was moving out to attack the enemy at Pittsburgh Landing. The father could not resist shouldering his musket and marching into the fight with his sons. He paid for his rashness with the loss of a leg.

A father and son, John C. Thompson, 70, and Flem, 13, enlisted in a north Mississippi company that fought at Shiloh. The old gentleman was a lawyer, who, when asked why he joined up, replied that he had talked and voted for secession and now felt that he ought to fight for the cause. Though wounded, he survived Shiloh only to fall at Chickamauga in the midst of a charge on Snodgrass Hill.

The Southerners were coming to fight for many reasons. Some were romantics. A Tennessean of Patrick Cleburne's command, George T. Blakemore, wrote that he "volunteered to fight in defense of the sunny South, the land of roses, . . . and for my Melissa, Ma and Sister, and all other fair

271

women. . . ." Henry M. Doak described himself as a "soldier of fortune—eager for the fray. . . ." When he heard a great battle was expected near Corinth, so anxious was he for a fight that he arose from a sick bed and headed west on the first train in order not to miss it. He got to Shiloh in time—in time, after six years' instruction on the violin with German and French masters, for a rifle ball to shatter his left hand.

J. M. Lashlee came from Camden, Tennessee, to join the Confederates. He was a man opposed to slavery and to secession, who enlisted with the Rebels, as did many others, only because the Union army had invaded his state. For Lashlee the memory of the second day of the battle would hold an unlikely nostalgia—one all its own. For there on the battlefield, wounded, he would meet a young girl from near Iuka, Mississippi, by the name of Emma Dudley. And he would marry her.

Another soldier who reached Corinth in time to hear the guns of Shiloh but too late to take part in the fight was brief about his reasons for joining the Confederates. He said simply: "Our liberties are threatened, our rights endangered." He was perhaps echoing the Memphis *Daily Avalanche* which was calling forth every armed, able-bodied man to the "scenes of a great and decisive battle" in the struggle for "Southern Independence." The New Orleans *Daily Picayune* was likewise sounding the theme of a great "struggle for independence" without which there would be "nothing left . . . for which a free man would desire to live." The New Orleans paper was in fact running a series of articles under the heading "Chronicle of the Second American Revolution." Its editorials were also fervently declaring that the situation now facing the South was the "crisis of the Confederate cause." Governor Pettus of Mississippi proclaimed that the decision to be faced was "liberty or death."

Many Southerners, of course, fought to protect the "peculiar institution" [slavery]. . . . Some Confederates even took selected Negroes along with them as personal body servants when they went to war. A man who fought at Shiloh later recounted a gory but impressive occurrence he witnessed involving a young Rebel officer and his slave. As the officer rode into battle on the first day of the fight, a cannon shot decapitated the young man. The Negro servant almost immediately caught his master's horse, and put the lifeless body upon it. Then the Black man moved off the battlefield, going slowly to the rear with the remains in the saddle and he behind on the horse, steadying the animal while they made their way back toward Corinth. The witness was convinced that the slave was taking his dead master's body back home for burial.

Every type of man seemed to be represented among the soldiers gathering at Corinth. Like all armies the Confederates had their gamblers. Some had a mania for cockfighting, scouring the country for fighting cocks and whenever the opportunity offered, staging a contest and betting on the outcome. "There were five or six men, mostly officers, who were ring leaders in this sport," remembered James I. Hall, who was convinced that the Almighty took a dim view of their activities. "In the Battle of Shiloh," he wrote, "they were all killed and although I remained in the army three years after this, I do not remember ever seeing or hearing of another cock fight in our regiment. . . ."

Some of those who were coming to join the Rebels were in love. Confederate Captain Benjamin Vickers of Memphis, Tennessee, was no doubt thinking much of the time abut his fiancee, Sallie Houston, also of Memphis, as he marched to the defense of the South at the Battle of Shiloh. There in the midst of one of the many Rebel charges he suffered a mortal wound. The young lady, even though she knew he was about to die, insisted upon their marriage, which was solemnized ten days after the Battle, and a few days before his death.

There were men who came to pillage and plunder. Major General Braxton Bragg, commanding the Confederate Second Corps, was particularly disturbed by "the mobs we have, miscalled soldiers." He complained to General Beauregard that while there was "some discipline left" in those troops from the Gulf (Bragg's own command) there was "none whatever" in the rest of the army. He further stated that "the unrestrained habits of pillage and plunder" by Confederate soldiers about Corinth was making it difficult to get supplies, and, worse yet, reconciling the people to the approach of the Federals "who certainly do them less harm." The troops were even "monopolizing or plundering the eating and sleeping houses" on the railroads. The forty-five-year-old Bragg, with his lowering brow, haggard, austere, no-nonsense appearance, was determined to do something about the pillaging and he quickly gave substance to his growing reputation as a severe disciplinarian. One of the Rebel soldiers wrote that Bragg's name became a "terror to deserters and evil doers," claiming that "men were shot by scores." Another said he hanged sixteen men on a single tree.

The last two statements were, of course, wild exaggerations, but it was soon after the Shiloh campaign, on the retreat from Corinth, that an incident occurred which did much to stamp Bragg as a stern, unreasoning disciplinarian. Bragg gave orders that no gun be discharged lest the retreat route be given away, and set the penalty of death for disobedience. Subsequently a drunken soldier fired at a chicken and wounded a small Negro child. The soldier was tried by court martial, sentenced to be shot, Bragg approved, and the man was executed. Some of the facts of the actual event were soon twisted, or ignored, however, and the story circulated that because a Confederate soldier shot at a chicken Bragg had the soldier shot—a soldier for a chicken. Although he was falsely maligned as a result of this incident, there is no denying that many of the soldiers thought he was unreasonably strict. Even in the earlier Mexican War, where Zachary Taylor's statement at the Battle of Buena Vista had helped make Bragg famous ("Give them a little more grape, Captain Bragg"), somebody hated Bragg enough to attempt his destruction by planting a bomb under his tent. Bragg was undoubtedly right, however, about the Rebel army at Corinth being in need of more discipline.

Some of those gathering at Corinth were despondent. Jeremy Gilmer wrote of the "confusion and discomfort—dirty hotels, close rooms, hot weather—and many other disagreeable things." And no doubt many were thinking of the possibility of death. One man confided to his diary: "e'er I again write on these pages, I may be sleeping in the cold ground . . . as a battle is daily . . . anticipated."

Although they were a mixed lot, there was one quality shared by nearly everyone in the Confederate army and a sizeable part of the Union army also: they had little if any experience as soldiers. It has been stated that "probably 80 percent of each army had never heard a gun fired in hatred." The estimate may be about right for the Rebel army but not for the Union force. Three of the five Federal divisions which fought at Shiloh had also seen action at Forts Henry and Donelson. There was a smattering of men in the Confederate ranks who thought of themselves as veterans, usually because they had been in one battle or heavy skirmish, but most were green. And there would not be enough time or resources to train them properly. General Leonidas Polk, in his official report, stated that one company of artillery, because of "the scarcity of ammunition, had never heard the report of their own guns."

Many of the officers, elected by their soldiers, or appointed by state governors, were not better prepared than the men in the ranks. A Confederate brigadier general said later that before Shiloh he had never heard a lecture or read a book on the science of war, nor seen a gun fired. At least he could appreciate the necessity to learn, whereas among the enlisted men were many who could see no need for target practice; after all, they thought, they already knew how to shoot!

The top Rebel commanders were attempting to bring organization and discipline out of the chaos, but the necessity for haste in attacking the enemy came to seem imperative, finally overriding all other considerations.

Meanwhile, in the Union camp, although the new recruits and even some of the commands that fought at Forts Henry and Donelson were in need of better organization and discipline, most of those gathering in the Blue ranks at Pittsburgh Landing were not short on confidence. Excited by the recent victory at Fort Donelson, which had been climaxed with the surrender of nearly 15,000 soldiers in Gray, some of the Federals believed they were moving in for the *coup de grace*. A feeling of victory was in the air. That some of the Union soldiers coming up the Tennessee River to Pittsburgh Landing had not fought at Fort Donelson made little difference. The sense of pride in that triumph was contagious, and now the Union army "from private to commanding general" knew, in the words of a soldier in the Sixth Iowa Infantry, that a great battle was shaping up "for the mastery and military supremacy in the Mississippi Valley." With new Springfield muskets, good clothing, fine camp equipage, and wholesale rations, and inspired by music from "splendid bands and drum corps," the troops in his regiment were "happy and supremely confident," he said.

A Northerner in the Fifteenth Illinois agreed. "The weather was delightful," he wrote. "Spring had just begun to open. . . . We all knew that a battle was imminent" but the victory at Fort Donelson "had given us great confidence in ourselves. . . ." Alexander Downing of the Eleventh Iowa recorded in his diary: "The boys are getting anxious for a fight." Division Commander Major General Lew Wallace told his wife in a letter that the enemy was disorganized and demoralized and that the war, if pushed, could not last long. General Grant, writing to his wife and obviously misinterpreting the Southern will to resist, said the "'Sesesch' is . . . about on its last legs in Tennessee. A big fight" would soon occur which, "it appears to me, will be the last in the west." Many a man in the ranks, like William Skinner, was echoing the same sentiment. Skinner wrote his sister and brother on March 27, 1862: "I think the rebellion is getting nearly played out, and I expect we will be home soon." The same theme was found in the letters of some people who were writing to the soldiers. Mrs. James A. Garfield, wife of the thirty-two-year-old man then serving in Buell's army who would become the twentieth President of the United States, was telling her husband: "If our army accomplishes as much this month as during the past month it seems as though there will not be much left of the rebellion."

Some Union men were so confident that the Confederates were demoralized and giving up that they seemed to be looking for a sizeable number of Southerners to swell their ranks. A correspondent travelling with the army wrote, with evident satisfaction, of an alleged 150 or so men from Hardin County who joined the Federal army at Savannah. This does not seem particularly hard to believe since there was much Union sentiment in that county.

If the soldiers read the Northern newspapers, and many of them did (Chicago papers were available at the landing about a week after publication), they would have found it difficult to escape the conclusion that the war was about over. Through the latter part of February and March the headlines were continually recounting dramatic Union successes and some of the editorials were fervent in implying, and occasionally actually stating, that the war could not last much longer. A corespondent of the Chicago *Times* who interviewed Confederate prisoners from Fort Donelson at Camp Douglas, reported that many of the Confederates were weary of war, that they declared the cause of the Confederacy was lost, and that it was useless to fight any longer. A few days later the same paper was reporting that the administration of Jefferson Davis was being bitterly denounced by even the Richmond newspapers.

The Cincinnati *Gazette*, on April 3, reported a great dissatisfaction in the Rebel ranks. Many Confederates, coming in from Corinth, Mississippi, were deserting to the Union army assembled at Pittsburgh Landing, the *Gazette* observed, and many more would desert if they could. The *New York Times* in big headlines was day after day heralding the triumphs of Union armies, noting that in London the capture of Fort Donelson had caused a change in British opinion and a rise in United States securities. Even the pro-Southern *London Times,* anticipating the demise of the Confederacy, was quoted as saying "There are symptoms that the Civil War can not be very long protracted."

Although Northern papers occasionally carried warnings that some signs indicated that the Confederate will to resist was still alive, such articles were often buried in the corner of a second or third page or else virtually obscured by the general optimism exuding from the continual accounting and recounting of Union triumphs.

Not only were some of the Union soldiers overconfident; there were also men gathering at Pittsburgh Landing who were so inexperienced and naive about war that they seemed to be enjoying a holiday. They banged away at flocks of wild geese from the steamboat decks as they came up the Tennessee River. It was all like "a gigantic picnic," one wrote. And some of them were getting wild, such as those men in the Twenty-First Missouri Infantry who were firing from the decks of their steamer as it moved up the river, aiming their guns at citizens on the river banks. Grant labelled the conduct "infamous" and preferred charges against the colonel of the regiment.

A correspondent from the *Chicago Times* traveling with the army thought that some of the soldiers had no respect for anything. He was appalled by their morbid curiosity, when, debarking at Pittsburgh Landing and finding some fresh and rather shallow graves—the evidence of a small skirmish early in March—some of the troops, with pointed sticks and now and then a spade, removed the scanty covering of earth, which in most cases was less than a foot deep, exposing the bodies of the dead, with remarks such as: "He keeps pretty well," and "By golly! What a red moustache this fellow had!"

The Union army, like the Confederate, had many very young soldiers in their ranks. A sixteen-year-old boy in the Union army would remember, sometime during the Battle of Shiloh, passing the corpse of a handsome Confederate, blond hair scattered about his face, with a hat lying beside him bearing the number of a Georgia regiment. Seeing the boy was about his own age, he broke down and cried.

A fourteen-year-old Yankee, Private David W. Camp, of the First Ohio Light Artillery, was said by his captain to deserve particular mention, having served "with the skill and bravery of an old soldier during the entire engagement." The captain further added, "I did not for a moment see him flinch."

Years later, Charles W. Hadley of the Fourteenth Iowa recalled one of the most affecting events of his war experience occurring in the area of prolonged and fierce fighting which became known as the "Hornet's Nest." He watched as a small boy, mounted on a fine horse, was suddenly lifted from the saddle by an exploding shell and dropped lifeless upon the ground.

The youngest of all usually were the drummer boys, among whom was Johnny Clem, ten years old, who went along with the Twenty-Second Wisconsin Infantry, and whose drum was smashed at Shiloh, the exploit winning him the name "Johnny Shiloh"; he later became still more famous as the drummer boy of Chickamauga and retired from the army in 1916 as a major general.

With the rapid concentration of so many men at Pittsburgh Landing it was inevitable that accidents would occur, some of them fatal. A soldier in the Fourteenth Iowa who had just come up the river on the steamer *Autocrat* watched as a soldier on the *Hiawatha* fell into the Tennessee close to Pittsburgh Landing and drowned before anyone could reach him. He was not the only one to suffer such a fate, for several drownings have been recorded. General Charles F. Smith, a crusty, square-shouldered, old officer who played a leading role at Fort Donelson as a division commander, and for a while afterward replaced Grant as the army's commander, slipped and fell while getting into a row boat and skinned his shin. Infection set in which forced him to relinquish his command while the buildup at Pittsburgh Landing was in process, and in about a month he was dead.

Many of the men in Blue who left records in letters, diaries, and memoirs revealing why they fought, said they did so for the Union. But of course, and again like the Confederates, the Federals had their share of soldiers seeking glory, adventure, and plunder. [Historian] Clement Eaton has suggested that it is "highly probable that the typical soldier, Northern or Southern, had no clear idea why he was fighting." It must have seemed to him, especially when he left for war as many did, with the hometown looking on, bands playing, girls waving, and small boys watching with awe and envy, that he fought for something splendid and glorious. The cheers told him so. And the realization assured him of his own individual worth and greatness; but, at the same time, he fought for something, whether "Southern Rights" or "the Union," that must also, at times, have seemed vague and intangible. Perhaps the most concrete thing for which the soldier fought, mentioned time and time again by the warriors on both sides, was "his country."

Regardless of why they were in the army, many of the Union troops, despite the recent successes and their confidence that more would soon follow, found that army life on the whole was dull, monotonous and unpleasant. When the exhilarating, but all too brief periods of interstate camaraderie through card playing, gambling, wrestling, joking and singing were over, the soldier still brooded, worried, got sick, and thought of loved ones back home. There was too much drill and routine, rain and mud. Sanitation was bad, with logs serving as latrines, and sickness and diarrhea (a correspondent remarked that no person could really claim to be a soldier who had not experienced the latter) were rampant at times.

Perhaps above all there was loneliness. An unknown soldier of "Co. C." of an unknown regiment was keeping a small, pocket-size diary, pathetic in its brief entries revealing utter boredom. Again and again, he set down such comments as: "Weather cold and unpleasant. Nothing of any importance"; "In camp . . . no drill. Nothing new"; "Drill today . . . boys sitting by fires." Toward the latter part of March, entries begin referring to "Beautiful morning," "Beautiful spring day," and "Weather pleasant," but the evidences of loneliness and boredom are still present. The pages are blank after March 29, except for one. There appears a final entry—in a different hand: "Killed in the evening by the exploding of a bombshell from the enemies battery." The entry is on the page for April 6.

One of the men who fought for "his country" at Shiloh and experienced something of the loneliness and sickness which was so common to all was forty-year-old Brigadier General William H. L. Wallace. Recently appointed as leader of the Second Division of the Union army, he was an Ohio-born, Illinois-educated lawyer who had served in the Mexican War as an adjutant. When the Civil War began he entered the service as a colonel of Illinois Volunteers. He fought at Fort Donelson, handled himself well, and was promoted to Brigadier General of Volunteers following that battle. Popular and respected by his men he was a natural choice when Grant had to find a new division commander to replace the ailing General C. F. Smith.

On March 8, Wallace told his wife in a letter that he had been quite ill for several days and prayed for the "strength and wisdom to enable me to do my whole duty toward the country in this her hour of peril." In this and other letters he spoke often of his longing for the war to end, and how much he wanted to see his wife and all the family once more. Ann Dicky Wallace, twelve years younger than her husband, must have found his loneliness especially touching, for she decided to go south and visit him. Wallace had told her not to attempt the trip and friends and relatives warned that she would not be allowed to pass, that all civilians were being turned back. Ann was not easily persuaded to change her to course once she had made up her mind.

The daughter of Judge T. Lyle Dicky, one of the most successful lawyers in Illinois, she may have thought her father's influence would help her get through. Most important in her decision, however, was her determination to see "Will" again. She had known her husband since she was just a small girl when Will, as a young lawyer, had visited many times in her father's home. Often he had taken an interest in the bright child, sometimes suggesting books for her to read, sometimes watching her ride her pet pony, or engage in some other sport, and on occasion just sitting and talking to her.

When Will returned from the Mexican War he made the pleasant discovery that little Ann had become a charming young lady of fifteen. When she was sixteen he pledged his love and asked her to become his wife. Soon after her eighteenth birthday they were married.

Now, after all the years she had known him, it did not seem right to Ann for Will to be away, undergoing hardship, sickness, facing danger and possible death, while she remained passively at home. "Sometimes, Will, I can hardly restrain myself," she wrote on March 21. "I feel as if I must go to you, more so when I think of you sick. It seems wrong to enjoy every comfort of a good home and you sick in a tent. Is it indeed my duty to stay so far back and wait so anxiously?" Three days later she dispatched another letter in the same vein. And in a few more days she was on her way south.

On the morning of April 6 Ann Wallace was just arriving at Pittsburgh Landing on a steamboat—her coming still unknown to her husband. As she was putting on her hat and gloves, readying to walk from the boat to her husband's headquarters, she could hear a great deal of firing in the distance. It was first explained to her that this probably involved nothing more than the men on picket duty exchanging a few shots with some Rebel patrol. A captain in the Eleventh Illinois who was on board suggested that perhaps it would be better for him to first find out how far it was to General Wallace's headquarters, for it would be better for Mrs. Wallace to ride if the distance were great.

As she waited for the captain to return, the sounds of firing seemed to be growing more pronounced. In less than thirty minutes, she thought, the captain was back with news that it looked like a major battle was shaping up. Ann's husband had already taken his command to the front, and now it was too late for her to see him. There seemed to be nothing she could do except settle down on the steamboat and wait—disappointed, frustrated, fearful for Will's safety as well as for her other relatives who were in the army. In addition to her husband, Ann's father, two brothers, two of her husband's brothers, and several more distant relatives were all fighting on the field of Shiloh.

Late in the evening a man from back home in Illinois came up to her. She thought he looked worn and depressed. He had been wounded though not seriously. "This is an awful battle," he said. "Yes, but these fresh troops will yet win the day," she replied. He reminded her that she had many relatives in the battle and could not expect that all of them would come through safely. Ann's reply, as she remembered it, was that they had all come safely through the Battle of Fort Donelson, and her husband, now a division commander, should be in a comparatively safe position. The friend then repeated his earlier comment, "It is an awful battle," and then, looking at him carefully, she realized what he was trying to tell her. Her husband had been stricken down while making the defense at the "Hornet's Nest" which proved to be so vital to the salvation of the Union army.

About that time her brother Cyrus, who had been with her husband when he fell, came in and gave her some of the details. He explained how he and another man tried to bring the body back to the landing, but could not as the Rebels were closing in around them. In her grief Ann, who could not sleep, spent most of the night in helping care for the wounded who lay all about her.

About ten o'clock on Monday morning her spirit was wonderfully lifted as news came that Will had been found on the battlefield, still breathing. She had rushed to the adjoining boat where they had brought him. He was wet and cold, his face flushed, and the wound in his head was awful looking. Ann clasped his hand and, though those standing around doubted, was convinced that he immediately recognized her, if only for a moment. He was removed to Savannah where Ann stayed with him constantly. Her hopes for his recovery grew brighter for a while. But then it gradually became obvious that his condition was growing worse, and he was mortally wounded. He breathed his last on Thursday night. She later wrote how thankful she was that he had not died on the battlefield and that she was able to be with him during those final hours.

When the battle was over the Federal army was forming burial details and digging mass graves into which they were stacking the dead bodies in rows, one on top of another. The stench of the dead was sometimes almost unbearable, and the battlefield was filled with ghastly scenes, like in the Hornet's Nest where fire had taken hold in the leaves and grass, burning the flesh from around the set teeth of some of the dead, leaving them with a horrible grin. There were scenes of wonderment, like that of a big Northerner, still gripping his musket, and a young Southerner, revolver in hand, who lay up against one another in a death embrace, having shot each other at virtually point blank range, yet neither face showing any expression of pain or anger.

But unquestionably, there were feelings of bitterness which would not subside for generations. Among the relatives coming to claim the bodies of their dead kinfolk was Samuel Stokes Rembert, III. He drove a team of horses and a wagon from his farm in Shelby County, north of Memphis, to Shiloh and somehow found the body of his eldest son, Andrew Rembert, a private in the Confederate army. Andrew's body was brought back and buried on the homeplace. Some years later Andrew's brother Sam erected a monument to his memory. That monument, still a striking sight today, is in the form of a kneeling angel, and stands eleven or twelve feet in height. But more startling than the white angel suddenly looming up in the midst of the forested area, is the bitter epitaph, which reads: "Three generations of Remberts. To my dear parents and loving sisters and my noble, gentle, brilliant and brave brother, killed for defending home against the most envious lot of cut throats that ever cursed the face of this earth."

One of the men who was walking over the battlefield in those days immediately after Shiloh was James A. Garfield. Wandering out beyond the Union lines with his pickets he came upon a group of tents in which there were about thirty wounded Rebels, attended by a surgeon and a few soldiers. He found dead men lying right in among the living. Sight and smell, he said, were terrible. It was soon after this that he was moved to write, in a letter sent back home, "The horrible sights that I have witnessed on this field I can never describe. No blaze of glory, that flashes around the magnificent triumphs of war, can ever atone for the unwritten and unutterable horrors of the scene of carnage."

DOCUMENTS

A Black Soldier Writes to President Lincoln, 1863

MORRIS ISLAND, S.C.
SEPTEMBER 28, 1863

YOUR EXCELLENCY ABRAHAM LINCOLN:

Your Excellency will pardon the presumption of an humble individual like myself, in addressing you, but the earnest solicitation of my comrades in arms besides the genuine interest felt by myself in the matter is my excuse, for placing before the Executive head of the Nation our Common Grievance.

On the 6th of the last Month, the Paymaster of the Department informed us, that if we would decide to receive the sum of $10 (ten dollars) per month, he would come and pay us that sum, but that, on the sitting of Congress, the Regt. [regiment] would, in his opinion, be allowed the other 3 (three). He did not give us any guarantee that this would be, as he hoped; certainly he had no authority for making any such guarantee, and we cannot suppose him acting in any way interested.

Now the main question is, are we Soldiers, or are we Laborers? We are fully armed, and equipped, have done all the various duties pertaining to a Soldier's life, have conducted ourselves to the complete satisfaction of General Officers, who were, if anything, prejudiced against us, but who now accord us all the encouragement and honors due us; have shared the perils

SOURCE: James Henry Gooding to Abraham Lincoln in Herbert Aptheker, ed., *A Documentary History of the Negro People in the U.S.* (New York: Citadel Press, 1951), 482–484.

and labor of reducing the first strong-hold that flaunted a Traitor Flag; and more, Mr. President, to-day the Anglo-Saxon Mother, Wife, or Sister are not alone in tears for departed Sons, Husbands and Brothers. The patient, trusting descendant of Afric's Clime have dyed the ground with blood, in defence of the Union, and Democracy. Men, too, your Excellency, who know in a measure the cruelties of the iron heel of oppression, which in years gone by, the very power their blood is now being spilled to maintain, ever ground them in the dust.

But when the war trumpet sounded o'er the land, when men knew not the Friend from the Traitor, the Black man laid his life at the altar of the Nation,—and he was refused. When the arms of the Union were beaten, in the first year of the war, and the Executive called for more food for its ravenous maw, again the black man begged the privilege of aiding his country in her need, to be again refused.

And now he is in the War, and how has he conducted himself? Let their dusky forms rise up, out of the mires of James Island, and give the answer. Let the rich mould around Wagner's parapets be upturned, and there will be found an eloquent answer. Obedient and patient and solid as a wall are they. All we lack is a paler hue and a better acquaintance with the alphabet.

Now your Excellency, we have done a Soldier's duty. Why can't we have a Soldier's pay? You caution the Rebel chieftain, that the United States knows no distinction in her soldiers. She insists on having all her soldiers of whatever creed or color, to be treated according to the usages of War. Now if the United States exacts uniformity of treatment of her soldiers from the insurgents, would it not be well and consistent to set the example herself by paying all her soldiers alike?

We of this Regt. were not enlisted under any "contraband"* act. But we do not wish to be understood as rating our service of more value to the Government than the service of the ex-slave. Their service is undoubtedly worth much to the Nation, but Congress made express provision touching their case, as slaves freed by military necessity, and assuming the Government to be their temporary Guardian. Not so with us. Freemen by birth and consequently having the advantage of thinking and acting for ourselves so far as the Laws would allow us, we do not consider ourselves fit subjects for the Contraband act.

We appeal to you, Sir, as the Executive of the Nation, to have us justly dealt with. The Regt. do pray that they be assured their service will be fairly appreciated by paying them as American Soldiers, not as menial hirelings. Black men, you may well know, are poor; three dollars per month, for a year, will supply their needy wives and little ones with fuel. If you, as Chief Magistrate of the Nation, will assure us of our whole pay, we are content. Our Patriotism, our enthusiasm will have a new impetus, to exert our en-

*The term *contraband* refers to fugitive slaves who often worked as laborers for the North. (Eds.)

ergy more and more to aid our Country. Not that our hearts ever flagged in devotion, despite the evident apathy displayed in our behalf, but we feel as though our Country spurned us, now we are sworn to serve her. Please give this a moment's attention.

Andersonville:
". . . death stalked on every hand," 1864

. . . The prison was a parallelogram of about two to one as to its length and breadth, about eighteen acres at this time—it was enlarged July 1st to about twenty-seven acres—and one-third of this not habitable, being a swamp of liquid filth. This was enclosed by wooden walls of hewn pine logs, from eight to ten inches square, four feet buried in the ground, eighteen feet above, braced on the outside, cross-barred to make one log sustain the other, and a small platform making comfortable standing room for the guards, every one hundred feet, with above waist-high space below the top of stockade, reached by a ladder. A sloping roof to protect the guards from the sun and rain had been placed over them. Later in 1864 the second line of stockade was built and a third was partly built for protection if attacked by Federal troops, it was said, but we knew it was to discourage us from "tunneling"—the distance being too great. The Florida Artillery had cannon stationed at each corner of the stockade, thus commanding a range from any direction; four guns were so placed near the south gate and over the depressed section of stockade at which point the little stream entered the enclosure.

The "dead line" so much talked of and feared was a line of pine, four-inch boards on posts about three feet high. This line was seventeen feet from the stockade walls, thus leaving the distance all around the enclosure an open space, and incidentally reducing the acreage inside and giving the guards a clear view all about the stockade or "bull pen," the name given it by its inventor—the infamous General Winder. He was the friend of Jefferson Davis, who named him as a "Christian gentleman," and he was the architect and builder of this wooden Hell. . . .

Inside the camp death stalked on every hand. Death at the hand of the guards, though murder in cold blood, was merciful beside the systematic, studied, absolute murder inside, by slow death, inch by inch! As before stated, one-third of the original enclosure was swampy—a mud of liquid filth, voidings from the thousands, seething with maggots in full activity. This daily increased by the necessities of the inmates, being the only place

SOURCE: "Hell and the Survivor: A Civil War Memoir," *American Heritage,* vol. 33, no. 6 (October/November 1982), 78–93. Copyright 1982 by American Heritage, a division of Forbes, Inc.

accessible for the purpose. Through this mass of pollution passed the only water that found its way through the Bull Pen. It came to us between the two sources of pollution, the Confederate camp and the cook house; first, the seepage of sinks; second, the dirt and filth emptied by the cook house; then was our turn to use it. I have known over three thousand men to wait in line to get water, and the line was added to as fast as reduced, from daylight to dark, yes, even into the night; men taking turns of duty with men of their mess, in order to hold their place in line, as no one man could stand it alone, even if in the "pink" of physical condition; the heat of the sun, blistering him, or the drenching rains soaking him, not a breath of fresh air, and we had no covering but Heaven's canopy. The air was loaded with unbearable, fever-laden stench from that poison sink of putrid mud and water, continually in motion by the activity of the germs of death. We could not get away from the stink—we ate it, drank it and slept in it (when exhaustion compelled sleep).

What wonder that men died, or were so miserable as to prefer instant death to that which they had seen hourly taking place, and so preferring, deliberately stepping within the dead line and looking their willing murderer in the eye, while a shot was sent crashing into a brain that was yet clear.

The month of June gave us twenty-seven days of rain—not consecutively, but so frequently that no one was dry in all that time. Everything was soaked—even the sandy soil. Still, this watery month was a blessing in disguise as it gave water, plenty of which was pure to drink. The boast of Winder was that the selection of this spot for his Bull Pen was the place where disease and death would come more quickly by "natural causes," when a removal of two hundred feet east would have placed us upon a living, pure, deep and clear stream of water, properly named "Sweetwater Creek," which had we been allowed to utilize would have saved thousands of lives—but no, that was not the intent of its inventor. To kill by "natural causes" was made more possible by this location. . . .

The average deaths per day for seven and a half months were 85. But during the months of July, August, September, and October the average was 100 per day. One day in August, following the great freshet,* I counted 235 corpses lying at the south gate and about. Many of those had been smothered in their "burrows" made in the side hill in which they crawled to shield themselves from sun and storm; the soil, being sandy, became rain-soaked and settled down upon the occupant and became his grave instead of a protection. Others, who had no shelter, in whom life was barely existing, were rain-soaked, chilling blood and marrow, and life flitted easily away, and left but little to return to clay. These holes or burrows in both the flats and up the north slope were counted by thousands; no doubt there

*A *freshet* is a great overflowing of a stream caused by heavy rains. (Eds.)

were some that never gave up their dead, the men buried in their self-made sepulcher. No effort was made to search unless the man was missed by a friend.

Such were Winder's "natural causes"!! . . .

Recollections of War, 1875

The dead in this war—there they lie, strewing the fields and woods and valleys and battle-fields of the South—Virginia, the Peninsula—Malvern Hill and Fair Oaks—the banks of the Chickahominy—the terraces of Fredericksburg—Antietam bridge—the grisly ravines of Manassas—the bloody promenade of the Wilderness—the varieties of the *strayed* dead, (the estimate of the War Department is 25,000 national soldiers kill'd in battle and never buried at all, 5,000 drown'd—15,000 inhumed by strangers, or on the march in haste, in hitherto unfound localities—2,000 graves cover'd by sand and mud by Mississippi freshets, 3,000 carried away by caving-in of banks, &c.,)—Gettysburg, the West, Southwest—Vicksburg—Chattanooga—the trenches of Petersburg—the numberless battles, camps, hospitals everywhere—the crop reap'd by the mighty reapers, typhoid, dysentery, inflammations—and blackest and loathsomest of all, the dead and living burial-pits, the prison-pens of Andersonville, Salisbury, Belle Isle, &c., (not Dante's pictured hell and all its woes, its degradations, filthy torments, excell'd those prisons)—the dead, the dead, the dead—*our* dead—or South or North, ours all, (all, all, all, finally dear to me)—or East or West—Atlantic coast or Mississippi valley—somewhere they crawl'd to die, alone, in bushes, low gullies, or on the sides of hills—(there, in secluded spots, their skeletons, bleach'd bones, tufts of hair, buttons, fragments of clothing, are occasionally found yet)—our young men once so handsome and so joyous, taken from us—the son from the mother, the husband from the wife, the dear friend from the dear friend—the clusters of camp graves, in Georgia, the Carolinas, and in Tennessee—the single graves left in the woods or by the roadside, (hundreds, thousands, obliterated)—the corpses floated down the rivers, and caught and lodged, (dozens, scores, floated down the upper Potomac, after the cavalry engagements, the pursuit of Lee, following Gettysburg)—some lie at the bottom of the sea—the general million, and the special cemeteries in almost all the States—the infinite dead—(the land entire saturated, perfumed with their impalpable ashes' exhalation in Nature's chemistry distill'd, and shall be so forever, in every future grain of wheat and ear of corn, and every flower that grows, and every breath we draw)—

SOURCE: *The Complete Works of Walt Whitman* 1 (New York: G. P. Putnam's Sons, 1902): 137–139.

not only Northern dead leavening Southern soil—thousands, aye tens of thousands, of Southerners, crumble to-day in Northern earth.

And everywhere among these countless graves—everywhere in the many soldier Cemeteries of the Nation, (there are now, I believe, over seventy of them)—as at the time in the vast trenches, the depositories of slain, Northern and Southern, after the great battles—not only where the scathing trail passed those years, but radiating since in all the peaceful quarters of the land—we see, and ages yet may see, on monuments and gravestones, singly or in masses, to thousands or tens of thousands, the significant word *Unknown. . . .*

Chapter 16

Reconstruction and Free Plantation Labor

The Civil War eliminated slavery but left undecided the question of what agrarian labor system would replace it in the devastated South. Peter Kolchin's essay "Free Plantation Labor" describes how Alabama freedmen (former slaves) and their erstwhile masters established relationships to maintain the productivity of the land. As you read, consider the aspirations, fears, and misunderstandings that governed the behavior of blacks, Southern whites, and Southern-based representatives of the federal government working for the Freedmen's Bureau. Although salaried agricultural labor and tenant farming made an appearance on Alabama plantations, it was sharecropping that came to dominate agriculture in that state and much of the rest of the South. Sharecropping ultimately proved an unproductive system of land management, crushing black farmers and their families under a yoke of debt and poverty for generations to come. Yet, as Kolchin's essay points out, both blacks and whites initially found the system attractive. Why?

The first document is a letter from a freed slave to his former master. The letter speaks eloquently of the conditions and humiliations that he had endured in the past and also of the better life that he has built for himself. How would you describe the general tone of the letter?

Although even the most tenacious plantation owners recognized that slavery was finished and that the South needed a new system of labor, few white Southerners could accept the freedmen as social and political equals. In 1865–1866, Southern politicians established Black Codes to ensure white supremacy. The second document is the Black Code of St. Landry's Parish, Louisiana. To what extent does this document support the claim of some Northern Radical Republicans that the Black Codes amounted to nothing less than the continuation of slavery? The code explains part of the motivation for the passage of the Reconstruction amendments and laws by the Republican-controlled federal government. It also provides clues to the fate in store for Southern blacks after 1877, when the last federal troops left the South and Reconstruction ended.

The third document consists of letters from two Northern schoolteachers, who were among the hundreds who traveled south after the war under the auspices of the Freedmen's Bureau and several private philanthropic agencies. What do these documents and the Kolchin essay indicate about the goals of the newly freed blacks? What actions did the freedmen take to achieve their objectives?

Beginning in the 1890s, the freedmen lost the rights and opportunities they had won during the ten years following the Civil War, as Southern whites began systematically to disfranchise blacks and to institutionalize segregationist and discriminatory practices. Whites prohibited blacks from voting, segregated them in public life, denied them justice in the courts, and placed their children in underfunded "colored schools." Although blacks never accepted these conditions as permanent, over half a century would pass before their march toward full equality resumed with the promise of significant success.

ESSAY

Free Plantation Labor

Peter Kolchin

I

Despite the migration of Negroes to Alabama's towns and cities, the most important question to blacks in 1865 concerned the role of the rural freedmen. The end of the Civil War found general confusion as to their status.

SOURCE: *First Freedom: The Responses of Alabama Blacks to Emancipation and Reconstruction,* Peter Kolchin. Copyright © 1972 by Greenwood Press. Reproduced with permission of Greenwood Publishing Group, Inc., Westport, CT.

"You have been told by the Yankees and others that you are free," one planter declared to his Negroes in April 1865. "This may be so! I do not doubt that you will be freed in a few years. But the terms and time of your ultimate freedom is not yet fully and definitely settled. Neither you nor I know what is to be the final result." Even if free, the Negroes' position in society remained to be determined. Presumably they would continue to till the land, for agriculture, especially cotton, was the mainstay of the state's economy and would continue as such for years. But it was not clear under what new system the land would be cultivated.

In the spring of 1865, before the arrival of Freedmen's Bureau officials, Union officers played the greatest role in establishing the new order. Throughout the state, they informed whites that the Negroes really were free and gathered blacks together to tell them of their new rights. "All persons formerly held as slaves will be treated in every respect as entitled to the rights of freedmen, and such as desire their services will be required to pay for them," announced Lieutenant Colonel C. T. Christensen in a typical statement from Mobile.

The army also served as the precursor of the Freedmen's Bureau in establishing the new agricultural labor system, according to which freedmen were to work under yearly contracts with their employers, supervised by federal officials. Varieties of this contract system had already been tested in certain Union-occupied portions of the South before the end of the war, and in April Thomas W. Conway, general superintendent of freedmen for the Department of the Gulf, arrived in Montgomery to inaugurate it in Alabama. But it was late summer before the Freedmen's Bureau was fully established throughout the state, and until then the task of supervising relations between planters and freedmen rested primarily with the army. Officers advised blacks to remain on their plantations "whenever the persons by whom they are employed recognize their rights and agree to compensate them for their services." Similar circulars, although not always so friendly in tone, were issued from other parts of the state. Brevet Major General R. S. Granger ordered that all contracts between freedmen and planters must be in writing. He added bluntly that "[t]hose found unemployed will be arrested and set to work." But officers were usually vague in recommending what the compensation of the freedmen, or their working relations with planters, should be. Conditions varied widely from one location to another during the first few months after the war as individual army officers, Freedmen's Bureau officials, and planters exercised their own discretion.

Observers generally noted a demoralization of labor during the spring and summer of 1865, which they frequently associated with the early migration of freedmen. Upon his arrival in Montgomery, Conway noted a "perfect reign of idleness on the part of the negroes." Other Bureau officials joined planters in declaring that blacks either would not work or would at best make feeble symbolic gestures toward work. Southern whites, and some Northern ones as well, complained that Negroes refused to work and were "impudent and defiant." In one Piedmont county, the commander of the local militia warned that "[t]he negroes are becoming very impudent and unless something is done very soon I fear the consequences." White Alabamians frequently confused black "impudence" with outright revolt, but organized violence did occasionally occur.

Events on the Henry Watson plantation, a large estate in the blackbelt county of Greene, illustrate the behavior of freedmen during the first few months after the war. "About the first of June," wrote John Parrish to his brother-in-law Henry Watson, who was vacationing in Germany, "your negroes rebelled against the authority" of the overseer George Hagin. They refused to work and demanded his removal. As Parrish was ill at the time, he induced a friend of Watson's, J. A. Wemyss, to go to the plantation and attempt to put things in order. "He made a sort of compromise bargain with the negroes," Parrish reported, "agreeing that if they would remain he would give them part of the crop, they should be clothed and fed as usual, and that Mr. Hagan [sic] should have no authority, over them. . . . All hands are having a good easy time, not doing half work." Six days later Parrish reported that "they have again rebelled." When Wemyss informed them firmly that they must submit to the overseer's authority, at first they "amiably consented," but soon they once again objected—"their complaints were universal, very ugly"—and seventeen of them left for nearby Uniontown, where a federal garrison was stationed. Meanwhile, a Freedmen's Bureau agent had arrived in Greensboro. Parrish brought him to the plantation, where he "modified the contract in the negroes['] fav[or] & made them sign it with their marks." The modified contract granted the laborers one-eighth of the crop.

When Watson finally returned from Germany to take charge of matters himself, he was totally disgusted with what he found. The Negroes "claim of their masters full and complete compliance on their part," he complained, "but forget that they agreed to do anything on theirs and are all idle, doing nothing, insisting that they shall be fed and are eating off their masters." Finding such a state of affairs more than he could tolerate, he decided to rent the plantation to overseer Hagin and "have nothing to do with the hiring of hands or the care of the plantation." Hagin, in turn, later broke up the plantation and sublet individual lots to Negro families.

II

Southern whites, long accustomed to thinking of their slaves as faithful and docile servants, were quick to blame outsiders for any trouble. As early as April 1862, a north Alabama planter had noted that the Union soldiers "to a great extent demoralized the negroes. . . . The negroes were delighted with them and since they left enough can be seen to convince one that the Federal army[,] the negroes and white Southern people cannot inhabit the same country." After the war, planters continued to complain about the harmful influence of the army. The presence of black troops was especially unpalatable to former slave owners. "[N]egroes will *not work* surrounded [by] black troops encouraging them to insubordination," complained one outraged resident of a blackbelt community.

Although Alabama whites were deeply humiliated by the presence of Yankees and black troops in their midst, there was little foundation to the complaints about outside agitation. Indeed, federal officials often cooperated directly with planters and local authorities in attempting to keep blacks in line. Army officers urged Negroes to stay on their plantations. Freedmen's Bureau agents frequently assisted in keeping order, too. "My predecessors here worked with a view to please the white citizens, at the expense of, and injustice to, the Freedmen," complained a shocked Bureau assistant superintendent shortly after his arrival in Tuskegee. "They have invariably given permission to inflict punishment for insolence or idleness, and have detailed soldiers to tie up and otherwise punish the laborers who have, in the opinion of the employers, been *refractory*." [Freedmen's Bureau] Commissioner [O. O.] Howard later explained that the Bureau "came to the assistance of the Planters" and succeeded in making the blacks "reliable laborers under the free system." He added that "[t]he good conduct of the millions of freedmen is due to a large extent to our officers of the Army and the Bureau."

A more substantial cause of the demoralization of labor was the mistrust existing between freedman and planter. Where this mistrust was minimal— that is, where planters and freedmen had relatively close ties and where planters readily acknowledged the changed condition of their relations— Negroes continued to work well. More often than not it was the small planter, who worked in the field beside his employees and knew them personally, who managed to remain on good terms with them. But few planters were willing to accept all the implications of the overthrow of slavery. "Thus far," pronounced the state's leading newspaper [*Daily Selma Times*] in October, "we are sorry to say that experience teaches that the negro in a free condition will not work on the old plantations." Another newspaper agreed that freedom had made the blacks "dissatisfied, listless, improvident, and unprofitable drones." Throughout the state, whites refused to believe that Negroes would work without the compulsion of slavery.

Some planters continued to hope that emancipation could either be rescinded or delayed, and "consequently told the negroes they were not free." Others recognized the de jure passing of slavery and concentrated on making the condition of the freedmen as near as possible to that of slaves. Upon his arrival in Montgomery, Conway noted that "the Planters appeared disinclined to offer employment, except with guarantees that would practically reduce the Freedmen again to a state of bondage."

Early contracts between planters and freedmen reflected the disbelief of whites in the possibility of free black labor and their desire to maintain slavery in fact, if not in name. Some planters reached "verbal agreements" with freedmen to continue as they had, without recompense. It was also relatively easy, before the Freedmen's Bureau was firmly established, for planters to lure former slaves into signing contracts that essentially perpetuated their condition. "Today I contracted with Jane and Dick to serve the remainder of the year, such being the federal law," Sarah Espy of the mountain county of Cherokee wrote in her diary in July. "I give them their victuals and clothing, the proceeds of their patches[,] and they are to proceed as heretofore." Similar contracts were made in other regions, and numerous Freedmen's Bureau officials reported upon arrival at their posts that Negroes were working without pay. The practice was summarized in a report to [Assistant Commissioner Wager] Swayne: "We find that the agreements they [the freedmen] have been working under (some of them since last April) are merely a paper drawn up by their later owners," wrote Captain J. W. Cogswell, "in which the negro promises to work for an indefinite time for nothing but his board and clothes, and the white man agrees to do nothing."

When some compensation was provided, as was the case more often than not, it almost always involved a share of the crop. There seems to have been little or no experimentation with wage labor during the first few months after the war. The initial reason for the immediate widespread adoption of sharecropping was simple: the defeated South did not have sufficient currency to pay laborers in cash. Cropping provided a convenient mode of paying freedmen without any money transactions.

Partly for the same reason and partly from tradition, most early contracts specified that food and medical care would be provided by the planter. In addition to being a continuation of the old plantation paternalism, this provision also conformed to the wishes of the Freedmen's Bureau. Shortly after his arrival in Montgomery, Swayne drew up a list of proposed labor regulations. One was that "[p]art of the compensation is required to be in food and medical attendance, lest the improvident leave their families to suffer or the weak are obliged to purchase at unjust rates what they must immediately have." The concern of the Freedmen's Bureau for the welfare of the freedmen, superimposed upon the legacy of slave paternalism and combined with the shortage of currency, insured that early contracts would give Negroes, in addition to their share of the crop, "quarters, fuel, necessary clothes, [and] medical attendance in case of sickness."

Although the size of the shares freedmen received in 1865 varied considerably, it was almost always very small. W. C. Penick agreed to pay his laborers one-quarter of the crop, but such liberality was rare during the summer of 1865. More typical was the contract between Henry Watson and his more than fifty adult blacks, which promised them one-eighth of the crop. In other cases shares varied from one-quarter to one-tenth of the crop.

In addition to appropriating the greater portion of the freedmen's labor, planters were concerned with maintaining control over their lives. "I look upon slavery as gone, gone, gone, beyond the possibility of help," lamented one planter. He added reassuringly, however, that "we have the power to pass stringent police laws to govern the negroes—This is a blessing—For they must be controlled in some way or white people cannot live amongst them." Such an outlook did not necessarily represent a conscious effort to thwart the meaning of freedom, for whites had been conditioned by years of slavery to look upon subservience as the only condition compatible with Negro, or any plantation, labor. Nevertheless, the effect was the same. Early contracts often included provisions regulating the behavior of laborers. A typical one provided that "all orders from the manager are to be promptly and implicitly obeyed under any and all circumstances" and added "[i]t is also agreed that none of the said negroes will under any circumstances leave the plantation without a written permission from the manager." If any of them quit work before the expiration of the contract, he was to forfeit all his wages. Some contracts gave planters authority to whip refractory Negroes.

It is only as a response to such attempts to perpetuate slave conditions that the seeming demoralization of black labor can be understood. Although whites pointed at idle or turbulent Negroes and repeated that they did not comprehend the meaning of freedom, the lack of comprehension was on the part of Alabama's whites. Blacks lost little time in demonstrating their grasp of the essentials of freedom and the tactical flexibility their new condition provided. Just as many felt compelled to leave their old plantations immediately after the war to prevent old relations from being perpetuated, so did they find it necessary to establish at the outset that they would not labor under conditions that made them free in name but slave in fact.

III

In December 1865 events reached something of a crisis as planters continued to strive for a return to the methods of prewar days and blacks continued to resist. Planter-laborer relationships were tense during the summer and fall, but with contracts entered into after the war due to expire on 31 December, the approach of the new year heralded an especially difficult time. Negroes now had the experience of over half a year as freedmen in dealing with planters. They also had the backing of the Freedmen's Bureau, which, if generally ambivalent about the precise position of the freedman in Southern society, refused to sanction his essential re-enslavement. The culmination of the demoralization of labor and the mass migrations of 1865 was the refusal of many blacks to contract for the following year.

One reason Negroes were slow to contract was that many of them expected the plantations of their ex-masters to be divided among them at the start of the year. While this idea proved to be a total misconception, it was neither so ludicrous nor so far-fetched a notion as white Alabamians portrayed it. Southern whites themselves had contributed greatly to the expectation by warning during the war that defeat would result in the confiscation of their lands. Commissioner Howard had originally intended to turn over confiscated and abandoned lands to the freedmen, and it was only when President Johnson directly countermanded this policy in the autumn of 1865 that the Bureau reversed itself and began restoring the lands in its possession to the original owners. As the end of the year approached, Freedmen's Bureau officials carefully explained to Negroes that they were not to be given land and advised them on contract for moderate wages.

White Alabamians responded to the black desire for land by exaggerating the extent to which the freedmen expected confiscation, playing up every minor incident, and predicting ominously that New Year's would bring a black uprising. They complained of Negroes arming themselves, and in at least one area whites organized armed patrols to defend themselves against an imagined impending Negro insurrection. Other observers, however, denied any threat of an uprising, and according to [reformer] Carl Schurz rumors were "spread about impending negro insurrections evidently for no other purpose than to serve as a pretext for annoying police regulations concerning the colored people."

The refusal of the freedmen to contract in December in no way presaged a rebellion, but merely expressed their reluctance to repeat their unhappy experience of the past half-year. Without careful Freedmen's Bureau supervision, the contract system threatened to become little more than an opportunity for whites to take advantage of illiterate and ignorant blacks. As Swayne wrote, with what turned out to be something of an underestimation of the abilities of the newly freed slaves, "[c]ontracts imply bargaining and litigation, and at neither of these is the freedman a match for his Employer." For this reason, the assistant commissioner [Swayne] reported, planters "so vigorously demanded contracts there was danger they would not undertake to plant at all without them."

That the fears of insurrection consisted chiefly of groundless rumors became evident when New Year's day passed without the slightest hint of trouble. To the astonishment and relief of whites, freedmen rushed to contract during the first few days of 1866 and then settled down to work. "The praiseworthy conduct of the negroes has surprised many," declared the Selma *Morning Times* in an editorial that typified the general white response. The demoralizing effects of emancipation about which whites had complained so bitterly vanished in a matter of days. "One thing is obvious," recorded a surprised planter; "the negroes, who are hired are farming and working much better than any one predicted they would work." Other white Alabamians agreed. From Tuskegee, the local Freedmen's Bureau agent boasted that "the Freedmen have commenced work with such a zeal as to merit the praise and approbation of the Planters. Planters say to me [']my negroes have never done so well as they are doing now.[']"

But if planters rejoiced that their laborers were hard at work, the freedmen had won a signal victory that was noticed by the more perceptive whites. "I think the negro hire was very high," complained future Democratic Governor George S. Houston; "[I] never had any idea of paying that much for negroes." He was right. Gone were the days when a typical contract gave the laborers one-eighth of the crop, or merely bed and board. By refusing to contract until the last moment, the freedmen had thrown their prospective employers into a panic and forced a significant alteration in the terms of the ultimate settlement. Although neither so well concerted nor organized, the process had essentially the same effect as a massive general strike.

Aside from the presence of the Freedmen's Bureau, which made blatant cheating by planters more difficult, the prevailing shortage of labor proved an inestimable boon to the freedmen. In 1866, as throughout most of the early postwar period, the pressure was on the planter to find laborers rather than on the Negro to find employment. Freedmen could feel relatively free in refusing to contract on what they regarded as unsatisfactory terms or in leaving employers with whom they were unhappy. Labor stealing, or enticing freedmen to change employers for higher wages, was a persistent complaint among planters. Occasionally, blacks were even able to strike for higher wages, as in the mountain county of Cherokee, "where they bound themselves together, under a penalty of fifty lashes, to be laid on the naked back, not to contract to work for any white man during the present harvest, for less than two dollars per day."

As had been the case in 1865, the terms of working arrangements varied widely among plantations. Both the lower and upper limits of the pay scale, however, were substantially higher than they had been. Half, or perhaps slightly more than half, of the contracts provided for a division of the crop. In such cases, the laborer almost always received a larger share than he had in 1865. Although there are examples of freedmen receiving as little as one-sixth of the crop, the prevailing portion—when, as was usual in 1866, the laborer provided nothing but his own labor—was one-quarter. For the first time, many planters contracted to pay their employees money wages rather than a portion of the crop. A typical small planter recorded that he paid his eight field hands an average of ten dollars per month for men and fifty dollars a year for women, in addition to food. In other cases where Negroes worked for wages, the rate of compensation usually ranged from seven to fifteen dollars per month for men, and somewhat less for women.

IV

The economic disadvantage of sharecropping to the Negro became evident in 1866 as the bright prospects of winter and spring faded in the summer. By August the cotton crop, which once seemed so promising, had been reduced by unseasonal rains to half its usual size, and autumn saw the second straight crop failure. As the extent of the disaster became clear, whites across the state began to decide that free blacks were not working well after all. The *Clarke County Journal,* for example, noted that although freedmen had labored satisfactorily during the winter and spring, now they seemed stubborn and lazy. "What is the matter with the freedmen?" it queried.

The contract system provided innumerable opportunities for friction between planters and freedmen—especially sharecroppers—in time of crisis. True, there were occasional touching instances when planters looked after former slaves. One white wrote to Swayne that an ex-slave of his who had left him after the war "because he would not 'feel free' if he did not" was "about to be imposed upon by an unprincipled man, who is about to employ him for the next year for far less than he is worth. . . . Please write to me," begged the distressed planter in a letter asking the assistant commissioner for advice. "I am willing to put myself to some trouble to protect my former faithful slave." Most planters, however, were primarily interested in receiving the maximum possible labor from the freedmen at minimal cost, even if it involved cheating, violence, and brutality.

The most common complaint of the freedmen was that either after the main labor on the crop was done or when it came time to divide the crop, planters would drive them off the plantations, frequently charging them with some technical violation of contract. Unlike wage earners, who were relatively secure, sharecroppers could be discharged and deprived of any compensation whatsoever. Temporary laborers could then be hired either by the day or week to finish up any remaining work. From Greene County, in the blackbelt, a Freedmen's Bureau agent reported "I find many, many men who employed them [freedmen] are arresting them . . . in a large majority of cases without cause" and sending them to sit in jail until the crop was sold. Although in some instances Bureau officials, or even the courts, mediated between planters and freedmen and were able to secure for the latter some payment, many injustices went unnoticed or unredressed.

The cyclical pattern established in 1865–1866 was repeated with some variations the following year. In December 1866, blacks once again were reluctant to contract. Although many of them now had the additional experience of being cheated out of their share of the crop, the absence of any illusions over the possibility of land confiscation enabled most blacks and planters to come to agreements more quickly and with less bitter feeling on both sides than they had the previous year. By spring, whites were rejoicing over Alabama's good fortune and praising her Negroes for their hard work and reliability. "The freedmen, according to universal testimony, are working better than they did last year," reported the *Daily Selma Messenger* with satisfaction.

There was an almost universal return to sharecropping in 1867, although a very few planters and freedmen continued, despite the shortage of currency, to experiment with wages. Some Freedmen's Bureau officials, who felt that Negroes fared better economically on wages, and some white Alabamians, who supported the system under which blacks were most carefully supervised, continued to advocate wage labor. With very few exceptions, however, planters and freedmen ignored their pleas. Arrangements granting the laborers one-quarter of the crop were most widespread, although in a few instances freedmen contracted to provide their own food and receive half the crop.

Sharecropping triumphed because both planters and freedmen favored the system. To the average planter it continued to be a more feasible labor system than wages, if for no other reason than the shortage of currency. In addition, many whites felt that shares gave blacks an interest in the crop, thus providing them with an incentive to work. Most blacks apparently preferred cropping, despite the economic disadvantages, because it allowed them greater control of their own lives. Because of his interest in the crop, the sharecropper required less supervision. In contrast to the wage laborer, who was a hired hand clearly in a subordinate position to his employer, the cropper was the partner of the landowner in a joint business venture that provided the freedman with opportunities for greater individual discretion, dignity, and self-respect. For this reason, Negroes considered the cropper a notch above the wage laborer in the social scale. "I am not working for wages," declared one freedman to his employer, as he explained why he had a right to leave the plantation at will to attend political meetings, "but am part owner of the crop and as I have all the rights that you or any other man has I shall not suffer them abridged."

V

As in 1866, the cotton crop of 1867 was a poor one. By fall, planters had once again begun to complain about the inefficiencies of freedmen as laborers. "The cause of the cotton crop being so inferior is the inefficiency of labor and the bad season [is] more on account of labor than anything else," lamented George Hagin, the ex-overseer who had rented Henry Watson's plantation. "There has been a few of the old negroes that lived on the place before that have worked very well but the younger ones are worth nothing." A correspondent of the Union Springs *Times* proclaimed free labor a failure.

Once again, planters drove freedmen from their homes without pay. "Negroes are now being dismissed from the plantations[,] there being nothing more for them to do," explained one blackbelt resident. He added calmly that "[t]hey will all be turned loose without homes[,] money or provisions[;] at least no meat." From the northwest corner of the state, 114 Negroes appealed for assistance to Major General John Pope, who in April had assumed command of the Third Military District,* comprising Alabama, Georgia, and Florida. They explained that "unless some person in whom we can place the utmost confidence be appointed to superintend the settling up of our affairs, we do not feel that justice will be done us." In 1867, for the first time, many blacks were also fired for voting Republican or attending political meetings.

Occasionally, through unusual persistence or intelligence, blacks were able to enlist the aid of the Freedmen's Bureau and resist arbitrary discharge. Bernard Houston, a sharecropper on an Athens plantation, told his landlord, "I shall not suffer myself to be turned off[,] and under legal advice and the advice of assistant Commissioner of [the] Freedmans Bureau I shall stay there until the crop is matured[,] gathered and divided according to contract." The planter protested lamely that he objected to the Negro's being "disobedient" and denied that politics had anything to do with the situation, but a month later he complained to Swayne that the freedman was "yet on the place acting in utter and entire disobedience of orders & the necessary discipline of the plantation."

In numerous other cases, freedmen were less fortunate. Freedmen's Bureau agents tried to come to the assistance of persecuted blacks, but there were simply too few agents for the job. Furthermore, since the procedure for handling grievances was not clear, Bureau representatives were not sure how best to dispose of them. Some turned cases over to the civil courts. In general, however, this method proved unsatisfactory. "[B]esides the slow process of the Law, there stands in the way the difficulty of obtaining counsel," explained one Bureau agent. "The Freedmen as a general thing have no mean[s] to pay a fee: consequently they submit to the swindle simply because they cannot purchase justice." The sub-assistant commissioner at Huntsville sent discharged freedmen back to their plantations and told them to stay there. In other locations, officials tried to mediate between laborers and planters. "I notify the parties concerned to appear at this office together, and try either to effect an understanding, or a settlement," explained one Bureau official. He reported that he had "so far been fortunate, to prevent any injustice to be done." But for every such settlement, many other grievances undoubtedly went unheard.

The cumulative effects of three years of substandard crops became increasingly evident during the late autumn and early winter of 1867–1868, a period of considerable tension because of the meeting of the Radical Constitutional Convention in December and the election to ratify the new constitution in February. The problem was no longer that freedmen were reluctant to contract, but rather that planters were unwilling or unable to plant. Their

---

*Provisions of the First Reconstruction Act of 1867 divided the former Confederacy—Tennessee excepted—into five military districts, each under a commander responsible for protecting life and property. (Eds.)

universal reaction to poor crops and low profits was to plan to cut back on planting operations. Unemployment among Negroes threatened to reach serious proportions for the first time since the war. . . .

VI

Hidden behind the daily monotony of agricultural labor, significant changes occurred in the lives of black plantation workers during their first few years of freedom. These changes were evident both in their relations with their employers and in their relations with each other. All of them can, with little inaccuracy and only slight ambiguity, be called moves toward independence. These moves, as much class as racial in nature, represented not only the desire of blacks to be free of white control, but also of ex-slave plantation laborers to be free of planter control.

"Freedom has worked great changes in the negro, bringing out all his inherent savage qualities," proclaimed the Mobile *Daily Register* in 1869. Certainly a growing physical restlessness and self-consciousness among black plantation workers —reinforced by the political emancipation brought about under congressional Reconstruction—were very evident. They were no longer willing to be imposed upon by their former owners. From the end of the war laborers, such as those on the Henry Watson plantation, had revolted against working under their old overseers. But the increasing number of white complaints of Negro "impudence," "insolence," and "insubordination," and the increasing readiness of black laborers to resort to violence and organization when faced with an unpalatable situation, testified to their growing self-assertiveness and confidence. In December 1867, for example, planters in Russell County, who were forced to cut back on planting operations because of poor crops the previous year, complained that their laborers were "seizing and holding property upon some of the places. They are generally armed." A year later, a revolt in the same area had to be put down by military force.

This desire of agricultural laborers for independence, which led them to choose sharecropping over wages even though they usually fared better economically under a wage system, was one of the greatest causes of other changes in modes of life and labor on the plantation. Before the war, field hands on large plantations had usually lived in rows of cabins grouped together. They had worked together in a slave gang, under the authority of an overseer and perhaps a driver. Their lives had been, by and large, collective. After the war, black plantation laborers quickly indicated their preference for a more individual form of life. They objected to working under the control of an overseer. They also objected to the regimented nature of the work gang and the Negro quarters. These had been accepted "in the days of slavery, when laborers were driven by overseers by day, and penned like sheep at night, and not allowed to have any will of their own," reported one Freedmen's Bureau agent. "But now, being *free* to think and act for

299

themselves, they feel their individual responsibility for their conduct, and the importance of maintaining a good character." He noted that fights frequently broke out among Negroes forced to lie among others against their will.

Many planters found it necessary or useful to break up the former slave quarters and allow laborers to have individual huts, scattered across the plantations. The process was far from complete by the end of the 1860s, but the trend was unmistakable. As early as the spring of 1867, an article in the Montgomery *Daily Advertiser* described certain changes that had occurred in the appearance of one plantation community. "You do not see as large gangs together as of old times, but more frequently squads of five or ten in a place, working industriously without a driver," wrote the correspondent. "Several large land owners have broken up their old 'quarters' and have rebuilt the houses at selected points, scattered over the plantation. . . ."

Although most black sharecroppers continued to provide only their labor and receive food and clothing in addition to their usual quarter of the crop, the late 1860s saw the introduction of a new cropping arrangement that would, in a matter of years, be widely adopted. Early in 1868, a Freedmen's Bureau official noted that there "does not seem to be as much uniformity in the tenor of contracts as last year." He wrote that although "some give the freedmen one-fourth of the crop and provide rations as was customary last year . . . others give one third of [the]crop, and require the laborers to furnish their own rations; and some give one half, the laborers bearing an equal share of the expense." The result was to remove the cropper still further from the wage laborer, and accentuate his role as a partner of the planter in a joint business venture.

Such changes in working and living conditions were sometimes fostered by planters themselves. Some, like Henry Watson, found it impossible to adjust to a new situation in which they did not have total control over their labor force. Under such circumstances, it was tempting for them to adopt whatever system would permit the least contact between employer and laborer, even if it resulted in more of the very independence that so troubled them. A correspondent from the blackbelt county of Hale reported to the Mobile *Daily Register* in 1869 that "everything appears experimental. . . . Many planters have turned their stock, teams, and every facility for farming, over to the negroes, and only require an amount of toll for the care of their land, refusing to superintend, direct, or even, in some cases, to suggest as to their management."

By the late 1860s, then, old patterns of agricultural relationships had been irreparably shattered, and the outlines of new ones had emerged. The logical culmination of emancipation for the plantation workers—the acquisition of their own land—remained for most an illusory dream. But within the confines of the plantation system great changes had occurred in the lives of the black laborers. They themselves had helped bring about most of these changes by demonstrating that they were not willing to continue in a position of complete subservience to their former owners. As one white planter lamented succinctly of the freedmen, "[T]hey wish to be free from restraint." That wish was a potent one in the years immediately following the Civil War.

DOCUMENTS

A Letter
"To My Old Master," c. 1865

TO MY OLD MASTER, COLONEL P.H. ANDERSON,

BIG SPRING, TENNESSEE

Sir: I got your letter, and was glad to find that you had not forgotten Jourdon, and that you wanted me to come back and live with you again, promising to do better for me than anybody else can. I have often felt uneasy about you. I thought the Yankees would have hung you long before this, for harboring Rebs they found at your house. I suppose they never heard about your going to Colonel Martin's to kill the Union soldier that was left by his company in their stable. Although you shot at me twice before I left you, I did not want to hear of your being hurt, and am glad you are still living. It would do me good to go back to the dear old home again, and see Miss Mary and Miss Martha and Allen, Esther, Green, and Lee. Give my love to them all, and tell them I hope we will meet in the better world, if not in this. I would have gone back to see you all when I was working in the Nashville Hospital, but one of the neighbors told me that Henry intended to shoot me if he ever got a chance.

I want to know particularly what the good chance is you propose to give me. I am doing tolerably well here. I get twenty-five dollars a month, with victuals and clothing; have a comfortable home for Mandy—the folks call her Mrs. Anderson—and the children—Milly, Jane, and Grundy—go to school and are learning well. The teacher says Grundy has a head for a preacher. They go to Sunday school, and Mandy and me attend church regularly. We are kindly treated. Sometimes we overhear others saying, "Them colored people were slaves" down in Tennessee. The children feel hurt when they hear such remarks; but I tell them it was no disgrace in Tennessee to belong to Colonel Anderson. Many darkeys would have been proud, as I used to be, to call you master. Now if you will write and say what wages you will give me, I will be better able to decide whether it would be to my advantage to move back again.

SOURCE: L. Maria Child, *The Freedmen's Book* (1865).

As to my freedom, which you say I can have, there is nothing to be gained on that score, as I got my free papers in 1864 from the Provost-Marshal-General of the Department of Nashville. Mandy says she would be afraid to go back without some proof that you were disposed to treat us justly and kindly; and we have concluded to test your sincerity by asking you to send us our wages for the time we served you. This will make us forget and forgive old scores, and rely on your justice and friendship in the future. I served you faithfully for thirty-two years, and Mandy twenty years. At twenty-five dollars a month for me, and two dollars a week for Mandy, our earnings would amount to eleven thousand six hundred and eighty dollars. Add to this the interest for the time our wages have been kept back, and deduct what you paid for our clothing, and three doctor's visits to me, and pulling a tooth for Mandy, and the balance will show what we are in justice entitled to. Please send the money by Adam's Express, in care of V. Winters, Esq., Dayton, Ohio. If you fail to pay us for faithful labors in the past, we can have little faith in your promises in the future. We trust the good Maker has opened your eyes to the wrongs which you and your fathers have done to me and my fathers, in making us toil for you for generations without recompense. Here I draw my wages every Saturday night; but in Tennessee there was never any pay-day for the Negroes any more than for the horses and cows. Surely there will be a day of reckoning for those who defraud the laborer of his hire.

In answering this letter, please state if there would be any safety for my Milly and Jane, who are now grown up, and both good-looking girls. You know how it was with poor Matilda and Catherine. I would rather stay here and starve—and die, if it come to that—than have my girls brought to shame by the violence and wickedness of their young masters. You will also please state if there has been any schools opened for the colored children in your neighborhood. The great desire of my life now is to give my children an education, and have them form virtuous habits.

Say howdy to George Carter, and thank him for taking the pistol from you when you were shooting at me.

FROM YOUR OLD SERVANT,
JOURDON ANDERSON

The Black Code of
St. Landry's Parish, 1865

Whereas it was formerly made the duty of the police jury to make suitable regulations for the police of slaves within the limits of the parish; and whereas slaves have become emancipated by the action of the ruling pow-

SOURCE: U.S. Congress, *Senate Executive Document No. 2* (Washington, D.C., 1865), 93–94.

ers; and whereas it is necessary for public order, as well as for the comfort and correct deportment of said freedmen, that suitable regulations should be established by their government in their changed condition, the following ordinances are adopted, with the approval of the United States military authorities commanding in said parish, viz:

SECTION 1.   *Be it ordained by the police jury of the parish of St. Landry,* That no negro shall be allowed to pass within the limits of said parish without a special permit in writing from his employer. Whoever shall violate this provision shall pay a fine of two dollars and fifty cents, or in default thereof shall be forced to work four days on the public road, or suffer corporeal punishment as provided hereinafter.

SECTION 2.   *Be it further ordained,* That every negro who shall be found absent from the residence of his employer after 10 o'clock at night, without a written permit from his employer, shall pay a fine of five dollars, or in default thereof, shall be compelled to work five days on the public road, or suffer corporeal punishment as hereinafter provided.

SECTION 3.   *Be it further ordained,* That no negro shall be permitted to rent or keep a house within said parish. Any negro violating this provision shall be immediately ejected and compelled to find an employer; and any person who shall rent, or give the use of any house to any negro, in violation of this section, shall pay a fine of five dollars for each offence.

SECTION 4.   *Be it further ordained,* That every negro is required to be in the regular service of some white person, or former owner, who shall be held responsible for the conduct of said negro. But said employer or former owner may permit said negro to hire his own time by special permission in writing, which permission shall not extend over seven days at any one time. Any negro violating the provisions of this section shall be fined five dollars for each offence, or in default of the payment thereof shall be forced to work five days on the public road, or suffer corporeal punishment as hereinafter provided.

SECTION 5.   *Be it further ordained,* That no public meetings or congregations of negroes shall be allowed within said parish after sunset; but such public meetings and congregations may be held between the hours of sunrise and sunset, by the special permission of writing of the captain of patrol, within whose beat such meetings shall take place. This prohibition, however, is not intended to prevent negroes from attending the usual church services, conducted by white ministers and priests. Every negro violating the provisions of this section shall pay a fine of five dollars, or in default thereof shall be compelled to work five days on the public road, or suffer corporeal punishment as hereinafter provided.

SECTION 6.   *Be it further ordained,* That no negro shall be permitted to preach, exhort, or otherwise declaim to congregations of colored people, without a special permission in writing from the president of the police jury. Any negro violating the provisions of this section shall pay a fine of ten dollars, or in default thereof shall be forced to work ten days on the public road, or suffer corporeal punishment as hereinafter provided.

SECTION 7.   *Be it further ordained,* That no negro who is not in the military service shall be allowed to carry fire-arms, or any kind of weapons, within the parish, without the special written permission of his employers, approved and indorsed by the nearest or most convenient chief of patrol. Any one violating the provisions of this section shall forfeit his weapons and pay a fine of five dollars, or in default of the payment of said fine, shall be forced to work five days on the public road, or suffer corporeal punishment as hereinafter provided.

SECTION 8.   *Be it further ordained,* That no negro shall sell, barter, or exchange any articles of merchandise or traffic within said parish without the special written permission of his employer, specifying the articles of sale, barter or traffic. Any one thus offending shall pay a fine of one dollar for each offence, and suffer the forfeiture of said articles, or in default of the payment of said fine shall work one day on the public road, or suffer corporeal punishment as hereinafter provided.

SECTION 9.   *Be it further ordained,* That any negro found drunk within the said parish shall pay a fine of five dollars, or in default thereof shall work five days on the public road, or suffer corporeal punishment as hereinafter provided.

SECTION 10.   *Be it further ordained,* That all the foregoing provisions shall apply to negroes of both sexes.

SECTION 11.   *Be it further ordained,* That it shall be the duty of every citizen to act as a police officer for the detection of offences and the apprehension of offenders, who shall be immediately handed over to the proper captain or chief of patrol.

SECTION 12.   *Be it further ordained,* That the aforesaid penalties shall be summarily enforced, and that it shall be the duty of the captains and chiefs of patrol to see that the aforesaid ordinances are promptly executed.

SECTION 13.   *Be it further ordained,* That all sums collected from the aforesaid fines shall be immediately handed over to the parish treasurer.

SECTION 14.   *Be it further ordained,* That the corporeal punishment provided for in the foregoing sections shall consist in confining the body of the offender within a barrel placed over his or her shoulders, in the manner practiced in the army, such confinement not to continue longer than twelve hours, and for such time within the aforesaid limit as shall be fixed by the captain or chief of patrol who inflicts the penalty.

SECTION 15.   *Be it further ordained,* That these ordinances shall not interfere with any municipal or military regulations inconsistent with them within the limits of said parish.

SECTION 16.   *Be it further ordained,* That these ordinances shall take effect five days after their publication in the *Opelousas Courier.*

Dedicated Teachers,
Determined Students, 1869

RALEIGH, N.C., FEB 22, 1869

It is surprising to me to see the amount of suffering which many of the people endure for the sake of sending their children to school. Men get very low wages here—from $2.50 to $8 per month usually, while a first-rate hand may get $10, and a peck or two of meal per week for rations—and a great many men cannot get work at all. The women take in sewing and washing, go out by day to scour, etc. There is one woman who supports three children and keeps them at school; she says, "I don't care how hard I has to work, if I can only sen[d] Sallie and the boys to school looking respectable." Many of the girls have but one decent dress; it gets washed and ironed on Saturday, and then is worn until the next Saturday, provided they do not tear it or fall in the mud; when such an accident happens there is an absent mark on the register. . . . One may go into their cabins on cold, windy days, and see daylight between every two boards, or feel the rain dropping through the roof; but a word of complaint is rarely heard. They are anxious to have the children "get on" in their books, and do not seem to feel impatient if they lack comforts themselves. A pile of books is seen in almost every cabin, though there be no furniture except a poor bed, a table and two or three broken chairs.

MISS M. A. PARKER

CHARLOTTESVILLE, VA., OCT. 17, 1866

Mrs. Gibbins (a colored native teacher) is very much liked by the colored people here. Her nature is so noble, that she is not so liable to stimulate petty jealousy among her people as many might under similar circumstances. . . . I think she is doing well in her new sphere of duty, especially in the matter of government. She has a kind of magnetism about her which is a good qualification for a teacher. She is really a fine reader of easy readings, and I should choose her to prepare scholars for me in that line, from among nine-tenths of those engaged in this work, so far as I have known her. She intends to pursue her studies in the evening with my help.

ANNA GARDNER

SOURCE: Edward L. Pierce, "The Freedmen at Port Royal," *Atlantic Monthly* 12 (September 1869):306–307.

PART II

Suggestions for Further Reading

For general social and economic changes before the Civil War, several books are useful. Among them are Robert Wiebe, *The Opening of American Society: From the Adoption of the Constitution to the Eve of Disunion* (1984); Sean Wilentz, *Chants Democratic: New York City and the Rise of the American Working Class, 1785–1850* (1984); Daniel Walkowitz, *Worker City, Company Town: Iron and Cotton-Worker Protest in Troy and Cohoes, New York, 1855–1884* (1978); Alan Dawley, *Class and Community: The Industrial Revolution in Lynn* (1976); and Howard Gitelman, *Workingmen of Waltham: Mobility in Urban Industrial Development, 1850–1890* (1974). Those interested in delving further into the subject of Thomas Dublin's essay will want to consult *Transforming Women's Work: New England Lives in the Industrial Revolution* (1994). For economic and political issues during this period, see Charles Sellers, *The Market Revolution: Jacksonian America, 1815–1846* (1991).

On the removal policy of American Indians to the West, see Ronald Satz, *American Indian Policy in the Jacksonian Era* (1975). On removal itself, see Arthur DeRosier, *The Removal of the Choctaw Indians* (1970), Wilkins Thurman, *Cherokee Tragedy: The Story of the Ridge Family and the Decimation of a People* (1970), and John Ehle, *Trail of Tears: The Rise and Fall of the Cherokee Nation* (1988). For background knowledge of Cherokee history and culture, William G. McLoughlin, *Cherokees and Missionaries, 1789–1839* (1984), is excellent. On assimilation, see Henry E. Fritz, *The Movement for Indian Assimilation, 1860–1890* (1963).

On the westward movement generally, particularly recommended is Richard White, *"It's Your Misfortune and None of My Own": A History of the American West* (1991), and two studies by Ray Billington: *The Far Western Frontier, 1830–1860* (1956) and *Westward Expansion* (1974). See also John D. Unruh, Jr., *The Plain Across: The Overland Emigrants and the Trans-Mississippi West, 1840–1860* (1979). For women and the West, consult John M. Faragher, *Women and Men on the Overland Trail* (1979), and Julie Roy Jeffrey, *Frontier Women: The Trans-Mississippi West, 1840–1880* (1979). A vivid description of family life in the Oregon Territory is included in Lillian Schlissel, Byrd Gibbens, and Elizabeth Hampsten, *Far from Home: Families of the Westward Journey* (1989). For the frontier as experienced by children, see Eliot West, *Growing Up with the Country, Children on the Far Western Frontier* (1989).

There is a growing literature on women's history. Two general works of value are Alice Kessler-Harris, *Out to Work: A History of Wage Earning Women in America* (1982), and Carl Degler, *At Odds: Women and the Family from the Revolution to the Present* (1981). On plantation women, see Catherine Clinton, *The Plantation Mistress* (1982), and Ann Firor Scott, *The Southern Lady: From Pedestal to Politics, 1830–1930* (1970). On women in American culture, consult Ann Douglas, *The Feminization of American Culture* (1977); Nancy Cott, *The Bonds of Womanhood: "Woman's Sphere" in New England, 1780–1835* (1977); Mary Ryan, *Cradle of the Middle Class: The Family in Oneida County, New York, 1790–1865* (1981); and Katherine Kish Sklar, *Catharine Beecher: A Study in American Domesticity* (1973). On women factory workers, see Thomas Dublin, *Women at Work: The Transformation of Work and Community in Lowell, Massachusetts, 1826–1860* (1979), and for black women, see Jacqueline Jones, *Labor of Love, Labor of Sorrow: Black Women, Work and the Family from Slavery to the Present* (1985). Especially interesting on the relationships of black men and white women is Martha Hodes, *White Women, Black Men: Illicit Sex in the Nineteenth Century South* (1997).

For religion in early-nineteenth-century America, an older but useful work is Whitney Cross, *The Burned-Over District: A Social and Intellectual History of Enthusiastic Religion in Western New York, 1800–1855* (1950). A more recent examination of the same region is Michael Barkun, *Crucible of the Millennium: The Burned-Over District of New York in the 1840s* (1986). See also Paul Conkin, *Cane Ridge: America's Pentecost* (1990), John B. Boles, *The Great Revival* (1972), and Charles A. John, *The Frontier Camp Meeting* (1955). For a comprehensive study of revivalism, consult William McLoughlin, *Modern Revivalism: Charles Grandison Finney to Billy Graham* (1959). A more recent view is found in Paul E. Johnson, *A Shopkeeper's Millennium: Society and Revivals in Rochester, New York, 1815–1837* (1978). For a biography of the era's most famous evangelist, see K. J. Hardman, *Charles Grandison Finney* (1987). An outstanding work on nineteenth-century Southern religion is Christine Leigh Heyrman, *Southern Cross: The Beginnings of the Bible Belt* (1997).

For immigration before the Civil War, see David Gerber, *The Making of an American Pluralism: Buffalo, New York, 1825–1860* (1989), and Brian C. Mitchell, *The Paddy Camps: The Irish of Lowell, 1821–1861* (1988). Other accounts are Jay Dolan, *Immigrant Church. New York's Irish and German Catholics. 1815–1865* (1975); Robert Ernst, *Immigrant Life in New York City, 1812–1863* (1949); Oscar Handlin, *Boston's Immigrants, 1790–1880: A Study in Acculturation* (1970); and Lawrence McCaffrey, *The Irish Diaspora* (1976). A highly regarded study of women immigrants is Hasia R. Diner, *Erin's Daughters in America: Irish Immigrant Women in the Nineteenth Century* (1983). An important survey of Irish emigration is Kirby Miller, *Emigrants and Exiles: Ireland and the Irish Exodus to North America* (1985). A classic study of anti-immigrant sentiment is Ray Allen Billington, *The Protestant Crusade, 1800–1860: Study of the Origins of American Nativism* (1938). More recent are Dale T. Knobel, *"America for Americans": The Nativist Movement in the United States* (1997) and Tyler Anbinder, *Nativism and Slavery: The Northern Know-Nothings and the Politics of the 1850s* (1992). Ethnic culture in the Midwest is examined in Jon Gerdje, *The Minds of the West: Ethnoculture in the Rural Midwest, 1830–1917* (1997).

For reform movements, useful general works are Alice Felt Tyler, *Freedom's Ferment* (1944), and Ronald G. Walters, *American Reformers, 1815– 1860*

(1978). On the antislavery movement, see Louis Filler, *The Crusade Against Slavery* (1960); Blanche Glassman Hersh, *The Slavery of Sex: Feminist-Abolitionists in America* (1978); and Eric Foner, *Free Soil, Free Labor, Free Men: The Ideology of the Republican Party Before the Civil War* (1970). For studies of the movement to improve care for the mentally ill, see David J. Rothman, *The Discovery of the Asylum: Social Order and Disorder in the New Republic* (1971), and Gerald Grob, *Mental Institutions in America: Social Policy to 1875* (1973). On the women's rights movement, the reader will profit from Ellen C. DuBois, *Feminism and Suffrage: The Emergence of an Independent Women's Movement in America, 1848–1869* (1978). Studies of the crusade for public schooling include Carl F. Kaestle, *Pillars of the Republic: Common Schools and American Society, 1780–1860* (1983); Lawrence A. Cremin, *American Education: The National Experience, 1783–1876* (1981); and Frederick M. Binder, *The Age of the Common School: 1830–1865* (1974). An important revisionist view is found in Michael Katz, *The Irony of Early School Reform* (1968).

Surveys of the several utopian movements may be found in Michael Fellman, *The Unbounded Frame: Freedom and Community in Nineteenth Century Utopianism* (1973); Mark Holloway, *Heavens on Earth* (1951); and Raymond Muncy, *Sex and Marriage in Utopian Communities: 19th Century America* (1973). Two recent accounts of American utopias are Stephen Stein, *The Shaker Experience in America* (1992), and Spencer Klaw, *Without Sin: The Life and Death of the Oneida Community* (1993).

The literature on antebellum slavery is extensive. Two recent works are Brenda E. Stevenson, *Life in Black and White: Family and Community in the Slave South* (1996), and Wilma King, *Stolen Childhood: Slave Youth in Nineteenth Century America* (1996). Standard works are John Blassingame, *The Slave Community: Plantation Life in the Antebellum South* (1972); Eugene D. Genovese, *Roll, Jordan, Roll* (1974); Herbert Gutman, *The Black Family in Slavery and Freedom, 1750–1925* (1976); Kenneth Stampp, *The Peculiar Institution* (1956); and Leslie Owens, *This Species of Property: Slave Life in the Old South* (1976). An account of slavery in one community is Charles Joyner, *Down by the Riverside: A South Carolina Slave Community* (1984). Those interested in the role and place of women in plantation society should turn to Elizabeth Fox-Genovese, *Within the Plantation Household: Black and White Women of the Old South* (1988). For free blacks in the South, consult Ira Berlin, *Slaves Without Masters: The Free Negro in the Antebellum South* (1975), and Michael Johnson and James Roark, *Black Masters: A Free Family of Color in the Old South* (1984). For the North, see Leon Litwack, *North of Slavery: The Negro in the Free States* (1961). A compelling survey of the history of slavery in America is Peter Kolchin, *American Slavery, 1619–1887* (1993).

The best introduction to the Civil War is James McPherson, *Battle Cry of Freedom: The Civil War Era* (1988). McPherson has also written an account of the soldiers' view of the war: James McPherson, *For Cause and Comrades: Why Men Fought in the Civil War* (1997). Other works on this topic are two by

Bell I. Wiley: *The Life of Johnny Reb* (1943) and *The Life of Bill Yank* (1952). Also for northern soldiers see Richard Moe, *The Last Full Measure: The Life and Death of the First Minnesota Volunteers* (1993). Consult also Reid Mitchell, *Civil War Soldiers: Their Expectations and Their Experiences* (1988), and Gerald F. Linderman, *Embattled Courage: The Experiences of Combat in the American Civil War* (1988). The experiences of black soldiers are described in Dudley R. Cornish, *The Sable Arm* (1966). For treatments of the home front, consult Robert Meyers, *The Children of Pride* (1972) for a Southern view. See George Winston Smith and Charles Burnet Judah, *Life in the North During the Civil War* (1966), and J. Matthew Gallman, *The North Fights the Civil War: The Home Front* (1994) for the Northern view. For contributions of women to the war effort, see Mary E. Massey, *Bonnet Brigades* (1966). Benjamin Quarles, *The Negro in the Civil War* (1953), reveals the impact of the war on blacks.

On Southern black Americans after the Civil War, consult two works by Eric Foner: *Nothing But Freedom: Emancipation and Its Legacy* (1983) and his impressive *Reconstruction: America's Unfinished Revolution, 1863–1967* (1988). See also John Hope Franklin, *Reconstruction After the Civil War* (1961); Leon Litwack, *Been in the Storm So Long: The Aftermath of Slavery* (1979); and Howard Rabinowitz, *Race Relations in the Urban South, 1865–1890* (1980). On black poverty, see Jay R. Mandle, *The Roots of Black Poverty* (1978). C. Vann Woodward, *The Strange Career of Jim Crow* (1966) remains an important work. Very comprehensive is Leon F. Litwack, *Trouble in Mind: Black Southerners in the Age of Jim Crow* (1998).